9.11.

THE CONSULTANT'S CRAFT

Improving Organizational Communication

THE CONSULTANT'S CRAFT

Improving Organizational Communication

SECOND EDITION

Sue DeWine
Provost, Marietta College

BEDFORD / ST. MARTIN'S
Boston ◆ New York

For Bedford/St. Martin's

Executive Editor, Communication: Patricia Rossi

Associate Editor: Jeannine Thibodeau

Senior Editor, Publishing Services: Douglas Bell

Production Supervisor: Dennis Conroy

Marketing Manager: Richard Cadman

Project Management: Books By Design, Inc.

Text Design: Lee Goldstein

Cover Design: Lucy Krikorian

Composition: Thompson Type

Printing and Binding: RR Donnelley & Sons Company

President: Charles H. Christensen

Editorial Director: Joan E. Feinberg

Director of Marketing: Karen R. Melton

Director of Editing, Design, and Production: Marcia Cohen

Manager, Publishing Services: Emily Berleth

Acknowledgments

Pages 19–20: "A Consulting Story from Patrice Buzzanell." Patrice M. Buzzanell. Reprinted with the permission of the author.

Acknowledgments and copyrights are continued at the back of the book on pages 476–478, which constitute an extension of the copyright page.

To Mike, Leigh Anne, and James

*While I was teaching others how to be consultants,
they were teaching me how to be a mom.*

PREFACE

Organizations have changed tremendously since the first edition of this book. As a result, consulting in organizations has undergone changes, which I have tried to reflect in this new edition. For example, during the last five years of the twentieth century, communication technology changed the very nature of work in the organization. Not only are consultants now using technology to assist their clients, but they are advising their clients about the impact technology has on human interaction. Consequently, one of the new chapters in this edition is "Technology and Training and Consulting" (Chapter 7). Another major impact on the way organizations do business and on consultants is the globalization of work. Another new chapter is "Globalization and International Consulting" (Chapter 16), written by my colleague, Mary Eicholtz.

At the same time, many of the skills I developed early in my consulting practice remain essential. Helping clients focus on issues that are preventing them from moving forward still takes great skill in human communication and understanding of the process, as well as understanding that particular business's environment and competition. Therefore, while I have updated references, added new stories on consulting, and included "lessons learned" from well-known and effective consultants around the country, I have maintained the essential ingredients of what makes a consultant successful. I have also kept those portions I feel give readers a sense of the intangible aspects of advising and helping corporate executives reach their goals.

I chose to retain the foreword by W. Charles Redding, who is often referred to as the "Father of Organizational Communication." Certainly his early writings did a great deal to launch the field of organizational communication. I was constantly stimulated by the challenges he regularly issued to researchers. I treasure the dinners we had with colleagues at conventions and our interactions when one of us served as a speaker and the other was in the audience. Charles has left us, but his memory and what we learned from him will live forever. I believe this foreword was one of the last things he wrote before his death in 1998.

I have also kept the introduction by Richard H. Brown. At the time he wrote it, he was vice president of Ameritech. Since then he has gone on to assume three CEO positions and currently is chair and CEO of EDS, the second-largest provider of computer services. In 2000 the company revenues approached $20 billion with 140,000 employees in fifty-five countries. Brown continues to advance his belief that the communication skills he learned as an undergraduate at Ohio University are serving him well as he leads a Fortune 100 company into the millennium.

The following story remains one of my favorites. It has helped me understand what I bring to a consulting assignment. It will help you assess the "value" you bring "to the table" and assess that value for your clients.

> One afternoon a woman of average means caught sight of Picasso in a restaurant. She had always admired his paintings but had never been able to afford one. She decided to be bold and ask him for a sketch: "Excuse me, but I have always been a great admirer of your paintings, and when I saw you in this restaurant I couldn't help but come up and tell you so. You would do me a great honor if you would simply sketch some scene from this restaurant on a napkin. I would treasure it forever." Picasso took the napkin and in less than three minutes had sketched a scene from the restaurant. The woman was delighted. "I'm willing to pay you for this small sketch. How much would you want?" Picasso replied, "My fee is $50,000." The woman was astonished. "How could you charge $50,000 for a three-minute sketch?" she asked. "But my dear lady," he replied, "you are not paying for the three-minute sketch. What you are paying for is sixty years of experience!"

I have tried to put my knowledge and background as a consultant into this book, so that in buying the book you are also paying for my thirty years of experience. The examples and stories are true and happened to my colleagues and me in the course of trying to solve human problems in organizations. I have also tried to pass on what I have learned by teaching consulting and training to undergraduates for those thirty years, and to PhD students for the last twenty years. However, you can't learn to be a consultant just by reading this book. You must add hundreds of hours of observation in organizations, with talented consultants, to the insights you learn here. I spent many hours observing Martha Langdom-Dahm and Gordon Lippitt. They were the first of many colleagues with whom I worked, but I remember them especially because we no longer have the opportunity to observe them in action but must remember the skill they demonstrated.

This book can serve as the primary text in an organizational communication or consulting course or as a companion text in organizational development, management, and human resource courses in communication and business schools. It would be useful to MBA programs and in adult education as well as public administration courses that focus on human resource development. It will be helpful to the 75,000 trainers and human resource managers who are members of the American Society for Training and Development. Organizational managers who may be members of the American Management Association may also want to try these techniques and strategies.

The book is written from the point of view of the individual who will have to function in an organizational setting and wants to figure out ways to interact with others that will make him or her very effective. It is also directed to those individuals who will be, or are, in positions that require them to help others learn these techniques (e.g., trainers, internal consultants, and human resource managers).

Part I provides an overview and basic definitions. *Part II* describes assessment techniques used by communication specialists to help identify communication problems in organizations. *Part III* presents a variety of training and consulting strategies, and *Part IV* identifies ways to correct communication problems encountered by the manager or communication specialist. Anyone who hopes to be an effective human resource or communication manager must be a model of effective communication before transmitting any skills to others. *Part V* presents evaluation methods for the trainer and consultant, and *Part VI* discusses professional development, so the consultant or communication manager is continually able to demonstrate desired skills.

This text offers a practical approach to solving communication problems to persons who will be, or are, managers and individuals responsible for human resources.

Acknowledgments

This second edition was written in my office at Ohio University and at home in the kitchen (while it was being remodeled), the dining room, and the office. I took it with me when I traveled to Bangkok for graduation ceremonies for the School of Interpersonal Communication at Ohio University's PhD students, to Australia while my daughter and I scoped out where she would be living for several months, and to conventions in various parts of the United States. I wrote parts of it on a laptop computer in hotel rooms and on planes. I finished proofreading it after I had accepted a new position as provost at Marietta College. All the time I was taking on new consulting clients I was wondering if this would turn out to be a good story for the book! I have deleted all references to real people and if clients see themselves in any of these stories, it will be because the described behaviors are familiar.

In addition to my husband, Mike, my daughter, Leigh Anne, and my son, James, to whom this book is dedicated because of their unending support of my writing and career, several other people made significant contributions to this second edition. Mary Eicholtz, my graduate advisee, has shown great ability as a consultant and trainer and in fact I have turned over to her many clients when my work schedule became too full. She assisted with updating the references and is the author of Chapter 16, "Globalization and International Consulting." I look forward to many years of continued collaboration with her. Another individual who was always willing to help with some of the details of the text was Sue Manderick. She has been a friend and colleague for many years and I appreciate having her in my life. Special friends like my sister, Lynda; Claudia; Mary; and Anita continue to be my sounding boards. Melissa Gibson did me a great favor when she suggested hosting a panel focused on this book at one of our national conferences and invited input for the second edition from those who had used the first. That was a wonderful start to making decisions about what to include in this second edition. Every time I thought I would drop something, someone would tell me it was one of his or her favorite parts of the book!

My publisher, Bedford/St. Martin's, asked the following individuals to review the text and I used their comments to guide me in making revisions: Patrice Buzzanell, Purdue University; Steven Maddan, Clemson University; Lisa Newman, University of Cincinnati; Gordon Rowland, Ithaca College; and Dudley Turner, University of Akron. Their suggestions were excellent. In particular, I would like to recognize the comments of Patrice Buzzanell. She was thought provoking and complete in her praise and suggestions for changes. When Patrice makes a suggestion, I listen. She is a very talented editor! Patricia Rossi at Bedford/St. Martin's and I toasted this project in New York at the beginning and again at its conclusion. Her constant gentle pressure kept me going and got me back on track when I needed it most. I was writing another text at the same time and Patricia's role was to remind me not to lose sight of this one. Her assistant, Michael Bagnulo, provided input at critical stages in the process.

Of all my writing projects, this book continues to give me the most pleasure. The stories I tell about clients reinforce for me the notion that no matter what positions they hold or personalities they possess, people everywhere want to enjoy being at work. Improving our ability to communicate will make our work more productive, rewarding, and enjoyable.

SUE DEWINE

CONTENTS

Chapter 5

How Do We Know What We Have When We Have It? *Data Analysis*   **66**

■ *PART III*

TRAINING AND CONSULTING STRATEGIES AND TECHNIQUES   **83**

Chapter 6

Using Training Techniques   **84**

Chapter 7

Technology and Training and Consulting   130

Chapter 8

Designing Consulting Interventions   142

■ *PART IV*

CORRECTING COMMUNICATION FAILURES   187

Chapter 9

Isn't Anyone Listening?
Using Active Listening Techniques   188

Chapter 10

Why Are Meetings So Boring and Unproductive?
Managing Meetings   **206**

Chapter 11

When Your Client Asks:
"How Can I Face This Audience?"   **242**

Chapter 12

Can This Group Work as a Team?
Team-Building Techniques   **272**

Chapter 13

How Do You Tell Clients What Kind of Job They Are Doing?
Using Descriptive Feedback   **304**

FOREWORD

W. Charles Redding (1914–1994)
Professor Emeritus, Purdue University
West Lafayette, Indiana

Improving organizational communication, the subtitle of Professor DeWine's book, epitomizes the reasons why it deserves our closest attention. To say that we live in an organizational world has become a truism. Thus, when any of the innumerable organizations touching our lives fails to function properly, we can expect to experience a variety of pains, both material and emotional, until the necessary improvements are made. Regardless of which particular organizational theory (if any) we happen to entertain, we must acknowledge one axiom: In every instance of organizational malaise that comes to mind, at some time and in some way, human communication behavior has been significantly involved. Indeed, there are those scholars who have persuasively made the case that a communication failure is at least one of the basic sources underlying *every* organizational failure.

As members of organizations, who among us can honestly report having never endured some sort of damage associated with such phenomena as insensitive supervision, confusing instructions, fruitless meetings, deceptive announcements, vicious defenses of "turf," biased (or entirely omitted) performance evaluations, misleading reports, empty promises, backstabbing tête-à-têtes with the boss, privacy-invading questions, sexist or racist harassment, scapegoating memoranda, clumsy explanations, paucity of information, conflicting orders, ambiguity (both intentional and unintentional), worship of inane regulations, refusal to listen to bad news, and rejection of innovative ideas—not to mention stubborn reliance upon autocratic, downward-directed messages in general? (Space limitations prohibit a complete inventory of evils.)

Yet to be considered are those problems we commonly experience in encounters, not as "insiders" but as "outsiders," with a host of organizations: government agencies, supermarkets, banks, labor unions, advocacy groups, insurance companies, professional societies, mail-order houses, educational institutions, publishers of journals, utility companies, manufacturers, and so on. As nonmembers of these organizations, we appear in such roles as customers, clients, suppliers, dealers, and, of course, taxpayers. Hence, we are all too familiar with the innumerable frustrations associated with the label "red tape," including unanswered inquiries, pedantic adherence to esoteric rules, incomprehensible prose, condescending (even insulting) statements, evasive explanations, refusals to accept responsibility, inconsistent assertions from different sources, violations of common courtesy, and so on.

Does this book claim to offer neat solutions to all these problems? Such an experienced and sophisticated consultant as Professor DeWine would vigorously reject any such suggestion. Indeed, one of the merits of the book is the author's emphatic insistence that communication failures in the organizational context are typically complex and rarely, if ever, amenable to formulary quick fixes. However, while carefully eschewing cookbook approaches, the author presents a great wealth of specific techniques designed not as magic cure-alls, but as helpful suggestions for the aspiring consultant.

I have not attempted a precise count of the number of times the reader is provided convenient lists of various items, such as principles, techniques, advisories ("tips"), self-assessment questions, and the like. Here is a sampling:

- "Principal skills" the consultant must have (Chapter 1)
- "Training skills"—31 of them! (Chapter 2)
- Pros and cons of data collection methods (Chapter 4)
- "Classic errors" in data analysis (Chapter 5)
- Major training methods (Chapter 6)
- "Consulting interventions" (Chapter 8)
- Several supplementary lists of guidelines, procedures, and methods (Chapter 8)
- Reasons for meetings, and techniques for improving meetings (Chapter 10)
- "Emergency kit" for making oral presentations (Chapter 11)
- Self-administered "challenge readiness inventory" (Chapter 11)
- Criteria for evaluating the impact of training (Chapter 17)
- Criteria for evaluating the effectiveness of consulting interventions (Chapter 18)

As the foregoing titles suggest, this book is amazingly comprehensive. Perusing its pages, I thought of the varied consulting assignments I myself had undertaken over the years—all the while regretting that no such book was available to me as I was starting out in the 1950s. The more I reflected, the more I became convinced that almost no problem I have ever encountered has been overlooked by Professor DeWine. When we recall that she has had more than thirty years of experience as a consultant, this is hardly surprising. In fact the book, while not pretending to be more than a practical guide, even addresses some topics one would expect to find in a full-blown treatise—elements of what could be regarded as groundwork for a "proto-theory" of communication consulting.

I should like now to single out several features of the book that, in my judgment, merit special attention.

1. The practice of consulting is positioned in a frame of contemporary scholarship and research in the field known as "organizational communication." The reader is given to understand that consulting does not exist in a vacuum—as a bag of tricks totally unrelated to theoretical underpinnings.

   The author does not devote a major segment of the book to a point-by-point exposition of basic concepts in organizational communication, but rather draws attention to a number of concepts, principles, and research findings, always taking care to demonstrate their relevance to consulting problems. The reader is left in no doubt that communication consulting can never be regarded as casual moonlighting for the dilettante but that it is serious business, requiring of the practitioner nothing less than a sophisticated understanding of research in human communication theory, organizational behavior, and management. Although the author is convinced that consultants will be more successful if they apply the principles she expounds, she gives absolutely no encouragement to those innocent souls who would like to believe that reading her book is a painless substitute for a thorough grounding in the appropriate disciplines.

2. Among both theorists and practitioners there has always been confusion regarding four significantly different, but overlapping, forms of helping interventions: teaching, counseling, training, and consulting. Unquestionably, in many consulting assignments, counseling, training, and teaching are all occurring simultaneously; in some other assignments, the consultant is acting almost exclusively as a teacher, as a trainer, or as a counselor. I am convinced that many unhappy episodes in consulting result from the failure, on the part of the consultant, the client, or both, to grasp the important differences that hold among these four activities. It is fortunate, then, that Professor DeWine has given careful thought (especially in Chapter 2) to this problem, emphasizing the crucial fact that consulting, when properly conducted, is one of the "helping" professions. She follows through in later chapters by focusing especially upon two of the most common tasks that consultants undertake: training and teaching. For both of these the reader will find a wealth of specific, down-to-earth suggestions.

3. The practitioner is advised how to "design consulting interventions" (Chapter 8), in terms of four basic categories: diagnostic, process (including confrontation and negotiation), problem solving, and decision making. Any consultant who has neglected to think through the ramifications of these categories is headed for serious trouble.

4. A topic that may come as a surprise in a book about consulting is represented by Chapter 11, "When Your Client Asks: 'How Can I Face

This Audience?'" In some respects this chapter may be regarded as merely a summary of familiar principles of public speaking. But it is also much more. Three elements are especially noteworthy. The first offers an "emergency kit for presentations," an amazingly comprehensive inventory of devices for dealing with just about every glitch that has ever bedeviled a public speaker. It includes, for example, such items as paper towels, extension cords, rolls of masking tape, transparency pens, headache medications, magnifying glasses, scissors, flashlights, envelopes with stamps, single-edge razor blades, and dimes (for removing jammed slide trays).

The second presentation tool is a "speaker's checklist." Among scores of items are these: coat racks in "secure" locations, tables for hand-outs, ready access to restrooms, window blinds, a marked script or cue sheet for projectionists, lectern lights, easels, and tape for door latches (not to recapitulate Watergate, but to preserve silence during late arrivals!).

The third is a self-administered "challenge readiness inventory" (borrowed from a Synergy Group newsletter). It invites prospective speakers, using a ten-point scale, to rate their predicted "comfort levels" when confronted by sixteen speaking situations. Sample questions are: "Present a proposal or sales talk with appropriate documentation to a client group"; "Deliver a 5- to 10-minute, all-purpose, amusing, and motivating talk to groups from 3 to 3,000"; and "Present a one-minute television editorial on the benefits your industry brings to society."

Devices such as these vividly illustrate Professor DeWine's rare ability, derived from her many years of experience "in the trenches," to provide detailed, hands-on advice to beginners as well as veterans in the consulting profession.

5. The author's treatment of feedback, a staple of communication textbooks, is unusually helpful when it offers excellent guidelines for giving and receiving feedback. I have learned, from painful personal experience, how thin the ice is when a consultant sets out to provide survey findings to a client organization whose members cannot tolerate bad news. Professor DeWine's suggestions should help practitioners to deal with such hazardous situations.

6. An especially provocative chapter (14) is devoted to a question frequently asked but seldom answered (at least in print): "How do I cope with difficult people?" The chapter, not surprisingly, offers no surefire formulas. Indeed, its candor is commendable for acknowledging that consultants must face up to the inevitability of failure in their dealings with a certain number of difficult people. Given this constraint, Chapter 14 offers sage, experience-based advice.

7. Chapter 18 contains absolutely essential material, namely, criteria for evaluating consulting interventions. Four points of view are

considered: the consultant's effectiveness, the consultant's own satisfaction, the client's satisfaction, and long-term outcomes of an entire project. Since every aspect of consulting demands careful consideration of ethics, it is noteworthy that many of the criteria in this chapter require the consultant to confront ethical issues.

8. Finally, the book is jam-packed with *specific real-life examples*, drawn from Professor DeWine's thirty years of consulting experience.

I now ask the reader to recall that, as an academic field, "organizational communication" is young. Organized graduate curricula have been in existence only since the 1950s (in fact, many were established as late as the mid-1970s). Ironically, a case could be made that communication *consulting* has a longer history than does the academic field of organizational communication itself. Both professorial and nonacademic entrepreneurs were offering their services as communication consultants (under a variety of labels, to be sure) at least as far back as the 1920s. In fact, Dale Carnegie—thought to be the first communication consultant—got his start as a speech instructor at a New York City YMCA in 1912. The 1920s saw the appearance of textbooks (including Carnegie's in 1926), advertised as teaching aids to be used in helping business and professional clients to improve their on-the-job communication skills. After the Second World War, skills training, aimed as it was at individual effectiveness, expanded into efforts to improve the functioning of an entire organization. However—until now—there has been no comprehensive guidebook for those who serve as communication consultants to organizational clients.

In a paper published some years ago (1979), discussing communication consulting as one of the helping professions, I warned that the consultant "occupies a role which always has the potential of doing irreparable damage to many persons," adding that even surgeons are "in a position to hurt fewer individuals than are many organizational consultants." I still hold this opinion, but, with the sage guidance Professor DeWine offers in this book—in which she reveals all her trade secrets—I have no hesitation in predicting that communication consultants will be far more likely to do good, and far less likely to do harm, than would otherwise have been the case.

Keeping all this in mind helps one to appreciate the special importance of this book. To say that it fills—and fills admirably—a long-standing void is to indulge in understatement.

INTRODUCTION

Richard H. Brown
Chair and CEO of EDS

A friend of mine, a high school teacher, once commented to me: "Just because you tell them something doesn't mean they know it." He knew that teaching, like all communication, is more than a random toss of the ball. If there's no catch, there's no communication. Business author Brent Filson highlighted this important truth when he wrote, "Communication isn't simply moving information. It's moving people by using information; it's transmitting a conviction from one person to another." Sue DeWine's book, *The Consultant's Craft: Improving Organizational Communication*, certainly follows this adage. It's not just about information; it's about affecting people. Every part of this excellent text on organizational communication is firmly grounded in the way people think, how they react to information, and how they interact with each other.

My experience as a business executive absolutely supports this approach. There are many ways to describe a business enterprise. For example, there is a legal description, such as you would find embodied in its articles of incorporation. There are material descriptions that describe the business in terms of its capitalization, its assets, or its sales revenues. There are functional definitions that tell you what the business does, what needs it meets, and what products or services it provides. But if you are looking to understand what a business truly is, and how it really works, I believe the most pertinent starting point is to define it from the human angle. Simply put, before it is anything else, a business is a group of people organized around a common goal.

When a business is understood this way, the universal importance of organizational communication becomes clear. It is not only a discipline for specialists, but a core element of leadership. After all, whether you're talking about the CEO or a shop foreman, leadership is at base a matter of influencing people to agree on and pursue a goal. The leader knows that people do the job and that motivation is essential if people are to do it well.

This is where you will most often find the difference between a mere manager and a manager who is also a leader. The leader is always aware that the job is being done by people. Leaders tend to be behavior- and people-centered, whereas mere managers can often be mechanistic and thing-centered. In his seminal work, *American Spirit: Visions of a New Corporate Culture*, Lawrence M. Miller tells us that leaders appeal to their people for contributions to customers, to the public interest, and to the long-term goals of the corporation, but managers tend to push the team with quantified, short-term objectives. Leaders give energy to an enterprise by defining purpose, and managers steer the energy. Leaders define success in terms of product and service achievements, and managers define it by numbers.

At the all-important point where decisions have to be executed and goals have to be achieved, leadership becomes essentially a matter of communicating—communicating the goal and communicating the enthusiasm needed to achieve the goal. Certainly this means that the most effective leader will be a consummate communicator. But it also means a leader must promote good communication among all the groups and individuals in the organization. There must be communication up and down and across the business. Leadership, therefore, implies some expertise in the techniques of using information to move people. As I see it, the greater the number of managers in a business who are good communicators, the better the leadership in that business, and the better its performance is likely to be.

As its title implies, *The Consultant's Craft* is a book for consultants and about consulting. The perspective throughout tends to be that of an outside consultant who works with a business on an ad hoc basis to address specific communication issues. But Professor DeWine makes it clear from the beginning that this is also a book for those managers within a business whose official responsibility is to ensure good communication in their organizations and for executives who know that human resources are the key to an organization's success. I would go further, and say that this is a book for every manager. Is each of us not responsible for some aspect of the process of communication? And should we not all know and use, at least to some extent, the techniques of organizational communication? To my mind, *The Consultant's Craft* is indeed a treatise on the process of communicating, but it is also by extension a treatise on a key aspect of management and leadership.

This book can serve as a corrective for the belief that internal communications is one of the "soft" disciplines, to be handled by the corporate communications or human resources department or perhaps by an outside consultant, but certainly not by those with the more "serious" task of running the business. Explicitly or implicitly, every part of the book supports the thesis that good communicating is critical to good management and good business performance. No one can read this and come away thinking that communication is separate and apart from the other facets of managing a business, or believing that it is anything other than "serious," or convinced that it is "someone else's job." In fact, at one point the author suggests that communication skills could become part of the management performance appraisal process.

Similarly, the manager who thinks effective communicating is always easy will be in for a surprise. Professor DeWine's analysis of problems and her comprehensive treatment of solutions illustrate the attention to depth and detail that must go into the process of communicating. The reader will gain new respect for the science of communication, as it becomes clear how complex and demanding it can be. Important communication decisions will be less likely to be tossed off casually, or made on the basis of whim or fancy.

My perspective in reading *The Consultant's Craft* was that of a businessperson, and so is my reaction to it. I am not a consultant. But if I were a consultant—or a student preparing for a career in organizational consulting—I am sure I would be just as pleased with this book. Professor DeWine has compiled a summary of the best in current thinking on her topic, and at the same time she has created a thoroughly detailed, hands-on manual, rich with illustrations and examples from her long experience as a consultant. It can serve as a textbook for the novice or a reference for the practitioner.

American business has come a long way since the days when hierarchical authority structures and mechanistic measurements were the norm for management. Today, most managers have learned they must attend to human factors, to motivation, to the quality and process of information flow. Professor DeWine's book is testimony to the progress that's been made in this regard and a contribution to further progress.

PART *I*

Overview

*T*his section of the book provides some basic definitions of the individuals for whom this book is written. Who in the organization is likely to be working on human communication problems? If you are hired as an outside consultant, how do your activities affect internal managers who may be working on the same problems?

Chapter 1 presents an example of a CEO with whom I worked and the human communication problems she faced. Chapters 2 and 3 identify the differences among training, consulting, and other helping professions. Throughout the book are personal examples and stories about clients with whom I have worked for the past 25 years. I have also included self-assessment instruments, evaluation forms, short articles, and intervention materials that I expect readers to pull out and use in a variety of settings.

Part I provides the foundation for sections that follow. Once you can identify how this material applies to you, it will be apparent how you can use the techniques.

Chapter **1**

THE CRAFT OF CONSULTING

Our deepest fear is not that we are inadequate.
Our deepest fear is that we are powerful beyond measure.

Anonymous

The word *craft* is used purposefully in the title of this book. Consulting takes more than extensive organizational knowledge, training and experience in organizations, and a set of complex skills. Being a consultant to an organization and its leaders takes all of this and more. Consulting is a craft that also takes some less defined abilities like intuition, curiosity, sincerity, and a keen awareness of the power one possesses in changing the lives of others.

Defining Craft in the Consulting Context

This chapter begins the process of defining the craft of consulting, but some of the attributes needed for this craft cannot be taught. I hope if you don't already have these special abilities you will know when to seek help from people who do. The following story demonstrates some of the attributes needed by the external consultant as well as the internal consultant who, regardless of job title, may be a manager, a human resources specialist, or a communication specialist.

> Early in 2000 a client contacted me to help instill in her staff a sense of interdependence. Sarah Tanley[1] was CEO of a large health-care facility where each practitioner had his or her own patients; however, they belonged to a group practice plan, which required that they adhere to some principles of operation. While each had a unique style of providing service, they all had to meet group practice standards so the group as a whole could survive. One health-care provider, Jake Shonborn, longed for the days when he could take enough time with each patient so the patient's questions could be answered and he could know the patient as a whole person in a specific family context. Janice Nettles, another health-care provider, managed to see twice as many patients per day as Jake did and

still felt she was able to provide good service while increasing productivity.

How could Sarah manage to integrate these two diverse approaches to providing health care to the region? Sarah could call on the expertise of the Human Resources Manager, who was skilled at conflict resolution, or she could ask Rob Harnish, one of the health-care providers who had served as a mediator for the group in the past because of his special abilities, or she could select someone outside the system. As you read about some of the more difficult problems Sarah Tanley faced, try to place yourself in the position of the individual who has been asked to help resolve them.

Organizations are plagued with a variety of persistent communication problems. In more than 25 years of consulting activity, I have worked with organizational members who did not clearly communicate expectations for new employees, gave miscues about work to be done, were involved in bitter interpersonal battles, did not know how to give positive *or* negative feedback, modeled poor listening behaviors, misused group decision-making techniques, and were generally described as poor communicators. Of course it is easier to identify these problems in others than in ourselves! My job as a consultant is not only to help solve these problems, but to develop the skill in others to solve the problems themselves. In that sense the techniques and strategies discussed in this book are useful for the consultant and the manager as well. In fact, any number of individuals in the organization with better-than-average communication skills could intervene and help resolve such dilemmas.

Individuals in the organization who are able to assess communication variables effectively and who can design methods for smooth information flow throughout the organization will be the organizational leaders in the future. These individuals may be in staff positions, like the staff consultant available to Sarah Tanley, or may be people like Sarah herself who are in line management positions and have acquired communication skills to deal with human relations problems described in the opening of this chapter. Throughout this text these individuals are referred to as "communication specialists" or "communication managers." Communication managers spend a great deal of time dealing with people problems.

Many authors have indicated the importance of controlling information in the organization. As Goldhaber, Dennis, Richetto, and Wiio reported in 1979, ". . . we are experiencing a revolution in which decision-making power is rapidly shifting from traditional decision makers (the line organization) to traditional knowledge workers (the staff organization). We propose that those responsible for interpreting that organizational environment have emerged as the true controllers of the organization and that the future will, if anything, further solidify their organizational power" (p. 4). Later, Goldhaber (1986) asserted, "Communication is essential to an organization. Information is vital to effective communication. Persons who control information control power" (p. 6).

As these authors predicted, in today's world the acquisition and use of organizational information determines, in large measure, the amount of influence any individual has. In other words, the more you know, the more likely it is that you can be effective.

With the advent of new communication technologies, the focus on information power is even more striking. In fact, Everett Rogers suggested this will change the structure and power base of the entire organization. "The new information technologies allow the restructuring and/or destructuring of organizational communication" (Rogers, 1988, p. 443). Thus, new technologies increase the importance of information power sources. These information power sources can be anywhere in the organization where individuals are knowledgeable about the flow of messages and can change the system when communication patterns are causing a decrease in organizational effectiveness.

Communication consultants are particularly well-suited to increasing organizational effectiveness because so much depends on how well organizational members are able to communicate and use relevant information. Thus the process of developing or increasing one's ability to assess and intervene in the communication system can be enhanced by examining the variables involved in organizational communication. It will be easier for Sarah Tanley to build a team among her staff if she has some general idea of the communication process.

Organizational Communication and the Communication Manager

Organizational communication is a discipline that seeks to help individuals understand the central nature of communication in all aspects of organizational work. The following definition of organizational communication is a modified version of one developed by Fred Jablin (1990, p. 157). In another publication my co-author, Dan Modaff, and I defined organizational communication as "the process of creating, exchanging, interpreting (correctly or incorrectly), and storing messages within a system of human interrelationships. The phrase 'system of human interrelationships' is critical to this definition. Communication is a human activity. It takes place only because human beings form relationships, which are sustained by certain communication practices. . . . Misunderstandings occur when the interpretation of the message is decidedly different from the intended message" (DeWine & Modaff, in press).

Communication in any environment is an interactional process in which persons share meaning verbally and nonverbally. The communication manager must be very sensitive to the fact that communication is *irreversible, unrepeatable,* and *reciprocal.* Consequently, the communication manager in the organization understands that once a message has been sent and received, he or she can neither erase the effect of that message nor ever repeat the message in exactly the same way. Because communication is a dynamic, ever-changing process, one can never move backward. Finally, people tend to respond in a manner similar to the way others talk to them. Consequently, the communication process builds on the interaction of two or more people.

For example, I worked with a manager who told her assistant, "You worked out much better than I expected!" The assistant was offended because he felt that meant she had not had a high opinion of him initially. There was no way the manager could take back what she had said; her only course was to listen carefully, demonstrate understanding of the assistant's feelings, and send new supportive messages. Those first words could not be erased, but they could be neutralized. We are not able to repeat a communication experience. The reciprocal nature of the interaction, with the sender becoming the receiver of feedback, makes the process continuous.

In an **organization** there is a sense of interdependence among members who occupy positions in a hierarchy and attempt to achieve common goals. A hierarchy may be quite informal, but there is always some division of labor and some sense of who makes the final decisions. In any organization communication is effected by a complex network of individuals in a unique organizational environment. Sarah's staff are independent, each with his or her own clients. Yet they work in an organizational structure and depend on individuals in that structure to provide support services such as a data base for client information, a processing center to handle client information, and a company wisely investing its money. They need each other and yet still need to be independent.

Organizational communication is the process by which messages are sent, the monitoring of the types of messages sent, the values associated with those messages, the amount of information conveyed, the rules and norms under which messages are sent, and the organizational variables that affect the process such as structure and outcome measures. Those very structures and outcome variables make organizational communication different from family communication, for example.

Values are communicated along with the content of a message. For example, the first nonfamily member to head a small, previously family-owned company unintentionally sent messages that suggested he did not accept the values held by the family. When he did not renew sponsorship of a local Little League baseball team, he unwittingly sent a message that he was not interested in the community and the employees' families. Employees saw this as a sign of a "hard-nosed" manager who did not care about their welfare, when quite the opposite was true. Each message we send carries a set of values we are communicating.

Communication managers/specialists spend a large portion of their time managing human interactions and developing human potential in the organization. They are information managers in that they monitor the process by which messages are sent and received. Their job title may be "manager" or "administrator" who has the ability to monitor this process, or they are "staff personnel" whose primary job function is to develop human potential in the organization. They also work with managers to develop their potential for solving human communication problems. Sarah Tanley is a communication manager. There may also be an individual in the corporate office in a staff position who is responsible for developing human resources. "The consultant must work jointly with the manager so that the manager can learn to see the problem for him- or herself, share in the diagnosis and be actively involved in creating a solution" (Coghlan, 1988, p. 27).

Application of Organizational Communication Principles

The opening case presents a number of communication issues. Individual goals seem to be in opposition to group goals, causing defensive communication, and motivational problems exist as well. In addition, violations of communication rules and climate norms have caused tension among the staff members.

The process of assessing the impact of such variables and developing programs for improving the communication process is the focus of this book. Later chapters identify effective methods for determining what communication variables are disrupting the exchange of messages among persons in the organization. A communication manager or consultant needs to be able to effectively apply these methods to enter or intervene in the system and create change.

Intervention

The term **intervention** refers to an action taken by an individual or a group of persons designed to interrupt and change some ongoing human process. For example, one staff I worked with had established a pattern of very cold and unresponsive behavior in the office. They did not talk to each other informally or even greet one another. In order to "intervene" and change that process, I asked that every staff member go out of his or her way each morning to greet every co-worker.

Attitudes follow behavior. I believe you must change behavior first and then attitudes. This simple suggestion obviously did not solve all the interpersonal problems plaguing this group, but it began a process where people paid more attention to the way they dealt with each other. It was an attempt to *intervene* in the system and begin the process of change.

In the case of Sarah, one intervention was suggested: fire and rehire. In one sense, the manager then loses two valuable components—the time invested in training these individuals and their knowledge of the company and its product. Sometimes this loss is less damaging than the potentially negative impact the individual might have on the system. The manager might also choose to ignore the problem under the belief that the best way to help people is to get out of their way and let them solve it themselves.

Another solution may be for the manager to restructure job responsibilities so those who are capable of handling larger responsibilities are given increased assignments, and those less capable are isolated so their impact is minimized. Communication managers look at the total system and how human communication is presently operating. After carefully assessing communication needs, they design and implement intervention strategies to combat nonproductive behavior.

Assessment

In the case of Sarah Tanley the organizational communication manager (who might be Sarah herself, an internal staff member, or an outside consultant) would assess the flow of communication among the health-care practitioners using a number of techniques and instruments described in later chapters. For example, a communication audit might be administered. A **communication audit** can determine where communication problems exist and is similar to a financial audit in that each one uses a battery of techniques and instruments (see Chapter 8 for further discussion of audits).

In essence, communication managers recognize that "information is power" and the ability to successfully handle important messages in the organization increases an individual's visibility. Training others to handle communication problems also enables the communication manager to have greater control over organizational outcomes.

Communication managers also recognize that there are *no simple answers when dealing with human behavior.* Communication managers can only *provide choices* and generate a better understanding of *probable consequences* of our actions. When I actually worked with the individuals presented in the case study, changes occurred only after a complex assessment process. Specific assessment processes are covered in the next several chapters.

Skills Needed by the Communication Manager

Communication managers need people-oriented skills with a focus on human resource development. Huse (1985) articulated this focus when he talked about the organizational development manager. If one replaces the phrases "organizational development consulting" and "change agent" with "communication manager," the emphasis remains the same:

> Certainly, OD [Organizational Development] consulting is as much a person specialization as a task specialization. The change agent must not only have a repertoire of technical skills but must also have the personality and interpersonal competence to be able to use himself or herself as an instrument of change. Regardless of technical training and/or accreditation, the consultant must be able to maintain a boundary position, coordinating between various units and departments and mixing disciplines, theories, technology, and research findings in an organic rather than mechanical way. The practitioner is potentially the most important OD technology available. (p. 452)

Eight Principal Skills

To be successful with human resource management, communication managers must have eight skills. These skills enhance an individual's interpersonal competence (Huse, 1985).

First, communication managers must be *eclectic* in that they choose from a number of "systems" or "doctrines." In this sense, the effective communication manager does not have one way of working with people, but instead is sensitive to the needs and values of others. Effective managers choose from a variety of styles to find those that will mesh best with established styles. This is not to say that individuals can change their basic personality structures as they move from group to group in the organization. Communication managers, however, need to have a contingency style of communication and make modest adaptations to the situation.

Second, communication managers must see themselves as *facilitators* of change. In this way, they assist or help the change process but may not serve as the agent of change. They prod where necessary and "back out" of the system when their presence would inhibit action.

Third, communication managers must be *situational experts*. This means they must be able to develop new problem-solving strategies that are generated *out of the situation* rather than being predetermined. Managers must be "tuned in" to the needs and special issues being expressed in each situation and creative enough to be able to adapt human development processes to the particular needs of that setting.

Fourth, communication managers must have *assessment* skills. They must have at their disposal survey methodologies, interview and observational techniques, and other tools for assessing the communication system at work, and they must know which tools will be most effective in a particular situation. In order to improve the communication system one must have a good understanding of how communication presently flows throughout the organization.

Fifth, communication managers must be a cross between *process managers* and *lay technicians*. To monitor the process effectively, managers must have a good understanding of the technical components. This does not mean that they are skilled technicians, but they should have a layperson's comprehensive understanding of how various technical components unite in the system to effect the whole.

Sixth, communication managers must be able to *identify internal resources*. If the "natural resources" of the organization are not utilized, then the organization is not able to develop human potential on its own. Communication managers must be keenly aware of the expertise among organizational members that may not have been tapped.

A seventh, very important characteristic for managers is the ability to *network* throughout the system. In this capacity, communication managers must have a good sense of what they do and do not know, as well as the ability to create a network among other managers and use resources uncovered in the system. This helps to establish a support system throughout the organization that will help human development processes continue to be productive.

The eighth skill requires that communication managers *recognize* when a part of the system no longer needs their continuous support and assistance, and *when termination of the relationship* with either a subunit or a system *is appropriate*. Communication managers who continue to be facilitators when the group or unit has taken over those functions on its own can be destructive to the process.

Communication managers are always training organizational members to take over the job they are doing at any one time. We can summarize these abilities by saying a **communication manager** must be

- an eclectic practitioner
- a facilitator
- a situational expert
- an assessor
- a process specialist/lay technician
- a resource identifier
- a network developer/user
- a temporary associate

The consultant may have all these characteristics and still not be successful unless the organization is supportive and the consultant is perceived as credible.

To test your ability to recognize these skills in yourself, a check list has been developed for your use (see Form 1.1). Ask a colleague or client to complete the form for you and compare their responses to your own. As you assess your capabilities and strive to improve your ability to work as a communication manager, this knowledge of the "status quo" will help you determine which areas to address first.

ASSESSMENT INSTRUMENT FOR ORGANIZATIONAL COMMUNICATION SPECIALISTS

Directions

Mark each statement on a scale of 1 to 5 in terms of how characteristic that quality is of the individual named below. Base your response on your observation of this individual's behavior in the organizational setting.

1 = not characteristic at all

2 = occasionally characteristic

3 = neutral

4 = somewhat characteristic

5 = very characteristic

_____ (name of person being observed)

_____ 1. tends to use a contingency style of leadership, meaning this individual uses whatever style is most appropriate for the group or individual involved.

_____ 2. is most often a facilitator of change rather than causing change or operating on his or her own.

_____ 3. is more comfortable creating new approaches to problem solving that arise from the situation itself, rather than planning the problem-solving method prior to identifying the level and depth of the problem.

_____ 4. has the skills necessary to assess the communication system in the organization; knows which instruments to use to collect various types of data and can successfully analyze that data so that recommendations can be generated.

_____ 5. has enough technical knowledge of the organizational system to understand the language of the system and can relate his or her knowledge to specific technical problems.

_____ 6. is a process manager in that she or he is extremely sensitive to the ways in which things are accomplished in the organization; is able to highlight the process being used during interactions.

_____ 7. has a good ability to assess what he or she does not know and can link others to resources that may be useful to solving problems when she or he is unable to help directly.

_____ 8. is able to identify internal resources for a group so that it can make the best use of the available human potential.

_____ 9. has a knowledge of intervention techniques that can improve communication once problem areas have been identified.

(Continued)

**ASSESSMENT INSTRUMENT FOR ORGANIZATIONAL
COMMUNICATION SPECIALISTS** *(Continued)*

_____ **10.** can recognize when he or she is no longer needed by the system or unit of the system and is sensitive to smooth termination of that working relationship while allowing for follow-up and a continuation of the system's internal support system.

Scoring

A score of 45 to 50 indicates a perception that you possess these skills to an extensive degree.

A score of 35 to 44 indicates an above-average perception of demonstration of communication manager skills. You need to identify those areas most in need of development and concentrate your efforts there.

A score below 35 indicates a low perception of communication manager skills. The fact that you are reading this textbook is an indication of your attempt to increase these skills, or it may be an indication that you don't feel these skills are necessary to the communication manager. If you are just learning these skills, a low score should be expected. Return to this self-assessment after you have finished the book. If your scores and the scores of the colleague or client vary tremendously, ask for input from several others. If your perceptions are markedly different from theirs, you have valuable feedback. As you continue to read, attempt to apply the skills to yourself and your own working environment. Use those skills and techniques that seem most useful and effective in that particular environment.

Activities of Communication Managers

Farace, Monge, and Russell (1977) developed an interesting outline of actual activities that are typical of the communication manager's job in the organization. These activities include

- interacting with other managers to develop communication strategies and policies.
- supervising the planning and production of internal and external communication programs.
- devising communication programs for organizational units to facilitate production.
- modifying and expanding the job-performance appraisal system to reflect communication skills.
- preparing manuals that outline policies and procedures and developing and implementing communication training programs.

These are all programs that can be developed and implemented by an internal communication manager with or without the help of external managers. *External communication managers* are experts in the field of communication who are not a part of the organizational system but who come into the system on a temporary basis to assist with some specific communication program.

There are advantages and disadvantages to both internal and external communication managers. A discussion of some of the approaches taken by both internal and external communication managers will help clarify the roles of each.

The Consummate Trainer

Spaid (1989) has outlined ten characteristics of what he calls the "consummate" trainer. The consummate trainer

1. has experience in virtually all tasks and techniques of the entire range of training methodology and can carry out these activities at an acceptable level of proficiency, but prefers and performs some of them exceptionally well.
2. orchestrates the parts of training with an acute awareness of the impact of the whole.
3. is flexible and versatile and open to change, from one training session to another and from one subject to the next.
4. takes risks and can submerge ego for the good of the group and the training.

5. can generate excitement in training, through a sense of drama.

6. has a sense of humor, which is applied to self as well as to others.

7. does his or her own homework and keeps on learning.

8. exhibits patience with learners and with self.

9. has enough independence and toughness of mind not to be overcome by fads and untested theories.

10. respects wisdom, as not knowledge alone or experience alone, but each informing the other (pp. 18–19).

If the trainer has all these characteristics, then he or she will be part magician, vaudeville act, teacher, counselor, and comedian. But most of all, he or she will be an outstanding trainer.

Internal and External Communication Specialists: A Comparison

Communication managers may be permanent members of the organization working internally or external consultants called in to provide expertise that the company lacks. Both roles have several things in common aside from their focus on the management of human resources.

Common Factors

First, *both internal and external communication managers must work with others who are a permanent part of the system.* They need access to information sources and rules and norms under which communication normally occurs.

Second, *both can be called in or imposed on* the organizational members by forces outside those immediate groups. As a consequence, they can both sometimes suffer from individuals' perceptions that they are "spies" for upper management, especially if there is mistrust between upper management and the group with whom the consultants are working. After all, they reason, if upper management hired this person to work with the group, that person must have been told what to look for. It is important for both the internal and external communication manager to establish a high level of trust with the client members.

Third, *both need to play multiple roles* and may need to shift from time to time from trainer to advocate to planner. The ability to be flexible in a variety of contexts is critical for the communication manager. Finally, *both want to be successful!*

Internal Communication Specialist		External Communication Specialist
+	Knowledge of client system	−
−	Objectivity	+
−	Greater flexibility due to low impact of problem on daily routine	+
+	Known quantity	−
−	Seen as valuable resource	+
−	Leverage with respect to involvement	+
+	Access to evaluation and successful intervention	−
−	Smooth termination	+

FIGURE 1.1   Pluses and Minuses of Internal and External Organizational Communication Specialists

needed by management in the formulation of policies and long-range plans; to assist management in developing and implementing policies; to assist management in establishing sound organizational plans, including objectives, functions, responsibilities, authorities, and relationships; and to recommend, coordinate, and perform the analysis, planning, design and installation of the systems. (Spechler & Wicker, 1980, p. 27)

For communication managers, these activities all have some relationship to human resource development.

Third, Spechler and Wicker also stated the *internal manager must be located on the organization charts* so that the operating management has a great sense of control over the change process. The consulting group's location on organization charts is an indication of how seriously top management takes its function.

Fourth, there must be a *"change orientation"* within the organization, which means organizational members must be willing to look at themselves critically and adopt new systems if necessary. In addition, the internal managers *must be professionally qualified* and willing to maintain a *continuous education of themselves.* Spechler and Wicker pointed out that such managers may be seen as a threat and thus need to sell their programs by using a well-developed marketing program. There must be an *emphasis on performance measurement* since these specialties could be a great aid to the organization in developing a strong performance-appraisal system. Often these conditions do not exist and while that may prevent overall company change programs, individual consulting can be done with less-than-ideal support.

Finally, the organization must be *willing to evaluate the success* of the internal managers' programs based on an analysis of the costs and benefits of the work performed. This evaluation should be a part of the design from the very first step so that every stage of the process can be included.

It should be obvious from the previous discussion that both the internal and external communication managers have the potential for advantages and disadvantages associated with their roles. Individuals in either of these roles can use the techniques and materials in this text effectively.

It is my belief that in order to mitigate the negative results of either role and to magnify the positive attributes of both, an internal/external communication manager *team* should be developed whenever possible. This requires the internal communication manager to be continually aware of those outside the organizational system who might be helpful in developing specific communication assessment/intervention programs. Communication managers, both internal and external to the organization, need a variety of skills to make their jobs more likely to have successful outcomes.

Because of the communication explosion of the last 25 years, organizations are realizing that their own communication is big business. Many top-level executives believe if business is to survive and enhance public opinion, it must have the capability to respond effectively. How well a company meets its communication needs determines not only its public image, but also the bottom line on its annual reports. Top-level management is beginning to understand the need to devote as much careful attention to internal and external communication as it devotes to product management and capital investment. Successful executives are developing a new awareness of the need for industry to communicate with many more elements of society than ever before. They also recognize the vital role that communication plays in the day-to-day management of a company. Once there is widespread recognition of the need to communicate effectively to influence the public and political climate in which business operates, the communication manager's position will be even more critical to the functioning of the organization.

The following story from Patrice Buzzanell points out the essential function of communication in any consulting assignment. The story situates communication at the center of this organization's attempt to establish better career development opportunities for its employees. It is a good story to end the first chapter because Patrice rediscovered "just how much organizational communication researchers can contribute to corporate functioning."

—————— **LESSONS LEARNED** ——————

A Consulting Story from Patrice Buzzanell

Patrice Buzzanell is an associate professor at Purdue University. She typically works with engineers and engineering managers on career management interventions and trends.

Years ago I was invited to gather data and prepare executive summaries and presentations for a telecommunications company in the midwestern United States. My contact was the director of electronic engineering, a very bright and talented man who seemed to have a knack for locating and joining telecommunications companies at the edge of explosive growth and who seemed to thrive in this kind of challenging and turbulent environment.

Members of this organization prided themselves on their innovativeness, their engineering management talent, and their desire to devise means to recruit, retain, and recognize technical expertise, particularly through professional career ladders and appropriate rewards (i.e., those means of compensation and perks that would be considered desirable by technical experts, such as lab equipment, time to do a sabbatical at a university research center, and budgetary discretion and decision-making power for their project teams that were equivalent to levels of similarly ranked executives).

The corporation flew me in for a preliminary presentation to the president, vice presidents, directors, and other top officers. I had access to company documents and to executives' and engineers' time as I learned the culture and politics of this corporation. Then the executives set up the group data-gathering sessions around the engineers' work schedules and provided supplies, refreshments, and publicity to indicate the degree to which the corporate executives were interested in obtaining survey results.

The experience was enlightening to me for a number of reasons. It reinforced my beliefs in the power of social scientific studies to obtain useful information for corporations and in communication as central to effective organizational functioning. My presentations enabled them to

- target areas where they needed to communicate better their commitment to professional employees and projects. Some suggested interventions included.
  - project team and one-on-one meetings to discuss career options, particularly avenues devised over the past year by a high-powered team of executives and engineers

- consideration of a career development office in the Human Resources Department to signal commitment to each employee's career
- funding for brochures outlining newly created career paths, means of obtaining key learnings to enable job bidding, and probable timetables and compensation packages

- incorporate mentorship roles at critical junctures, such as during the transition from technical expert to engineering manager.
- reduce the rapidity of restructurings because of the negative effect on morale, innovativeness, work productivity, and retention.
- focus on internal career information source development. Clusters of specific sources were associated with intent to leave and potential voluntary turnover of those managers and engineers the corporation most wanted to retain.

The experience also was enlightening because it reinforced just how much organizational communication researchers can contribute to corporate functioning. These organization members had spent many thousands of dollars designing a "perfect" career system, yet they forgot that their time was wasted unless they effectively communicated both the details of the system and their commitment to it. The recommendations I listed didn't seem especially earth-shattering to me but they made a huge difference to the people who were trying to create (and live in) a "better" working environment. This consulting experience gave me confidence that I knew a lot. And recognizing just how much we can contribute is different from the academic experience in which you often are aware of how much you don't know.

Patrice can be reached through the Department of Communication at Purdue University (1366 LAEB, W. Lafayette, IN 47907-1366) or <pbuzzanell@sla. purdue.edu>.

Note

1. The names have been changed to protect the privacy of the people involved.

Additional Resources

DeWine, S., & Modaff, D. (in press). *Organizational communication: Foundations, challenges, and misunderstandings.* Los Angeles: Roxbury.

Dryden, G., & Vos, J. (1997). *The learning revolution.* Auckland, New Zealand: The Learning Web.

Eisenberg, E. M., & Goodall, H. L. (2001). *Organizational communication: Balancing creativity and constraint* (3rd ed.). New York: Bedford/St. Martin's.

Putnam, L. L., Phillips, N., & Chapman, P. (1996). Metaphors of communication and organizations. In S. Clegg, C. Hardy, & W. Nord (Eds.). *Handbook of organizational studies* (pp. 375–408). Thousand Oaks, CA: Sage.

Chapter 2

DEFINING TRAINING AND CONSULTING

■ **HELPING PROFESSIONS**

■ **TRAINING SKILLS**

■ **CONSULTING SKILLS**
Definitions of Consulting
Approaches to Consultation

■ **CAREER OPTIONS**

Lessons Learned: Clarify Your Role

ADDITIONAL RESOURCES

Make no mistake. The communication industry is booming. In-house communication managers are having a hard time finding qualified people, consultants and freelancers have more work than they can handle, small communication agencies are springing up all over the place.

Crescenzo, 1998

*H*uman resource training and consulting are big business. The reason is that managers probably spend more time coping with human relationships and individual behavior problems than they do making decisions about company policies, system maintenance, and organizational outcome issues related to products and services. These human relationships are the core of the organization. Without strong working relationships the company cannot exist. Training and consulting, as discussed in this book, refer to ways in which human behavior can be modified both from inside the organization, by managers, and from outside the organization, by external consultants.

Helping Professions

Training, consulting, and coaching are part of the helping professions. Teaching and counseling are other examples of helping professions. All five focus on assisting others to function more effectively in their personal and professional lives. A comparison of the five will clarify the unique focus for training and consulting.

Training is the direct delivery of skills, through some formal process, to enhance human performance. These skills can be technical knowledge applied to the organization's product or service, or relationship skills applied to working with, and directing the work of, others.

Consulting is entering or intervening in a system to stop some destructive human process and to improve the ability of the organization to function. The destructive process may be affecting the organization's ability to produce quality products, provide prompt services, or function without high turnover and disputes.

Both of these activities (training and consulting) can be delivered by internal employees or external trainers/consultants. The activities of both can be adapted by internal managers as well. Parts II, III, and IV of this book provide specific techniques and suggestions that could be used by anyone facing human relationship problems in the organization and wishing to improve its general work climate. Individuals actively working on human relationship issues and becoming skilled at managing communication issues are referred to as "communication managers."

Figure 2.1 provides a comparison of training and consulting to various other types of helping activities. It is critical for the communication manager to understand how the focus shifts, who is involved in the process, how psychological distance changes, and if expectations increase depending on the type of help being presented.

As helping professions, consulting, training, teaching, counseling, and coaching all focus on human behavior and attempt to enhance individual performance. While they have these things in common, they also differ in dramatic ways so that the process of each is quite different.

Focus is the specific aspect of human behavior the communication manager is addressing. A communication manager may be a teacher, a counselor, a trainer, a coach, or a consultant. A *teacher* is trying to enhance the *knowledge* level of students; a *counselor* wants to help an individual cope with *emotional stress;* a *trainer* is *imparting skills* so that a job can be completed more competently; a *coach* is helping an individual improve his or her *performance;* and a *consultant* is assisting individuals to address *work issues* that when resolved will result in better organizationwide performance and a more positive organizational climate.

Theoretical Issue	Consulting	Training	Teaching	Counseling	Coaching
Focus	issue	skills	knowledge	people	performance
Number of players	3 or more	3 or more	2	2	2
Psychological distance	distant	sometimes close; sometimes distant	sometimes close; sometimes distant	close	close
Follow-up	constant	not responsible	not responsible	sometimes occurs; sometimes doesn't	constant
Who defines problems	together	client	teacher	sometimes client; sometimes counselor	together
Nature of problems	work-related	work/personal	personal	personal	work
Entry issues	great	minimal	medium	great	great

FIGURE 2.1   The Training / Teaching Matrix

The *number of players* changes across these various activities. Consulting and training involve at least three people: the trainer/consultant, the participant, and the individual(s) with whom the participant is working. Usually the goal of training and consulting is to help individuals work more effectively with others and to pass along the skills learned so the performance of those they work with improves as well. For example, a training session for managers on time management ultimately is designed to have the managers not only improve their own time management skills but to assist those they manage to do the same. Teaching, coaching, and counseling involve a more direct delivery with just two people directly involved: the teacher, coach, or counselor and the person receiving the help or education. Although the teacher usually lectures to a group of 15 to 40 people, the relationship is between the teacher and each individual student in the class.

Psychological distance determines how intense and intimate the relationship may get. Counseling is the most interpersonally intense of all the helping activities. Because the counselor and the client are dealing with emotional and personal issues, the process is necessarily a direct connection between the counselor and client. The intensity of this relationship may cause clients to transfer some of their emotional reactions to the situations they find themselves in, to inappropriate feelings of closeness to the counselor. Coaching is as close as counseling but not as intense, since the focus is work performance rather than personal issues.

Teaching and training involve a mixture of more and less distance between the helper and the person being helped. In both cases there are times when the trainer and teacher are imparting knowledge, and the psychological distance is great. There are also times when both the trainer and the teacher are asked to assist an individual to improve his or her performance and, in working with the individual, the teacher or trainer may uncover personal problems preventing the person from performing well.

In consulting, the relationship is usually more distant since the consultant is assisting with the resolution of problems that involve many others beyond those with whom the consultant has direct contact. Often, the consultant is helping the teacher or the trainer determine how to cope with the issues raised by the individuals with whom they must work.

The *follow-up* expected of the trainer and teacher is low. It is expected that the individual who is trained is responsible for her or his own learning, and usually the teacher or trainer is not expected to follow up on the day-to-day use of that knowledge. In sharp contrast, the consultant and coach are often hired especially to follow up on problem solving and to determine how effectively managers are applying solutions to problems. The counselor does not own the problem; however, his or her involvement in the solution is a mixture of direct and indirect follow-up. On a continuum from follow-up being expected to no follow-up at all, the consultant and coach would be placed on the high end of the continuum, the teacher and trainer on the low end, and the counselor in the middle.

Who defines the problem can be a very important determination to make early in the relationship. In training, the client usually defines the problem. A trainer is asked to develop a workshop on supervisory skills and does so. In this case the client has determined that supervisory skills need to be improved. Even when the trainer conducts a needs analysis, this assessment is very abbreviated compared to the problem assessment conducted by the consultant or coach. In fact, often the client and the consultant together focus their entire effort on identifying problems. The teacher is similar to the trainer in that one person defines the problem, only in this case it is the teacher. The teacher, in consultation with state, district, and school guidelines, determines the material to be covered in each class setting.

Depending on the type of counseling being conducted, there may be a mixture of client/counselor definition of problems. For example, a counselor using the approach developed by Sigmund Freud, which was very analytical, would define the problem without collaboration with the client. "Psychoanalysis" is a system of psychology that stresses the unconscious and requires the counselor to analyze for the client what the problems may be. A counselor following the approach developed by Alfred Adler would define the problems in consultation with the client. "Adlerian psychology" is a personality theory in which "two equals cooperatively tackle the education task" (Mosak & Dreikurs, 1973, p. 74). Finally, a counselor using Carl Rogers's approach of acceptance and supportiveness would help the client to define the problem him- or herself. Rogers's "client-centered psychology" has as its central hypothesis that "the growthful potential of any individual will tend to be released in a relationship in which the helping person is experiencing and communicating realness, caring, and a deeply sensitive nonjudgement understanding" (Meador & Rogers, 1973, p. 119).

Another significant difference is the *nature of the problem.* In counseling the nature of the problem is personal; in consulting and coaching it is work-related. If a consultant finds a client pursuing personal issues, the consultant should refer the individual to a counselor or focus on only those aspects of the personal issue that affect work performance. Both training and teaching may be a mixture of the two; however, trainers and teachers should not act as psychological counselors unless trained to do so.

Finally, *entry issues* vary depending on the needs of each situation. Entry issues are those questions that come up during the first encounter with the client or the persons with whom the manager is working. Since the trainer is usually with the participants for a short time, entry issues are minimal and mostly relate to building credibility so the skills that are delivered will be accepted. The teacher is with the student for a longer period of time and thus must build credibility over a period of weeks in order to maintain interest. Since the counselor deals with emotional personal issues, and the consultant and coach address sensitive organizational problems, all three must spend a great deal of time building the trust of the client so that the client will be open and share information necessary to aid diagnosis. Knowing these differences, individuals engaged in training and consulting must possess certain unique skills. These unique skills are examined in the rest of this chapter.

Training Skills

A director of training needs specific kinds of skills that vary from consulting skills. One of the best sources to identify those skills is the American Society for Training and Development (ASTD). In November of 1981 (and revised in 1999), the National ASTD Professional Development Committee and the ASTD National Board of Directors commissioned the ASTD Training and Development Competency Study. The charge of the study was "to produce a detailed and updated definition of excellence in the training and development field in a form that will be useful to and used as a standard of professional performance and development" (McLagan, 1983, p. 2). "After consulting with numerous experts and ASTD committees, one of the products of the study was a definition of training which is the following: Identifying, assessing, and through planned learning, helping develop the key competencies which enable individuals to perform current or future jobs" (McLagan, 1983, p. 25).

Thirty-one competencies were identified for the training professional (McLagan, 1983, pp. 38–68):

1. *Adult learning understanding*—knowing how adults acquire and use knowledge, skills, and attitudes. Understanding individual differences in learning.

2. *AV skill*—selecting and using audio/visual hardware and software.

3. *Career development knowledge*—understanding the personal and organizational issues relevant to individual careers.

4. *Competency identification skills*—identifying the knowledge and skill requirements of jobs and tasks.

5. *Computer competence*—understanding and being able to use computers.

6. *Cost-benefit analysis skill*—assessing alternatives in terms of their financial and strategic advantages and disadvantages.

7. *Consulting skill*—helping individuals recognize and understand personal needs, problems, alternatives, and goals.

8. *Data reduction skill*—scanning, synthesizing, and drawing conclusions from data.

9. *Delegation skill*—assigning task responsibility and authority to others.

10. *Facility skill*—planning and coordinating logistics in a cost-effective manner.

11. *Feedback skill*—communicating opinions, observations, and conclusions so that they are understood.

12. *Futuring skill*—projecting trends and visualizing possible futures and their implications.

13. *Group process skill*—influencing groups to both accomplish tasks and fulfill the needs of their members.

14. *Industry understanding*—knowing the key concepts and variables that define an industry or sector (i.e., critical issues, economic variables, inputs, outputs, and information sources).

15. *Intellectual versatility*—recognizing, exploring, and using a broad range of ideas and practices. Thinking logically and creatively without undue influence from personal biases.

16. *Library skill*—gathering information from printed and other recorded sources. Identifying and using information specialists and reference services and aids.

17. *Model-building skills*—developing theoretical and practical frameworks which describe complex ideas in understandable, useful ways.

18. *Negotiation skill*—promoting win-win arguments while successfully representing a special interest in a decision situation.

19. *Objectives preparation skill*—preparing clear statements which describe desired outputs.

20. *Organization behavior understanding*—seeing organizations as dynamic, political, economic, and social systems which have multiple goals; using this larger perspective as a framework for understanding and influencing events and changes.

21. *Organization understanding*—knowing the strategy, structure, power networks, and financial position of the specific organization.

22. *Performance observation skills*—tracking and describing behaviors and their effects.

23. *Personnel–HR field understanding*—understanding issues and practices in other HR areas (organization development, organization job design, human resource planning, selection and staffing, personnel research and information systems, compensation and benefits, employee assistance, labor-union relationships).

24. *Presentation skills*—orally presenting information so the intended purpose is achieved.

25. *Questioning skill*—gathering information from and stimulating insight into individuals and groups through the use of interviews, questionnaires, and other probing methods.

26. *Records management skill*—storing data in an easily retrievable form.

27. *Relationship versatility*—adjusting behavior in order to establish relationships across a broad range of people and groups.

28. *Research skills*—selecting, developing, and using methodologies for data collection and analysis.

29. *Training and development field understanding*—knowing the technological, social, economic, professional, and regulatory issues in the field; understanding the role Training and Development (TD) plays in helping individuals learn from current and future jobs.

30. *Training and development technique understanding*—knowing the techniques and methods used in training; understanding their appropriate uses.

31. *Writing skills*—preparing written material which follows generally accepted rules of style and form, is appropriate for the audience, [is] creative, and [which] accomplishes its intended purpose.

Both the trainer and the consultant need these skills. These actions are referred to as "interventions." Entering an ongoing process and causing change is intervening. An *intervention* is a specific technique used by the trainer or consultant to cause that change.

Redding (1979) identified two ends of a continuum of consulting interventions. At one extreme are those things classified as training that are specific, technical, hands-on skills. At the other end are those things categorized as consulting, which are broad-based, conceptual skills. The first type of intervention includes activities such as assisting with the improvement of an organizational in-house publication and presenting a workshop or seminar to improve specific skills. Redding suggested these activities fall under the skills-oriented areas of human resources development.

The second type of intervention includes working on organizational problems such as conflict between line and staff, communication climate, and the development of an employee communication program. As Rudolph and Johnson (1983) pointed out, "Even though Redding's approaches categorize consulting into two neat packages, obviously times exist when consulting activities shift along the continuum from one area to another. An employee's attitude survey, for example, could be identified as an intervention step in an organizational development project rather than an activity in the skills areas of human resource development" (p. 2). While skills may shift from one end of the continuum to the other, consulting has its own unique set of behaviors and activities.

Consulting Skills

The skills needed in consulting depend on the definition of the process. Previously, consulting was defined as intervening to stop some destructive process in an organization. In addition, consulting is a *temporary helping process* that should be *voluntary* and focuses on solving a *work-related human or organizational problem.* The key words in that definition are "temporary," meaning consulting is not a permanent part of the organizational life; "helping," since it is essentially a problem-solving process; "voluntary," meaning people should not be required to participate as a condition of employment; and "work-related," suggesting that it focuses on work rather than personal issues.

Definitions of Consulting

Lippitt and Lippitt (1986) defined consulting as "a two-way interaction process of seeking, giving, and receiving help aimed at aiding a person, group, organization, or larger system mobilizing internal and external resources to deal with problem confrontations and change efforts" (p. 1). This definition attaches significance to the internal as well as external resources that are available and the need to draw upon those resources to solve problems for the organization.

Rudolph and Johnson (1983) identified the difference between organizational development and human resource development. Organizational development deals in the broadest context with the totality of planning, organizing, leading, and controlling compared to human resource development, which is focused more narrowly on dealing with the functions of a manager from a situation-oriented, technical, educational, and/or problem-solving perspective. They suggested, "Communication consulting is most often viewed as a component of human resource development even though dealing with the management process. The primary job of the communication consultant is to apply communication principles and concepts to specific situations as one means of helping the organization meet its objectives relative to its human resources" (p. 5).

To focus on communication specifically as a consulting activity may be ignoring a great deal of potential data, or it may mean centering the activity on that which is more important than all other actions. Goldhaber (1986) suggested that communication consulting is part of the larger area of organizational development, while Pace and Faules (1989) discussed human resource development and suggested that this is really the area for communication consulting. Pace and Faules's position is more nar-rowly focused.

The perspective of this book is articulated in Daniels and DeWine (1991). That treatise clearly identifies communication as the central activ-ity of organizational processes. "[P]ower, leadership, and all the other req-uisite variables with which consultants work are created and sustained in the language and discourse of organization members" (p. 2). Katz and Kahn (1978) added to this conclusion when they suggested, "Communica-tion is the very essence of a social system or organization" (p. 428). Thus, from my perspective, the manager, consultant, trainer, or communication manager who attempts to change human behavior does so by using com-munication as both the tool to intervene and the target of the change ef-fort. Communication becomes both the tool and the target for solving human problems. An examination of approaches to consultation is appro-priate, starting with communication as the central activity of human re-source development.

Approaches to Consultation

Sherwood (1981) identified two approaches to consultation: (1) the client presents the consultant with a problem for solution, to which the consultant provides a recommended solution or alternatives; and (2) the client asks the consultant to both define the problem and offer recom-mended solutions. Sherwood suggested this latter case is the *physician's* approach: a client presents a set of symptoms and the consultant must first make a diagnosis and then prescribe a remedy. Rather than either of these approaches, Sherwood recommended a collaborative approach to organizational consultation where the organization, not the boss, is the client in all the following phases.

1. Identification of problems
2. Conceiving solutions or actions
3. Implementation
4. Follow-up

"To say that the organization is the client means that the consultant works together with the boss to define a meaningful organizational unit, one that includes the boss, with which the consultant will work" (p. 5).

Sherwood went on to point out that traditional approaches to consult-ing often assume that the client has already effectively identified the prob-lem or that it is the consultant's responsibility to decide the nature of the problem. In a collaborative approach, the consultant works with the client to arrive at a joint understanding of problems facing the organization. He reminded us that consultation must remain a management responsibility.

Lippitt and Lippitt (1986) defined the consultation relationship as a voluntary relationship between a professional helper and a help-needing system, in which the consultant is attempting to give help to the client in the solving of some current or potential problem, and the relationship is perceived as temporary by both parties. Also, the consultant is an outsider and not a part of any hierarchical power system in which the client is located (p. 17).

The approaches taken by Sherwood and Lippitt and Lippitt were closely aligned with the approach taken by organizational development (OD). Over the years OD has gone through a transformation. "In the early years, the major thrust of many OD programs was to emphasize such factors as involvement, participation, and ownership. The expression of feelings, the creation of trust, and the reduction of defenses were high on their agendas. But today's dilemmas are even harder to deal with: autonomy vs. control; innovation vs. no surprises; participation and ownership vs. meeting deadlines; and job security vs. excess employees through job design" (Argyris, 1999, p. 240).

Writers often refer to OD as the major focus of consulting activities. OD is concerned with increasing the competence and health of an entire organizational system or subsystem. It typically involves diagnosis of organizational problems and implementation of meaningful and lasting organizational change. In the course of stimulating organizational change, OD specialists may call upon different intervention strategies such as team building, career planning, process consultation, and role analysis (see French & Bell, 1990).

Organizational development differs from training and development in that the latter is concerned primarily with improving the self-awareness, skills, and motivation of individual organizational members. Although an OD effort might involve employee development, it would do so only as a part of its larger objective of improving the competence of the units that constitute the total organization. Some of the intervention techniques that OD specialists use are also used by trainers for developing individual managers.

Chapter 6 discusses the strategies used by trainers and Chapter 7 discusses those used by consultants. I began this chapter by contrasting training and consulting with three other helping processes: teaching, coaching, and counseling. Skills needed by trainers and approaches to consulting help identify when each of these activities is most appropriate.

Since this book is directed toward the communication manager, either as an internal or external helper and as a trainer or consultant, we need to explore the specific career options and activities of such a position.

Career Options

I have been using the term *communication specialist* to refer to an individual who has the skills and knowledge to act as an outside consultant or as an internal manager. What makes that person a communication specialist is the ability to focus on human communication problems and successfully apply the interventions discussed in this book. The job titles such an individual may have include, but are not limited to, the following:

Human Resource Manager

Trainer

Chief Executive Officer

Accounts Executive

Independent Consultant

(For more examples of jobs appropriate for a communication specialist, see DeWine and Modaff, in press, chap. 12.)

Harry Dent (1995), a consultant and author, suggested nine behavioral skills one must cultivate in the new economy to avoid what he calls "job shock," or the rapid changes in job descriptions as companies embrace change of all kinds. The nine skills are grouped as follows into three categories—problem-solving skills, people skills, and integrative skills:

Problem-Solving Skills

1. Become results-oriented.
2. Be proactive.
3. Think creatively.

People Skills

4. Know yourself.
5. Become sensitive to the needs of others.
6. Increase your tolerance level.

Integrative Skills

7. Expand your ability to communicate.
8. Sharpen your business skills.
9. Get a grasp on information technologies (1995, pp. 191–192).

These skills allow individuals to succeed where others have failed. Being able to resolve conflict, help groups stay on task, assist others in problem solving, run effective decision-making meetings, and improve communication skills of managers and employees all contribute to one's ability to be an effective leader. Whether you are using these skills to advance your own career or to help others succeed, you will be more successful if you recognize which of your own skills and behaviors could be improved.

─────── LESSONS LEARNED ───────

Clarify Your Role

One of the first things I say to a client is an attempt to define my expertise. I usually begin with a statement like the following:

> Although I have studied your industry (I always do my homework), I am *not* an expert in the pharmaceutical industry (or tire molds, or manufacturing). You are the content experts in your field. What I am an expert at is the process you go through to decide how to produce new products and services and sell them. I am a process specialist. I focus on the human process of communication and decision making. My job is to draw from all the expertise that already exists in this group and make sure your communication behavior enhances your organization's work.

This is the answer I give when a client asks, "What is organizational communication?" or "What does a consultant actually do?" I am a process specialist and the tools explained in this book could be used to improve any human process whether you are an internal consultant or manager or an outside consultant. Never make the mistake of claiming to be an expert in the industry in which you are working unless, of course, you are. Since I have spent my career in academic institutions and been an administrator for 12 years, when I work with university faculty or administrators, I can claim expertise both in their communication process as well as in their business. But when I work with manufacturing companies, retail, government, or even telecommunication companies, I do not want the clients to think they are hiring an expert in that industry. When I work outside my "content" area, I claim expertise only in the human communication process. Knowing the expertise you have—and do not have—is probably the most important lesson to learn first.

───────────────────────────────

Additional Resources

Arnold, W. E., & McClure, L. (1996). *Communication training and development* (2nd ed.). Prospect Heights, IL: Waveland Press

Bergquist, W., Merritt, K., & Phillips, S. (1999). *Executive coaching: An appreciative approach.* Sacramento, CA: Pacific Soundings.

Block, P. (2000). *Flawless consulting: Guide to getting your expertise used* (2nd ed.). San Francisco: Jossey-Bass.

Robinson, D. G., & Robinson, J. C. (1995). *Performance consulting.* San Francisco: Barrett-Koehler.

Chapter 3

STAGES OF THE CONSULTATION PROCESS AND DEVELOPING INITIAL CREDIBILITY

*When we walk to the edge of all the light we have and take that step
into the darkness of the unknown,
We must believe that one of two things will happen:
There will be something solid for us to stand on,
Or
We will learn how to fly.*

Teller (first name unknown)

*U*nderstanding the stages of consultation will make us more prepared for the unexpected.

Stages of the Consultation Process

The stages of consultation begin with the first giant step into the unknown. Ronald Lippitt and Gordon Lippitt, two of the most well-known consultants from the 1970s and 1980s, identified seven stages of the consulting relationship that are still accurate today:

1. Developing a need for change
2. Establishing a consulting relationship
3. Clarifying the client problem
4. Examining alternative solutions and goals
5. Transforming intentions into actual change efforts
6. Generalizing or stabilizing a new level of functioning or group structure
7. Achieving a terminal relationship with the consultant and a continuity of change ability (1986, p. 19)

Initiation and Entry

The first contact with a client is usually a brief indication of the commitment being requested and the establishment of a date for the first meeting to discuss the feasibility of working together. At that first meeting the consultant must ask some critical questions. Here's an example of how that conversation might develop:

> "We would be interested in having you work with us in developing a series of strategic planning meetings over the next six months."

The First Meeting

The following are the issues that the consultant must have the client address:

1. Where is the client in the process?

    Have they already done some strategic planning? Are you coming in after they have made some mistakes that you must help them recover from, or is this the beginning of the process when no one has prior notions of the outcome?

2. *Has the client used a consultant in the past and with what success?*

    Find out about failed attempts to work with this group. When I have forgotten to ask this question, I often learned that a client turned to me after other consultants had been unsuccessful, either due to their ineptness or the client's inability to accept change. Don't ever go into a contract "blind."

3. *What is the client's goal?*

    To be successful in helping the client as a result of the consultation, you must know what he or she wants. Therefore, be sure to get a clear answer to this question.

4. *What is preventing this group from getting there on its own?*

    Here you begin to uncover the issues central to the consultation. What obstacles are preventing them from succeeding without your help? Some clients have very little awareness of their problems and the biggest part of your job may be helping them identify exactly the issues they need to resolve. Other clients have a clearer idea about what they need help with, and still others think they know and don't.

Developing a Contract

Besides the questions about the relationship with the client system, you need to clearly establish the *amount of time* you will agree to work with the client and the *fee you will charge.* I frequently commit to a certain date and then suggest that we reevaluate at that time the need for continuing the relationship. Any time I have not been specific about the length

Communication Consultants
190 Longview Heights
Athens, Ohio 45701

Telephone: 740.593.7539   **Email:** dewine@eurekanet.com

The following is a statement of understanding between Communication Consultants and XYZ Organization about the goal of the consultation project, length of time involved, and fees to be paid.

Communication Consultants agrees to conduct interviews with the top management team, consisting of 21 individuals, during the first three weeks of February 2000. Those interviews will serve as the basis of a goal-setting and team-building retreat to be held on two consecutive days in March 2001. Two co-facilitators will conduct the retreat, which will focus on issues raised during the interviews. The goal is to end the retreat with action steps leading to an effective strategic plan.

Consulting fees will be $100 per hour per consultant for the interviews, and $3,500 for the two-day retreat. Expenses (travel and lodging) will be covered by the client. An assessment by the client and consultant will be conducted immediately following the retreat to determine what follow-up steps should be taken. The consultants will provide an executive summary of the action steps agreed to at the retreat and it will be distributed to participants within one week following the retreat.

Signed _____ Date _____

FIGURE 3.1   A Sample Contract

of time or the eventual outcome, I ended up being committed to a project or client long after I thought it was necessary. It is wise to negotiate and sign a contract. See the sample contract (Figure 3.1).

In these early stages you are establishing a relationship with the client and determining when and how decisions will be made as you proceed to implement the contract. The client is testing whether he or she can trust you, and you are determining if this group is ready for a consultation. I am always surprised at how quickly clients begin to reveal controversial and confidential issues that exist among people in the group. There have been times when they have told me more than I want to know! Unless I am serving as a counselor, I want the conversation to focus on work-related issues, not personal problems. However, if those personal issues are affecting the work of the group, then it is important to understand that variable. Two additional issues need to be discussed in the early stages of the consulting relationship: how decisions will be made and your expenses.

It is very important to resolve issues related to who will make decisions about how data are collected and analyzed at the beginning of the consulting process. Ideally, the consultant would have control of the data-collection process as long as it does not disrupt normal operations.

In one situation my colleagues[1] and I were asked to conduct a series of focus groups. We were operating under one definition of *focus groups* and the client was operating under another. What we had in mind were private groups where participants were guaranteed anonymity. What the client had in mind was more like product interviews, which would be videotaped and turned over to the client. In this situation, we decided that our agreement to complete this contract would depend on our being allowed to conduct the interviews as we thought best. In other words, if the client insisted on having the interviews videotaped, he would have to find other consultants to do them. After a discussion with us, the client agreed to let us, the experts, determine the best way to collect the data.

In the initial discussions you must expect to address consulting fees and the expenses you incur. In one instance I made clear that my consulting fee did not include travel expenses and that since I would be subcontracting with five other consultants, they would have travel expenses. The client agreed to pay them. However, she thought that meant driving expenses. I should have made clear at that point that one of the consultants I was hiring would be flying in for the workshop, and I would expect her airfare to be covered. Since it was my mistake, I took the expense out of my own consulting fee. You can't afford to make that kind of mistake very often!

Data Collection

The next stages of the consultation process involve collecting data, analyzing the data, and deciding how to present the information to the client. Chapters 4 and 5 give a detailed account of data-collection methods and analysis techniques. Based on the analysis, some form of intervention or training takes place next. Chapters 6 through 16 present material to use in the intervention and provide you with a wide variety of tools and strategies for working with clients. One model for determining the best intervention for a particular situation is the "Consulcube."

Applying Skills to Resolve Issues: The Consulcube™ Model

Blake and Mouton (1976, 1983, 1989) developed a model that identifies not only skills needed by consultants but likely issues and circumstances under which one might be addressing those issues in a consulting relationship. We know that communication managers and consultants may be asked to resolve sensitive organizational problems.

Redding (1979) stated, "It is common knowledge that some communication consultants deal with extremely sensitive and high-risk problem situations; for example: line-staff conflicts, superior-subordinate malfunctions, participative decision making, employee publication practices, etc." (pp. 348–349). He cautioned that communication consultants need a broad perspective in order to deal with such sensitive issues: "The consultant who lacks a sophisticated grasp of systems approaches will almost certainly either waste the time and money of the client with innocuous trivia or dangerously mislead the client into believing that *'in vacuo'* tinkering will solve profound problems" (p. 349).

Levels of the Organization

Blake and Mouton's "Consulcube" provides the type of framework called for by Redding (see Figure 3.2). First, the consultant will enter the organization at a particular level by working with an individual, a group, among groups, throughout the organization as a whole, or between organizations (identified as "units of change" in the Blake and Mouton model). Any intervention into a system creates change. Certain interventions are more effective at the micro than at the macro level in the organization.

Intervention Approaches

Blake and Mouton have identified five broad categories of interventions: acceptant, catalytic, confrontation, prescriptive, and theory and principles. The **acceptant style** of intervention is one in which the consultant acts as a sounding board for the client—similar to Carl Rogers's counseling style of helping individuals. The consultant accepts the problem as the client presents it and tries to be responsive to the client's needs. An example from my own consulting business is a group with whom I had been working for some time providing communication skills training. The client called and asked that I help cope with the violent death of a co-worker. My intervention was to be an accepting listener. I could not suggest "solutions," but could only provide a sounding board for their frustration and sadness. On the diagram, square E-1 identifies the intervention of acceptance being used when the issue is power or authority. Square A-1-1 is when the problem of authority is dealt with at the individual level. The letters and numbers in the square are only used to identify a particular square.

The **catalytic style** is similar to the use of the word in chemistry: the catalyst enables chemicals to react with one another. The consultant who

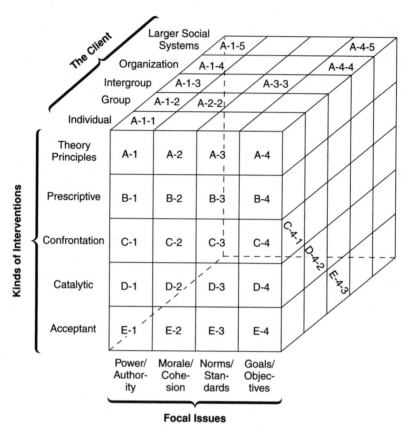

FIGURE 3.2　The Consulcube™ From Robert R. Blake & Jane Srygley Mouton, *Consultation: A Handbook for Individual and Organization Development* (2nd Edition). Reading, MA: Addison-Wesley Publishing Co., Inc., 1983, p. 11. Copyright © Scientific Methods, Inc. Reproduced by permission.

uses a catalytic style of intervention causes individuals to interact and communicate in order to solve problems. When I worked with a group of women who felt they were not being heard by their male bosses, I ran a workshop for the entire group in which I spent most of my time focusing on the process and simply calling their attention to the way in which they were all interacting. My presence alone caused some interaction to occur about why they needed an outside communication manager at all! I served as a catalyst to generate communication between males and females about their styles of interacting.

A **confrontation intervention** is one in which the consultant directly confronts contradictory information or behaviors. "A consultant who operates in a confrontational mode pinpoints for the client inappropriate, invalid, or unjustified values and gets him or her to face up to a reality in the values domain which was previously unrecognized, ignored, disregarded, or rejected" (Blake & Mouton, 1989, p. 224). A CEO who says he has an "open-door policy" and is not available four days out of five may have to be confronted with the information about his lack of accessibility versus what he would like others to believe about his style.

Prescriptive interventions are those that provide the answer for the client. This is a doctor-patient model where the communication manager collects the data and makes a diagnosis. "A prescriptive consultant not only identifies what the real need is but also specifies the actions necessary if the client is to escape from self-defeating behavior cycles" (Blake & Mouton, 1989, p. 296). Its success depends on the client's *willingness* and *ability* to follow the diagnosis. Clients may be *able* to perform the tasks requested, but refuse to do so, because they are not convinced those tasks are necessary or helpful. Or they may be *willing,* but lack the necessary skills to carry out the recommendation from the communication manager.

I once recommended that a client needed to have regular staff meetings so everyone would understand new policies. They were willing to do so, but the leaders of the group lacked the skills necessary to run an effective meeting, and these meetings soon evolved into wasted time (see Chapter 10 for details on running effective meetings). They were *willing* but *unable* to carry out the recommendation. Another client, who had the ability and resources to implement a performance review process, needed to be convinced that this was a necessary process before he would be willing to carry it out. He was *able* but *unwilling* to implement the suggestion.

Finally, Blake and Mouton (1989) identified **theory and principles** as a type of intervention. With this approach, the consultant or communication manager uses a theoretical approach to understanding issues. "Theory-based interventions engage a consultant in those activities necessary to assist a client in acquiring a theory basis for governing individual action. The client is freed from blind reliance on common sense and conventional wisdom and is enabled to see situations more objectively by avoiding the distortions that subjective attitudes, beliefs, and untested convictions can produce" (p. 381). I find this to be the least used of the five types of interventions.

Categories of Issues

The third dimension of the Consulcube involves the identification of four broad categories of issues with which consultants deal: *power/ authority, morale/cohesion, norms/standards,* and *goals/objectives*. These categories are broad enough that most human relationship problems can fit under one or more of them. Decisions made by top-level officials without input from those who must implement the decisions might be an issue of power and authority. Adding a large number of new members and losing old members of a work team may lead to a problem of morale and cohesion. An individual who acts inappropriately in an office setting may be ignoring norms that have become a part of the organization's culture. Finally, I frequently find that various individuals in the organization have separate goals that sometimes conflict with the organization itself, leading to problems of goals and objectives.

Application of the Model

The Consulcube is formed by placing these three dimensions along three places on a cube, creating squares that cross levels of the organization and potential issues with an intervention approach. Some crossings are not appropriate. For example, when the issue is morale, confrontation usually would not be the most appropriate intervention. Nor would working with the total organization provide many opportunities for an acceptance style of interaction. However, other squares help guide the consultant when he or she is choosing an appropriate method to approach the problem. For example, a problem of individual morale might call for an acceptance intervention, while some power issues must be confronted directly by the consultant.

In choosing an appropriate intervention, most often I use a collaborative model of consulting. As Kurpius (1978) suggested, "When following the collaboration mode the consultant's goal is to facilitate the consultee's self-direction and innate capacity to solve problems. As a result, the consultant serves more as a generalist than a technical expert. His [her] major efforts are directed toward helping people develop a plan for solving problems" (p. 19). With this philosophy, the client and the consultant determine together what the issue is, how it can be solved, and what both the client and the consultant can do to resolve it. This type of joint diagnosis ensures a greater likelihood of acceptance for the solution.

The communication manager is an individual who focuses on the potential for increased human performance and uses a variety of skills to tackle many organizational problems. I have used the terms *communication manager, communication specialist,* and *communication consultant* interchangeably in this chapter. All three terms are used throughout the book. All three refer to individuals who focus attention on the development of better communication throughout the organization.

These first three chapters have served to provide a framework for what follows. Understanding the role of the communication manager in the resolution of common communication problems will guide the following discussion. The next part of this book identifies communication problems by discussing how to conduct needs assessments and analysis, and intervention strategies that can be applied to those problems. Part III provides solutions through specific communication techniques. I hope these will help you learn new "frameworks" in which to place problems, as well as alternative ways of coping with them.

━━━━━━━ LESSONS LEARNED ━━━━━━━

The Most Important Question to Ask the Client

I have found that the most important question to ask the client in the initial stages of the consultation is, "What have you already tried?" I remember quite clearly the time I forgot my own golden rule. I had been asked to conduct a communication audit of a large health-care facility. I hired five consultants to assist me in completing approximately 50 interviews and analyzing the data from more than 500 employees. We had met with union representatives and explained the purpose of the data collection. Management wanted to improve the communication system in the organization and find out what additional channels of communication could be used to inform employees of changes in policies and practices. We had scheduled 43 of the interviews and they were to begin on a Wednesday morning at 6 A.M. and continue through the night shift until midnight that night. The interviewers all showed up, but only two of the interviewees made their appointments. We thought, bad night. We'll try again. We went through five schedules, increasing the number we interviewed by only five. By this time we had put many hours into a project without generating much of a return. I also had to pay the consultants for their time regardless of the number of interviewees who showed up, and I had already quoted the client a final fee. This project was getting costly in more ways than one. Clearly, something was terribly wrong. I scheduled another meeting with the union representatives and top-level management.

The answers they gave did not seem to cover the complete lack of involvement in this process. People were "busy," it was the time of the year, some forgot, and so on. I didn't believe these excuses explained the large percentage of no-shows. Finally I made a connection through a colleague to a person who had not participated and asked to talk to her. Because she trusted my colleague and he told her I would never reveal her name, she agreed to talk with me. What I discovered was that two years ago another consulting firm had been hired to "talk to folks" about how to make their jobs more challenging and interesting. Interviewers claimed interviewees' names would not be used. However, job titles that were used were attached to certain individuals. The resulting recommendation to management was that 20 percent of the jobs were duplicative and needed to be eliminated. Management eliminated 32 positions in the following weeks citing the "consultants' report" as evidence for their actions. Many of the current employees had family members and friends who had lost their jobs the last time a "consultant" had said, "Just tell me what your job is like." Obviously, they weren't about to open themselves up to another outsider.

The questions I forgot to ask during the initial meetings were "What have you already tried? Have you ever used a consultant? With what results?" It is absolutely imperative that you find out who has been there before you. As with the introduction you are given as you get up to do a presentation, you must work with the impression the introducer creates of you whether you like it or not. Every consultant who has come before you in effect "introduces" you and indirectly has an impact on your success.

So, what did we do? We delayed the project until we could meet with the entire union and distribute copies of the interview guide and questionnaire. When they asked that certain questions be dropped, we dropped them. When they asked for confidentiality, we went to elaborate lengths to ensure that the interviewers didn't even know the names of the individuals they were interviewing. And we agreed to let the union leadership review the report prior to giving it to management to ensure that no names were listed. Was management comfortable with these steps? Not completely, but those were the conditions for our continued involvement in the project. I had to be ready to walk away from the project and lose money on it if management would not agree to allow us to keep all names of employees confidential.

There are still times when I get caught up in a discussion of the issues facing the organization and I forget to ask these important questions. However, I always find a way to go back to top management and find out if interventions have been used that had a negative impact on the organization. I need to know what fears I am going to have to overcome. This lesson cost me weeks of time and energy and I've never forgotten it.

Note

1. The colleagues were Mary Eicholtz, Todd Holm, Linda Simpson, Alax Matveev, and Brian Ralph, who were part of a graduate-level consulting class I was teaching. Students in the class work with a client throughout the course and use the intervention techniques we cover in class.

Additional Resources

Biech, E. (1999). *The business of consulting.* San Francisco: Jossey-Bass/Pfeiffer.

Blake, R. R., & Mouton, J. S. (1989). *Consultation* (2nd ed.). Reading, MA: Addison-Wesley.

Lippitt, G., & Lippitt, R. (1986). *The consulting process in action* (2nd ed.). San Diego: University Associates.

Schein, E. H. (1999). *Process consultation revisited: Building a helping relationship.* Reading, MA: Addison-Wesley.

PART *II*

Identifying Communication Problems

*P*art II explains the first step in solving human communication problems in organizations: identifying the problem. You can't apply solutions until you understand fully the dimensions of the problem with which you are dealing. The very first thing a consultant or communication manager must do is a needs assessment to determine individual as well as organizational needs.

This section of the book is divided into two chapters: Chapter 4 discusses data collection techniques, and Chapter 5 explains some simple data analysis procedures. Data collection and analysis absolutely must be a part of the consultant's repertoire of skills. The techniques are not difficult to acquire. The reader who has no background in data analysis, however, may want to explore the additional resources listed at the end of the chapters for more information about statistical design. This discussion will give you a good start toward learning the techniques.

Chapter *4*

CONDUCTING NEEDS ASSESSMENTS

Don't try to play hard ball if you haven't got a glove!

Quoted in Zemke and Kramlinger,
Figuring Things Out, *1989, p. 4*

Your recommendations to the client must be supported with facts and observations that are believable, or you shouldn't be in the business of making recommendations. The way in which you collect data is the subject of this chapter and the analysis of data is discussed in the next chapter.

One of the consultant's most significant contributions is to be a neutral observer of organizational life. Organizational members are caught up in the processes of the organization and therefore are not able to disengage themselves in order to make clear, unbiased observations.

Recently I embarked on a six-month contract with a small university to assist with a strategic planning process. My colleague and I agreed to coach the chair of the strategic planning committee and facilitate the planning meetings. At the first meeting with the chair and two other committee members, we started collecting data about the group's activities. The first thing I noticed was that any time the chair mentioned the university president's name his voice became hushed and he looked over his shoulder at the wall that separated the conference room from the president's office. Later some knowing looks passed between the committee members when I asked what would be the president's involvement in the process. I learned that the president had announced his resignation and would have no role in the strategic planning. These early cues made us more alert about issues relative to who would be involved in the process and who actually had the power to make decisions during the remainder of the president's "lame-duck" term. In short, we began collecting data immediately upon entering the room for that first meeting.

The consultant's job is not only to identify the problem but to separate it from symptoms and uncover solutions that frequently lie buried in the minds of organizational members. In this sense, the consultant or communication specialist acts like a detective. Steele's (1985) comparison of consultants and detectives highlights the importance of diagnosis for both. One of the major activities of both a detective and a consultant is an extensive search for clues and evidence. Both the consultant and the detective have two reasons for collecting evidence. One is to understand what has occurred and the second is to make a case.

Both the detective and the consultant have temporary involvement in a system or group of people. They establish a network of relationships for the duration of the case. A consultant or detective may be quite central to several of these relationships and may be very important at the time, but then that consultant or detective moves on to a new case.

Both a consultant and a detective are independent of the group they are studying and yet there are many attempts by individuals to incorporate them into the group. Both have a keen sense of intuition and a sense of the dramatic. They are on center stage and they must control the timing of events. The first step, for both of them, is recognizing a problem when they see one.

How Do We Know When a Problem Exists?

To the degree there is a gap between "where we are" ("A") and "where we want to be" ("B"), we have a problem area. The challenge is planning how to get from "A" to "B." The wider the gap, the greater the distance we must travel to achieve our goals. Thus, the first steps for the consultant are to describe the organization in its current state and then help the organization determine its immediate and long-term goals.

We also know a problem exists when, as Davis (1986) suggested, behavior moves out of the range an observer would consider reasonable in the circumstances. This may be behavior by an individual or by groups of people. Of course, what is "reasonable" to one person may be "out of range" to another! There must be some agreed-upon standard of behavior to which employees will be held accountable.

Davis goes on to point out five pitfalls in problem identification that are quite useful for consultants to remember:

1. *Mistaking symptoms for the underlying problem.* Symptoms may point to the existence of a problem but if you waste time solving the symptoms you may not touch the actual issue.

2. *Accepting without question the opinions of others* concerning the problem. Because the people you talk with may very well be a part of the problem, you must not be in a hurry to reach conclusions until the evidence triangulates or doubles back on itself and supports earlier versions of the story.

3. *Assuming the problem is a person.* It is unrealistic to believe the problem is exhibited by a single person. If the consultant focuses on only one person without examining the surrounding people, events, and environment, then the analysis is quite isolated.

4. *Killing the messenger* as a reaction to bad news. Sometimes the messenger is mistaken for the bad news itself. To the degree individuals

in the organization blame the messenger, future reports will be less likely to filter up through the organization.

5. *Overlooking multivariate causes.* The consultant needs to look at all contributing variables listed above plus more.

These general guidelines suggest the need to keep searching for answers even when the problem solver thinks all symptoms have been answered. Making assumptions that lead to untested solutions is dangerous. My rule of thumb is to keep collecting data until it starts to become repetitive. I have also learned that part of the job the client is paying me to do is help articulate issues. The first contact usually mentions some vague need to improve "communication." That could mean anything from writing clearer memos to examining dysfunctional interpersonal relationships to reworking unclear job descriptions. The consultant usually begins with a series of questions that need answers.

Bell and Nadler (1985) suggested 13 questions that the consultant might explore in order to develop an organizational diagnosis:

1. Is there a well-defined, widely communicated statement of organizational mission or purpose?

2. Do employees have clear work goals or objectives?

3. Is there an organizational structure that provides for adequate span of control and balanced allocation of resources?

4. Are there training activities that provide employees with the competencies they need?

5. Is there a process for ensuring the right people are in the right work roles?

6. Does the organization have effective ways of ensuring that employees get performance feedback?

7. Do employees have a way to determine the priority of their work objectives to enable them to put the greatest energy on the most important tasks?

8. Is there a method for communicating management information needed to achieve work objectives?

9. Does the organization have a process that allows employees to contribute to the development of work objectives?

10. Are there methods for employees to be appropriately rewarded for their contribution?

11. Do employees have the tools and aids they need to perform their work?

12. Is there a process that ensures employees have the freedom they need to perform their work efficiently?

13. Are job descriptions up-to-date and communicated to employees? (pp. 156–157)

These questions can serve as the basis for building a series of inquiries into organizational life. The communication consultant tends to focus on issues related to organizational relationships and the ability to send and interpret messages, while a financial consultant may focus on the balance sheet. The talented consultant knows that when issues arise that need to be addressed by persons with expertise other than their own, additional individuals should be called on to help solve problems. No consultants should attempt to solve problems for which they have no training or expertise.

It is helpful to use a framework to conduct an assessment of an organization's potential problems. One author has developed six broad categories for diagnosis and titled this model "Six Places to Look for Trouble with or without Theory" (as cited in Harrison & Shirom, 1999). The six categories are:

1. *Helpful mechanisms* refers to the adequacy of internal procedures like budgeting, information management, and communication.
2. *Relationships* covers relations both within and among organizational units, including conflict resolution arrangements.
3. *Strategy* addresses the clarity of goals and if they are agreed upon. Do the goals fit the resources and environments?
4. *Structures* means how work is divided.
5. *Rewards* and equitable allocation process. Do important tasks have incentives?
6. *Leadership,* which is at the hub of all other activities, refers to the ability of someone to keep all other areas in balance. (pp. 101–102)

Sampling Procedures

When the consultant is working with a large organization (i.e., more than 100 employees), it is unreasonable to expect that every person can be interviewed or included in the data analysis. This would take unlimited funds and time, both of which are highly valued commodities. Therefore, the consultant must determine a method for **sampling** the population that will ensure that the individuals included in the sample are representative of the rest of the group.

If you sampled only the daytime workers in a plant, or you talked only to the managers or only long-time workers, imagine the slanted view you would get of the organization. There are two principal ways to select subjects: random sampling and stratified sampling.

Random Sampling

The "random" in "random sampling" does not indicate a haphazard approach to selecting respondents. In order to make sure that the procedure is indeed **random sampling,** every person in the population must have an equal chance of being selected. Therefore, you cannot start with the beginning of the alphabet and stop when you have enough because those whose names begin with letters at the end of the alphabet would not have an equal chance of being selected.

The most correct way to select respondents is to use a table of random numbers which is included in any standard statistics book. This table indicates which numbers to use given the total number of respondents you want. They have been generated by a computer to be absolutely random and would select respondents in the population at all points.

Another convenient way to select random respondents is to determine how many respondents you want (5 to 10 percent of the population is reasonable with large organizations) and divide the number of respondents you want into the total number of organization members. The result will indicate how many people to skip. For example, if you are working with an organization of 500 people and you want a 10 percent sample, or 50 people, divide 50 into 500 and the result is 10. This means you should select every 10th person to be included.

The final test of random sampling is to compare your sample demographics with the population demographics. If there are 60 percent females and 40 percent males in the total population, then your sample should approximate that distribution. Also check length of employment, age, salary level, positions, and previous training. Since you hope to generalize to the total population, the sample must be as similar to that population as possible. Otherwise, you can draw conclusions only about this unique small subset of the total group.

Stratified Sampling

The second major technique is called **stratified sampling.** If you want special subgroups represented in the sample, you could divide the population into those subgroups and then do random selection from the subgroups. For example, if you want to make sure you include an equal number of long-term employees and new employees, you could divide the list of organization members into these two groups and then draw an equal number of respondents from each group, randomly.

Data Collection Methods

The questionnaire and the interview are probably the most frequently used methods for collecting data about the organization. While these are the most used, they are not always used correctly and may not be the best ways to get the desired information. This section outlines suggestions for developing questionnaires, interview guides, observation techniques, critical incidents, and organizational outcome data. The next chapter identifies the best ways to analyze the data collected with each of these techniques.

The Questionnaire

Consultants develop questionnaires by identifying broad categories to be studied and then construct questions within these categories. Well-executed questionnaires are a useful form of data collection but they are not the best source of data in every situation. The communication consultant must know when, as well as how, to use questionnaires. The first step is to develop a content matrix.

CONTENT MATRIX

The first step in developing a questionnaire is to define the broad general categories of interest or concern. The questions are generated by developing a matrix of possible areas to explore. Researchers identify these areas from past research; practitioners identify them from past research as well as preliminary discussions with corporate leaders about areas of concern.

For example, an employee survey on satisfaction with the decision-making process used in the organization might include the categories of interest shown in Figure 4.1.

Depending on the desired length of the questionnaire (and the shorter the better!) the matrix in Figure 4.1 would generate at least nine questions covering three levels of decision making in the organization across three characteristics of decision making. This matrix ensures that each aspect

	Effectiveness of Decision	My Involvement	Follow-Up
Upper management's decision-making practices	1	2	3
My unit's decision-making practices	4	5	6
My immediate supervisor's decision-making practices	7	8	9

FIGURE 4.1   Content Matrix for Questionnaires

listed vertically is analyzed by each characteristic listed horizontally. Thus, a question in square 1 might read: "How effective are decisions made by upper management?" compared to a question in square 9, "Does my manager follow up on decisions in a timely fashion?"

STRUCTURING OF QUESTIONS

The second step in developing the questionnaire is to structure the questions following these guidelines:

1. *Ask only one question at a time.* For example, a question like this: "Does your manager make effective decisions, and do you feel upper management follows up on decisions made at lower levels?" provides no useful data. You do not know which is the more salient bit of information in the question: my manager's decisions or upper management's follow-up practices.

2. *Use simple and unbiased wording.* A question written like the following: "Do you feel there is a lack of adequate follow-through on decisions made by upper management?" is not only one-sided, but confusing.

3. *Avoid negative wording.* Some negatively worded items are necessary to control for response biases; however, double negatives and leading questions are out of bounds. "Do you not believe that decisions are poorly made in the organization?" is confusing and misleading. However, it is much clearer if respondents are asked the degree to which they agree or disagree with the statement, "Decisions seem to take a long time to be made in this organization."

4. *Use questions that can be easily tabulated for computer scoring but also allow space for comment,* particularly when you are asking for answers that are not objective. You are losing a great deal of information if you do not allow respondents to make clarifying comments.

The structure of the questionnaire is very important. Place a few easy and interesting questions at the beginning to gain respondents' interest, your most important questions in the middle, and demographic items at the end. You do not want the demographic items up front in case they make respondents hesitant to answer for fear of revealing who they are. At the end of the questionnaire, they can always choose not to respond to some demographic questions and not affect content items.

The consultant should always create at least two different questionnaires with the items in a different order. Since respondents get tired of answering questions, the last questions on the questionnaire may be answered with less thought or not at all. You don't want the same questions to always be responded to in this way. Therefore, with different orders respondent fatigue will be distributed across items more equally. Be aware that even this procedure will not necessarily protect the data from being influenced by the order in which it was collected. The consultant must always help the client analyze the results carefully.

As mentioned earlier, some items must be worded negatively so that respondents do not respond routinely. Also, the same information must be asked for more than once to check the validity of answers. When scoring these negatively worded items, remember to reverse the score on those items or you will have "garbage"!

While there are several types of forced-choice questions, I prefer making statements and using **Likert-type scales** for responses. These are five-point scales on which respondents can indicate their opinions or beliefs in a quantifiable way. The following is the standard scale in use:

1 — strongly agree

2 — agree

3 — neither agree or disagree

4 — disagree

5 — strongly disagree

Other anchor points that have been used successfully include:

almost never true, rarely true, occasionally true, often true, almost always true

very characteristic, somewhat characteristic, neither characteristic nor uncharacteristic, somewhat uncharacteristic, very uncharacteristic

inadequate, somewhat inadequate, adequate, more than adequate, excellent

not at all, to a slight extent, to a moderate extent, to a large extent, to a very large extent

Additional types of scaling include rank ordering (used when you want to determine which answers are most important to respondents) or yes/no questions. I find yes/no questions the least useful because they limit, to such a great extent, the amount of information you receive.

ADVANTAGES AND DISADVANTAGES OF QUESTIONNAIRES

The advantages of using a questionnaire are that it is the easiest and least expensive way to collect large amounts of data and include diverse populations in a short period of time. Questionnaires can also be standardized so that the data can be quantified easily and summarized. Finally, you can ensure anonymity for the respondents to questionnaires.

The disadvantages are the lack of "rich" data, particularly if forced-choice items are used. Also, if you are surveying a population that is frequently tapped for questionnaire completion, you may get a low response rate. At one time researchers felt that unless you received about an 80 percent response rate, your data were so nonrepresentative of the population as to be unusable. Indeed, some types of surveys need close to 100 percent response for any meaning to be extracted from them. However, today one feels fortunate to receive a 30 to 40 percent response rate from randomly mailed surveys.

Interviews

The interview provides a rich source of data for the consultant. In fact, interviews are the way in which the consultant begins any data collection. From the first meeting with the client, the consultant should be using good interviewing techniques to try to uncover the areas of concern for the organization.

THE INTERVIEW GUIDE

The first step is to develop the interview guide. This set of questions can be developed in a way similar to the construction of the content matrix used for questionnaires, although the questions are usually more open-ended. *The interview guide can be used to help determine areas of concern and thus use open-ended questions, while the questionnaire should be used more to confirm issues and thus use more closed questions.*

In developing the questions, follow the same guidelines for language as recommended for questionnaire items and invite the subject to talk. A question such as, "Does upper management follow up on decision making in this organization?" will not invite as much comment as, "What is your sense of how decision making takes place in this organization? Cite some examples that illustrate your response."

An interview guide should include the main questions to ask as well as indicate follow-up questions that might be used to probe for more information. For example, a main question might be, "How frequently do you like to receive feedback about how you are doing your job?" with a series of possible follow-up questions such as, "Is once a week too much? Would you rather receive this information in written form or face-to-face?"

THE OPENING STATEMENT

Second, the interview must develop the "opening statement." This includes not only the purpose for the interview but answers questions the respondent may be thinking but will not ask. Rossett and Arwady (1987) identified these concerns on the part of the respondent as questions of *intent, competency, propriety,* and *broader impact.* Respondents want to know why they are being interviewed, whether the interviewer is an expert who will have access to this information, and what will be done as a result of the interview. One of the most difficult situations is one in which previous interviews have brought about no noticeable changes. Respondents will be discouraged about participating again, only to find that their comments do not matter. Worse still is the situation in which previous data collection techniques have brought about the disappearance of jobs!

NOTE TAKING

Third, the interviewer must develop some form of note-taking procedure. Audio- or videotaping the interview is the most comprehensive way to collect the data and is used frequently when a complete data set is desired. The three principal drawbacks are (1) the intimidation felt by the respondents even when they give their permission, (2) the overwhelming amount of information, and (3) the labor-intensive transcription process that takes place later. The cost, as well as cultural considerations, often prevent companies from using this method.

Using some form of brief note taking during the interview can work well. The interviewer would be wise to leave time between interviews to fill out the notes taken. If notes are not amplified immediately, facts begin to fade, and one can easily confuse respondents' answers.

AVOIDANCE OF BIAS-INDUCING BEHAVIOR

Fourth, the interviewer must be aware of behaviors that will cause biases on the part of the respondent. The rule of thumb is to be as unobtrusive as possible. This refers to the interviewer's appearance as well as suggesting, in any way, agreement or disagreement with the respondent's answer.

A FAVORABLE ATMOSPHERE

Finally, select a time and place that enhance your chances of getting open, honest responses to your questions. This means a private space, free from distractions, at a time that is convenient for the respondent. If you are interviewing a person during the busiest part of the day or week, the respondent's mind will be on the tasks left to do that day, rather than on your questions. Let your interviewees determine the best time for the interview.

Practice interpersonal responsiveness by beginning the interview with some nonthreatening questions that help you to know the person with whom you are speaking. Starting with ridiculous comments on the weather is insulting. Both the interviewer and the interviewee know why they are there, and while the first questions should not be the most difficult or controversial, they should indicate your intent not to waste time and should clearly point out the purpose of the interview. A sample interview guide used to collect information on decision making in the organization is shown on the next page.

The open-ended questions are followed by probing questions for examples and details of their general conclusions. It is in the examples that you will acquire some of the richest data and information. You might simply say, "Could you give me an example of that?"

ADVANTAGES AND DISADVANTAGES OF INTERVIEWS

The advantages of the interview include adaptability and richness of data. These are also the major disadvantages. Adapting the interview to each interviewee makes it very difficult to compare data across subjects, and the richness of data may make the analysis stage so overwhelming as

---

■ **SAMPLE INTERVIEW GUIDE**

Good morning! My name is Sue DeWine and I am working with the Human Resource Department to study the decision-making process at your organization. I am a researcher and consultant and I have worked with companies like yours for the past 25 years.

I would appreciate your candid remarks since no names will be attached to any information collected. The more open you are the better able I will be to help determine how to improve the decision-making process.

I will be writing a report and making recommendations to the Vice President for Human Resources when I have completed the interviews. Each participant will receive a summary of those results and at any time you may contact me if you have questions or concerns about the process we are using.

First, tell me how long you have been in this business and your length of employment at this organization.

During your time with this organization, how would you characterize the decision-making process used here? For example, when are you consulted about decisions being made?

With whom do you consult when you have decisions to make?

What do you particularly like about working here?

How would you like things to be different about the way in which decisions are made?

to render the consultant unable to draw conclusions. The selection of a questionnaire or interview is determined by a number of factors, such as length of time to complete data collection and detail needed to answer the questions of interest. Rossett and Arwady (1987) have developed a chart that summarizes the advantages and disadvantages of both (see Figure 4.2).

Observations

Observations of individuals on the job are probably the most realistic, though time-consuming, activity in which a consultant can participate. Davis (1986) suggested four methods of observation: (1) observe by walking around and taking notes on people and activities; (2) observe from a fixed location without being seen; (3) observe from a fixed location with the knowledge of the subjects that they are being observed; and (4) ob-

	Interviews			Print Surveys	
	In Person		Telephone	Small *N*	Large *N*
Factors	Individuals	Small Groups			
Anonymity of Sources	None	None	None	Some	High
Cost	Depends on number, distance, length	Depends on number, distance, length	Depends on length, number, and cost of calls	Low	Usually high, especially in development of instrument
Follow-up Questions	Good opportunity	Fair opportunity	Good opportunity	Some or none	None
Response Rate	High	High	Usually high	Depends on quality of questions and anonymity	Usually low
Ease of Analysis	Depends	Depends	Depends	Easy with preparation	Depends on quality of questions and data analysis preparation
Risk	Some	High; need group skills	Some	Some; print endures	High; many people receive and print endures

FIGURE 4.2   Needs Assessment Tools   From A. Rossett & J. W. Arwady, *Training Needs Assessment*, Englewood Cliffs, NJ: Educational Technology Publications, 1987, p. 77. Reprinted by permission.

serve and also interact with the person (or persons) being observed. The interaction will focus on asking for more information about a certain task.

The first step is to determine the purpose of the observation and the length of time necessary to make the observation. Early in the process a decision must be made about how much information to give the person being observed. If not at the beginning, then at some later time it is very important that individuals be fully informed about the intent of the process. I would not agree to observe individuals without their knowledge. I find that once I am around long enough, they ignore me and my presence is not disruptive.

Second, a method for taking field notes must be developed. Field notes require coding schemes that will be useful to you at a later date. For example, the time of day and the amount of time passed during each observation may be important. As with interview notes, it is absolutely critical you spend some time immediately following the observation clarifying your own notes. Otherwise, they will be more useless than useful to you.

Third, you must become as unobtrusive as possible. This means you cannot participate in the conversation being observed to offer suggestions or solutions! Nor should you do anything that will call attention to your presence (by wearing clothes that are obviously out of place with the culture or by responding nonverbally to things you observe by laughing or chuckling at humorous events).

To be a good observer you must distinguish between the content of what you see and hear and the process of the event. Chapter 8 discusses the technique of process observation. This is the most frequent type of observation in which you will engage and takes a great deal of skill and talent. You must be a naturally curious individual with keen insight, patience, and tact.

Critical Incidents

Critical incidents are extensive examples individuals are asked to write out. Zemke and Kramlinger (1989) outlined step-by-step procedures for collecting critical incidents. John C. Flanagan, a World War II military psychologist, was actually the designer of this data collection tool. He was asked to determine why so many training planes were crashing. He decided to ask pilots exactly what they had done incorrectly and described the process as "soliciting war stories." In a sense, when you use critical incidents in the organization you are "soliciting war stories" about life in that organization.

> Critical incidents are reports or descriptions of things people in the study population report having done or have been observed doing by others. These incidents are classified by supervisors or other knowledgeable subject matter experts as effective or ineffective in achieving the desired

job results. These descriptions can take the form of stories, anecdotes, reports, or observations related by superiors, peers, subordinates, or by qualified observers. The incidents can be analyzed bit by bit, collectively, or both. (Zemke & Kramlinger, 1989, p. 129)

Having organizational members tell stories about life in the organization provides the consultant with an understanding of issues that no other method can generate. Many organizational researchers are now studying organizational culture by living in the organization for a period of time and asking for stories from its members. Being a good listener is a key to the effectiveness of this technique.

Organizational Outcomes

Organizational outcome data include all the publications produced by the organization as well as personnel files and records. It could even include what Greiner and Metzger (1983) referred to as "routine data." The following is a sample of some of the routine data they collected and conclusions it led to.

An analysis of memos circulated in the top management revealed the power structure of the organization through the listing of names of recipients at the bottom.

A client claimed that his plant was promoting good young managers out of the plant to other parts of the company. An analysis of the personnel records showed this not to be the case; in fact, managers with high appraisal ratings were being kept back, and those with low ratings were rotated out.

A CEO who was well-read in management theory lectured the consultants on how participative he was in running the company—until the consultants examined his calendar pad to find that he remained in his office 95 percent of the time and seldom held a meeting.

A consultant hired to design an alcoholism program for a company found the participants for the program by analyzing time clock records to see who was chronically late on Mondays.

All of these techniques lead the consultant to insights about issues organizational members may face and be unwilling, for a number of reasons, to articulate. In the end, the consultant should use a variety of methods to arrive at the clearest picture of where the organization is and where it wants to be. The next chapter describes the methods for analyzing the data. Often the consultant collects a great deal of material and then doesn't know quite what to do with it!

--------------- LESSONS LEARNED ---------------
What's Wrong with My Data?

Early in my graduate education I learned that data are only as good as the questions you are asking. If you don't ask the right questions, then all the data you collect are meaningless. The statistical packages you use will still give you accurate-looking results even if the question you asked was illogical. Often the organization, as well as the consultant, start out asking one question and end up with answers to another one. Let me give you an example.

A colleague of mine was hired by a major consulting firm to reduce their turnover rate. For five years the turnover rate had been increasing and it was costing the organization a great deal in replacement costs, to say nothing of knowledge drain. His charge was to find out why the turnover rate had steadily increased. He developed an extensive survey to measure all kinds of outcome variables, including absenteeism rate, time to promotion, percentage of educational benefits used, percentage of employees with stock options, and general demographic information on employees. What this gave him was a broad profile of the employees of this organization. He could answer such questions as, "How many of our employees have taken advantage of educational opportunities in the past five years? How many times has each employee, or subgroups of employees, been absent during the past year? What is the average time it takes an employee to get his or her first promotion? What is the educational background of our employees? What training programs have they participated in?"

In short, he got lost in the data and lost sight of the original question. He still could not answer why turnover rates had steadily increased. First, he was asking the wrong questions, and second, he was asking the wrong people. He should have asked former employees why they had left the organization. That seems so obvious and yet I have seen individuals make this mistake time and again. You have to keep asking yourself two questions: "What is it I am trying to find out?" and "What is the most direct way to answer that question?"

Additional Resources

Downs, C. (1988). *Communication audits.* Glenview, IL: Scott Foresman.

Downs, C., DeWine, S., & Greenbaum, H. (1994). Organizational communication instrumentation. In R. Rubin & H. Sypher (Eds.), *Instrumentation in communication.* New York: Longman.

Rossett, A., & Arwady, J. W. (1987). *Training needs assessment.* Englewood Cliffs, NJ: Educational Technology Publications.

Chapter **5**

HOW DO WE KNOW WHAT WE HAVE WHEN WE HAVE IT?

Data Analysis

- **CLASSIC ERRORS IN DATA ANALYSIS**
- **EFFECTIVE DIAGNOSIS**
  Objectivity
  Feedback versus Handback
- **FREQUENCIES AND HYPOTHESIS TESTING**
- **CONTENT ANALYSIS AND GROUNDED THEORY**
- **MULTIPLE APPROACHES**
- **TIPS FOR ANALYZING RESULTS**

Lessons Learned: *A Primer on Statistics: Do Numbers Lie?*

ADDITIONAL RESOURCES

All statistics do . . . is help you crunch large amounts of information into usable numbers.

Ron Zemke and Thomas Kramlinger,
Figuring Things Out, *1989*

*I*ndividuals without statistical training are sometimes intimidated by the language of statistics. I have always believed that a few simple rules for data analysis, spoken in "plain English" can be followed by anyone and will allow anyone to interpret the data that have been collected. The techniques discussed in this chapter are designed to help you avoid making some of the following mistakes about data available to you.

Classic Errors in Data Analysis

Metzger (1989) identified what he called classic errors in data analysis. These lead to false conclusions about how to solve problems before you really know what the problem is!

> *Slot machine management*—when managers lose hope, they often enter a "valley of despair." In the valley, it appears that the only way out is to be extremely decisive, so they start making a lot of decisions quickly, as if loading nickels into a one-armed bandit, but they seldom line up three cherries, and these frantic efforts only make things worse. (p. 176)

For example, jumping to a decision to eliminate an internal newsletter because the first time employees were surveyed about it they indicated slight dissatisfaction, is ill advised. More information is necessary.

> *Freudian hydraulics*—as people's normal impatience gets worse and worse, it can become a powerful psychological force that makes people absolutely unable to wait, so they try to make something, *anything,* happen and push unrealistically hard until it does. Such approaches take a heavy toll. (p. 176)

The need to cut costs often produces such pressure. In one case a corporate executive felt pressured to demonstrate his ability to make tough decisions, so he cut all travel by employees instead of making a more careful decision about what travel was necessary and what could be delayed.

Because of this "edict" the executive lost credibility since some of the travel was directly related to increased revenue.

> *The charge of the light brigade*—this is management's propensity to keep right on doing whatever is running the firm into the ground simply because management has so much invested in the existing systems of values and tenets that it cannot face the enormous impact of its error. It is an ego trap of immense proportions. (p. 176)

The adoption of new technology, discussed in Chapter 7, frequently leads to such poor decision making.

One of my golden rules is to make sure clients really want the answers to questions they are asking. I repeat this phrase often, "Don't ask the question if you aren't ready to hear the answer." No matter how often I repeat this, there are still clients who act surprised because they don't get the answers they want.

In one instance some of my graduate students[1] and I worked with the state supreme court collecting citizens' opinions about the supreme court. In five major cities throughout the state we conducted focus groups asking citizens what their concerns were with that state's legal system. Many comments were thoughtful and related to changes that would make the legal system more accessible and understandable to the general population. We also received many follow-up phone calls and letters from individuals claiming particular judges and lawyers were corrupt. Interestingly enough, a few names continually were raised by people who had had what they perceived to be negative experiences with the courts. We did not pass along any information related to specific individuals, but instead tried to focus on general themes for improvement in the system itself that were repeated in different parts of the state. One example was putting information about the court system on-line (on the World Wide Web) so citizens could read about court procedures and know what to expect when they went to court. Another idea was training for jurors that would prepare them better to participate in the legal system.

It became clear when we presented our report that the citizens' commission that had been charged with conducting this study was interested in citizens' opinions even though there were answers some lawyers on the supreme court did not want to hear. Some of the lawyers had asked a question that they really did not want to hear the answer to. They had not prepared themselves, despite our warning, for answers that would challenge their thinking about how the system was working.

Effective Diagnosis

It is critical once the data are collected that very careful analysis takes place so that hasty conclusions and solutions are not implemented. Greiner and Metzger (1983) identified qualities that the consultant must have in order to carry out an effective diagnosis. Most important is objectivity. I have often worked with clients who were so desperate to find a solution, any solution, that they grabbed the first plausible explanation they stumbled upon. Often they were correcting a symptom, not a cause. Consequently, the solution did not fix the problem but provided only temporary relief.

Objectivity

Consultants cannot believe every opinion expressed to them by clients' employees. Nor can they take sides with executives. They need to be independent and step back from the "trees" to see the "forest." Second, they must have an intense curiosity. "Consultants must be nosey, looking behind symptoms and superficial explanations. They are puzzle solvers who must love the challenge of a messy and ill-defined problem." Third, they must demonstrate the art of being able to see a pattern running through many pieces of evidence. Client problems rarely have simple explanations. Finally, the consultant must treat each situation as new and unique, not as an exact replica of their last engagement (Greiner & Metzger, 1983, pp. 29–30).

What makes this process difficult is the fact that while the consultant and client are collecting data they are generating it and changing it at the same time. In other words, the minute we begin to examine an organization, it begins to change and we contribute to that change! Therefore, we must always be aware of our own actions as we collect and analyze the data.

Feedback versus Handback

The consultant's job is not over until the client has some useful action steps to take. Don't confuse data feedback with data "handback" (Bowers & Stambaugh, 1986, p. 45), which occurs when

> . . . tabulated information simply is returned to supervisors and managers who don't know how to use it effectively. Data handback produces pernicious and irrelevant effects. Feedback needs to be a thorough and systematic process supported by trained facilitators in order for it to work well. You cannot hand a group a summary of their survey results and expect them to handle it well without outside help. (p. 45)

For example, in one communication audit the head of the unit being audited was identified as an isolate and the cause of much of the frustration among staff members. At the same time a division in the group was causing decision making to be almost impossible. To "hand back" that information without first preparing the unit head and providing a plan of action steps to correct these problems would serve only to make the problem more awkward. Feedback must take the form of positive steps that the group members can implement.

TABLE 5.1

MATCHING DATA ANALYSIS TECHNIQUES TO DATA COLLECTION METHODS

Data Collection Method	*Data Analysis Technique*
Questionnaires	Frequencies tables, central tendency figures, range, variance, hypotheses testing
Interviews and critical incidents	Content analysis
Observations	Behavioral frequency counts, grounded theory
Outcome data	Multiapproaches

The information becomes feedback when it is delivered in the context of how to minimize negatives and emphasize positives. Without that context, you are simply handing off the information without a framework in which to understand and act on it.

Table 5.1 shows the data analysis techniques I suggest for each of the data collection methods discussed in Chapter 4, so the consultant will be able to provide "feedback," not "handback."

Frequencies and Hypothesis Testing

The scales used on the questionnaire determine the type of analysis possible. For example, most demographic data produce a **nominal scale,** meaning you are simply counting the number of items or observations in any one category. Suppose you want to conduct a workshop on gender issues in the organization, and you want to know the number of females at each level of the organization. By asking the respondents to indicate their sex and level of employment, you would simply count the number in each category.

In a second type of scale, an **ordinal scale,** the data can be placed logically in rank order. For example, when studying gender one might ask men and women what their preferences are for sending messages in the organization (e.g., memos, meetings, interviews, email, newsletters, etc.). Each response is ranked by the respondent from lowest to highest preference. The number of observations for each sex can be counted but the categories themselves cannot be added or multiplied.

The third type of scale is an **interval scale** in which distances between the responses have meaning. The Likert-type scales defined earlier are used for interval data, where "strongly agree" is defined as higher on the scale than "agree." For example, one might ask respondents to indicate how effective they think various forms of communication are: "Sending memos is an effective way to communicate with people in this organization" with responses ranging from "strongly agree" to "strongly disagree." Different from either nominal or ordinal scales, these data can be added, subtracted, multiplied, and divided.

A **frequency table** simply lists the number of responses for each item and **measures of central tendency** describe one characteristic of the data. The **mode** identifies the most frequent number in a series of numbers, the **medium** indicates the middle number in a series of numbers, and the **mean** is the average of a series of numbers. For example, suppose respondents were asked how often they talked with their supervisors during an average week. The answers for the nine fictional subjects were the following: 2, 2, 3, 4, 4, 5, 5, 5, and 9. The mode is 5, the medium is 4, and the mean is 4.33. Probably the most meaningful statistic is the mean, or the average number of times individuals talked with their supervisor during a week. It can be calculated only for interval data. **Variance,** or the way the numbers vary around the mean, and **range,** or the highest and lowest numbers, are simply other ways to indicate the variability of the data. The range in our example is from 2 to 9.

In order to test hypotheses, one can use simple **t-tests,** which are statistical tests for the difference between two sets of scores. **Analysis of variance** tests for differences among three or more scores. There is a chance that the mean (or average) score for two groups will be different by a few points but not be statistically significant; thus these tests provide a valid answer. The "Additional Resources" section at the end of this chapter includes a short article written for human resource department (HRD) practitioners (Maiorca, 1991) and a text with a brief "statistics emergency kit" (Zemke & Kramlinger, 1989). These two sources provide the simplest, yet most thorough, description of basic statistics I have found.

Content Analysis and Grounded Theory

Content analysis is a systematic analysis of text. For example, journalism researchers might collect editorials that appeared during a certain period of time, in major newspapers, on a particular topic. Adjectives used, topics included, or arguments presented might be counted and summarized. Conclusions could be reached about the treatment various newspapers gave to political topics or candidates.

In one study (Hale, Cooks, & DeWine, 1992) the transcription of the Clarence Thomas hearings for appointment to the Supreme Court were analyzed. Specifically, Hale, Cooks, and I conducted a content analysis of the senators' questioning of both Thomas and Anita Hill. We made comparisons between the language used, arguments presented as a preoration to their questions, and themes the congress members reinforced by the style and content of their questions. We discovered significant differences in the way in which these two people were introduced, allowed to answer, and treated during the hearing.

Usually in content analysis, categories are predetermined and examples are found in the text that fit those categories. In **grounded theory,** the categories emerge from the text itself, thus the theory or conclusion is "grounded" or based on the data, not predetermined.

Examples of occasions when a consultant might use the grounded theory technique include the following:

- an analysis of promotional material used by the organization in order to determine how it presents its goal or mission
- an examination of critical incidents written by employees and identifying themes expressed by a majority of the respondents
- content analysis of performance appraisal forms before and after some intervention into the organization

This technique sounds simple and easy to do, and yet I believe it is the most difficult. When one has an abundance of data, finding insightful and meaningful themes is the goal.

Behavioral frequency counts involve simply listing, in a logical order, behaviors that are observed for one particular person or one specific task. Then a category scheme can be applied or developed in similar fashion to content analysis or grounded theory. This is not based on perception but on actual observed behavior.

Multiple Approaches

Outcome data are pieces of information collected by the company that will ultimately reveal how human behavior has changed as a result of some intervention. Absentee rates, turnover percentages, number of manufacturing errors, and safety records are examples of outcome data. There are two important steps to analyzing these data: first, getting access to them, and second, understanding the conditions under which they were collected. For example, absentee data need to be considered in light of times of the year and general wellness of a community. Outcome data can provide very clear evidence of the impact of interventions on actual goals for the organization or they can be "garbage," depending on how many other variables can be controlled.

Tips for Analyzing Results

The following are techniques I have used to collect and analyze results. There are many pitfalls along the way to a good data analysis, and these suggestions may help you avoid some of them.

- *Keep a log of ideas and observations as the project progresses.* Your chronological notes will be extremely useful to you as the project progresses.

- *Highlight notes in the margins of the flow diagrams.* As a part of your field notes you may be diagramming information and work flow. Notes that help you understand your diagrams will be critical.
- *Don't give your client more of a presentation than is required to inform, persuade, or initiate action.* Sometimes a consultant overwhelms the client with information. It is better to provide only enough data at a time that can be fully understood and acted upon.
- *The written report should include nine sections:*
  1. the executive summary
  2. project background
  3. objectives and scope
  4. methods
  5. analysis
  6. findings and conclusions
  7. recommendations
  8. expected benefits
  9. implementation guide (O'Shea, 1986, pp. 239–240)
- *Enhance the readability of your report.* You should
  - write short reports.
  - arrange material for emphasis.
  - avoid long, complex paragraphs and sentences.
  - avoid jargon.
  - use active voice and direct, descriptive words rather than euphemisms.
  - use pictures and graphs.
  - use numbers selectively (O'Shea, 1986, p. 245)

If the written report is not clear, clean, and crisp, your recommendations may be ignored. The way in which the ideas are presented determines how much "noise" is present when the client is listening to your suggestions.

- *Remain neutral as much as possible as you analyze the data.* Your greatest advantage is your lack of history and perceived lack of agenda as you collect and analyze data.
- *Keep the data confidential.* You need to be able to say to participants that they will never be identified individually. I always destroy identifying information. In one case the client wanted all information collected, including names of participants. I told the client I would not ask for participants' names, only demographic information. Therefore, I would not be able to turn over any identifying information.

Remember the example of a client named Sarah Tanley introduced in Chapter 1? Following an all-day retreat with that group I wrote the following report (Form 5.1). The written report needs to clearly identify the next steps and who will be held accountable for implementing these steps.

SUMMARY OF HEALTH-CARE
PRACTITIONERS GROUP PRACTICE RETREAT

February 17, 2000
Facilitator: Sue DeWine

The physicians and administrators associated with the _____
met from 8:30 until 4:30 to discuss issues relative to the group practice.
The goal of the retreat was to identify issues relative to maintaining interdependence among physicians in the _____.
The morning discussion focused on answering these three questions:

1. What makes a group practice?
2. What are the particular challenges and opportunities in operating a
   group practice?
3. Why be a part of a group practice?

Six major themes emerged from this discussion:

1. Quality of Care: Access Issues
2. Continuity of Care
3. Environment/Cultural Issues (space limitations)
4. Group Identity (communication to external market)
5. Managing Diverse Practice Styles
6. Accountability

Although dozens of ideas were expressed, the following represents those
ideas that could most easily be turned into action items.

Action Items and Responsibilities

Promote loyalty to group practice.

Referrals to colleagues could be assisted by
- patient information cards listing physicians in practice that physicians would hand to patients with instructions like: "When I'm not
  available, you would see one of these colleagues of mine."

(Continued)

SUMMARY OF HEALTH-CARE
PRACTITIONERS GROUP PRACTICE RETREAT *(Continued)*

- an information sheet listing special interest areas of physicians distributed to physicians only.

  responsibility: _____

  timeline: immediately

  Explore printing a physicians' directory
  responsibility: Communications office

Improve quality of information.

Need to increase the quality of information passed from one physician to another for referrals and follow-up.

Discussion focused on keeping more thorough patient files/notes; suggested exploring the possibility of some sort of automated service for patient notes.

Follow-up: no assignment; however, exploration of cost of automated service should be investigated.

Explore feasibility of "health-care groups" in family medicine (other groups should at least analyze current structure).

Would dividing family medicine into smaller health-care groups make operation more effective?
  responsibility: Subgroup Task Force
  timeline: by mid-March a preliminary discussion and report back to physicians

Improve communication among physicians.

Facilitate more informal conversations among doctors.

- Occasional informal lunch?

- Monthly dinner?

- Town hall meetings?
  responsibility: _____ will explore various options and host at least one such event within 1–2 months.

  Increase training for clinic staff.

- Issues raised included increasing staff members' knowledge of physicians' schedules, increasing general helpfulness of staff and personal responsiveness of staff to patients.

(Continued)

75

SUMMARY OF HEALTH-CARE
PRACTITIONERS GROUP PRACTICE RETREAT *(Continued)*

- Protocol issues: phone calls from and to physicians in acute cases and staff sensitivity and ability to differentiate between routine calls and **critical** calls.
  responsibility: _____-staff training

Decrease dependence on part-time staff so physicians and staff know each other and staff is more consistent.
  responsibility: _____ -exploration of options with administrators and use of sick time and incentives to encourage better service.

Mix offices up and/or hold joint meetings so physicians are not isolated by practice.

No assignment made. This idea needs further exploration.

Group identity: Consider new name to reflect more accurately our educational focus and for marketing purposes.

Does our name accurately reflect who we are? Would another name help attract clients?

1. Add questions to patient questionnaire to determine patients' attitudes about our identity and our name.
   responsibility: _____
2. Task force uses these data to begin exploring feasibility of a name change.
   responsibility: _____ Second Subgroup Task Force

Monthly reports of physicians' productivity.

Physicians will review and identify discrepancies and alert administrative staff; new computer system should make this more accurate.

Strategic planning on expectations and accountability.

Accountability standards need to be set for everyone: physicians, administrators, staff, hospital.

Short-term and long-term goals/expectations need to be discussed.
  responsibility: a task force, yet to be named

(Continued)

SUMMARY OF HEALTH-CARE
PRACTITIONERS GROUP PRACTICE RETREAT *(Continued)*

General Ideas for Future Continued Discussion

Scan annual reports into email distribution so units have access to activities in each group.

Improve continuity of care with nurses, improving patient relationship with nurses.

Establish baseline standards for practice and tie to compensation.

Explore issues like scheduling to capacity, include DNKA analysis, scheduling active coverage (identify time off as early as possible).

Identify standards for collections.

Attempt to tie productivity more closely to payments (long lag time).

Identify short-term changes in procedures that could increase profits.

Incorporate physicians' input in hiring and evaluation of staff/nurses.

"Idea Board" Issues

The following questions/issues were raised and due to a lack of time could not be fully answered at the retreat. Individuals have been identified who have agreed to provide to all physicians the information requested within a relatively short period of time.

For physicians' eyes only. . . .

1. Identify the percentage of a physician's salary that comes from the practice, and instructional support.

   Question: How do we make salaries reflect workload percentage?

2. Show the breakdown of expense increases over the past 1 to 2 years (i.e., percentage of the increase due to new hires, one-time-only expenses for technology, etc.).

3. What operations (practices, routines, and ways of doing things) are not cost effective?

4. What amount of money is spent on nonpracticing physicians serving as administrators?

5. Describe ER expenses.

Kelley (1986) pointed out several pitfalls that inexperienced consultants often run into in collecting data. When consultants encounter these problems, their data are suspect, and their analyses may be based on inaccurate or incomplete information.

1. They fail to discuss with the source the purpose of the data collection; consequently, the source provides inaccurate or inappropriate information.
2. They fail to understand the source and its biases. Every source has an awkward and limited perspective.
3. They fail to understand how the source gathered its own data. This contributes to the source's bias and may affect the data's validity.
4. They fail to plan ahead in order to obtain what is needed the first time. Returning to the scene because of an oversight creates an air of incompetence.
5. They fail to document everything they read, see, or hear immediately. Memory is short.
6. They fail to reflect on the data gathering process. Are they covering each facet of the problem? Are there gaps in the data? Are they jumping to conclusions that bias their efforts? Are the data well organized? (p. 169)

In the final analysis, the consultant must draw on years of experience working with human beings in organizations in order to make an accurate assessment of conditions as they exist. Listening carefully to clients enables the consultant to provide them with many answers and possible solutions they are unable to suggest themselves for a variety of reasons. This stage of the consulting process is essential for any follow-up intervention. Interventions without careful data analysis fail and can leave the organization worse off than before the consultant or communication specialist entered it.

Once the needs assessment has been completed, the next step is to plan an intervention or training proposal. This must come from the data analysis itself rather than being preplanned or superimposed. The old adage about a boy who receives a new hammer and goes around looking for things to bang on is never more true than when individuals have training or consulting interventions in mind and attempt to make them fit whatever data have been collected.

Chapter 6 discusses a variety of training techniques. Keep in mind that you cannot simply pull a technique out of context and apply it, like the hammer, to anything in sight. The technique or intervention must be selected carefully based on what the data reveal about the organization and the people in it.

———— LESSONS LEARNED ————

A Primer on Statistics: Do Numbers Lie?

Only if they are misused and misinterpreted. Statistics help us summarize large amounts of information into usable numbers. When we begin to draw conclusions from those numbers we have to be very careful not to go beyond what the statistics are telling us. Few researchers deliberately lie. But when research is published, especially in advertisements, the data are presented in ways that support what the author wants you to believe. A set of data does not necessarily result in a single conclusion. People can easily misinterpret the data they gather. Here are some humorous examples:

- "On all my birthdays so far, I have been less than 35 years old. So by induction, on all my future birthdays, I will be less than 35 years old."
- "Statistics indicate that one out of four babies born is Chinese. We have three children now, so we expect our next child to be Chinese."

These are obvious misinterpretations. However, some invalid conclusions are more difficult to uncover. The following are five critical questions you should ask of reports you read and of those you produce. If you are presenting your own data, you should be able to answer these questions about the data. The answers to these questions serve as only a "primer" in statistical analysis. Many clients expect you to qualify your recommendations with sophisticated statistical analysis. A basic statistics course is necessary for beginning consultants and more advanced statistical training will give consultants even greater opportunities to work with clients.

1. **Can this information be generalized to the population at large?**

   A sample is drawn from a population for the purpose of representing the population. Only to the degree that the sample is representative of the population can you apply the data to a larger group (i.e., are the demographics of the respondents in one unit of the organization typical of the rest of the organization in terms of race, sex, age, occupation, and income?). Be careful to apply your results only to the sample unless you can demonstrate a high degree of similarity between the sample and the population.

2. **How do we interpret the mean?**

   The mean is the simple average of the scores. Scales typically have four to ten possible responses. The mean can be distorted by "outliers," or responses that are extremely different from the rest of the sample. For instance, your data might be unreliable if a small group of respondents answered every question with "5" or "strongly disagree." When reporting results, be careful to examine the data for unusual responses that might mask your data.

3. **How much does a questionnaire tell us about people's attitudes?**

   I always remind clients that survey data only represent how individuals feel at one moment in time. Their responses may be affected by random occurrences. For example, if you interviewed individuals soon after the organization announced a merger, or a layoff occurred, or sticker prices had significantly increased or decreased, these factors would certainly affect responses on any kind of survey about the organization. Responses are influenced by needs of the moment, events immediately preceding participation, and even the way in which you may have approached the participants to ask for their participation. Therefore, we should think of survey data as a "snapshot" of attitudes to stimulate discussion and analysis of the problem, rather than a concrete profile of attitudes.

4. **Has social desirability affected you results?**

   Social desirability is the degree to which respondents have answered the way in which they think the researcher wants them to respond. Everyone wants others to think well of him or her. Often, in survey data, it becomes obvious to the respondent what is the most "desirable" answer. The researcher needs to either eliminate any suggestion that one type of response is desired, or be more cautious in writing conclusions because she knows respondents may have given her exactly what she may have wanted.

5. **Has the research been conducted following standard ethical guidelines?**

   The National Research Act outlines three ethical guidelines that should be followed by any researcher:

   - *Voluntary participation* should be guaranteed if at all possible. Some field research subjects are not afforded the opportunity to volunteer or to refuse to participate. However, each subject who is interviewed should do so voluntarily.
   - *No harm should come to participants.* The clearest example of harm to participants concerns the revealing of information that would embarrass subjects or endanger their home life, friendships, or jobs. It is also possible for subjects to be harmed psychologically. The problem of "inflicted insight" concerns unsought self-knowledge; the person now knows things about himself or herself that he or she would rather not know. An example is the Milgrim studies where subjects thought they were administering serious electrical shocks to others.
   - *Anonymity and confidentiality* should be guaranteed unless the participants have agreed to the release of their responses. A re-

spondent is considered anonymous when the research cannot identify a given response with a given respondent. Anonymity often ensures accuracy of responses. People are more likely to be truthful if their responses are anonymous.

We are credible only to the degree that we report our data responsibly and carefully. Remember, people will believe what we tell them!

Note

1. The colleagues were Mary Eicholtz, Todd Holm, Linda Simpson, Alax Matveev, and Brian Ralph, who were part of a graduate-level consulting class I was teaching. Students in the class work with a client throughout the course and use the intervention techniques we cover in class.

Additional Resources

Frey, L. R., Botan, C. H., Friedman, P. G., & Kreps, G. (1991). *Investigating communication: An introduction to research methods.* Englewood Cliffs, NJ: Prentice-Hall.

Maiorca, J. J. (1991). Basic statistics for the HRD practitioner. In W. Pfeiffer & W. Jones (Eds.), *The 1991 annual: Developing human resources* (pp. 245–265). San Diego: University Associates.

Reinard, J. C. (1994). *Introduction to communication research.* Madison, WI: Brown & Benchmark.

Zemke, R., & Kramlinger, T. (1989). *Figuring things out: A trainer's guide to needs and task analysis.* Reading, MA: Addison-Wesley.

PART *III*

Training and Consulting Strategies and Techniques

*P*art III provides a collection of some of the most effective training and consulting techniques I have encountered. I have tried to include all the information necessary so that you could implement these techniques after reading their description. However, reading about a technique and actually performing it may be very different.

Chapter 6 reviews eight major categories of training methods; Chapter 7 focuses on technology and consulting; and Chapter 8 discusses numerous consulting techniques under several broad categories. These are techniques I have used, along with hundreds of others, for more than 25 years. The ones I have included are the ones that have been consistently effective. No matter who the group is (top-level executives, first-line employees, university faculty, high school students, government workers, social service employees), these strategies have helped them become more aware of human communication problems and how to solve them.

Chapter *6*

USING TRAINING TECHNIQUES

The 2000 ASTD State of the Industry Report found a continuing increase across all firms in employer-provided training in the United States, as measured by the amount spent on training. Among those firms identified as benchmarking organizations, about 76% of employees eligible for training are receiving it. In comparison, the Training Investment Leaders (identified by ASTD as "cutting-edge" firms) are providing training for nearly 97% of eligible employees. At the leading firms, few employees are not being trained.

McMurrer, Van Buren, and Woodwell, 2000, pp. 42–43

*T*raining is big business. In 2000 The American Society for Training and Development had 70,000 members, whose professional careers are in the field of training, from every state in the United States and in 150 countries. Training has become another arm of the education system and is a very demanding activity. In 1995 ASTD reported $55 billion spent on training in the United States alone.

I sometimes think adults have a shorter attention span than young children. I recently watched a group of children in a room filled with Lego blocks of all sizes become absorbed for over an hour in building imaginary high rises, yet I have also often watched trainers lose adult audiences' attention after only 30 minutes. The difference is involvement. No one was lecturing to those children about how to put the blocks together. They were learning by doing. Adults get as bored as children when they are talked *at* rather than invited to get involved more actively in the learning process. Adults are just *usually* more polite about it.

This chapter presents a variety of techniques to get participants "involved" in the training process. These techniques range from simple strategies that make lectures more exciting to complex situations. Ultimately, the success of any training technique depends on the skill of the trainer. The selection of a technique depends on overall program objectives, amount of time available, costs of implementing the technique, facilities, and availability of equipment and materials. One of the basic tools of training is the lecture.

Lectures

The word *lecture* conjures up a stern father trying to explain to his child the difference between right and wrong, or a professor reading from her yellowed notes to a class of students, half of whom are sleeping. Yet the lecture can be one of the most effective ways to get important information across to the trainees, but it should be used sparingly and with some creativity.

Limitations of Lectures

"Traditional teaching operates on the false belief that learning is consumption . . . the teacher is the vendor and learning is a matter of storage. That's incorrect. Knowledge isn't something you absorb—it's something you create. It's an active process, not a passive process." (Alonzo, 1998, p. 55). This author goes on to report the historical basis for this belief:

> In the front part of the brain there is an area that governs problem-solving ability and motor skills. These two functions are attached. Physiologically, movement and problem solving are connected. The brain is an old mechanism. In the past, our ancestors were always moving. Our brains developed in an environment where humans were moving while solving problems. The concept of being sedentary while you learn is a very recent development. (p. 56)

Wexley and Latham (1981) described the purpose of lectures as the "attempt to train employees by focusing primarily on their cognitions" (i.e., thoughts and ideas) (p. 127). The major disadvantage of the lecture is the one-way nature of the presentation, where information flows only from the trainer to the trainee. The learner becomes a passive listener. Wexley and Latham criticized the lecture technique for being "deficient for teaching job-related skills that can be transferred from the learning situation to the actual work situation. What can be transferred from the lecture to the job must almost always be limited to cognitive principles, rules, and factual information" (p. 128). They also suggested that the lecture technique may be threatening to individuals who have limited educational, social, or economic backgrounds.

Finally, the lecture typically ignores differences among trainees' abilities, interests, backgrounds, and personalities. When selecting a training format, the trainer must consider the participants' learning styles as well as the complexity of the material being presented.

Advantages of Lectures

Smith and Delahaye (1987) identified advantages and disadvantages of using lectures in training programs. Advantages are the low cost and the fact that most adults have been taught by this method and are familiar with it. The lectures can conserve time, can allow the trainer to present information in an orderly fashion, and can accommodate a large audience. It does require speaking ability on the part of the trainer; trainers who are comfortable with this style of delivery can capture the participants and make them want to learn and participate in the training session.

Features of Dynamic Lectures

The most important principle of developing dynamic lectures is to keep them short. In a training session a lecture usually shouldn't last more than 15 to 30 minutes. If more cognate material needs to be presented, break it into smaller sections. Trainers are fond of calling this activity a "lecturette."

The lecture needs all the elements of a good public speech: an *attention step* that makes the audience want to hear more, *a need step* that tells them specifically why this information is relevant to them, *a variety of appeals* including logical, emotional, and ethical, and *a conclusion* that summarizes the primary objective and makes one final appeal. The presentation should be filled with examples and illustrations tying the trainees to the topic. Chapter 11 provides more specific information on public presentations, much of which is relevant to short lectures in training sessions as well.

Using Visual Information

We know that audiovisual aids, when used properly, can enhance a training program. For example, Sredl and Rothwell (1987) suggested that about 80 percent of learning occurs through sight alone, 10 percent through hearing, 5 percent through touch, and 5 percent through smell and taste. "The more that senses are stimulated, the more information is reinforced and likely to be retained. Stimulating more than one sense at the same time dramatically increases recall" (p. 124).

Form 6.1 (pages 89–91) presents a worksheet for selecting media. The issues to consider are quite helpful and should give any trainer the best guidance for selection of media.

Effectiveness of Visual Aids

Wexley and Latham (1981) suggested that audiovisual techniques be considered in the following situations: (1) when there is a need to illustrate how certain procedures should be followed over time, (2) when there is a need to expose trainees to events not easily demonstrated in live lectures (e.g., a visual tour of a factory, open-heart surgery), (3) when the training is going to be used organization-wide and it is far too costly to ask the same trainers to travel from place to place or assemble everyone in one location, and (4) when audiovisual training is supplemented with live lectures or discussions before and after the sessions. "Well-developed audiovisuals can arouse strong, drive-producing responses, especially when effective instructors are employed. Audiovisuals also clue or attract trainees' attention by using their unique features, like instant replay, slow motion, animated cartoons, time-lapse photography, and close-ups" (p. 134).

The following guidelines are suggested to determine if the use of videos or films will enhance the learning situation (American Society for Training and Development, 1988):

- Does the program meet your needs analysis requirements? Does it tie into the learning objective in the training session, or is it merely entertaining?
- Are the program style and approach appropriate for the age group, cultures, experience, and education level of your learners?
- Is the program attention-getting and, if appropriate, motivating, or is it dull?
- If characters and situations are shown in the program, are they realistic or ridiculous? Does the dialogue sound natural or contrived?
- Does the program portray a work environment similar to that of your learners?
- Are the job problems portrayed in the program similar to those encountered by your learners, or are the problems shown irrelevant?
- If the program is about job behaviors, does it include examples of both desired and undesired behaviors?
- Does the program include enough information on how to improve job performance?
- Does the program include only a digestible amount of information, or would learners suffer from information overload?
- Is the program terminology consistent with that used in the rest of the training session?
- Does the program periodically summarize information and emphasize the essentials?
- Is the program conducive to postviewing discussion?
- What could the program accomplish in training that could not be done more simply or inexpensively with another film, video, or training method?
- Is the program accompanied by print materials that support the program content?
- Is the program accompanied by information validating the effectiveness of the program?
- Is the film or video in good physical shape; will it run smoothly?

WORKSHEET FOR MEDIA SELECTION

Directions: As you consider choice of media, work through the questions on this worksheet. Check an answer in the center columns to each question in the left column. Finally, at the end of the worksheet, make a media selection.

Issues to Consider	Yes (√)	No (√)	See Remarks (√)	If Yes, Eliminate (or Consider Carefully) Use Of:	If No, Eliminate (or Consider Carefully) Use Of:
1. Will instruction be delivered to a group?	( )	( )	( )	• Computers for instruction • Printed material • Audiotape, unless properly amplified • Videotape, unless projected on large screen	• Blackboard • Ceramic board • Felt board • Magnetic board • Overhead • Opaque • Rear screen projection • Slides
2. Do learners have any preference for certain media? Are they opposed to certain media?	( )	( )	( )	(Fill in as appropriate)	
3. Are instructional objectives primarily cognitive?	( )	( )	( )	(Fill in based on your preferences)	• Computer-based instruction • Overhead • Blackboard • Felt board • Ceramic board • Magnetic board • Opaque • Rear screen projection • Slides
4. Is there a great deal of time available for preparing media? materials?	( )	( )	( )	(Fill in based on your preferences)	• Film • Professional audiotape • Professional videotape • Computer-based instruction • Slides

(Continued)

89

WORKSHEET FOR MEDIA SELECTION *(Continued)*

Issues to Consider	Yes (√)	No (√)	See Remarks (√)	If Yes, Eliminate (or Consider Carefully) Use Of:	If No, Eliminate (or Consider Carefully) Use Of:
5. Is funding available for the most expensive media-based materials?	( )	( )	( )	(Fill in based on your preferences)	• Professional films, audio-tapes, video-tapes • In-house computer instruction
6. Are facilities adequate for most any kind of media?	( )	( )	( )	(Fill in based on your preferences)	(Fill in as appropriate)
7. Are raw materials available such as blank videocassettes?	( )	( )	( )	(Fill in as appropriate)	(Fill in as appropriate)
8. Is in-house talent, skilled in all types of media, available?	( )	( )	( )	(Fill in as appropriate)	(Fill in as appropriate)
9. Is necessary equipment available (or obtainable)?	( )	( )	( )	(Fill in as appropriate)	(Fill in as appropriate)
10. Will frequent revision be necessary?	( )	( )	( )	(Fill in as appropriate)	(Fill in as appropriate)
11. Other (specify: _____)	( )	( )	( )	(Fill in as appropriate)	(Fill in as appropriate)
12. Other (specify: _____)	( )	( )	( )	(Fill in as appropriate)	(Fill in as appropriate)

(Continued)

WORKSHEET FOR MEDIA SELECTION *(Continued)*

SELECTION OF MEDIA

Which one medium or group of media would be appropriate?

REMARKS

Are there reasons to take different action? If so, explain and tell how any anticipated problems will be overcome.

Source: From H. J. Sredl & W. J. Rothwell, *The ASTD Reference Guide to Professional Training Roles and Competencies, 1&2,* New York: Random House Professional Business Publications, 1987, pp. 129–131. Reprinted by permission.

Cautions in Using Visual Aids and PowerPoint

Arnold and McClure (1996) list a few simple rules for using audiovisual aids in training presentations:

1. Confine audiovisual aids to a single concept.
2. Make sure that every participant in the training session can see and/or hear the audiovisual aid.
3. Maintain control of your audiovisual aid by planning ahead for its use.
4. Watch out for Murphy's law: If something can go wrong, it will.

There are conditions that can significantly increase the cost of using visual media. Before you decide to invest in such media, consider some of the costs identified by Riblen (1983).

> The cost estimates for audiovisual materials are based on the use of professional support. If, for example, you were costing a film, we include a scriptwriter, a director, at least one technician, and studio time costs. The same would be true if we were considering video tape or video disks . . . . Costs for initial production of audiovisual materials are many times higher than for written materials. For that reason alone the decision to produce them should be carefully considered. The cost for changing these kinds of materials after they have been completed is also very high. So stable materials should be selected, as well as material that is to be presented to large numbers of people over a broad geographical area or at intervals in a few locations. The decision to include these kinds of audiovisuals in a training program should be taken seriously and made only if the costs can be justified . . . . Making large investments in materials that cannot be completely justified can do more harm to your presentation than good. (pp. 157–158)

I use the simplest form of audiovisual aids possible. They are aids, not the main focus of the presentation. When they become noticeable, then probably they are inappropriate. I use flip charts most often because they are simple and transportable, and they provide visual evidence of the group's accomplishments.

There are many sources of information about the use of audiovisual aids. One of the best is the ASTD Info Line (Spruell, 1987), in which a series of criteria are identified to help trainers select the most appropriate aids for any training session.

Video- and Computer-Aided Training

The advent of technology into the training room has dramatically changed some training programs. Computers are now being used for decision-making meetings, and video conferences have become a cost-effective way

to bring people together. Companies realize the usefulness of video confer-
encing for introducing new products and policies. These can be brought
into the field office without bringing all the field managers into a central
location.

John Hancock Financial Services of Boston has relied on business television networks to bring its 17,000 employees closer together.

> This company—whose insurance business alone has $32 billion in assets—
> has used an in-house television studio for more than 20 years. Yet by up-
> grading its equipment to handle live transmissions, John Hancock's group
> and retail insurance companies . . . have realized advantages in savings in
> travel costs, reaching 30 times as many people for each class, and a de-
> creasing need to take seminars on the road to regional locations for weeks
> at a time. (Gerwig, 1991, pp. 6–7)

The traditional classroom is no longer the only place training can take
place. As Romiszowski and deHaas (1989) point out, distance learning
can take place via computers with the advantages of

> classrooms open 24 hours a day and you never find a closed door when
> you want to speak to your tutor. It means a more democratic environment
> for group interaction, in the sense that all people are equal because they
> have the same possibilities and tools to communicate their thoughts. In-
> terruptions can be made at any time. Even reactions to past messages be-
> long to the possibilities. (pp. 8–9)

Some uses of computers and video involve group decision making.
Computer-mediated decision making tends to remove the impact of status
and position power in small group discussions. It also has the potential
to remove some of the fear of being evaluated immediately. It equalizes
verbal contributions so those who are less verbal have an equal chance of
being "heard"; however, it may introduce unequal treatment due to writing styles and abilities.

Some suggestions for using technology in training and consulting include the following:

- Discuss with the client the potential change in communication messages when they are sent via technology rather than face to face.
- Use techniques that will help make the training more personal,
  even though the participants may be seeing you on a large screen
  instead of in person. The instructor will have to work harder at
  calling people by name and making personal comments that indicate the instructor knows the class members.
- Try to offer options to the students that will make them feel more a
  part of the class rather than audience members. For example, they
  might want the class broken into short lectures with certain times
  for interaction with the instructor and personal phone conferences.

- If possible, visit each site at least once so students have personal contact with the instructor.
- Encourage small group interaction and group presentations so that the participants feel a sense of commitment to each other.

Trainers need to be competent to use video conferences and computer-mediated training techniques if they want to be able to meet the demands of modern business. A discussion of on-line training is developed in the next chapter on technology and training techniques.

One experienced trainer, Anita James (2000), who uses technology to enhance her presentations, makes these practical recommendations when using PowerPoint:

1. Do not use more than one idea per slide or transparency.
2. List a maximum of 5 to 7 lines per slide or transparency.
3. Use a maximum of 4 to 6 words per line.
4. The minimum font size should be 24 point; maximum size is 42 to 44 point.
5. The font should be sans serif (e.g., Arial, Univers, Helvetica).
6. Do not print vertically.
7. Use no more than 3 or 4 colors on a single slide or transparency.
8. Keep diagrams and charts simple (i.e., minimal lines).
9. Remember, visual aids should enhance a presentation, not *be* the presentation.

Self-Assessment Instruments

Many trainers use **self-assessment instruments** as a part of the training program. These tools range from personality inventories to opinions about how the group or organization is currently functioning. These self-assessment instruments can be found in a variety of places, but the instrumentation books and annual handbooks published by University Associates (Pfeiffer and Jones, 1972–2000, and later published by Jossey-Bass/Pfeiffer) are the best resources. A review of organizational communication instruments provides another resource that includes the instruments (Downs, DeWine, & Greenbaum, 1994).

Benefits and Hazards of Self-Assessment Instruments

The benefits of using self-assessment instruments include helping participants to understand group or individual behavior theory, providing feedback about one's own behavior from a nonpersonal source, allowing nonthreatening comparisons with "norms" or the rest of the group, and providing a common language for discussions.

The hazards of using self-assessment instruments include the fear some people have of being "exposed" and not wanting to talk about their own behaviors, presentation of more feedback than individuals want or are able to handle, development of a nit-picking session on the instrument itself, and the facilitator's presentation of the results as the "only answer."

Effective Use of Self-Assessment Instruments

To avoid these pitfalls, the facilitator must set the appropriate climate. Introduce the instrument as merely a "snapshot" of individuals' behavior at one point in time. Clarify that there are no right or wrong answers and that this instrument only provides a "mirror" to hold up and see how much is reflected. When consultants start using instruments to guide all behavior and all future interventions, dangerous assumptions are operating. Instead, these instruments must be used to stimulate discussion about what is going on in the group and how each individual may be reacting to that group. Instruments should never be used as a strict categorized system in which to place individuals for future reference.

The underlying principle of the instrument must be explained. Try to select instruments that do not imply there is one right way to be. The administration of the instrument must be clear and without confusing directions. Make the scoring of the instrument as simple as possible with score sheets set up so that very little instruction must take place.

The results should be interpreted in the context of the focus of the particular group setting. Avoid playing "dime store psychologist." Your job is not to psychoanalyze anyone, but merely to have each individual think carefully about his or her own behavior.

If the group gives you permission, posting the results can be very revealing. It is not necessary to post individual results, but in the aggregate, individuals can see where they fit into the group picture. It is critical that the facilitator spend enough time discussing the results so that participants can use the information to improve their ability to function in the group.

Case Studies

A **case study** is a narrative or short story about some organizational issue. Case studies can be rather simple, including only the basic information, or very complex, including a complete financial report and history of the organization. The use of case studies in training sessions provides real-life examples of problems or issues the trainees are asked to analyze. The case study approach to learning was originally developed by the Harvard University Business School.

One author suggests that using real-life cases in international business communication training provides students the opportunity to do the following:

1. Experience the international and cross-cultural issues and problematic situations confronting international business managers and discover different cultural patterns and meanings,

2. analyze the issues and problems in light of the business theories and research,

3. develop appropriate strategies and implementation plans for coping with communication problems, and

4. develop persuasive and analytical skills as they communicate their case study results. (Zhao, 1996, p. 11)

Studying a case involves discovery, problem solving, and collaboration. There are a number of excellent case study books from which to select cases, including the most well known, the Harvard Business cases. For particular focus on communication issues, see Gary Peterson's (2000) or Beverly Sypher's (1990, 1997) texts about communication case studies.

Types of Case Studies

According to Ronstadt (1980), Harvard M.B.A. candidates prepared between 500 and 700 business cases before graduating. The case studies include the following types:

1. *Highly structured or technical problem-solving cases.* These are short case studies with a small amount of information. The best solution is often available, and the student or reader applies some kind of formula to find an answer.

2. *Structured vignettes.* These are used in introductory management courses at the graduate and undergraduate levels. They may vary in length. A best solution usually does not exist, but the student is expected to identify and apply several concepts to solving the case.

3. *Long, unstructured cases or problems/opportunity-identifying cases.* Here the reality of the situation is reflected by supplying all or nearly all of the relevant information.

4. *Ground-breaking cases for advanced M.B.A., doctoral, or executive management classes.* The business situation is totally new, and not all problems have been identified.

Effective Use of Case Studies

A retired professor from Harvard who was in part responsible for the development of this training technique suggested the following eight tips when using case studies:

- Take responsibility for classroom leadership. This should not turn into a massive nondirective interview.
- Do not let the participants "beat a dead horse."
- If a sideline discussion is important, let it be developed if time is available.
- Insist that participants state positions and conclusions.
- Indicate when analysis is moving in the right directions.
- As facilitator, serve as a "sounding board" for ideas and analysis.
- Ask participants to list major topics and then ensure they are covered in the discussion.
- State the objectives of the case study and be enthusiastic. (Christensen, 1987, pp. 9–14)

Cases should be selected for the main issue they present and the degree to which that issue addresses problems the group may be facing (James & DeWine, 1990). They can be used with individuals or in groups. There is seldom a right or wrong answer but rather cases are used to have participants consider factors important to making decisions.

Tracey (1989) suggested that the major advantage to using case studies is that "the products of thinking in case studies are more relevant to the experiences of the trainees because they must inject their own perceptions, attitudes, and feelings into the case" (p. 258).

Maier, Solem, and Maier (1975) identified important contributions of the case method to training, including the following:

- It discourages making snap judgments about people and behavior.
- It discourages believing in or looking for the correct answer.
- It graphically illustrates how the same set of events can be perceived differently.
- It destroys any smug generalizations one might have about right versus wrong answers, management prerogatives, the attitude of labor, the best methods of discipline, the younger generation, the place of women in management, and many other issues.
- It trains one to discuss things with others and to experience the broadening value of interaction with one's equals.

- It stresses practical thinking so that such considerations as cost, convenience, deadlines, attitudes of top management, and the feelings of other persons prevent solutions from becoming idealized.

- It causes doubt as to whether there really are basic human relationship principles. (pp. 1–2)

Two excellent examples of extended case studies that address organizational communication issues are those by Goodall (1989) and Tompkins (1992). In both books, each chapter represents a different case study or a different segment of the same case. Their insights and observations are thought-provoking. Parts of these books would be very useful in a training session that focuses attention on communication issues. To appreciate the case study technique from a trainee's perspective, try working through the case of "B. Parker and Company" at the end of this chapter (pages 120–128). The content of this case will also give you insights into communication problems that a consultant might face.

Tracey (1989) pointed out the major disadvantage of using case studies: "A considerable amount of time is required for trainees to read, digest, and discuss all the materials in a case report" (p. 258). Case studies can be fairly simple, like the one at the end of this chapter, or so complex and detailed that they take more than 200 pages to explain! "Managing after the Merger" is another example of a case study and its analysis.

■ CASE STUDY:
MANAGING AFTER THE MERGER: FEEDBACK AT BAS

It was 5:30 in the evening on a Tuesday. Howard Deerfield, a Human Resource Manager, was leaving his office at Baker Allied Software (BAS) and going to his daughter's soccer game when the phone rang. Gary Blummer, the Director of Software Engineering and Services, sounded tense as he said, "Howard, I need to talk to you as soon as possible. We need to terminate one of my senior engineers and I need information about how to proceed. Calhoun Davis has to go!" Howard agreed to meet at 7 A.M. Wednesday with Gary. He turned out his office light and mumbled, "I wonder what's going on?"

One year ago, BAS purchased Millennium On-Line Software (MOS), a small, but high-potential software development company. No promises were made during the merger regarding the retention of MOS employees, but it was widely known that the primary value of MOS rested in its talented software designers and programmers. MOS was known in the software industry as a fast-paced, innovative company, while BAS was a highly structured, large organization with considerable market share. So far, BAS has made no cuts in staff, and the merger was going as smoothly as could be expected. However, in the last month Howard has noticed an increase in the number of employee relations incidents, including conflicts between employees and supervisors. Howard wasn't sure what was happening. He'd been through a merger before and knew that differences in organizational cultures just took some time to work out. However, the sharp increase in complaints and tensions among employees about all kinds of issues looked like the beginning of trouble. As Howard drove to the soccer game, he pushed these thoughts out of his mind.

Later that night, Howard made a quick phone call to Jessica Moore, Vice President of Engineering and Gary Blummer's boss. Jessica was aware of Gary's plans to terminate Calhoun, but admitted that she did not entirely approve of the action. In fact, she was the one who recommended to Gary that he talk to Howard about termination. Jessica said,

"If we fire Calhoun, we'll lose valuable experience and knowledge. In addition, if the competition hired Calhoun, they would have access to information about many of BAS's technical advances. I'm not sure what the problem is between Gary and Calhoun. I've tried to get Gary to talk but haven't had any luck. Maybe a neutral party, like you, could investigate the situation. Just in case, we'd need to bring in someone from Legal to check the writing of a severance agreement—if it comes to that—and make sure that Calhoun couldn't walk off with information and clients. I think it's great that Gary made an appointment with you. Fill me in tomorrow at lunch— my treat!"

When Howard arrived at BAS the next morning, Gary was already waiting outside the office with a half-empty cup of coffee. Gary didn't even wait to get inside Howard's office before he began talking. He blurted out, "Good, you're here. Let's figure out how we're going to take care of this termination." Howard sat down at his desk and said, "First, why don't you explain the situation to me."

Gary sighed and said, "Howard, it's best that Calhoun and I part ways. He has no loyalty to BAS. I've tried to find out what's really bothering him but haven't gotten anywhere. I've had it! I can't even talk to him—he's always complaining. There have been several incidents lately where Calhoun was even arguing incessantly against company policies."

"What types of policies?" interrupted Howard.

"He complains about every policy, but especially about performance appraisals. Look, I've had two meetings with Calhoun to sort through his complaints. We don't make any progress. It would be different if others raised the same issues, but I haven't heard a peep. At this point, I want to know how I can terminate legally and quietly."

Howard asked Gary if he had notes from his two meetings with Calhoun. Gary admitted that he did not have documentation and added that he hadn't intended to fire Calhoun at the time he scheduled those meetings. He was just trying to talk through what was wrong, but the situation had gotten progressively worse since then.

Gary stood up. "Look, Howard, I've been managing direct reports for quite a while now and I've never had a situation like this one with Calhoun.

(Continued)

I've got a lot of projects going on and can't afford to keep someone on my team who's so negative about everything."

As Howard walked Gary to the door, Howard said, "Gary, since performance appraisals are scheduled for next week, let's just hold off on terminating Calhoun. Let me take a look at some personnel files and talk to a few people. How about talking tomorrow?" Gary agreed and seemed to relax a little.

"It's a puzzle to me why Gary wants to fire Calhoun," Howard said to Jessica at lunch. "Gary's unit is producing well past expectations and really needs Calhoun's input. There have been a couple of complaints from direct reports in the past but nothing that couldn't be settled fairly quickly. He's also had very little turnover—so I don't get it."

They agreed to return to Howard's office and look at the rest of the files from Gary's project team. Back at the office, Jessica scanned the files and pulled out the project team and individual employee ratings. Howard took out a piece of paper and jotted down some figures in columns. He came up with what looked like a comparison table.

EXHIBIT A   Summary of Unit and Employee Ratings

	Top Management	Supervisor	Self	Peer
Robin	90%	70%	85%	80%
Stephanie	80%	65%	90%	80%
Cliff	75%	80%	75%	75%
Calhoun	85%	50%	90%	80%
Jamal	70%	90%	75%	90%

Included in all employees' files were copies of their last five annual performance reviews plus a special (top officer initiated) six-month review of Gary's unit after the merger between BAS and MOS. Each file also contained two years' worth of comments from 360-degree reviews. Prior to the merger, BAS and MOS both used 360-degree feedback, but asked different questions.

Source: Table adapted from K. Miller & K. Medved, Managing the manager, *Management Communication Quarterly* (2000).

Analysis of "Managing after the Merger: Feedback at BAS"

Jessica stopped reading aloud and closed the last file. "Well, Howard," she said, "what do you suggest?"

"It seems to me that you need to do some coaching with Gary on a number of issues including the performance appraisal process and an increased understanding of cultural mergers," said Howard. "Gary's notes about what he wants to talk about in the performance appraisal are not constructive and often highlight insignificant facts to suit his purpose. He is not using the performance appraisal process for the growth and mentoring of his engineers."

"Well, I know what I'm not going to do," Jessica responded. "I'm not ready to approve firing Calhoun, at least not until I have a better understanding of the problems between Gary and Calhoun. I think you're right. I need to coach Gary through this performance appraisal process next week. Long-term goals need to include improving Gary's ability to evaluate employees and conduct performance appraisals. A short-term goal might be to mediate a discussion between Calhoun and Gary to get the issues on the table and defuse the conflict. At this point, I don't have enough data to approve Gary's firing Calhoun. That's not to say that I won't eventually reach the same conclusion as Gary, but I need to take him through this process first. However, I have to be honest with you, Howard, and tell you that I don't feel confident in confronting Gary. Since I am new to BAS myself, I haven't really developed a long-term relationship with Gary and I think I could use some help."

"You know, Jessica, there are a lot of resources available out there. Let me do some research and get back to you."

During the next week, after using the help Howard identified, Jessica coached Gary through this set of performance appraisals with his engineers. Specifically, she helped him recognize the purpose of appraisals as one of employee mentoring and development. Jessica realized that it would take several sessions and conversations with Gary to reach this long-range goal. To work on the immediate problem of the conflict between Gary and Calhoun, she planned a meeting between the two of them for Monday at 10 A.M.

As Jessica reflected on what needed to be said at the meeting between Gary and Calhoun, she recognized that she needed to focus on how to increase the success of the software engineering team instead of individual issues that might be bothering either of them. Jessica began the meeting by saying, "The goal of this meeting is to identify issues important to your success as a team. The first thing we need to do is establish some ground rules. First, I will be taking brief notes and immediately following this meeting will write up my understanding of what we have discussed. I will then give each of you a copy to review. Is that all right?"

Both Gary and Calhoun nodded their heads.

"The second ground rule is that nothing we say to each other should be a personal attack. Let me give you an example. If I am upset with someone because she is frequently late to meetings, I might say, 'I can never depend on you to show up. How can I possibly feel confident that you'll do a good job when you always miss the meetings where we talk about the project?' " Jessica has been coached to get Gary and Calhoun to "buy into" the negative impact of words like "never" and "always." As they discussed this statement, she pointed out that it is more an attack against the person than a description of troublesome behavior.

"The third ground rule is that no decisions will be made today. The purpose of this meeting is to gather information, and we will reflect on this information before we come to any decisions."

During that first meeting, several issues were brought to the table. First, Gary expressed disappointment with Calhoun's lack of enthusiasm and constant criticism of BAS's policies. Calhoun, on the other hand, felt he was not being asked to contribute to the team and confessed to feeling that he might be threatening to Gary because he used to have the same job at MOS before the merger. Jessica's goal was to prevent them from reaching conclusions about the issues bothering them. Rather, she wanted them to engage in

(Continued)

active listening, provide examples of behavior, and paraphrase the issues. Her other role was to help them be specific. They were modestly successful.

Gary said to Calhoun, "You never have anything good to say about BAS."

Jessica interrupted him and asked Gary to rephrase his complaint using specific examples.

Gary said to Calhoun, "Last Wednesday, you said in an email that performance appraisals were a waste of time."

Calhoun replied, "That's not exactly what I said. To refresh your memory, I said performance appraisals in this company don't appear to be doing what they're supposed to be doing, and I asked what their goal was."

Jessica used this opportunity to talk through what changes in the process would make performance appraisals more productive for both of them. Later in the conversation, Calhoun said, "My peers rate me very highly but I don't seem to be able to please you. I just don't know what I have to do to be a contributing member of this team. I think I have a lot to offer BAS."

Gary was unable to respond. He seemed confused as to what Calhoun meant, but couldn't articulate his bewilderment in a way that would solicit more information from Calhoun for clarification.

Later Jessica had an opportunity to talk with Gary privately and to point out the following fact: "Gary, from the 360-degree performance feedback, it would appear that your perception of Calhoun, as well as Stephanie, is quite different from their peers. Stephanie received a rating of 90 from her peers but only 65 from you. Calhoun received a rating of 90 from his peers but only 50 from you. At the same time, Jamal received a rating of 75 from peers, but you gave him a rating of 90. Is it possible that you and the team members are using different criteria to evaluate each other? Perhaps you need to clarify those criteria and get the team to agree on indicators of success for your team."

Gary felt that Jessica might not really understand the dynamics of the engineering team and resented her subtle insinuation that his team wasn't communicating well. Nevertheless, he agreed to try to keep an open mind and explore the possibilities.

Jessica had been working with an outside consultant for some time and when she reported on the outcomes of several meetings with Gary and Calhoun, her outside consultant suggested the following: "Be careful that you are not taking Gary's problem on as your own. For example, I hear you talking more about the specific program than about Gary. When you focus more on the problem than on the person who is telling you about the problem, you begin to lose track of what the person is saying, having begun to think about the problem and its solution. The moment you begin to offer solutions to the problem while the person is still talking about the problem, you are usually no longer testing to see if the person has a clear idea about the nature of the problem or if he has identified his own solution to this problem. The moment you begin to worry about your own ability to solve the problem rather than focusing on the other person's ability to solve the problem, you are 'owning' the problem and you are no longer coaching the individual but trying to do his job for him. We know this is difficult to do sometimes, especially when you have ultimate responsibility for the outcome, but you need to try so that your managers can become more self-sufficient in their management skills."

This was hard advice for Jessica to accept. However, she realized she often worried about the problem long after the sessions with Gary rather than monitoring his progress in solving the problem himself. She made a call to Gary and suggested the following:

"Gary, I think you need to spend more time observing your team and how it works. I'd like you to delay the report I've asked you to do for me and instead take a day to shadow your team. I will ask you to do two things: suspend judgment and instead assume an attitude of innocence by giving each team member the benefit of the doubt. Second, take careful notes of what you observe, which I will ask you to share with me at our next meeting." Gary, a bit reluctantly, agreed to try Jessica's request.

When Gary and Jessica met following his day of observation her goal was to help him identify positive behaviors and attitudes he could reinforce for each team member and help him be specific in his description of those behaviors. Furthermore, she wanted to encourage Gary to suggest possible changes in any processes he observed and, if necessary, identify the consequences of continued unacceptable behavior. During the meeting, Jessica and Gary agreed on a six-month action plan for him that included (1) cultural merger training for his entire team, (2) an increase in team meetings from one per month to one every two weeks, and (3) within three months a list of criteria by which future performance appraisals would be conducted—agreed to by all team members. The action plan focused on improving the quality and quantity of communication between Gary and his team and among the team members. Furthermore, the plan was intended to increase the appreciation of how each organization did things in their cultures before the merger. Jessica hoped this approach would allow a smoother merger of the two cultures. Jessica and Gary agreed to meet again in one month to review the progress he had made on meeting these goals and to reassess his decisions about firing Calhoun.

Later that day, Jessica had the following phone conversation:

"Hello, Sue? This is Jessica. Well, you and Mary were right about the issues in this case. I just finished talking with Gary this morning. Your analysis of the previous evaluations was right on target. Your help was great. Now, I'd like to talk to you about James, who thinks he has a sexual harassment case on his hands. Yesterday, one of the secretaries came to him and described in detail an encounter with her supervisor that was unlike anything I have ever heard. . . ."

Review Questions

1. Were the roles Howard and Jessica played appropriate? What other interventions could they have tried?
2. If you were an outside consultant called in by Howard, what steps would you have taken?
3. What do you think the likelihood is that Gary and Calhoun will be able to continue to work together?

Source: From S. DeWine and M. Eicholtz, case analysis, *Management Communication Quarterly.*

Small Group Activities

Dividing training participants into small groups of five to seven people allows a more personal experience with other types of training techniques. For example, a simulation involving five people will allow everyone in the group to participate in either the discussion or the role plays in the simulation. In a group of 20 to 40 people, many people will be passive audience members. Small group activities personalize the training experience for all participants.

Bunker, Nochajski, McGillicuddy, and Bennett (1987), in their review of literature on training designs, concluded that "to be effective, skills training requires practice according to criteria, followed by performance feedback. When a new skill is learned, a small group may be a safe place to try it out" (p. 229). Many training techniques are "tried out" in group settings. Placing participants in small groups makes them feel more involved in the process.

A small group fosters interpersonal relationships among the group members. This increases the possibility that group members will get to know each other better and feel more comfortable with each other. People tend to want to help someone they like. Thus, the group becomes more cooperative. This makes consensus easier to reach. It is also possible that as they get to know one another they will increase their dislike for each other as well! However, I have found that during the initial stages of a group a "halo effect" is in operation. The halo effect suggests that people will give each other the benefit of the doubt in initial interactions and will suspend judgment in an effort to get along.

At the same time, groups have to watch out for "groupthink" (Janis, 1972). **Groupthink** occurs when a group becomes so dependent on its own information that members do not allow outside information, especially if it is contrary to their thinking, to enter the discussion.

Small groups' members must be careful that they do not defend one group member against another, that they do pay attention to the process they are using in making their decisions, that they don't allow so much social interaction that it interferes with accomplishing the task, and that interpersonal conflicts are not under the surface and never dealt with.

Ellis (1988) suggested the consultant or trainer needs to "guide rather than influence the group's activity" (p. 54). The facilitator must not present the ultimate solutions to the group because then the facilitator, rather than the group, "owns" the solution. Nor, at the same time, can the facilitator sit back and simply let the group move in any direction. "Guiding rather than influencing" is a good guideline to follow.

Structured Experiences

Structured experiences are exercises intended to allow individuals to try out behaviors in a relatively safe environment. Experimental learning is

most useful where intellectualization is not as effective as actually placing people in true-to-life settings.

Structured experiences are designed to engage participants in the
learning process. Another term used to indicate a shift to active participation in the training process is *accelerated learning*. This approach recommends using the learners' knowledge as a foundation for learning and reducing the negative stress sometimes associated with training, and
creates a collaborative environment that integrates both hemispheres of
the brain for greater creativity. This technique allows trainers to use real-
life experiences that engage the participants' multiple intelligences
(Greenbaum, 1999, p. 55).

Inexperienced trainers should not use structured experiences, and
yet that is the activity of choice for many training consultants. The problem with using "games" is that many trainers do not know how to analyze them properly once they are completed. A very well thought-out and
carefully orchestrated debriefing should occur after every structured
game and, in fact, often takes longer than the game itself.

Porter (1987) suggested a five-stage process for completing the debriefing following an activity. These stages are experiencing the activity,
data gathering, interpreting, generalizing, and applying (p. 69). During
the data gathering stage, participants are asked what happened during
the activity, including thoughts and feelings, and what people did or said.
The third stage, interpreting, asks individuals to "make sense of the data
reported in the preceding phase" (p. 70). The next stage, generalizing, is
"drawing out what the participants have learned and relearned" (p. 70).

The last stage, applying, may be the most significant of all the stages.
Here the trainer is asking participants how this experience can be used in
their everyday lives and how their new knowledge might influence or
affect the way they behave on a day-to-day basis. Sometimes the trainer
uses this stage to help participants make commitments to what they will
do with what they have learned, on the job or in their personal lives. In
my experience, processing the activity is much harder and demands
greater skills than running any activity. If the trainer is not highly skilled
at drawing out insights and helping people to understand their experiences, the activity remains just a game.

A facilitator should spend approximately twice as much time discussing the activity as was spent participating in the activity. This discussion first asks participants to explain to the whole group what they were
asked to do during the simulation. People always want everyone to know
why they were acting the way they were and that the behavior is not the
way they normally react. Only after everyone has had a chance to explain
what he or she was doing can you get the group to focus on the meaning of
the activity. What did they learn from this activity that they can now apply
to work or personal settings? How did they feel when people acted a certain way and how does that translate into everyday life? This discussion is

absolutely necessary, or the participants will end up thinking, "This was an interesting activity and kind of fun, but what does it have to do with anything else?"

Role Play

A **role play** is a description of a problem "acted out" by two or more individuals. It can bring out the "ham" in people, but for those who are more apprehensive, I would never use the term *role play!* Some will see this as silly.

There are two role-playing procedures. One is the multiple role-playing procedure, in which the entire group attending the training session is formed into role-playing groups, the size of the groups depending on the number of participants required for the particular case. All groups role-play simultaneously. This maximizes opportunities for the members of the audience to try new attitudes and behaviors and provides data from several groups so that the results can be compared.

The other procedure is single role playing, in which only one role-playing group performs while other members of the class participate as observers. An advantage to this is, since all persons observe a single performance, it is possible to discuss the details that led to a particular effect. Also, participants in the role play profit from the analytical discussion of their behaviors since they are often unaware of the effect of their actions on others. Finally, observers can develop sensitivity to the feelings of the performers.

There are also modifications of these two basic types:

Role reversals: participants begin the role play in one role and halfway through switch places with another participant and assume a different role. This is especially effective at helping individuals to experience another point of view.

Alter egos or doubles: one person plays a role and a second person stands behind the participant, providing advice and suggestions. In this way, the second person becomes the "alter ego" of the role player and helps the performer remember his or her role.

Rotation or fish bowl: I have found it quite useful to have individuals rotate through roles or have the entire group watch a role play (as if the participants are in a "fish bowl") and then ask the observers to make suggestions for the role players. For example, one role player is trying to use a new conflict management technique. I may stop the interaction and ask the observers if there are other things the person might say or do to help resolve the role play. I may ask someone who has a particularly good suggestion to take the place of the role player and act it out. This gets the entire group involved while providing one common experience for all to analyze.

Role plays should be strictly voluntary, because forcing a normally shy individual to "act out" will cause extreme stress for that person as well as those watching the experience! Don't force someone who is not inclined to be "on stage" to do so. Provide opportunities for one-on-one role plays or discussions about the situation for those individuals who are reluctant to perform in front of a group.

The importance of debriefing cannot be overemphasized. The facilitator must "make the point" or the whole exercise becomes fruitless. The debriefing should normally take as long or longer than the activity took to perform.

Figure 6.1 outlines Jones and Pfeiffer's (1979) identification of the extent to which role playing and other activities are experiential. At the extreme end of the continuum are "intensive growth groups." These activities involve many of the others described earlier; however, they also involve counseling, and I would not suggest that a trainer who has not had graduate-level training in counseling and/or psychology use this technique. Even then, the training should be specifically for this type of activity. Don't try it if you don't know what you are doing!

Simulations

In **simulations,** participants are asked to act out complex cases and roles in order to analyze an organizational problem. Simulations are attempts to re-create real social settings where individuals can have a true-to-life experience. The goal is to gain insight into one's own behavior.

Purpose of Simulations

Caplan and Darth (1987) summed up the purpose behind the use of simulation in training: "The idea behind laboratory education is quite simple: to provide a setting in which participants can exhibit behavior and in turn reflect on and learn from that behavior" (p. 137). Laboratory education, simulations, and hands-on experiences were developed as alternatives to more didactical methods in which an expert delivers information that is absorbed by the listeners. It is also an alternative to the case method, in which the instructor leads a discussion based on a post-mortem of an actual case. As Caplan and Darth suggested, laboratory education was "invented expressly to serve the purpose of creating a living laboratory in which participants put their own behavior under a microscope" (p. 237).

Examples of early simulations used by trainers certainly include the T-group (training group) from NTL (National Training Laboratories). After 40 years of use, it still offers advantages, despite the image problems this technique has had. During the 1950s and 1960s T-groups, or sensitivity training, was sometimes seen as therapy groups run by nonpsychologists.

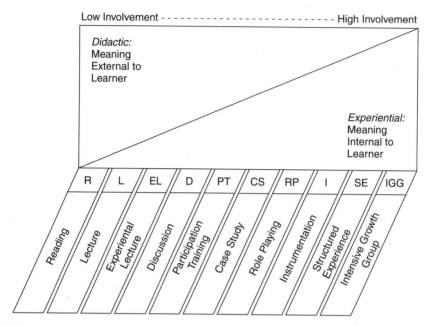

FIGURE 6.1   The Technology of Human Relations Training   From J. E. Jones & J. W. Pfeiffer, Role Playing, *The 1979 Annual Handbook for Group Facilitators,* San Diego: University Associates, 1979, p. 182.

An unskilled trainer asking probing, personal questions can do a great deal of damage.

An example of a simulation is "Looking Glass" (McCall & Lombardo, 1979). "Looking Glass" is a hypothetical, medium-size glass manufacturing corporation, complete with annual report, financial data, and glass products. The simulation creates an air of authenticity. The fictional company consists of three divisions, whose environments vary according to the degree of change. The simulation lasts six hours and is intended to represent a typical day in the life of the company. It begins by giving each participant an "inbasket" full of memos and materials. Contained in the collective inbaskets of the 20 participants are more than 150 different problems that participating managers must attend to. The problems vary in importance. During the simulation, there are often discrepancies between "what participants intend to do and what they discover later they actually do" (p. 147).

McCall and Lombardo pointed out limitations of this technique because a simulation removes participants from the present environment, and whatever is learned from the simulation must be adapted to the individual's current circumstances. Second, it is powerful, meaning that it exposes participants to an intensity that many of them may not be prepared for, and it is highly demanding in terms of staff preparation and time.

Boyer (1987) described a simulation approach for developing consultation skills. He suggested the advantages of using a simulation are that it "permits some simultaneous training in cognitive interpersonal and personal competence without the time commitments and complications that may accompany a practicum approach" (p. 149). A practicum approach is usually more like a semester-long class in which students take on roles for several weeks at a time in a simulated organization.

Boyer suggested that cognitive approaches typically emphasize cognitive skills more than interpersonal or personal emotional skills. They are easier to design, control, and implement. Simulations do provide substantial opportunities for participants to develop interpersonal and personal competence. The simulation approach may serve as a transition between the cognitive and practicum approaches. It is less labor-intensive, yet permits simultaneous development of cognitive, interpersonal, and personal skills. In addition, it can be used with less experienced participants.

A Sample of the Simulation Technique

The activity in Form 6.2 was developed for a graduate consulting class. Each participant takes a turn at playing the role of "consultant" with the same cast of characters. The interactions are videotaped for later review.

THE CONSULTATION SIMULATION

The Organization

Mead Mental Health Clinic is a community service agency serving a district of four counties. Its services include counseling and psychological services, career planning, crisis intervention–related workshops, and outpatient and inpatient care. It also provides educational services to inpatients, including continuing education for adults and regular educational services for school-age patients. On the staff are 39 professional workers and 72 hourly wage workers.

Background of the Problem

Mead Mental Health Clinic has long recognized that employees who are satisfied with their jobs enable a company to be successful. This philosophy, rather than a specific problem, led to the establishment of two-way communications. Over the years, the philosophy and the programs that reflect it have evolved to meet employees' changing needs, encompassing a variety of face-to-face, written, and other methods of communication. Every April and May since 1946, the Mead Mental Health Clinic has held a series of two-hour "jobholders meetings" in which management reports to employees on the company's financial health, business planning, wages and benefits, and other areas of general interest. Employees, in turn, are free to question any member of management, including the top administrator of the center. Some questions are submitted in writing, some are asked from the floor. Some are signed, some are anonymous. Whatever the question, a top-level administrator gives a spontaneous reply.

The Problem

The employees who attend these meetings respond very favorably to them. However, only 60 percent of the professional workers and 25 percent of the hourly wage workers attend. Top management would like to increase the percentage of attendance in hopes of increasing participation in decision making and policy development. *You have been called in as a consultant to help them attain this goal.* You have had two previous meetings with top management, which includes Center Director, Director of Clinical Services, Director of Educational Services, Supervisor of Nursing Staff, and Director of Personnel.

(Continued)

THE CONSULTATION SIMULATION *(Continued)*

Meeting Participants

Mr. Stan Leiber, Center Director: overall administrator with particular responsibility for financial operations. He enthusiastically supports this project and made the initial contact with the consultant.

Dr. Victoria Quarterly, Director of Clinical Services: a counseling psychologist who is skeptical about the success of the project as well as the effect of having an outsider come in as a consultant.

Ms. Margaret Coffman, Director of Educational Services: would like to be supportive of this project as long as it is not going to eliminate any of her educational programs or increase her workload.

Mr. Fred Williams, Supervisor of Nursing Staff: wants equal attention given to problems of the nurses as well as equal respect given to their input into decision making.

Dr. Chris Dotson, Director of Personnel: having designed three consultation workshops, he believes he can solve any problems the center has with no outside help. He feels he already knows why the attendance is at its present level and, if given the proper resources, feels he could solve the problem.

Design

Students are divided into groups of six with one person designated as the "consultant." Every 10 minutes students change roles until everyone serves as the consultant. While one group is being videotaped, another group is watching on closed-circuit TV. Each group also reviews its own tape.

Outdoor Games

One type of training activity is the use of physical activities that are usually held outside. These games can be quite engaging and place participants in an entirely different setting from their usual workplace.

I have used outdoor games with a variety of audiences, including a group of bankers who spent all of their time indoors working on sometimes tedious tasks. For three successive programs bank executives participated in team-building physical activities—always their favorite program among a variety of development topics. The uniqueness of the activity is attractive as long as you can get the participants to buy into setting aside their more "adult" selves and agreeing to "play" a little. I always remind them that no matter how successful we are today, and no matter what we have achieved, we need to remember we were all children and it's useful to tap into our "child" from time to time. This is one of those occasions.

One of the cautions is that the "games" can be perceived as fun but without a relevant point. It is critical that the facilitator take as much time processing the activity as the activity itself took to complete. Weaver (1999) defined such experimental activities as a unique synthesis of knowledge from the fields of learning theory, adult learning, and organizational development. Ropes courses are one example of this type of activity, but there are many other less physical activities that force participants to depend on each other and challenge teamwork. Forms 6.3 and 6.4 show two examples of outdoor games, "Rope-a-Leader" and "Eight-Pointed Star," that require limited physical activity.

ROPE-A-LEADER:
EXPERIENCING THE EMERGENCE OF LEADERSHIP

Goals

- To provide the participants with the opportunity to experience and observe the emergence of leaders from within a group
- To discuss the emergence of leaders

Group Size

Twenty to thirty-five participants in subgroups of five or seven

Time Required

Forty minutes

Materials

Twenty-five feet of ¼-inch rope, twine, or macramé cord for each subgroup

Physical Setting

Any area large enough so that all subgroups can work without disturbing one another

Process

1. Ask the participants to assemble in subgroups of five or seven. (Odd numbers work best.) Once subgroups have assembled, place a rope on the ground near each group. (*Note:* You may place ropes in several locations prior to beginning this activity.) (Five minutes)

2. Explain that the task of each subgroup is to use the rope to form "an absolutely perfect" circle on the ground. When finished, the rope should lie on the ground with no one touching it to hold it in place. Tell participants they may *not* talk to one another or to you during the activity and that you will be the final judge as to when they have accomplished the task. Tell them to begin, giving them no more than two or three minutes.

3. While subgroups are completing the task, walk around from subgroup to subgroup "judging" their work and being critical about the final shapes they have created.

4. After the circles have been completed, tell the subgroups to form a perfect square, then a triangle, a trapezoid, and an octagon. Remind the participants not to talk. (Ten minutes)

(Continued)

113

ROPE-A-LEADER:
EXPERIENCING THE EMERGENCE OF LEADERSHIP *(Continued)*

5. After all of the shapes have been completed say, "On the count of 3, point to the leader of your subgroup. Ready? 1, 2, 3." Ask members of each subgroup, in turn, how they selected that particular leader.

6. Reconvene the large group and lead a discussion based on the following questions:

   - How did the leadership evolve in your group?
   - How did other members of the group acquiesce to the leadership?
   - Did conflict occur in any groups? Why or why not?
   - How does what happened here compare to what happens in a typical work setting at your organization?

   (Fifteen minutes)

Variations

- This activity can be used for team building.
- At the end of the activity, the group can discuss what attributes of the leaders made the process work. List the attributes on a flip chart for a further discussion of leadership.

Submitted by John W. Peterson and Sherry R. Mills.

John W. Peterson and Sherry R. Mills are the founders and partners in Creative Training & Conference Management, Colorado Springs, Colorado. Both have master's degrees in education and have developed and presented workshops on a variety of topics throughout the United States.
The 1999 Annual: Volume 1, Training/© 1999 Jossey-Bass/Pfieffer

---

EIGHT-POINTED STAR

Summary

One or two groups of eight stand in a circle and toss a water balloon among them in the pattern of an eight-pointed star. Once this seemingly simple task is accomplished, participants are presented with a more challenging problem related to the star pattern they have learned. Observers are used.

Objectives

To explore communication, leadership, and problem solving

Materials

A bag of five moderately filled water balloons for each group of eight. (Only one balloon per group is needed but accidents do happen!)

Time Limit

30 to 45 minutes

Procedure

1. Briefly describe the activity and ask participants to form one or two groups of eight with one or more volunteer observers for each group.

2. Place a balloon in the middle of each group and instruct participants as follows:

   "Stand in a circle. Your initial task is to toss the water balloon among yourselves in the pattern of an eight-pointed star. The pattern must be continuous and involve all eight of you as points of the star. You may begin."

3. Give each observer a copy of "Instructions for the Observer."

4. When a group believes it has formed a pattern, tell the members that each person should throw the balloon to someone and receive it from another. These are the only two people in the circle whom the pattern should connect. If not, they have not formed the star correctly and must reassess.

5. If the group has succeeded in forming the star, tell the players their next task involves tossing the balloon to either the same person they threw it to or the person they received it from in forming the eight-pointed star. They should begin by throwing the balloon to one of these two people. That person is out and must give the balloon to someone who is not yet out. This person throws someone else out. When there is no one left to receive a throw, the process ends. The goal is to throw out as many people as they can, and they should keep trying to improve.

(Continued)

115

EIGHT-POINTED STAR *(Continued)*

   Challenge the group at some point with the fact that all eight can be eliminated.

6. Conduct a review and discussion.

Commentary

If you are using two groups, rely on the observers to let you know when a group has finished the first task. More than two groups requires an assistant or putting the observers in charge by giving them the instructions so you can roam from group to group.

Some groups have difficulty even with the first task and this is a pretty good indication of poor communication patterns and/or unproductive leadership struggles. If you sense these may be issues, use this exercise early on as a diagnostic and potential reference point for further training.

The solution involves a pattern of one person tossing the balloon to the third person away from him or her in a clockwise direction. If the points of a star are numbered from 1 to 8 (see Figure 1) the solution will be as

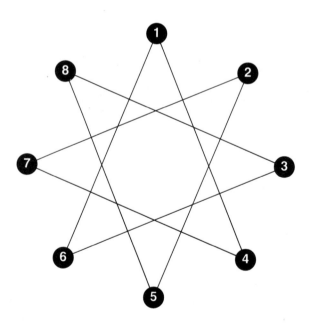

FIGURE 1   Eight-Pointed Star

(Continued)

EIGHT-POINTED STAR *(Continued)*

follows: 1 to 4, 4 to 7, 7 to 2, 2 to 5, 5 to 8, 8 to 3, 3 to 6, 6 to 1. Note also the pattern of always eliminating the last person to throw. During the review, ask what patterns were noticed. There are many pattern metaphors in this exercise that you can relate to any training theme you want.

Variations

1. Balls and other objects can be substituted.
2. Catches can be restricted to one hand and penalties can be assessed for each dropped and/or burst balloon.
3. With two or more groups it can become a competition in that time penalties are assessed for drops and/or bursts.

Instructions for the Observer

Note the leadership and communication patterns and anything that strikes you about the way participants solve the problem. Specifics to watch for are (1) visible communication aids such as drawing a star or forming a system (such as raising hands and then lowering them) to communicate who has or has not received the balloon, and (2) insights such as observations that the balloon cannot be thrown to an adjacent person and the person who starts must also be the one who completes the star.

Designing and Directing Training

Like their clients, trainers need training and practice to ensure that they perform their work well. In "practicing what they preach," trainers build on a body of knowledge about the design and direction of training activities. They also develop their own talents and skills.

Guidelines for Designing and Directing Training

To begin with, trainers should be realistic about the amount of time needed to design a training program. According to Zemke and Armstrong (1997), the U.S. Office of Personnel Management estimates the following preparation times for developing one hour of training:

Technical formal courses—5 to 15 hours

Self-contained training, ready for other trainers to use—50 to 100 hours

Conventional management development—20 to 30 hours

Technical on-site content—1 to 3 hours (p. 70)

Knowing the design stage will be costly in terms of time, you next turn your attention to criteria for selecting the components of the training.

Bunker and colleagues (1987) reviewed a large body of published material on training design and conclude the following guidelines based on categories of important principles of design.

The first category is initial activities. These initial activities are critical since adults need to "know the schedule, the rules of the game, and who the staff and other participants are" (p. 277). These activities set the climate for the entire workshop and establish the staff's role with the participants in the workshop.

The second category is establishing a collaborative participant-staff relationship. Their review indicates many authors emphasize that adults must be responsible for their own learning (Pfieffer & Jones, 1973). I recommend the staff put themselves in the participants' roles when designing a training event in order to understand the nature of a collaborative relationship.

Third, levels of activity and participation are planned. Many authors suggest that the degree to which there is active participation on the part of the attendees is something that needs to be decided early in the event. An underlying assumption is that "involvement and shared leadership increase commitment which in turn increases learning" (Bunker et al., 1987, p. 228).

Fourth, the trainer must maintain energy in the workshop. The staff's level of energy carries over and is expressed by the participants. Staff members should vary the activity type, length, and intensity so that participants do not get bored. All trainers must pay attention to building in time for breaks for the physical, as well as psychological, needs of the participants.

Fifth, the trainer must plan strategies to reduce resistance. Several authors deal with resistance as a part of the process of learning and of the change process and explain that it must be carefully understood. Finally, a variety of sequence patterns are recommended from less difficult to more difficult or from less risky to more risky. Most suggest that as the program progresses the trainer should gather data on how it is affecting the participants.

Lippitt and Lippitt (1986) suggested ten assumptions as guides in designing learning sessions:

- Every client group is unique.
- Within each group, participants show differences in readiness.
- The consultant should recognize the network already established within the client group and support its influence.
- The consultant should encourage learning through the formation of teams of peers.
- Client learners should have a major role in planning the design.
- The consultant should demonstrate how to build resources.
- The consultant should build mutual feedback processes.
- The design should promote follow-up.
- The design should teach methodological skills so that client learners can apply their training without having to rely on the consultant.
- The consultant's challenge is to help the client tie information to a variety of applications, like action planning, management plans, and risk taking.

Lippitt and Lippitt (1986) also identified traps in training designs. Some of the traps involve personnel, both the training staff and the client. Relying totally on one expert is a bad idea, as is allowing the participation of an inadequately prepared, unknown, and uncomfortable resource person. Not obtaining data about the client before the session, not involving the client in the planning, and not sharing the agenda can prevent the session from meeting the client's unique set of needs. Not dealing with the learners' feelings or allowing the expression of individual preferences, and using haphazard grouping patterns can also be damaging. Inattention to the details of the physical setup of the training site (for example, the seating arrangement, the working order of equipment, and the legibility of visual aids) or to the schedule (failing to devise a definitive way to begin the session, allowing long coffee breaks, having no plans for transitions) may have a negative effect. Even after a successful session, failure can result in the long run from skipping plans for follow-up or preparing inadequately for the recording and distribution of follow-up materials (pp. 108–109).

It is important that the trainer pay attention to all the small details that make a session go well. In a sense, it is like planning a mini-conference, with plans for food, seating, lighting, travel arrangements, and social programs. I always pay a great deal of attention to the environment in which I will be working because I believe the shape of the room, the places where people are sitting, lighting, and sound all have a great impact on the success of the meeting. But sometimes all the planning in the world will not prevent problems.

> A colleague and I were planning a full day retreat for the executives of a pharmaceutical company. This was the first time I worked with this consultant and I wanted to be sure we had thought of every detail. We had arrived at the hotel the night before, and at 10:00 P.M. found the room with the name of the organization on the door for the next morning. The room was not arranged as we had instructed and so we dismantled the room and spent till 11:30 P.M. rearranging it to fit the needs of this session. We found someone in housekeeping to provide new tablecloths to fit the new arrangement and were very pleased with the result. As we wearily approached the elevator, congratulating ourselves for coming in a night early and avoiding a disaster, we noticed on the bulletin board for the next day that the room we had just rearranged was scheduled for another organization! They no doubt had had the room arranged just the way they wanted it! Attending to every detail can still get you in trouble! We told the desk clerk the next morning that there must be some error on the bulletin board and actually the two rooms were switched and then spent the rest of the morning wondering, along with the group leader, why the hotel would have switched the rooms at the last moment! At the right opportunity, I will 'fess up!

■ **CASE STUDY: WHAT WOULD YOU DO?**
B. Parker and Company

The following case study gives you a chance to practice the concepts you've learned. After reading each section of the case, think about what's going on. Analyze why things are happening the way they are. Then go on to read and answer the review questions. Compare your answers with the next part of the case, which describes what happened as a result of what came before, or the action that was taken in that particular instance. Remember, the action taken and the decisions made in this case are not necessarily the only possible or justifiable ones. Rarely is there only one right answer to any business problem.

B. Parker and Company is an advertising firm located in Boston. It was founded in 1931 by Brendan Parker II and is presently run by his son, Brendan Parker III. Initially, the company handled only print media—newspapers and magazines. But as television and radio became more popular and more influential as advertising media, B. Parker and Company branched into T.V. and radio advertising. By 1963, B. Parker and Company had become one of the most sought-after firms in Boston. Over the years, B. Parker's creative department had collected a network of talented in-house and freelance writers and graphic artists. Their newspaper ads were catchy and bright, their T.V. and radio commercials witty and appealing. This year the company is celebrating its fiftieth anniversary.

Brendan Parker III is eloquent without being loquacious, and well-spoken with no hint of arrogance. He speaks well with others and presents his ideas clearly. He also listens carefully to what others have to say, and always with a sympathetic ear. It's an attribute and a skill that the entire company profits from.

Planning a Meeting

Brendan Parker was reasonably satisfied with the company's rate of growth and its prestige, but he felt it was time to get involved in bigger things. He wanted the company to plan on bidding for new accounts in the advertising market dominated by the larger New York agencies. He decided to lay the groundwork for the new marketing push by meeting informally with the company's managers to gather their reactions and pool their ideas. These included the production manager, Michael Fox; the creative manager, Lee Codman; the marketing manager, Lauren Casey; the finance manager, Sean Dennison; and the sales manager, Jane Monoson.

As B. P. sat down to prepare the memo announcing the meeting, the intercom buzzed. "Yes, Vanessa," he answered to his secretary.

"Mr. Parker, Jeb Stuart from Rockwell is on the line. May I put him through?"

"Vanessa, tell him I'm busy right now, but that I'll get back to him just as soon as I can. That'll give me a chance to glance through the Rockwell file."

As B. P. replaced the receiver, he picked up a file from his desk. B. Parker and Company had been having problems with this account from the beginning. Rockwell was what B. P. referred to as the "blue-blooded killer." It was an old company located in Connecticut. Rockwell was meticulous in its approach to everything, and its managers were perfectionists to the core. Although B. P. admired these traits, he found his dealings with Rockwell tedious. He knew it was an account that had to be handled delicately. It was an important account, one that would add to the prestige of his company if it was successful in its bid for the account.

After quickly reviewing the file, he called back Jeb Stuart.

(Continued)

"Hi, Jeb. Brendan here. Sorry I wasn't able to talk with you immediately. How are things going?"

"Fine, Brendan, fine," Jeb replied. "But questions concerning your campaign have cropped up in the minds of a few people here. They're matters of policy rather than approach, so I thought it best to speak with you personally."

"Right, Jeb. What seems to be the problem?"

Jeb and Brendan went on to discuss the problem for the next 20 minutes. In the course of the conversation, Brendan decided it would be best to meet personally with Jeb and other members of Rockwell. Except for the policy reservations Jeb referred to, Rockwell seemed ready to accept B. Parker's proposed advertising campaign. Brendan was determined to quell any remaining reservations Rockwell might have. The two men finished their conversation after agreeing that Brendan would meet with Jeb in Connecticut that afternoon.

Brendan buzzed Vanessa and asked her to book him on an early afternoon flight to Connecticut. He then quickly finished his memo to his managers. Brendan's memo is shown in Exhibit A.

EXHIBIT A   Brendan Parker's Memo

TO: All Managers
FROM: Brendan Parker
RE: New Marketing Strategies
DATE: March 15, 1981

There will be a mandatory meeting for all managers on Friday, March 17, at 3:00 P.M. in the informal conference room on the thirtieth floor. After a thorough appraisal of each department's performance, I have decided it is time to re-evaluate our position in the marketplace. You will be expected to provide input to help reshape our marketing policies.

Review Questions

1. Is Brendan Parker's message effectively conveyed by his memo? Why or why not?

2. Brendan Parker decided to hold an informal meeting. Does the tone of his memo reflect this? Is the tone formal or informal?

3. Is there any difference in the message Brendan Parker is *sending* and the one the managers are *receiving*? How do you think the managers will interpret the message?

4. Is the memo clear? Will there be any questions in the readers' minds when they've finished reading it? Will the managers attending the meeting be prepared for what Brendan Parker wishes to discuss?

5. How could this memo be improved, if at all?

Jane Monoson Gets Worried

After receiving the memo, Jane Monoson immediately went to Lauren Casey's office.

"Did you get the memo?" Jane asked as she walked into Lauren's office. Lauren nodded and said, "It was just put on my desk. I'm not quite sure what to make of it. I didn't think our position in the market was threatened in any way. Of course, our bid for the Batchelor account could have been rejected. B. P. was really counting on it—it's worth $2 million. B. P. always holds meetings if an account falls through."

"Oh, no," Jane moaned. "I gave that account to that new young exec, Paul Winthrop—the fellow we pulled in from the Wilmar Agency. Maybe I shouldn't have put him in charge of something so big so soon."

"I wouldn't worry too much yet, Jane," Lauren replied.

Jane stood up and said, "No. I'd better talk with Paul—see what kind of feedback he got from the people he's worked with at Batchelor's. Paul would have a better idea of what's going on with that account than anyone. Besides, I don't want to go to this meeting completely defenseless. Listen Lauren, I'd better see you later. I want to catch Paul before he heads out to lunch."

Jane returned to her office and phoned Paul's office. The call was put through to Madge, the account executives' secretary.

"Hi Madge, it's Jane. Is Paul anywhere in the building?"

"Sorry, Jane," Madge replied. "Paul just stepped out for a luncheon meeting. Can I leave him a message?"

Jane thought for a moment. "Yes, tell him to see me as soon as he returns. It's about the Batchelor account. A big problem has surfaced, and I have to talk to him."

Madge took down the message and reassured Jane she would pass it on to Paul immediately.

Review Questions

1. Brendan Parker's message has obviously been misinterpreted by Lauren and Jane. Where did the communication process break down? More specifically, at what point in the sender-receiver system was the weakness?

2. What do you think of Jane's reaction? Is she acting too hastily? Should she have waited until after the meeting before acting? Why or why not?

3. Should Jane have passed the message to Madge? Or should she have waited to speak with Paul personally?

4. What possible interference problems could there be in the transmittal of Jane's message?

The Anxiety Spreads

After failing to reach Paul, Jane decided to try B. P. personally. Maybe he can calm my fears, she thought to herself. She picked up the phone and called Vanessa, B. P.'s secretary.

"Hi, Vanessa, it's Jane. Is Brendan around?"

"Sorry, Jane," Vanessa replied. "Mr. Parker just left for a meeting with a client. Very urgent business, so I hear."

(Continued)

Jane groaned silently to herself. B. P.'s "urgent business" had to do with the Batchelor account, she thought. After thanking Vanessa, Jane phoned Michael Fox, the production manager.

"Mike , did you get the memo? What do you think B. P. wants? I tried calling B. P., but —"

"Jane! Slow down! I've seen the memo. We all have. I thought it was just a general meeting—an open forum. But after talking with the others, I'm beginning to worry. Sean, for one, is sure it means trouble. Now it sounds as though you think that, too."

"Mike, I think it's about the Batchelor account. I've been trying to get ahold of Paul Winthrop, who's handling the account. But Madge says he's at lunch. I'll see what I can find out from him when he gets back, and I'll keep you posted."

Almost two hours later, Paul Winthrop returned to his office, elated after his meeting with J. P. Stance, the executive representing the Batchelor Company.

"How're ya doing, Madge?" he greeted the secretary as he burst into the office. "A sunny day to match my feelings. Just about settled the big one— seems to be no competition out there. Dear J. P. did everything but sign the contract. All she's got to do is convince one more big wheel that we've got the talent they need, and the account is ours. Can't wait to tell Jane."

Madge sighed and said, "Paul, I hate to be the bearer of bad news, but Jane phoned while you were out. I don't know—maybe she spoke with that one big wheel J. P. Stance hadn't. Whatever it was, she sounded frantic. Said there was a major problem with the account. She wanted to see you as soon as you returned. Paul, really, I'm sorry."

Paul looked stunned. "Madge, I can't believe it! J. P. almost had her pen in her hand! She must know what's going on over at Batchelor's. I really didn't think she'd play games with me." He sighed. "I should have known. My first big one, on the line. I'd better see Jane right away."

A Measure of Relief

Paul rushed to Jane's office, apprehensive and nervous. He knocked on her door and walked in when he heard her "Come in." Right away he knew something was wrong from the look on her face.

"Have a seat, Paul," Jane said tiredly. "I'm not quite sure how or where to begin. I'm not even sure what to pin my concerns on. But I've been worried all day."

"Did you talk to the big wheel at Batchelor's—Mr. Bentley? I really didn't think J. P. would run me through the mill. I mean, Jane, she did everything but sign the papers! Listen, I reviewed our campaign again with her during lunch. She said that Batchelor was in dire need of our kind of exposure. Jane, she was almost pleading with me, instead of me with her! I really don't understand. I mean—"

"Paul, hold on! I haven't spoken to Bentley since our last meeting together at the Plaza. I called you because *I* wasn't sure of the status of the account. You see, I got this memo today from B. P. He seems concerned about our position in the marketplace. I immediately assumed our newest big account had been shot down. B. P. always holds meetings after a potential client falls through."

"Well, if that's all it is," said Paul, annoyed, "it's a good thing I didn't call J. P.! I was thinking about it before I came to see you. I really could have blown the account. Listen, do you mind my asking exactly *what* the memo said?"

"Why not?" Jane replied. "At this point, a second opinion may help."

Paul read the memo and handed it back to Jane. "Jane, granted, the memo sounds serious, but I think you're jumping the gun. I'd talk with the other managers—see what their reactions are. Listen, I'd better return to my office. I want to put a few polishing touches on the Batchelor presentation I was about to throw out the window."

Jane gave Paul an apologetic look. "Paul, I'm sorry. I suppose I was passing my worries on for nothing. Anyway, I should have waited to talk with you personally. And I probably should've kept my mouth shut until after the meeting. Well, I'll let you know what happens. And keep smiling. It sounds like you've done a great job with this account."

Review Questions

1. What breakdowns in the communication process do you see thus far?
2. What problems will these breakdowns present? What problems do you think will arise at the meeting?
3. What obstacles have hampered effective communication? What problems with interference (internal and external) have occurred?

The Meeting Begins

Two days later, Brendan Parker was in his office editing his notes and polishing his ideas for the meeting he had arranged. His secretary, Vanessa, walked in with a letter that needed his signature. B. P. smiled. He was in fine spirits.

"Well, Vanessa, looks like a great St. Patrick's Day. The Batchelor and Rockwell accounts went through smoothly. Batchelor's was so pleased with Winthrop's final presentation. With these accounts under our belts, I think we're ready for the New York competition. We'll show them Boston's brains are the brightest. Oh—by the way, don't let me forget to send a personal note of congratulations to Paul Winthrop. He did a tremendous job. Hmm—it's time for the meeting, isn't it? Have all the managers gathered in the conference room yet?"

"Yes, Mr. Parker. I was just going to bring in coffee. Do you have a cup, or should I bring an extra?"

"No, I'm all set, Vanessa. Thanks. Tell them I'll be in in a few minutes. I've got to make one more phone call."

All the managers had gathered in the conference room ahead of time and were impatiently waiting for Brendan to arrive. Sean Dennison, in charge of

(Continued)

finance, was nervously drumming his pen on the table. He turned to Michael Fox, who was sitting next to him, and said, "I wish B. P. would get here, already. I've gone over these notes so many times the figures seem blurred."

Michael smiled sympathetically. "I know, Sean. At this point, we're all a little on edge. But I still say that if it were a serious problem, surely at least one of us would already know about it."

Jane was sitting across the table, nodding her head in acknowledgement of something Lauren had said.

"You know, Lauren," Jane said, "the Batchelor account is really a smashing success. I feel horrible about Paul. I really had him terrified."

"Well, Jane, mistakes can happen," Lauren replied. "We often look for answers too quickly—even when we're unsure of what the question is."

Lee Codman, sitting next to Lauren, was resting his head in his hands. "God, I'm exhausted," he said to no one in particular. "First I was charging around the office trying to abate fears and calm nerves. Then I had to do an about-face and start congratulating everyone for their stupendous efforts on the Batchelor account."

Lauren looked at Lee and said, "You *look* tired. But then, we all do. We've all been a little jumpy the past couple of days. Look at Sean. He's walking the floor like an alley cat. Stop pacing, Sean," Lauren called out. "You're making me nervous."

Just then, the conference room door opened and Brendan Parker came striding in, sporting a huge grin. "Happy St. Patrick's Day from the happiest Irishman in Boston today. We're here to—" Brendan looked around at all of the managers gathered in the room. His grin turned to a look of bewilderment as five haggard, anxious faces stopped him in mid-sentence.

Review Questions

1. What has happened? Why is Brendan so confused? What are the managers demonstrating through their body language?

2. Think back on the events over the past two days at B. Parker and Company, and list the communication problems that have plagued:

    (a) Paul and Jane.

    (b) Brendan Parker and the managers.

3. Consider the communication style of each of the managers and Brendan. Which individuals could stand some improvement in communications skills? Specifically, how and in what areas should they improve?

B. P. Vows Improvement

"Why all the glum faces?" Brendan asked as he approached his chair at the head of the table. "We need more spirit in this room! We'll soon be high rolling with the big New York agencies!"

"What?" Jane cut in.

The managers looked at one another and then at Brendan.

"You mean we're expanding our market?" Lee Codman asked.

"Yes," Brendan replied. "You've all done incredible jobs. Your departments must have competent, talented people. B. Parker has put together a strong, talented group—one that's ready to meet New York head on."

Jane laughed softly, shaking her head in disbelief. "Brendan," she said, "we're here for the wrong reasons. Or, I should say, we're here prepared for battle. A lot of us assumed that you called this meeting because something awful had happened."

Brendan looked around the room. The looks on the other managers' faces confirmed Jane's statement.

"Well, I don't know what to say. You all received my memo," Brendan said. "How did you get such a wrong impression?"

Sean refused to be blamed for misinterpreting the memo. "Well, Brendan," he said, "when you wrote that we were going to 're-evaluate our position in the marketplace,' most of us assumed that you were referring to a major change in company policy, all right. But you have to understand there was no positive tone in your memo—no optimism or excitement."

"That's right, Brendan," Lee agreed. "We just weren't sure. And, of course, the situation became magnified when we started talking to one another."

Brendan pulled the memo he had written out of his folder. After reading it over, he said, "O.K. I can see your point. No guidelines. No definite statement. It is ambiguous. But why didn't you come and see me instead of whispering among yourselves? My door is always open—always has been."

"Is it really?" asked Lauren, boldly speaking up. "You've been inaccessible—out of town—until today. And in the little time you are here, it's not that easy to see you."

Brendan looked around at the nods and expressions of assent that punctuated Lauren's statements. "Looks like you're not the only person who feels that way, Lauren," he said soberly. He thought for a moment. "Maybe before we start talking about making headway in New York, we ought to talk about improving our position right here, among ourselves. After all, I believe that openness is really important to a creative company like ours. It's the flow of ideas and the criticism and changes that we make that keep us alive. Maybe we should take steps to improve communication in this company. So tell me: How do you think we can make the organization more receptive to accurate and free communication? And what can I do personally to keep misunderstandings like this one from happening again?"

Review Questions

1. How would you answer Brendan's questions if you were one of the managers?
2. Do you agree with Brendan's statement that communication is important to a creative company? Why or why not?

(Continued)

3. Would you say that B. Parker and Company's problems stem from the fact that the company is too open, or not open enough? Could it be both? Explain your answer.

Source: American Management Association. *Executive Skills*, 1978, pp. 13–16. Reprinted by permission.

LESSONS LEARNED

Training Techniques Most Likely to Succeed

The training techniques most likely to succeed are usually the simple ones with the least amount of structure. Some of the most complicated and well-developed training techniques allow the trainees to get lost in the details and miss the point. If I have four hours for a training session, I want at least two hours for "debriefing," or discussing the impact of a training technique and what participants should take from the experience. I always use the last half-hour to talk about how to take what they have learned back to the job site.

Role plays generated from the discussion are much better than scripted dialogues. You have to be able to see the opportunity and provide directions on the spot. And you have to know which participants would be willing to role-play in front of the group. I have made the mistake of putting someone on the spot and asking her in front of everyone else if she would try role-playing. In that position, it is very embarrassing for someone to refuse and yet it is worse to actually do it. Now I try to seek people out before the session and be sure I have their consent before I call on them.

Outdoor games are an excellent way to get groups to break old habits, such as sitting and listening but not participating. Having people move around and participate in some physical activity, even at a minimal level, has always worked for me. It gets participants talking to each other as they move from one place to another. The kinds of outdoor games I use never require a medical attendant! They are definitely low impact and participants can opt out at any time.

One time I had planned to use a ropes activity where each person on a team must get through a maze of ropes tied between two trees. Parts of the maze are easier than others to get through. Some you can easily step over and others a person must be lifted through. Once someone has gone through one part of the maze, that opening is closed to others. Usually teams that have the smallest people go last because they are the easiest to get over and can get through the more difficult openings. One group had a very large woman who wanted to wait until last. The only openings left were ones where a person would need to be lifted through. I realized too late the problem they would have. They succeeded in getting her through one of the openings but I have not used that activity again for fear someone would be embarrassed by this activity.

When planning training techniques, always consider the physical and psychological well-being of your participants. You want to get the point across but you don't want the participants to focus on something that didn't work or was too difficult for them. You also don't want them to leave thinking, "That was fun, but what did it have to do with anything I do at work?" Spend more time talking about the "message" behind the activity than conducting the actual activity.

Additional Resources

Auerbach, C. (1997). *The 1997 McGraw-Hill training and performance sourcebook.* New York: McGraw-Hill.

Biech, E. (2000). *The 2000 annual: Vol. 1. Training.* San Francisco: Jossey-Bass/Pfieffer.

Consalvo, C. M. (1993). *Training with outdoor activities.* Aldershot, NH: Connaught Training.

Fish (video). (1998). Burnsville, MN: ChartHouse International.

McArdle, G. E. (1999). *Training design and delivery.* Alexandria, VA: ASTD.

Peterson, G. L. (2000). *Communicating in organizations: A casebook* (2nd ed.). Boston: Allyn & Bacon.

Sypher, B. D. (1997). *Case studies in organizational communication: Perspectives on contemporary work life.* New York: Guilford.

Chapter 7

TECHNOLOGY AND TRAINING AND CONSULTING

- ON-LINE TRAINING
- VIRTUAL LEARNING COMMUNITIES
- USE OF EMAIL IN ORGANIZATIONS
- USE OF VOICE MAIL IN ORGANIZATIONS
- THE "HUMAN MOMENT"

Lessons Learned: Keep Ahead of New Technologies

ADDITIONAL RESOURCES

Few managers have thought through the full ramifications of this new technology. It introduces an open, democratic, and largely integrated communications system into organizations.

Adapted from Nicholas Carr, The Politics of E-Mail, *1998*

On-line and Web-based training are staples among training tools. PowerPoint, video conferences, and virtual organizations are a few of the forms of technology with which consultants must be comfortable. Not only must trainers and consultants be able to effectively integrate new forms of technology in their delivery of services, but they also may be helping clients use technology to enhance decision making and increase performance. Consultants are even being called on to help companies protect themselves from "disruptive technology."

Harvard Business School professor Clayton Christensen describes "disruptive technology" as a new product that sneaks into the established market. "The Internet is the Godzilla of sleuth attacks. Once a cumbersome tool wielded only by academics and nerds, today's Web challenges not just retailers but everyone from venerable giants to small operations. Stealth attacks are all around us" (Mack & Summers, 1999, p. 89). Consultants must be sensitive to technology's impact on the organization in terms of outcome variables as well as personal relationships.

Some have indicated that information technology changes the locus of knowledge and in the "eyes of many managers, this equates to changing the locus of power" (Thach & Woodman, 1995, p. 71). Information is power, and when many people have access to it the balance of power may be significantly altered. Consultants, especially communication consultants, can help managers be sensitive to, and respond to, how the introduction of technology changes procedures and human relationships. There is no doubt that technology is here to stay as part of the fabric of organizational life. It has certainly changed the way in which training is conducted.

In the 2000 ASTD State of the Industry Report, benchmarking service participants (those participating in the study) were spending 8.5 percent on technology as a learning tool while the training investment leaders (those firms identified as "cutting-edge" firms by ASTD) were spending 18.3 percent on such training technology. The organization reporting the most extensive use of learning technologies was the mutual fund company Van Kampen Investments, which delivers 57 percent of its training through technology (McMurrer, Van Buren, & Woodwell, 2000, p. 47). The top learning technology used by Van Kampen Investments was computer-based training; it and multimedia were the two most popular presentation technologies among all the participants in the study.

On-Line Training

One example of a learning technology, which is growing rapidly, is on-line training. On-line training is making a significant impact on training and consulting. Trainers must keep up with the on-line conversation among participants in the training group, which can be a challenge. Some on-line trainers provide suggestions for dealing with multiple questions from students at the same time. For example, the trainer could state at the outset that he or she will stop to read participants' chat questions every five minutes or after each module. Make these Q & A periods part of your design. Indicate that while you take the next minute to read your questions, you would like the students to note in a separate e-file or on paper the most important point from the last session. Then discuss those points after you have finished reading the questions (Training Directors' Forum, 2000, p. 2). This keeps the trainer in control of the training session and the discussion. The use of on-line training will increase as long as it is an effective cost-saving measure that does not significantly reduce the quality of training.

Virtual Learning Communities

Creative virtual learning communities are being used to enhance on-site training. One such program, "Management University," includes a resource center, a management forum, and an executive perspective (Newman & Smith, 1999, p. 45). A selection of relevant prescreened books, searchable cases, topics, issues, and a message board for managers to post questions on difficult management situations and get answers from people who have resolved similar problems, are all parts of the virtual learning community. This provides ongoing interactive learning long after the training session or consulting intervention has taken place. According to Hite (1999),

A virtual organizational system is built on temporary associations of talent, capabilities, and purpose. It is virtual in the sense that a large percentage of the parts and pieces that constitute the whole system are defined solely by a particular point in time, a place in the environment, and the purpose of the system at those points. At its most extreme, such a system can be compared with a gas that is contained in the same shape as its environment—a spherical chamber means the gas conforms to a spherical shape—a box means the gas takes the shape of the inside of the box. (p. 36)

This new structure can provide follow-up support for training programs long after the face-to-face training. Virtual learning communities and virtual organizations give consultants and trainers the potential to create alternative communication and educational patterns.

Use of Email in Organizations

Email has become the fastest way to distribute information in an organizational setting. Consider one employee's experience with email:

Harry was senior partner at a Boston law firm. He was representing a bank in a complicated real estate deal with the developer of a commercial property. Many of the details of the agreement were being worked out via email between Harry and the developer's counsel. At a key juncture, when a technical point about interest rates came up, the developer's counsel emailed Harry: "Of course your client won't grasp this, because he won't understand what we're talking about." When Harry's client read this message, which was mixed in with other documents, he became furious and nearly canceled the deal. Trying to patch things up, Harry met with the developer's lawyer, who was stunned to hear how his message had been misconstrued. "I was trying to be ironic!" the lawyer gasped in horror. "Your client is an expert in the field. Saying he didn't know what we were talking about was just my way of being funny. I can't believe what a misunderstanding this is!" (Hallowell, 1999, p. 62)

This kind of misunderstanding has happened to others. One employee I worked with thought he was sending a personal message to a colleague wishing him success in fighting a battle in the corporation against the "that SOB controller" and accidentally used the wrong distribution list. This private message was sent to the entire organizational distribution list, including "the SOB controller" and the company's president. In that sense, email is almost too easy. We send messages without thinking carefully, just to get the message off our desk and on to someone else's computer screen. We allow more informality in email messages than would be acceptable in a written memo. Therefore, when you want the message to sound more formal, more definite, a written memo distributed to mailboxes may convey that subtle message in a way that an email message cannot.

The use of email is perceived negatively sometimes because of the choice of that medium for the message. One such event occurred late in 1999 with the replacement of the CEO of a major corporation. Employees found out through the following email:

To: All _____ Personnel
Subject: Moving Forward

This past Sunday evening, _____ (CEO of the company) informed members of the senior management _____ that he had decided to retire, effective immediately. He will be joining a company that will be identified in a coordinated press release later today. Attached at the bottom of this note is a copy of the news release we are sending to news media globally.

In the last two weeks, _____ was presented with what he believes to be an extraordinary opportunity to lead a new business venture into the eCommerce world. He believes that our established, dominant place in the market coupled with the very favorable position in the arbitration make this the right time and the right choice for him to retire.

Today we began the transition to new leadership at _____. The _____ Committee of the Board has asked me to be the interim Managing Partner and CEO. I am honored to be asked and pleased to serve.

We are grateful for _____'s 11 years at the helm of our fine organization and we recognize that a transition of leadership was inevitable. As you know, we are experiencing the most successful year in our history, with revenues expected to exceed $9 billion. That success is directly a result of the hard work of each and every one of you.

Personnel in this Fortune 500 company were surprised to receive the news by email. They expected that vice presidents and partners would tell managers, who would then communicate this information in a more personal way. Later, managers did make phone calls to provide more information about changes that were expected in the company. A message needs to be distributed throughout a large corporation very quickly before employees read about it in the newspaper. It is difficult to decide which method is the quickest, most accurate, and most appropriate. As a communication consultant, it is your job to help clients choose the best communication channel for their circumstances.

Email can be a very efficient way to communicate, but it may not be the most appropriate in all circumstances. Sometimes more personal contact is necessary. Voice mail can be perceived as extremely responsive to customers or as a way to keep customers at a distance from the organization.

Use of Voice Mail in Organizations

Voice mail can help your client, as well as create a negative impression. More and more corporations have turned to voice mail to cut the costs of operators. Although it may cut costs, it also "costs" organizations in terms of public relations.

One of my challenges as a consultant is to help clients use technologies appropriately. I have developed several guidelines for organizations who want to provide better service to customers through the use of a voice-activated response system (see box "Tips for Using Voice Mail" on page 138).

One role of the consultant to a client who wants to integrate new technologies is to help the client anticipate possible problems. The consultant should pose questions like the following:

1. Since more information will be available and greater access will be possible, who controls the information and access to it?
2. What measures will be taken to protect sensitive data and people's privacy?
3. Will the technologies be used just to increase speed of business practices and reduce staff, or will people be retained to use the data and improve processes?
4. What are the potential psychological effects of interacting through a machine all day?
5. Will organizations have to plan and hold social functions after and during work hours to enable their employees to see and touch real people? (adapted from Thach & Woodman, 1995).

The "Human Moment"

It is quite clear that organizations will continue to be affected dramatically by the many changes in technology. The consultant can serve as a reminder that the human toll must be constantly assessed. The result of this significant increase in technology is to refocus our attention on what one psychiatrist has called "the human moment" (Hallowell, 1999, p. 58). He described this moment as "an authentic psychological encounter that can happen only when two people share the same physical space. I have given the human moment a name because I believe that it has started to disappear from modern life—and I sense that we all may be about to discover the destructive power of its absence" (p. 59). Hallowell indicated his business is made up of business executives who feel lonely, isolated, or confused at work. In the last ten years technological changes have made many face-to-face interactions unnecessary. However, people need human contact "to maintain their mental acuity and their emotional well-being. I make this assertion having listened to and counseled thousands of patients whose jobs have been sapped of human moments" (p. 60). Hallowell went on to recognize the benefits of technology while urging that we balance it with personal interaction.

> Technology has created a magnificent new world, bursting with opportunity. It has opened up a global, knowledge-based economy and unchained people from their desks. We are all in its debt—and we're never going back. But we cannot move forward successfully without preserving the human moment. The price we pay for not doing that is too high, for individuals and organizations alike. The human moment provides the zest and color in the painting of our daily lives; it restores us, strengthens us, and makes us whole. Luckily, as long as we arrange our lives properly, the human moment should be easy enough to preserve. All we have to do is take heed—and make it happen. (Hallowell, 1999, p. 66)

The following editorial highlights many of the problems customers have with voice mail.

■ **"SO YOU WANT TO TALK ON THE PHONE WITH A REAL PERSON? SORRY, YOU CAN'T."**

"We're sorry, but all the lines are busy. Please hold for the next available operator. Thank you for your patience. Remember, your call is very important to us."

Seriously.

If you'd like to listen to a continuous loop of music by the Bee Gees, push 1 now. If you'd like to leave a message that will undoubtedly be ignored, push 2 now. If you are ready to implode in frustrated anger, push 3 now. Like its cousin, road rage, phone rage raises blood pressure and causes outbursts. And as companies increasingly rely on voice-mail systems to handle customer service, more and more people are seething in silence or slamming down the phone.

A study conducted for Prudential Insurance Co. of America found that 41 percent of Americans (43 percent of men and 38 percent of women) surveyed admitted to "growing angrier by the minute" when put on hold. According to that study, 53 percent of respondents say they often hang up and try again when put on hold, while 56 percent say they do something else while waiting. About 12 percent of people who answered the survey say they often forgot why they called the number in the first place.

For some reason, Midwesterners are more irritated by phone jail than others. About 45 percent of Northeasterners said they hang up while on hold, compared to 58 percent of Midwesterners.

Mary Flowers, vice president of public relations for Prudential, said the company did the survey to help educate consumers and corporate clients on the frustrations of tangled phone systems.

Although he's only 14, Mather Fisher has had his share of phone rage. Fisher was one of dozens of readers who responded to a *Minneapolis-St. Paul Star Tribune* request for phone horror stories. Fisher said his latest outburst was over an incident involving an unnamed software company.

"I was put through several extremely long menus," Fisher said. "Then, after an hour and a half, someone finally picked up and asked, 'Do you still want to hold?' I figured I'd stayed on for so long, I've gotta be close. Wrong."

Two hours later, a technician finally picked up, Fisher said. "What?" the technician demanded. Fisher started to explain his problem, and the tech cut him off: "Reinstall it!" he yelled before disconnecting Fisher. "This was my tale of grim horror," said Fisher. "I got a little upset." Fisher was actually more controlled than many. Other respondents confessed—usually anonymously—to slamming down the phone, yelling obscenities, throwing household objects, and leaving nasty messages on the offending voice machine.

Technical support for computer companies was a popular target of phone-rage sufferers. So were banks, all government offices, cable companies, and the medical industry, especially HMOs. But by far the worst offenders, callers said, were the phone companies. Cinda Baxter echoed many when she expressed frustration with the phone company US West, which she dubbed "the worst offender in the Theatre of the Ridiculous."

"They have a simple plan," wrote Baxter. "Make your 411 call as impersonal and inaccurate as possible by requiring you to continually repeat, repeat, repeat—eventually at yell level—the city, then state, then name of the party you are looking for. After hollering at this supposedly functional computer over and over, it eventually reroutes you to an actual digitized computer voice that gives you a phone number in Bloomington . . . Indiana, that is (rather than Minnesota). And these people work in communications?"

Audrey Murphy, of Minneapolis, agreed. After waiting for an hour recently to discuss long-distance rates, she was cut off. Murphy, who when talking to real people has a pleasant voice and good sense of humor, admits to fits of anger when faced with phone jail.

"I was so furious I slammed down the receiver and yelled 'Damn you!'" she said. "At least in a car you can honk at someone, but on the phone you can't do anything." To top it off, Murphy received a letter from AT&T a few days later apologizing for not getting back to her. Its advice: "They said I should call them," Murphy said. "Needless to say, that letter went into the circular file."

Chester Eggen of Edina, Minn., offered this: "I think the phone company should offer free phone repair or free phones for people who smash their phones because they are so mad that they can't get through."

"Call any state agency and try to find a real person," Mickelson added, "You can't do it, I guarantee you."

(Continued)

> At least one expert expects phone rage to get worse before it gets better. Rahn Rampton, a publicist for Blue Pumpkin Software, a Silicon Valley company that creates software designed to speed up phone systems, said there are 100,000 call centers worldwide. But that number will surge to 300,000 by 2001, meaning more diverted calls and more anger.
>
> Published in *The Athens Messenger*, Dec. 10, 1999; Scripps Howard News Service; writer: Jon Tevlin. Reprinted with permission.

Isn't it ironic that we must now remind ourselves that we still need human interaction? As a communication consultant one of my principle goals is to bring key participants together in face-to-face sessions where the "human moment" is extended to the "prolonged human conversation." I use technology to *enhance* rather than *replace* human dialogue.

Here are my personal recommendations when creating voice mail messages.

■ TIPS FOR USING VOICE MAIL

1. *Always give the option of waiting for a human operator.* "Select '0' if you wish to talk with a customer service representative." No one should be exited out of the system without the option to talk to a real person about problems and for information not included among the options.

2. *Do not make the menu longer than four or five choices.* Nothing is more frustrating than to listen to six or seven options, select one, and then have to listen to another set of four or five options. If you want customers to call back, don't make them dread having to spend their time listening to your options.

3. *Make sure the voice sounds as natural as possible.* There is no need to speak very slowly, especially when the caller will have to listen to a long list of options.

4. *Do not say, "Your call is very important to us."* The customer doesn't believe it. Just say, "We'll get back to you as soon as we can," and then do it! How many messages go unanswered at your organization?

5. *Do not leave a long message* describing how to leave a message. We all know how to leave messages. Besides, the automated voice repeats what you've just said, which is "Leave a message at the beep."

═══ LESSONS LEARNED ═══

Keep Ahead of New Technologies

Unless your specialty is technology, it is next to impossible to keep "ahead" of new technologies. You can, however, help your clients make good decisions about its use. The following are a few lessons I have learned concerning technology and consulting.

1. **Help your clients avoid becoming "techno groupies."**

    You must find out how your clients are using technology to communicate and determine if the technology they have chosen has enhanced or created barriers to human interaction. I have seen corporations and individuals become what I call "techno groupies," meaning they purchase the latest technological fad without considering if it will really benefit their system. Recently a client eliminated a paper catalogue it used to send to customers, saying all the customers used the Web page anyway, so why bother? When sales dipped conspicuously, they sought advice from some of their best customers. They discovered that while most of the customers were aware of the Web page they much preferred to grab a catalogue or brochure and turn pages instead of scrolling down computer screens. The technology was available, the customers knew how to use it, but they simply preferred using something else. So they turned to competitors whose catalogues were on their shelves.

2. **Don't let technology overshadow your message.**

    Consultants who use technologies to enhance their presentations to clients need to be careful that the technology does not overshadow the point of the presentation. Many clients now expect that Power-Point will accompany an oral presentation. However, when the PowerPoint slides tell the entire message, the audience may wonder what contribution the speaker is making to the presentation. I have seen PowerPoint presentations so overshadow the message that the audience was impressed with the graphics, but left without any clear message or point.

3. **Using email definitely makes life easier.**

    Technology has definitely made our lives easier when it is used appropriately. Email is great for keeping in touch with large numbers of people quickly. Recently Dick Brown, CEO of EDS, had a major internal problem with a security leak about an important deal with a client. In a matter of minutes he was able to send an email to all 70,000 employees of EDS cautioning them about these kinds of issues (Brown, 2000). Brown usually sends an email message to all EDS employees once a week. In a situation where there is absolutely no way this individual could personally contact even 1 percent of the employees on a weekly basis, 100 percent of employees hear directly from the CEO. And he invites responses; he gets about 200 messages a day to respond to!

4. Technology has widened the gap between those with access and those without, at the same time that it has decreased the influence of physical presence.

According to research reported in *Newsweek* ("New Wired World," 1999), it is estimated that there are almost 200 million people on the Internet. This means that only 3 percent of the 6 billion people in the world have Internet access. There is a huge gap between the haves and have nots. At the same time, the use of computers and communication technology, like virtual organizations, has diminished the impact of race, sex, and physical appearance and to some extent equalized participation in decision making. This dichotomy between bringing people closer to equality and increasing the gap between those who use technology and those who do not is mind boggling. The communication consultant can make a significant contribution to understanding the impact of technology on human interaction.

This chapter on technology will be out of date as soon as I write it. As consultants we must be aware of how technology helps us provide services to our clients and how it changes the nature of work in the organization. We must constantly ask the question, "Is this new technology helping human beings make better decisions, or is it getting in their way?"

Additional Resources

Grodin, D., & Lindlof, T. R. (Eds). (1996). *Constructing the self in a mediated world.* Thousand Oaks, CA: Sage.

Hallowell, E. M. (1999). The human moment. *Harvard Business Review, 77*(1), 58–66.

Ludlow, P. (Ed.) (1996). *High noon on the electronic frontier: Conceptual issues in cyberspace.* Cambridge, MA: MIT Press.

McMurrer, D. P., Van Buren, M. E., & Woodwell, W. H. (2000, Jan.). Making the commitment. *Training and Development Journal,* 41–48.

Thach, L., & Woodman, R. W. (1995). Organizational change and information technology: Managing on the edge of cyberspace. In W. W. Burke (Ed.), *Managing organizational change.* New York: American Management Association.

Chapter 8

DESIGNING CONSULTING INTERVENTIONS

■ **ORGANIZATIONAL DEVELOPMENT AND INTERVENTION**
■ **CATEGORIES OF INTERVENTION**
■ **DIAGNOSTIC INTERVENTIONS**
Communication Audit
Survey Feedback
Performance Consulting

■ **PROCESS INTERVENTIONS**
Process Observation
Confrontation Meetings
Negotiation
Executive Coaching

■ **PROBLEM-SOLVING INTERVENTIONS**
"Wants" and "Musts"
"Best," "Worst," "Most Likely"
"Is" and "Is Not"
Search Conference

■ **DECISION-MAKING INTERVENTIONS**
Force Field Analysis
Synectics
Nominal Group Technique
The Delphi Technique
Strategic Planning

■ **DESIGNING AND DIRECTING A CONSULTATION INTERVENTION**
Lessons Learned: Consulting Interventions Most Likely to Succeed
ADDITIONAL RESOURCES

142

The problem with most [consultants] is that they don't understand their jobs. They try to take the horse to water and make it drink it. Their job is to make the horse thirsty.

Author unknown

*C*onsulting interventions are not designed to *make* clients change their behavior. They are designed to encourage others to *examine* how they are functioning and *consider changes*. Intervening into an ongoing system suggests major changes that will have a ripple effect throughout the organization. For that reason, one should intervene very carefully and only after consideration of the possible impact of that intervention, negative as well as positive.

Lippitt and Lippitt (1986) suggested: "One should not intervene to influence a group unless the impact will be at least neutral, if not positive, for each individual in the group" (p. 47). Stepping into an organization and simply being there changes the way individuals interact with each other.

You cannot ask an "innocent" question. "How are things going?" suggests that people ought to stop and think about how this organization functions. As any teacher knows, when you ask for assessment, you are bound to get it! It is highly unlikely that you will ever receive a response like, "Everything is just great! I love it here!" Even if people feel very positive about their work setting, when asked to assess it they search until they find something to say about how it could be better. Therefore, when you ask the question, you must be prepared to do something with the answer. Intervening into an ongoing system implies change. To intervene and do nothing is to make life worse than it was.

> "Sue, we want you to talk to our staff about their low morale and then give us some recommendations," said the two chief operating officers of the organization.
>
> When I heard this request, my response was, "With the first interview I conduct, you will be raising expectations by the employees that something will change. Don't invite me in unless you are prepared to make some immediate changes that indicate you have heard what they have tried to tell you or I will just make the situation worse! Higher expectations with no results are much harder to live with than low expectations with no results."

That is how I begin most initial conversations with potential clients. People expect to see some results from their participation in a change effort and they expect those results to show up rather quickly. This does not necessarily mean a major shake-up in the organization, but may in fact mean some small step that can be taken immediately to demonstrate that employees have been heard.

Intervening is sometimes asking the most obvious questions and making statements that seem so simplistic they make you wonder why you are there. Yet, individuals caught up in the politics of the situation are unable to ask those questions themselves. Questions such as, "Why are you doing it that way?" and comments such as, "It doesn't seem to be working," and "That doesn't make sense to me; please explain it to me," can lead to productive analysis of an ongoing process.

Organizational Development and Intervention

Organizational development is a form of direct intervention into the human potential of the organization. Beckhand's (1967) definition of organizational development remains the most appropriate: "an effort which is planned, organization-wide and managed from the top to increase organization effectiveness and health through planned interventions in the organization's processes, using behavioral science knowledge" (p. 20).

French and Bell (1990) defined an organization development (OD) intervention as "sets of structured activities in which selected organizational units engage in a task or a sequence of tasks where the task goals are related directly or indirectly to organizational improvement. Interventions constitute the action thrust of organization development; they 'make things happen,' and are 'what's happening'" (p. 113).

They go on to suggest some general guidelines that I think are quite useful for designing interventions. The intervention activity should be structured so that the following situations occur:

- The relevant people are there. The relevant people are those most affected by the problem being resolved.
- It is oriented to the problems and opportunities generated by the clients themselves.
- The goal and the way to reach the goal are clear. Few things demotivate an individual as much as not knowing what he or she is working toward or how the activity contributes to goal attainment.
- Successful goal attainment is highly probable. Expectations of practitioners and clients should be realistic.
- It contains experience-based learning as well as conceptual/cognitive/ theoretical–based learning. Learning through experience can be made

a permanent part of the individual's repertoire when it is augmented with conceptual material that puts the experience into a broader framework of theory and behavior.

- The climate of the activity is such that individuals are "freed up" rather than anxious or defensive. Setting the climate of interventions means that people expect "to learn together" and "to look at practices in an experimenting way so that we can select better procedures."

- The participants learn how to solve a particular problem and "learn how to learn" at the same time.

- Individuals can learn about both task and process. The **task** is what the group is working on, that is, the stated agenda. The term **process** refers to **how** the group is working and what else is going on as the task is being worked on.

- Individuals are engaged as whole persons, not segmented persons. This means that role demands, thoughts, beliefs, and feelings, not just one or two of these, should be called into play (pp. 114–115).

Categories of Intervention

Blake and Mouton (1989) identified major interventions in terms of their underlying themes. These include

- *Discrepancy intervention,* which calls attention to a contradiction in action or attitude that leads to exploration;

- *Theory intervention,* which uses behavioral science knowledge and theory to explain present behavior and assumptions underlying the behavior;

- *Procedural intervention,* which represents a critiquing of how something is being done to determine whether the best methods are being used;

- *Relationship intervention,* which focuses attention on interpersonal relationships (particularly those where there are strong negative feelings) and brings the issues to the surface for exploration and possible resolution;

- *Experimentation intervention,* in which two action plans are tested for their consequences before a final decision on one is made;

- *Dilemma intervention,* in which an imposed or emergent dilemma is used to force close examination of the possible choices involved and the assumptions underlying them;

- *Perspective intervention,* which draws attention away from immediate actions and demands and allows a look at historical background, context, and future objectives in order to assess whether the actions are "still on target";

- *Organization structure intervention,* which calls for examination and evaluation of structural causes for organizational ineffectiveness;

- *Cultural intervention,* which examines traditions, precedents, and practices—the fabric of the organization's culture—in a direct, focused approach.

There are many schemes for classification of interventions. Some experts divide them into diagnostic activities, team and individual activities, education and training, coaching and counseling, career counseling, and structural activities. French and Bell (1990) categorized interventions according to their focus on the individual or the group and on task versus process issues. Table 8.1 shows their categories. I have categorized interventions, according to the procedures used to carry out the intervention, into the following six areas:

1. *Diagnostic interventions:* communication audits, survey feedback
2. *Team-building interventions:* interpersonal interactions
3. *Process interventions:* process observation, confrontation meetings, negotiation
4. *Planning interventions:* strategic planning
5. *Problem-solving interventions:* defining problems, force field analysis, synectics
6. *Decision-making interventions:* nominal group technique, Delphi

TABLE 8.1

FRENCH AND BELL'S TYPOLOGY OF OD INTERVENTIONS BASED ON TARGET GROUPS

Target Group	*Types of Intervention*
Interventions designed to improve the effectiveness of INDIVIDUALS	Life- and career-planning activities Role analysis technique Coaching and counseling T-group (sensitivity training) Education and training to increase skills, knowledge in the areas of technical task needs, relationship skills, process skills, decision making, problem solving, planning, goal-setting skills Grid OD phase 1 Some forms of job enrichment Gestalt OD Transactional analysis Behavior modeling

TABLE 8.1

FRENCH AND BELL'S TYPOLOGY OF OD INTERVENTIONS BASED ON TARGET GROUPS *(Continued)*

Target Group	*Types of Intervention*
Interventions designed to improve the effectiveness of DYADS/TRIADS	Process consultation Third-party peacemaking Role negotiation technique Gestalt OD Transactional analysis
Interventions designed to improve the effectiveness of TEAMS & GROUPS	Team building—Task directed —Process directed Grid OD phase 2 Family T-group Responsibility charting Process consultation Role analysis technique "Start-up" team-building activities Education in decision making, problem solving, planning, goal setting in group settings Some forms of job enrichment and MBO Sociotechnical systems and Quality of Work/Life programs Quality circles Force field analysis
Interventions designed to improve the effectiveness of INTERGROUP RELATIONS	Intergroup activities—Process directed —Task directed Organizational mirroring (three or more groups) Structural interventions Process consultation Third-party peacemaking at group level Grid OD phase 3 Survey feedback
Interventions designed to improve the effectiveness of the TOTAL ORGANIZATION	Technostructural activities such as collateral organizations, sociotechnical systems, and organizational restructuring Confrontation meetings Strategic planning/strategic management activities Grid OD phases 4, 5, 6 Survey feedback Interventions based on Lawrence and Lorsch's contingency theory Interventions based on Likert's Systems 1–4 Physical settings

Source: From W. L. French & C. H. Bell, *Organizational Development: Behavioral Science Interventions for Organization Improvement,* Englewood Cliffs, NJ: Prentice-Hall, Inc., 1978, p. 122. Reprinted by permission. Not all of the interventions listed above are discussed in this book. The reader is directed to the original source for further elaboration.

The rest of this chapter provides examples of specific interventions in the diagnostic, process, problem-solving, and decision-making categories. Chapter 12 details team building and includes a variety of interventions to use with groups. Team building is such a pervasive intervention today that it needs an entire chapter devoted to its explanation along with examples and techniques. Strategic planning is another major intervention that I use frequently. For that reason I have devoted an entire chapter to the change process, resistance to change, and planning for change. Chapter 15 details strategic planning models and techniques.

Diagnostic Interventions

In Chapter 4, I discussed the development of questionnaires and the criteria by which to measure their validity. Any diagnostic intervention should also meet these criteria. The first diagnostic intervention combines survey research with feedback sessions and major organizational recommendations that make it a comprehensive intervention.

Communication Audit

A communication audit is one diagnostic intervention that has been used by the communication discipline for some time. The International Communication Association (ICA) Communication Audit is the most well known and still widely used package of diagnostic intervention tools.

> For many of us, the word audit elicits fear or irritation because of its association with the Internal Revenue Service. Basically, however, an audit is merely a process of exploring, examining, monitoring, or evaluating something. Accountants audit our financial records, physicians audit our health, professors audit our learning progress, and managers review, or audit, our level of performance . . . . A communication audit differs from other audits only in that it focuses primarily on communication, and, therefore, there are certain methodologies that may be applicable to it. (Downs, 1988, p. 3)

The International Communication Association is a professional organization dedicated to the study of communication processes in a variety of contexts. The Organizational Communication Division of ICA devoted more than five years to the development of the Communication Audit. The Communication Audit is actually a package of instruments used in the assessment of employees' perceptions of the communication process in their organization. The ICA Communication Audit has been used extensively in research and consulting in the years since its development. The advantages of the ICA Communication Audit are well documented: overcoming the use of single instruments, limited situationalism, small nonrepresentative samples, lack of standardization and norms, and limited measurement of actual behaviors—to name a few of the claims made by the audit's developers (Dennis, Goldhaber, & Yates, 1978; Falcione, Goldhaber, Porter, & Rogers, 1979; Goldhaber, Yates, Porter, & Lesniak, 1978) (see note 1, p. 156).

In an extensive study of the audit use (DeWine, James, & Walence, 1983), data suggest several conclusions about the ICA Communication Audit. First, the audit does appear to have the ability to identify or highlight communication problems and potential solutions in an organization. Aside from an awareness of obvious problems the audit appeared, for a majority of the people who used it, to provide viable alternatives, confirm the directions or courses management had charted, initiate creative thinking, or, in some instances, inspire administrators not to change the environment at all. Second, the data demonstrate that managers maintain their own form of organizational reality. The administrators select and accept issue analysis and recommendations from an audit according to their own perceptions of organizational reality and what is most appropriate for their organizations, regardless of the nature of the recommendations. The recommendations may function as a force to propel communication behaviors to a higher level of consciousness for the purposes of observation, assessment, and modification.

Sections of the audit cover the following areas:

Amount of information activity received about topics

Amount of information desired about these topics

Amount of information actually sent about topics

Amount of information desired to be sent about these topics

Amount of follow-up by people now

Amount of follow-up needed

Amount of information received from sources

Amount of information desired from these sources

Timeliness of information received from key sources

Organizational communication relationships

Satisfaction with organizational outcomes

Amount of information received from channels now

Amount of information desired from channels now

The questionnaire, in a revised format (DeWine & James, 1988), is included in its entirety (Form 8:1). The authors used a national and regional data bank to develop this revised form (see note 2, p. 157). In addition to this questionnaire, a communication diary, communication network analysis, and a critical-incidents form as well as interview schedules complete the "package" of diagnostic tools (Downs, 1988; Goldhaber & Rogers, 1979).

SURVEY OF ORGANIZATIONAL COMMUNICATION
(taken from DeWine & James, 1988)

Instructions

As you complete this survey, think of communication patterns as they currently exist in your organization. Do not consider how things have been in the past or how you hope they will be in the future, but how people communicate today. Try to think of interactions you have had with various people in your organization during the last 1 or 2 weeks and use these incidents as examples.

PLEASE MARK ONLY ONE RESPONSE TO EACH QUESTION.

You may find the following definitions useful as you answer the questions on this survey:

[Some of the terms it often helps to define include *communication, information, company policies, grapevine, middle management.*]

Receiving Information from Others

Below are types of information you may receive from various sources within your organization. Give each topic two scores. First, score each for how much of that information you get, if "3" is the average amount an employee gets. Then score each for how much you need to carry out your work activities in the best way you can.

Use the following scale:

1 = very little   2 = little   3 = some   4 = great   5 = very great

Topic	How Much I Receive	How Much I Need
How well I am doing my job		
My job duties		
Organizational policies		
Pay and benefits		
How technological changes affect my job		
Mistakes and failures of my organization		
Promotion and advancement opportunities in my organization		
Important new program, product, or service developments in my organization		
Specific problems faced by management		

(Continued)

SURVEY OF ORGANIZATIONAL COMMUNICATION *(Continued)*

Sending Information to Others

Below are types of information you may send to various individuals within your organization. Give each topic two scores. First, score each for how much of that information you send, if "3" is the average amount an employee gets. Then score each for how much you need to send to carry out your work activities in the best way you can.

Use the following scale:

    1 = very little   2 = little   3 = some   4 = great   5 = very great

Topic	How Much I Send	How Much I Need
Reporting what I am doing in my job		
Reporting what I think my job requires me to do		
Reporting job-related problems		
Complaining about my job and/or work conditions		
Requesting information necessary to do my job		
Evaluating [grading] the performance of my immediate supervisor		
Asking for clearer work instructions		

Follow-Up on Information Sent

Below are employees to whom you might send information within your organization. Give each topic two scores. First, score each for how much follow-up you get, if "3" is the average amount an employee gets. Then score for how much follow-up you need to send to carry out your work activities in the best way you can.

Use the following scale:

    1 = very little   2 = little   3 = some   4 = great   5 = very great

Topic	How Much I Receive	How Much I Need
Subordinates		
Co-workers		
Immediate supervisor		
Middle management		
Top management		

(Continued)

SURVEY OF ORGANIZATIONAL COMMUNICATION *(Continued)*

Interpersonal Communication Relationships

Below are different communication relationships you may have established within your organization. Give each topic one score that indicates the nature of the communication relationship in question, if "3" is the average amount for an employee. Use the following scale:

1 = very little   2 = little   3 = some   4 = great   5 = very great

Topic	
I trust my co-workers	
My co-workers get along with each other	
My relationship with my co-workers is satisfying	
My immediate supervisor is honest with me	
My immediate supervisor listens to me	
My relationship with my immediate supervisor is satisfying	
I trust top management	
Top management is sincere in its efforts to communicate with employees	
My relationship with top management is satisfying	

Organizational Outcomes

Below are topics concerning your satisfaction with working in the organization. Give each topic one score that indicates the degree to which you are satisfied with that topic, if "3" is the average amount of satisfaction for an employee. Use the following scale:

1 = very little   2 = little   3 = some   4 = great   5 = very great

Topic	
My job	
My pay	
My progress in the organization to this point in time	
My chances for getting ahead in the organization	
My opportunity to "make a difference"—to contribute to the organization's overall success	
My organization's system for recognizing and rewarding outstanding performance	
My organization's overall communicative effort	
My organization as compared to other such organizations	
My organization's overall efficiency of operation	
The overall quality of my organization's product or service	
My organization's achievement of its goals and objectives	

152

(Continued)

SURVEY OF ORGANIZATIONAL COMMUNICATION *(Continued)*

Channels of Information

Below are listed a number of channels from which you receive information about various aspects of your organization. Give each topic three sets of scores. Each set of scores should indicate the degree to which the information you receive from that source is *useful, accurate,* and *timely.* Remember that "3" is "some," "1" is "very little," and "5" is "very great."

Channels	Job-Related Information			Personal Issues			Organizational Information		
	Usefulness	*Accuracy*	*Timeliness*	*Usefulness*	*Accuracy*	*Timeliness*	*Usefulness*	*Accuracy*	*Timeliness*
Telephone									
The "grapevine"									
Written memos, letters									
Bulletin boards									
Internal publications (newsletters, etc.)									
Computers									
Magazines									
Newspapers									
Teleconferences									
Radio									
Television									
Speeches									
Films, videotapes									

SURVEY OF ORGANIZATIONAL COMMUNICATION *(Continued)*

Sources of Information

Below are listed a number of sources from which you receive information about various aspects of your organization. Give each topic three sets of scores. Each set of scores should indicate the degree to which the information you receive from that source is *useful, accurate,* and *timely.* Remember that "3" is "some," "1" is "very little," and "5" is "very great."

Channels	Job-Related Information			Personal Issues			Organizational Information		
	Usefulness	Accuracy	Timeliness	Usefulness	Accuracy	Timeliness	Usefulness	Accuracy	Timeliness
Face-to-face contact* between two people									
Face-to-face contact among more than two people									
Co-workers in my own department									
Individuals in other departments									
Immediate supervisor									
Department meetings									
Middle management									
Formal management presentations									
Top management									

*EXAMPLE: If you were reading the first question it would go like this: "How useful is job-related information you receive face-to-face with another person?"

SURVEY OF ORGANIZATIONAL COMMUNICATION *(Continued)*

Communicative Experience Form

As you have been recording your responses to the items in this survey, the questions may have brought to mind a recent work-related experience of yours in which communication was particularly effective or ineffective. Please respond to the questions below and give us a clear summary of that experience.

    A. To whom does this experience primarily relate? (Circle one)

        1. subordinate   2. co-worker   3. immediate supervisor

        4. middle management   5. top management

    B. Please circle the quality of communication you will be describing in the experience below (circle one):

        1. effective   2. ineffective

Describe the communicative experience, the circumstances leading up to it, what the person did that made him/her an effective or ineffective communicator, and the results (outcome) of what the person did. Please write legibly. THANK YOU.

Quality of Information

The following questions are provided so that you can be more specific in the responses you make. The questions are not the same as you have already answered and your responses should be a statement or statements rather than a number like "3."

1. When decisions are made in the organization that will affect your job, how do you find out about them? Who tells you? When are you told? How much information about the decision do you receive?

    _____

    _____

    _____

(Continued)

SURVEY OF ORGANIZATIONAL COMMUNICATION *(Continued)*

2. When changes are to be made in the organization (not related specifically to your job), how do you find out about them? When do you usually know about the changes? From whom?

_____

_____

_____

3. What types of information do you receive to let you know how your job relates to the goals of the total organization? How often do you get the information, if at all? From whom?

_____

_____

_____

Notes

1. The 13 subscales from the original ICA Communication Audit Survey (Goldhaber & Rogers, 1979):
Receiving Information from Others—Current
Receiving Information from Others—Needed

Sending Information to Others—Current
Sending Information to Others—Needed

Follow-up on Information Sent—Current
Follow-up on Information Sent—Needed

Sources of Information—Current
Sources of Information—Needed

Channels of Communication—Current
Channels of Communication—Needed

Timeliness of Information Received from Key Sources

Organizational Communication Relationships

Organizational Outcomes

(Continued)

SURVEY OF ORGANIZATIONAL COMMUNICATION *(Continued)*

2. An overall factor analysis combining the National Data Bank and the Regional Data Bank is available. It includes 30 organizations and over 5,000 respondents. The Regional Data Bank now includes data from over 30 organizations and over 6,000 subjects. Inquiries about the use of the Regional Data Bank should be directed to Dr. Anita James at Ohio University.

Survey Feedback

Survey feedback is one of the oldest and most frequently used diagnostic interventions. The consultant or manager systematically collects data about the organization and its members and then presents the data in a feedback session. Groups at all levels of the organization are involved in the data collection, analysis, and feedback. This is different from a research project, in which the data may be isolated from the day-to-day workings of the organization. From the moment you begin collecting the data, you are in fact changing the organization since organizational members are assisting with the collection process. French and Bell (1990) presented a comparison between the characteristics of survey feedback and the traditional use of attitude surveys in Table 8.2. The major difference is the involvement of organizational members in the survey feedback throughout the process versus only top management involvement in the traditional attitude surveys.

TABLE 8.2

TWO APPROACHES TO THE USE OF ATTITUDE SURVEYS

	Traditional Approach	*Survey Feedback or OD Approach*
Data collected from:	Rank and file, and maybe supervisors	Everyone in the system or subsystem
Data reported to:	Top management, department heads, and perhaps to employees through newspaper	Everyone who participated
Implications of data are worked on by:	Top management (maybe)	Everyone on work teams, with workshops starting at the top (all superiors with their subordinates)
Third-party intervention strategy:	Design and administration of questionnaire, development of a report	Obtaining concurrence on total strategy, design and administration of questionnaire, design of workshops, appropriate interventions in workshops
Action planning done by:	Top management only	Teams at all levels
Probable extent of change and improvement:	Low	High

Source: From W. L. French & C. H. Bell, *Organization Development: Behavioral Science Interventions for Organization Improvement,* Englewood Cliffs, NJ: Prentice-Hall, Inc., 1978, p. 122. Reprinted with permission.

Performance Consulting

Experts in the Human Resource field are promoting performance consulting because they believe that training programs must go beyond the classroom and determine the impact of training on employees' job performance. "For too long the HRD or training profession has focused on the activity of training . . . we must shift from focusing on what people need to learn (training) to what they must do (performance)" (Robinson & Robinson, 1995, p. 7).

Performance consulting may include training programs, but it also includes performance models (performance needed to achieve business goals) and guidance in addressing obstacles to work. Only when performance has changed in the desired direction has the performance consultant's role been completed.

Process Interventions

Process interventions make take one of four forms: process observation, confrontation meetings, negotiations, or executive coaching.

Process Observation

When the focus is on the process the group uses to carry out their tasks, then the intervention is most likely to be process observation (PO). PO is one of the cornerstones of communicative consulting. An individual who is able to objectively observe the group process, accurately and fairly report it back, and help the group cope with the things they discover about themselves, is truly a talented individual.

The following discussion comes as close as possible to describing how to carry this out; however, the best way to learn how to do it is to observe a master facilitator. I have spent hundreds of hours watching others manage groups effectively and ineffectively. I learned just as many helpful hints from those who did it poorly as I did from those who did it quite well. I often am negotiating a contract that includes the participation of an observer or person in training so that others may have carefully protected experiences while they are learning how to perform this extremely delicate intervention.

Process observation is the ability to watch group interaction, at both the verbal and nonverbal levels, in order to make accurate inferences about the health of the group's communication. In addition, observations must be presented to the group in a nonthreatening way. The goal is to help the group build a positive climate in which to form a cohesive team.

The key is to observe actual behavior (either the person's exact wording or nonverbal cues) and record it accurately. The second step is to reflect on what one is observing. Avoid classifying the behaviors as either "good" or "bad." The question to ask is, "What is this person doing that will help or hinder the group process? What could he or she do differently to enhance the efforts of the group?"

When the process observer is presenting feedback, the self-esteem of individual members should be enhanced. This may mean giving some feedback outside the group setting to a person who has some behaviors to correct. Also, focus should be on the group problem, not on individual people. The person's behavior is a problem, not the person. The group is there to solve a problem, not to evaluate people. Chapter 13 provides more details on the skills of providing feedback.

Greiner and Metzger (1983) discussed the difference between process consultants and content consultants. "Process consultants are the psychologists of the consulting trade whereas content consultants are the specialist surgeons. The process consultant offers no specific answers but rather asks lots of questions" (p. 20). On the other hand, the content consultant "takes direct action to verify the causes of a problem and then writes a report to support a set of specific recommendations. Content consultants believe they are better able to see the 'forest' for the 'trees' because they are independent and objective outsiders" (p. 21). In reality, either extreme is likely to be less effective than a combined approach. As Greiner and Metzger put it, "Most clients are not interested in hiring a psychiatrist to 'shrink' them, nor are they receptive to a professional lecture" (p. 22). Thus, process consulting must be part of a major intervention process.

Gabarro and Harlan (1976) defined process intervention and divided it into three distinct classes. The first is **conceptual inputs,** whose objective is to provide members of the client group with an organizing principle. This principle can help them see the distinctions between typical and optimal behavior.

Second is **coaching,** which Gabarro and Harlan defined as the process of assisting members of a client group to practice new behaviors with which they want to become proficient. Coaching interventions are most effectively made during the early, standard-setting phases of the consulting process—when they can shape the kinds and sequence of interpersonal communication early. Here the consultant would work closely with individuals to help them understand the consequences of their behaviors to the group and for themselves.

Finally, process observation can be used to heighten the client group members' awareness of the significance of the distinction between **content** and **process dimensions** of transactions in a group. It may increase the group's awareness of the implications and consequences of members' actions and provide a model of behavior that demonstrates how one can facilitate a group's movement in the direction of its objectives.

Metzger (1989) concluded:

> Nowadays as we have seen, the traditional content-based consulting approach is no longer readily accepted by many clients. Given the sophistication of most management teams today, it is unrealistic to think that con-

sultants should personally take charge and direct the solution for the client, while educating the client's managers on how this or that problem should be resolved. Such consulting approaches correspond to the old paradigm of mechanistic management. (p. 49)

Thus, the best approach may be to focus on the human process that group is using to carry out organizational tasks.

Schein's (1987, 1988) two volumes on process consultation provide one of the best sources on actual techniques used in process interventions. He explained the concept of process as "how things are done rather than what is done. If I am crossing the street, that is what I am doing, but the process is *how* [italics added] I am crossing: walking, running, dodging cars, asking someone to help me across because I feel dizzy, or some other way" (p. 39).

Schein (1988) clearly defines the kinds of interventions that a process consultant would be most likely to use starting with agenda setting, managing interventions, questions that direct attention to process issues, meetings devoted to process issues, and conceptual inputs on process-related topics. Actual solutions to management problems are not even listed because they would not be considered valid interventions in a process consultation model. A consultant who permitted himself or herself to become interested in a particular management problem in sales, marketing, or production would be switching roles from that of process consultant to that of expert resource. Becoming an expert resource can make a consultant lose effectiveness as a process consultant.

Schein goes on to say: "The process model starts with the assumption that the organization knows how to solve its particular problems or knows how to get help in solving them, but that it often does not know how to use its own resources effectively either in initial problem formation or in implementation of solutions" (p. 29).

The process model further assumes that inadequate use of internal resources or ineffective implementation results from process problems. People fail to communicate effectively or develop mistrust, engage in destructive competition, punish people they mean to reward and vice versa, fail to give feedback, and so on. "The job of the process consultant is to help the organization to solve its own problems by making it aware of the organizational processes, the consequences of those processes, and the mechanisms by which they can be changed" (Schein, 1988, p. 193).

Confrontation Meetings

A process consultant is needed to run a **confrontation meeting** between two groups or two individuals. It should be done in a "laboratory-type" setting where two conflicting groups come together and work through their tensions and frictions that have built up over an extended period of time. Since this can be quite intense, the consultant needs to have highly developed skills in counseling techniques and group process.

The first step is to set the climate for an open exchange of opinions, which may indeed differ. A series of activities helps to establish this climate.

Second, each group meets separately to identify how they perceive the other group and how they think the other group perceives them. Then the two groups are brought together and their perceptions are shared.

In one instance I was asked by the head of the unit to work with a group of mid-level female managers who "seem to think they are being mistreated although I can't for the life of me understand why. We have given two of them recent promotions and salary increases but it doesn't seem to satisfy them." I met with the women, then met with the top management team (all of whom happened to be male), and then had the two groups come together for a confrontation meeting. I asked the females to meet in one room and list all their perceptions of the males, and the males to do the same about the females. Then I also asked them to identify what they predicted would be the other group's perception of them.

When these four lists were compared, we discovered that the women thought the men would perceive them as not as serious about their work while the men did indeed see them as serious about their work, as evidenced by the belief that higher salaries would correct the problem. We also discovered that the men thought the women would perceive them as mistreating them when the women actually saw the men as unaware of how their actions were slowing down the progress of the group. Higher pay for two women was not solving the problem of lack of respect for all of them.

During the confrontation meeting I acted as the facilitator, reading the lists while they were developed and asking questions for clarity. It was an eye-opening experience because both sides learned their perceptions of how the other group viewed them were often wrong. Only after the two groups confronted their own misperceptions could we begin to work on pulling this team together again. As a result of these meetings, promotions took place and changes in personnel policy were developed. I can't say that internal attitudes changed because I don't believe any external force can cause attitudes to change; however, work behavior patterns did change, for the better.

The facilitator must be aware that feelings may be more intense during this session than in previous sessions. Second, if no action is taken as a result of the confrontation meeting, morale will be even lower.

Negotiation

Often, the consultant or communication manager ends up being the mediator or negotiator in interpersonal relationships, group conflict, and decision making. The communication consultant needs the same characteristics that are required for legal mediators who are trying to reach a settlement between disputing parties. Keltner (1987) identified ten skills needed by the mediator:

> *Credibility* and integrity of the mediator is the most basic tool of the mediator. The mediator must be accepted as a person who can be trusted, who thoroughly knows the process involved, and who relates well to the parties.
>
> *Empathy* means the mediator must establish rapport with the clients by trying to see the situation from each perspective. It is important that the mediator not have a predetermined outcome for the situation in mind.
>
> *Listening* is a basic skill. The mediator must listen not only for feelings but for content and to evaluate as well. This means the mediator must be able to read nonverbal cues as well as verbal cues.
>
> *Feedback* is a skill discussed in Chapter 13. The ability to provide information to clients without increasing their defensiveness is critical. Using feedback to see if you have received an accurate understanding of the individual's message is important to the establishment of positive relationships.
>
> *Interrogation* is the use of questions as an important part of the data-gathering process. It is also a part of the persuasion that goes on during a mediation process when the question itself may suggest a course of action.
>
> *Timing* for the mediator means knowing when to move forward, when to allow the other person to go on with his or her analysis, and when to make an analysis. The mediator needs a sense of when it is time to push the parties to resolution. If they are "pushed" too soon, the mediation will be unsuccessful.
>
> *Speaking skills* or the ability to converse informally with the parties in a clear, friendly, and useful fashion is important. The mediator must hold the attention of the clients.
>
> *Message carrying,* or taking ideas from one party to another, requires careful work. Some messages must be transferred as precisely as possible and others must be attenuated or modified in order not to upset delicate relationships being established.
>
> *Nonverbal communication* is an ever present part of the negotiation process. The observation of facial expressions, use of space, eye contact or lack of it, personal appearance, and other forms of nonverbal cues are very useful to the mediator in order to determine the attitudes of the parties.
>
> *Persuasion* is sometimes the final skill needed as the mediator tries to get resolution on the part of two disputing parties. If the parties are

going to reach a settlement, they must change the rigid positions they start out with.

Keltner identified seven stages in the mediation process:

1. *setting the stage* (establishing rapport and credibility);
2. *opening and development* (identifying ground rules and building trust);
3. *exploration of the issues:* isolation of basics (when the relative importance of issues is decided and clients state opening positions);
4. *identification of alternatives* (identification of other options);
5. *evaluation, negotiation, and bargaining* (matching needs with criteria previously established);
6. *decision making and testing* (when parties begin to make commitments);
7. *terminating the process* (mediator reviews the decisions made).

These steps become quite helpful when the session begins with little agreement or movement on either side.

Executive Coaching

Executive coaching is a combination of counseling and consulting. It is usually done one-to-one to provide support for executives in decision making and other problem-solving activities. It is a personal service for executives who want to achieve specific career goals. It is a highly confidential one-to-one relationship between an executive and a coach. Through face-to-face meetings, phone calls, and observation sessions, the coach helps the executive notice and change thought and behavior patterns that are preventing him or her from performing his or her best at work (O'Brien, 1997, p. 6).

One approach is the 360-approach or 360-assessment. Everyone who was important from the executive's past and present is interviewed in depth and then "hundreds of pages of data are fed back to the client during a three-day off-site session that usually includes the spouse" (Snyder, 1995, p. 31). This information can be very sensitive and is clearly not for everyone. A consultant should never enter into executive coaching without extensive training and knowledge of the counseling process.

Richards (2000) identified four guidelines for coaching executives and managers:

1. *Speaking from the heart* means finding statements that resonate with your core values and also forward some action or event in the organization's change process. Coaches should listen for these messages

as the executive speaks and help him or her identify statements that express something he or she feels passionately about.

2. *Framing an authentic role* refers to uncovering some existing part of ourselves rather than learning new behavior, for example, the child in each of us could be the role of grandparent as it might be applied to other settings. Too often we behave in stereotypical ways that do not serve us, or those around us, well. "Executives and managers are particularly prone to these mistakes because we have so many preconceived notions about how they are supposed to be" (p. 103).

3. *Making good use of your life* means remembering your life goals and the reasons you are doing what you are doing that extend beyond your self-interest.

4. *Aligning behavior with intention* can sometimes result in holding on to comfortable behaviors even when those behaviors do not advance our new intentions. "When our behavior does not align with our intentions and we have gone public with our intentions, we sow confusion at best, and mistrust at worst." (pp. 101–106)

Form 8.2 is one example of an interview guide that might be used by an executive coach.

SAMPLE INTERVIEW GUIDE: PURPOSES OF THE INTERVIEW

As a result of information obtained in this interview, you will be able to answer the following questions:

1. What are the major business needs facing this individual now and in the next two to three years?
2. What implications do these business needs have for the performance requirements of key positions within this individual's unit or area of responsibility?
3. What forces and factors, both within and outside the control of the individual, will challenge the accomplishment of business and performance goals?

As a result of this discussion, you and the individual will be able to determine what, if any, assistance you can provide to support the individual in meeting her or his business, performance, and work environment needs.

Prior to the Interview

Make an appointment with the individual. Indicate the following:

1. You want to learn more about the business goals and challenges of various individuals within the organization.
2. You are setting up an appointment with this individual for the purpose of discussing his or her business goals and challenges.
3. The interview will require approximately one hour.

Introductory Comments

Include the following items in the introductory comments:

1. The reason and purposes for the interview
2. How long the interview will take
3. How you will be using the information

> *Rationale:* It is important for the individual to understand why you are initiating this conversation. A key message to communicate is that you want to ensure that the work you do is directly linked to the business goals and needs of the organization; the individual can provide important information about those business goals. Additionally, indicate that this individual is a (prospective) client for your services and you want to ensure that you are meeting her or his needs.

(Continued)

SAMPLE INTERVIEW GUIDE: PURPOSES OF THE INTERVIEW
(Continued)

Questions Regarding Current Business Goals

Include the following questions:

1. What are the business goals for (select one) your group, unit, or department in the next year?
2. What measurements will you use to determine if the goals are achieved?
3. What are the forces *outside your control* that will make accomplishment of these goals difficult or challenging? (*Note:* You may want to provide an example such as changes in the economy or governmental regulations.)
4. What forces *outside your control* will help in accomplishing these goals?
5. What are the forces *within your control* that will make accomplishment of these goals more difficult? (*Note:* You may want to provide examples such as obsolete manufacturing equipment or a reward system that does not encourage people to focus on the business goal that was identified.)
6. What forces *within your control* will help in accomplishing these goals?

> *Rationale:* The most relevant business goals are those that must be achieved and supported right now; therefore, the interview begins by discussing the most current business needs. Remember, these are the operational goals for the unit, department, or group. It is important to know what should be occurring operationally and how it will be measured. You also want to identify forces or factors that may challenge the accomplishment of these goals.
>
> Frequently, we are asked why it is important for a performance consultant to know what forces exist outside the organization. After all, no one can do anything to change them. Perhaps the following example will illustrate why this type of information is vital.
>
> Prior to 1984, AT&T was the only long-distance telephone service available in the United States. If people needed this type of service, they telephoned AT&T to request it. The AT&T employee who answered the phone needed skills in taking orders to ensure that all information was recorded accurately.
>
> In 1984, AT&T was divested under orders of the U.S. government. This was certainly an external force that AT&T could not control. However, with divestiture came many competitors—MCI and Sprint, just to name two. Now choices were available to people in the United

(Continued)

SAMPLE INTERVIEW GUIDE: PURPOSES OF THE INTERVIEW
(Continued)

States who wanted long-distance telephone service. If the AT&T employee who answered the telephone still performed as an order taker instead of a salesperson, it is unlikely that AT&T could have achieved its business plan. The employee had to demonstrate the skills of asking questions, overcoming objections, and providing benefits.

The point of this example is that forces external to the organization have implications for the performance requirements of people in the organization. To fulfill our responsibilities as performance consultants, we must have knowledge of those forces and work with our clients to identify the implications for employees within the business.

(Richards, 2000)

Problem-Solving Interventions

The most difficult step in problem-solving interventions is defining the problem. The difficulty arises in part because of a confusion between symptoms and the problem. Using the following three techniques can help identify problems.

"Wants" and "Musts"

Ask the group to generate a list of problems or issues related to one problem. Use normal brainstorming techniques of not allowing any evaluation while the original list is being generated. After the list is developed, explain to the group that not all the items they have raised may be able to be addressed in this session. In fact, it is my experience that a group is usually not able to address every item that has been raised. It turns out that the group is ready to live with some issues if the most *critical* issue can be addressed. Next, go over each item on the list and ask the group the following question: "Is this an item that *must* be addressed in order to solve this problem or is this an item we *want* to address if possible but it is not as critical?" "Musts" are discussed immediately and "wants" are left for a later meeting or time.

"Best," "Worst," "Most Likely"

Often, when groups are trying to solve a problem, they are prevented from moving forward because of unrealistic fears of the things that might happen as a result of implementing a solution. Have the group identify the "worst" thing that could happen if this solution is implemented, the "best," and the "most likely" outcome. Once the group has listed the worst possible outcome, and you then address what is more likely to happen, the group often is able to handle the "worst" and understands what is more probable.

"Is" and "Is Not"

When defining the problem, it is sometimes useful to identify what it is not, or what it will not involve. For example, when a group was talking about low morale, they were talking about people being discouraged from trying new programs and policies. They were *not* talking about people treating each other fairly or unfairly, they were *not* talking about low trust, they were talking specifically about innovations and the system's inability to respond quickly to new ideas.

Watzlawick, Weakland, and Fisch (1974) suggested the notion of reframing a problem in order to solve it. They explained, "To reframe, then, means to change the conceptual and/or emotional setting or viewpoint in relation to which a situation is experienced and to place it in another frame which fits 'facts' of the same concrete situation equally well or even better, and thereby changes its entire meaning" (p. 95). They proposed a four-step approach to solving problems:

1. a clear definition of the problem in concrete terms
2. an investigation of the solutions attempted so far
3. a clear definition of the concrete change to be achieved
4. the formation and implementation of a plan to produce this change (p. 110).

In the first step, the translation of the problem into concrete terms turns a vaguely stated problem into concrete ideas and permits the critical separation of problems from pseudo problems. Second, a careful examination of any attempted solutions shows what kind of change should not be attempted and also reveals what maintains the situation in its current state. Finally, the tactic chosen to solve the problem must be translated into the group's own language.

Search Conference

A relatively recent intervention is the search conference. "A search conference is a participative approach to planning in real time that helps organizations to develop the capacity for active adoption to turbulent environments" (Anderson, 2000, p. 33). Employees at all levels should be involved in learning and planning so they stay abreast of the changing environmental demands. The search conference is normally a two-and-a-half day event that is usually held off-site in a retreat setting. Ideally 20 to 40 people are selected to participate based on their expertise, knowledge of the system, diverse perspectives relative to the strategic issue under consideration, and their potential for taking responsibility for implementation.

Usually issues are identified in the large group and later assigned to small groups for in-depth discussion and recommendations back to the large group. "As a whole community, participants scan their external environment, review their history, analyze the strengths and weaknesses of their current system, which provide a shared context for their most important tasks: the development of strategic goals and action plans" (p. 34).

In this context the participants conduct a broad and sweeping scan of their environment. Participants pool their perceptions of significant changes, emerging trends, and likely future demands. The intent is to "unfreeze" the system out of its complacency. "Dissatisfaction with the status quo builds as participants learn about the environmental demands on their system and the need to respond more effectively to such demands in the probable future" (p. 36).

Harrison and Shirom (1999) suggested that the search conference be "used more often in planning for sociotechnical interventions, but it can also be used as a diagnostic intervention . . . the outputs of Search Conferences are proposals for change that must then be negotiated with broad groups of stakeholders" (p. 99). These conferences are best applied in face-to-face problem-solving groups. This requirement restricts their applicability to large organizations unless participation is restricted to top management. That solution, however, undermines the possibility of broad employee involvement in diagnosis and planning for change.

Decision-Making Interventions

The difference between problem solving and decision making is that **problem solving** is a process to determine the reason or cause of a problem so that one can make appropriate decisions. **Decision making** is the process of selecting among a variety of alternatives which one would best solve the problem that has been identified.

Some typical types of decision making include decision by majority with voting or polling taking place; decision by minority, wherein a few somehow manage to influence the larger group; decision by formal authority in which one individual, because of position, makes the decision for the group; and decision by consensus, in which the group continues discussing the issue until everyone can "live with" the decision. Some specific interventions that assist with the decision-making process include the following techniques.

Force Field Analysis

Lewin (1951) originally developed **force field analysis,** the concept of identifying those forces that drive a group or individual to make a certain decision and those forces that are preventing that decision from being made. A group must know what the desired condition is and then must be able to identify what is preventing them from reaching that desired condition.

In order to change the current condition, Lewin suggests that driving forces could be increased, restraining forces could be reduced, or both. Lewin advises against simply adding more driving forces because that may increase tension and resistance. Thus, the best approach is to work on the most important restraining force and attempt to reduce it. Sometimes a detailed form helps a group complete all necessary steps for this analysis (see Form 8.3).

At a corporate board meeting, I helped top executives identify what was preventing them from performing as a team. The strongest restraining force was the fact that the previous CEO had encouraged competitiveness among his senior officers. In fact, each officer was evaluated on how he was able to increase his return on investment at the expense of other units in the organization. The main driving force was their loyalty to the company. Increasing their loyalty to the company would not overcome the block to working collaboratively, but reducing the competitiveness would.

FORCE FIELD ANALYSIS

Change Effort Analysis

Step A

We will use the force field analysis concept to analyze your problem. This concept states:

- Any function or item to be changed can be thought of as an ongoing process-in-equilibrium.

- The process may be described as operating at a particular level on a continuum running from "less" to "more," or "not so good" to "very good." This may be portrayed thus:

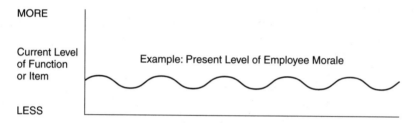

- The function or item always occurs in a tension system (or field of forces)—a system of forces opposing each other and stabilizing at the present level of the function. Different forces have different strengths or importance and may be so indicated by the *length* of the arrow.

  - The forces pushing the function in the direction of MORE are called driving forces.

  - The forces pushing the function in the direction of LESS are called restraining forces.

- A quasi-stable equilibrium exists when the strength of the forces tending to lower the level (restraining forces) are in balance with (or equal to) the forces tending to raise the level (driving forces).

(Continued)

FORCE FIELD ANALYSIS *(Continued)*

- Three processes are involved in changing the level of the function or item to a more desirable level:
  1. Diagnosis. Identifying all forces—driving and restraining—currently maintaining the present level.
  2. Unfreezing. Changing the different strengths of the individual forces.
  3. Refreezing. Stabilizing the forces at the new, desired level.

Step B

Construct a force field analysis for your change effort. Identify all the driving and restraining forces you can. These can be

- individuals,
- groups,
- forces and factors like tradition, pleasure, fear, and
- yourself. You may be both a driving and a restraining force.

The key at this stage is *full* identification of driving and restraining forces—often you will discover allies and restrainers you did not suspect.

Less		**More**
Driving Forces	Change Effort	Restraining Forces

Step C

Now assess the relative strength of each of the forces. One technique that might be helpful is to apportion 100 points to the driving forces and 100 points to the restraining forces. You cannot be accurately discrete but try

(Continued)

FORCE FIELD ANALYSIS *(Continued)*

to be as realistic as possible. It is conceivable, for example, for a single force to receive a weighting of as much as 90.

Step D

Three basic strategies for effecting change present themselves:

1. Add to the driving forces. This is generally less desirable since adding driving forces usually marshals more opposing forces and increases tension.
2. Remove, or reduce, restraining forces. This is usually more desirable—it is less obvious.
3. Add to the driving forces and work to eliminate or/and reduce restraining forces. This is probably the most frequently employed strategy.

We will concentrate on reducing or eliminating the restraining forces. It is fully recognized, however, that in your change effort you may find it highly desirable to consider adding to the driving forces.

Usually, you cannot attack all the restraining forces simultaneously. Some restraining forces are so rigid that they are almost impervious to change. Review the restraining forces you have identified.

- Which should you dismiss as not being amenable to change?
- Which of the restraining forces are most ready to change?
- Which of the restraining forces are not only amenable to change, but also have been assigned a significant weighting?

Step E

Consider the restraining forces you have identified as significant and vulnerable to change. We now consider which of these restraining forces we should attempt to change. Ask the following kinds of questions relevant to each force:

- Who in our system has access to the force I am trying to change?
- Which force, if I can change it, will have trigger-linkage—multi-causality?
- What are my resources for giving the kind of help that seems to be needed now or that may develop?
- Where do I and my group of change agents have the most leverage?

(Continued)

FORCE FIELD ANALYSIS *(Continued)*

Action Planning Steps

Step A

From where do you feel the support for this change in your organization must come? (Rank)

____ top management
____ professional personnel
____ middle management
____ supervisors
____ hourly workers
____ external consultants
____ external crises
____ internal crises
____ other

Step B

What are the best roles for you to assume in the change effort?

____ an educator
____ an advisor
____ a technician
____ an advocate
____ a trainer
____ a mediator
____ a coach
____ an expert on procedures
____ a doer
____ other

Step C

What new resistances can be expected and how can they be countered?

_____

_____

_____

_____

(Continued)

FORCE FIELD ANALYSIS *(Continued)*

Step D

Who are the "driving forces," and who needs to be involved/informed so that you don't alienate any of your supporters?

_____

_____

_____

_____

Step E

Are you clear with references to the action steps:

- What exactly is to be done and in what sequences?
- How is it to be done?
- Who is to do it?
- Where is it to be done?
- When is it to be done?

Step F

How can or should you terminate your role as a change initiator? When will the change be considered completed?

_____

Synectics

Prince (1970) and Gordon (1961) founded Synectics Incorporated in the late 1960s and early 1970s to promote the development and study of an intervention called **synectics.** Synectics groups are currently functioning, as are groups using some of the basic ideas developed as a part of this intervention. The purpose of the intervention is to provide individuals with a system for arriving at creative and innovative solutions to problems. It is a highly structured process that takes a group through several steps leading to solutions previously not imagined.

The two essential concepts to the process that can be applied in any group setting are *making the strange familiar* and *making the familiar strange.* Individuals usually feel threatened by something strange and unknown to them. Thus, an unusual concept must be made familiar so that concrete solutions can be considered. For example, one group was trying to design a solar-powered camping oven that would fold up. Some members could not imagine how such an item could fold up until someone described it as an "umbrella," a common article.

One application of synectics is for process improvement to arrive at ways to reduce the number of processing steps. By asking participants to imagine that they are part of a manufacturing process, they envision themselves as the part going through its daily routines. This allows the participants to look at the complete process from a unique perspective, contribute innovative solutions to an existing problem, and obtain the entire group's agreement on how to proceed with improvements (Weitz, 1995, p. 77).

I have frequently used parts of the synectics process to get a group "unstuck" from particular thinking styles and unproductive problem-solving methods.

Nominal Group Technique

Nominal group technique (NGT) was developed by Andrew H. Van de Ven and Andre L. Delbecq in 1968 (Van de Ven & Delbecq, 1971, 1974). Its purpose is to provide groups with a decision-making process that does not initially put people "on the spot," as brainstorming can do. There are six steps involved in this process:

1. Individuals suggest solutions to a problem independently and in writing.
2. Ideas are presented to the group members through a format that disassociates the idea from the person. The ideas are all listed on a flip chart and the leader goes through them without identifying

the ideas' authors. Evaluation of the ideas should not take place at this stage.

3. The ideas of all the group members are then discussed for clarification and now pros and cons may be presented. Again, the ideas have been separated from the people who proposed them so defensiveness will be minimal since the "cons" are about ideas, not the person himself or herself.

4. The group arrives at a decision by secret ballot. The members are asked to rank the ideas that have been proposed. This system reduces conforming pressures that often are present in an open discussion.

5. The preliminary vote is discussed. Each member can comment on selected items and raise any questions or issues for the group to consider.

6. A final vote is taken, again by secret ballot.

The advantages of this technique include:

- It ensures that ideas are collected from every member, in contrast to brainstorming or any oral method of discussion during which only the most vocal members of the group usually speak up.
- The ideas are problem-centered and all related to solving the problem rather than topics that get the group off track.
- It separates the idea from the person, thus reducing defensiveness.
- It forces all members to work and produce their share of the effort.
- The technique can accommodate a large number of participants.
- It forces equality of participation.
- It allows participation from all hierarchical levels.
- It is less costly and quicker than some other methods of problem solving.

Disadvantages include:

- Members may be "voting" on ideas they do not fully understand.
- The group is missing the synergy that sometimes occurs when group members talk together. One idea may lead to another if the discussion is allowed to continue.
- Some members may dislike writing ideas and have more difficulty expressing themselves in writing than orally.

The Delphi Technique

"Organizations employ a variety of strategies for bringing stability and certainty to their environments" (Pfeffer & Salancik, 1978, p. 70). One technique for increasing stability and reducing uncertainty is the Delphi Technique.

Delphi is used to predict future events and reduce uncertainty. Delphi was originated at the Rand Corporation in 1948. It was initially developed to provide the Air Force with information on the targets for a Soviet nuclear attack. Since the 1960s the Delphi has been used in a variety of settings and to help solve human communication problems.

Delphi is "a method for structuring a group communication process so that the process is effective in allowing a group of individuals, as a whole, to deal with a complex problem" (Linestone & Turoff, 1975): "an intuitive methodology for organizing and sharing expert forecasts about the future" (Weaver, 1971); and "an attempt to elicit expert opinion in a systematic manner for useful results" (Sackman, 1975).

Once a problem is formulated, an expert panel is selected and a questionnaire is developed. The "solution testing" involves submitting the results of the questionnaire to the panel as many times as it takes to gain consensus or until a minority opinion can be articulated. Then the group opinion of the panel is written and disseminated. The first version of the questionnaire usually consists of open-ended questions. The second questionnaire usually contains scaled items developed from the open-ended responses. Panel members are asked to prioritize their responses in light of the summary of the group response. In the last round the lowest ranked items are dropped. The process continues until consensus is reached.

An example of a successfully used Delphi was a small city government trying to prioritize the purchase of city equipment. The discussion had dissolved into factions advocating the purchase of equipment for the fire or police department. The arguments were no longer rational and had become personal attacks against various members of each department.

A Delphi technique was introduced to first collect information from experts in the field about the quality of equipment necessary for various tasks and the expected cost for acceptable equipment. This removed the discussion from personal attacks to factual information about equipment needs. Once the information was collected a second Delphi was used with the government officials, feeding back the information obtained and asking for their judgment about priorities. A list was developed for the purchase of equipment according to greatest need. Even after the decision was made, some of the interpersonal problems remained and were dealt with at a later time.

The advantages include having a panel of experts on a particular subject, having an opportunity to receive the opinion of every panel member, and, like NGT, allowing anonymous input. It is best used for complex issues and questions that require much thoughtful consideration. Like NGT, it keeps people focused only on the main issue at hand. It does, however, eliminate group dynamics and any synergy that might occur in a face-to-face group. Some panel members may be pressured to agree with the majority opinion and thus "groupthink" may occur.

Strategic Planning

Probably the intervention I use most frequently is strategic planning. The first step in implementing change is to plan the strategic planning meetings. Advice to companies planning strategic planning meetings, and to the facilitators attempting to assist them, includes the following:

1. Organize a preplanning meeting as a step in the overflow of decisions. Make sure participants know where inputs are coming from and where outputs will go.

2. Select a competent facilitator. Not all facilitators are equally effective. As a consultant you should not attempt to facilitate a strategic planning meeting unless you have had extensive experience working under the supervision of someone who has had such experience.

3. Start with a well-defined agenda that spells out task steps, estimated times, and expected deliverables. Participants need to know what they are going to do and what to expect.

4. Follow an effective methodology, which ensures that the needed information is available, group dynamics are taken care of, and sound strategic decisions are made.

5. Select participants carefully to ensure meaningful consensus and commitment of the management team, which will ease implementation.

6. Be professional in the environmental analysis of all relevant aspects of the industry.

7. Make sure the CEO delivers a clear message to the management team. Work with him or her to flesh out the guidelines the management team will use to produce a final strategic plan.

Give the meeting credibility by having the CEO endorse the output and update participants about the implementation of decisions (adapted from Flores & Fadden, 2000, p. 33).

In one strategic planning process for which I and a colleague served as consultants point 7 above was a bit tricky. The top two leaders of the organization announced their retirement and their replacements had not yet been found. At the same time, the governing board wanted a strategic team to develop a plan before their replacements were identified. Since these top two leaders were seen as "lame ducks," there was no CEO to endorse the planning process. I felt it was essential that the chairman of the board, who had requested this process, endorse the planning process to the entire organization. In essence, he was serving as the CEO in this situation; while the top two leaders had to be involved as well. I probably spent more time helping plan how to present the message, hopeful and alarming at the same time, than I did assisting with the planning process itself.

Chapter 15 provides details on the strategic planning process.

Designing and Directing a Consultation Intervention

One framework used to design interventions is the competing values framework, which consultants use to describe and understand the complexity of managerial work. Organizations are identified along a series of descriptors including flexibility control and internal and external focus. The results are four panels that characterize organizations by cooperative teams, responsive ad-hocracy, stable hierarchy, and rational firm (Brown & Dodd, 1998, p. 47). This model is probably as useful as any other. The primary purpose of any model to which you can compare an organization is to get its members to begin to think about how their organization operates, what helps them function successfully, and what patterns contribute to their dysfunction.

One way to evaluate the success of an intervention is to look at the criteria used by Peters and Waterman in their original 1984 text and by Peters in his follow-up work in 1988 and 1993 to identify excellent companies. These criteria could be applied to identifying outstanding consultants as well. The eight attributes that emerged to characterize the distinction of excellence are captured in the following phrases: (1) a bias for action, for getting on with it, (2) close to the customer, (3) entrepreneurship, (4) productivity through people, (5) hands-on, value-driven, (6) stick to the knitting, (7) simple form, lean stuff, and (8) simultaneous loose-tight properties (pp. 13–15).

Having a "bias for action" means being analytical in one's approach to decision making but not being paralyzed by that fact. "Close to the customer" suggests keeping in touch with the clients and understanding their needs. It is surprising how many consultants enter the client system with ready-made solutions that may not address the client's needs at all. "Entrepreneurship" means being innovative. For the consultant "productivity through people" implies fostering an attitude that human beings are the most important investment for the corporation. "Hands-on, value-driven" is explained through the words of Thomas Watson, who said, "The basic philosophy of an organization has far more to do with its achievements than do technological or economic resources, organizational structure, innovation and timing" (Peters & Waterman, 1984, p. 15). "Stick to the knitting" means "never acquire a business you don't know how to run" (p. 15). The consultant should be very careful about claims he or she makes about individual competencies. "Simple form, lean stuff" implies simple but eloquent designs for the system and for operating the organization. "Simultaneous loose–tight properties" combines a centralized and decentralized approach to interacting in the organization.

Table 8.3 will help you select which of the preceding interventions you might feel most comfortable integrating into your own client/consultant relationships. It identifies ten criteria to compare interventions. "Expediency" refers to how urgent the situation is and consequently how quickly the intervention should be implemented. Some interventions require a high level of skill on the part of the consultant, while others cannot be used unless the clients are fairly skilled at human interactions.

For example, Delphi technique requires experts in a particular field to participate. Size of the group, the organization's goals, and the financial costs are clear; however, you must also consider something less obvious. Emotional costs, such as the self-disclosure needed in a confrontation meeting, might be quite high. This is similar to risk level, which could mean making yourself vulnerable. The physical environment, as well as the formality of the situation, may be more supportive of certain types of interventions.

A human resource (HR) problem and an organizational development (OD) problem call for very different interventions. For example, role plays are effective for HR problems while Delphi is more effective for OD issues. Finally, some interventions (e.g., confrontation meetings) simply make individuals *aware* of problems while others (e.g., force field) work at solving problems. In short, the best intervention is the one you feel the most comfortable using , the one most acceptable to the client, and the one best suited to the situation.

Subsequent chapters address special communication problems you are likely to face.

TABLE 8.3

INTERVENTIONS COMPARED

	Audits	Survey	Team Building	Process Observation	Confront. Mgt.	Negotiation	Planning	Synectics	Force Field	Nominal Group	Delphi
Expediency	L	L	A-H	H	H	A-H	L	H	H	H	L
Skill Consultant	A	A	A	H	H	H	H	H	A	A	A
Skill Client	L	L	H	L	A	L	A	H	A	A	H
Size of Group	H	H	L	L	L	L	A	L	A-H	L-A	A-H
Cost—$$	H	H	A	L	L-H	L-H	A-H	A-H	L	L-H	A-H
Cost—Emotional	L	L	A-H	A-H	H	H	A	A	A	A	L
Risk Level	L	L	A	A	H	H	A	H	A	A	A
Formal vs. Spontaneous	F	F	F-S	S	F	F	F	F	S	S	F
HR vs. OD	OD	OD	HR	HR	HR	HR	OD	HR	HR	HR	OD
PS vs. Awareness	Aw	Aw	Aw	Aw	PS	PS	PS	PS	PS	PS	PS

Key: H = High, A = Average, L = Low, F = Formal, S = Spontaneous, OD = Organization development, HR = Human resource, PS = Problem solving, Aw = Awareness raised

LESSONS LEARNED
Consulting Interventions Most Likely to Succeed

One of the most critical mistakes a consultant can make is taking the client's definition of the problem as given. Of all the interventions discussed in this chapter, those that help you diagnose the problem are the most important. Your major contribution as an outside consultant is often to provide an objective diagnosis of the problem. Communication audits and interviews are the primary ways I discover the challenges the group is facing. Nevertheless, even when you insist on conducting some form of diagnosis before planning any other intervention, you can be fooled.

In one situation I met with the executive team of an organization to plan a retreat for all administrative staff. Over several days we had ten hours of group interviews with this team, and I thought I had a good understanding of the issues they were facing. They needed to create a sense of team in order to launch a new service. The problem was that units of the organization had been fairly independent up to this time; now they needed to become more dependent on each other and collaborate. We designed a rather extensive team development retreat that lasted 12 hours. The retreat accomplished quite a bit, I thought. There were commitments made to help these groups come together, promises to collaborate, and very specific assignments agreed to in order to create a unified effort. Twenty-four hours after the retreat, five of the retreat participants were fired. Top management had been planning this all along and wanted this retreat to get the rest of the group ready to work together. Everyone felt betrayed, including me. Despite the fact that I had conducted what I considered to be rather extensive group discussions to uncover the dominant issues with this group, I was as surprised as everyone else that the true purpose of the whole effort was to downsize the executive level of the organization. Sometimes consultants are used as scapegoats.

In another situation I was asked to spend several weeks helping a small college do strategic planning. I conducted interviews with about 20 percent of the participants and discovered they had two major issues to resolve before they could agree on goals and objectives. There was a great deal of tension on campus between faculty and students over one particular student activity. The college also had a significant increase in commuter students and had not learned how to incorporate them into the student body. In fact, college administrators weren't sure they wanted to. I recommended a "town meeting" prior to the strategic planning process to get these two issues on the table and hear both student and faculty opinions. I facilitated the town meeting, which had to be controlled carefully so that all opinions were heard but no one was allowed to dominate the discussion. Following that town meeting were smaller group meetings focusing on some of the same issues. Once the strategic planning committee had more input from all over campus, it was better prepared to begin discussions on goals and objectives. Operating in a vacuum is never a good idea.

Another intervention I use frequently is force field analysis. It is an excellent visual representation of what is moving the group forward and the most important challenges in their way. It really gets at the heart of most issues. It is also something very easy to introduce without a lot of explanation. The group immediately identifies its most difficult challenges and can quickly choose which one to work on first. Often, the intervention does not have to be elaborate, but may be a simple process that helps a group prioritize issues and solutions. Before this analysis, the problem may seem insurmountable and too difficult to tackle.

Additional Resources

Blake, R. R., & Mouton, J. S. (1983) *Consultation* (2nd ed.). Reading, MA: Addison-Wesley.

Facilitation skills (1998). Phoenix, MD: Brainstorm Dynamics.

Reddy, W. B. (1995). *Intervention skills: Process consultation for small groups and teams.* San Diego: Pfeiffer.

Schein, E. H. (1999). *Process consultation revisited: Building a helping relationship.* Reading, MA: Addison-Wesley.

PART IV

Correcting Communication Failures

When a group asks me to work with them, chances are they are experiencing intergroup conflict and weak communication skills. This section of the book contains a wealth of stories and examples from my consulting practice. These eight chapters cover solutions to the most typical communication problems that I have encountered. Chapter 9 provides specific techniques for increasing listening ability, Chapter 10 suggests some simple but powerful strategies to improve meetings, while Chapter 11 explains how to help others prepare dynamic presentations. Chapter 12 includes team-building strategies, and Chapter 13 discusses one of the most important skills for a consultant: how to provide feedback in a nonthreatening manner. Chapter 14 describes everyone's nightmare: dealing with difficult people and conflict situations. Chapter 15 addresses the problems encountered when any change is introduced in a system. Finally, Chapter 16 focuses on the unique challenge of international training and consulting.

This section is very practical and skills-oriented. The techniques are fully described, and you are encouraged to apply all of my "trade secrets" to enhance human communication in organizations!

Chapter **9**

ISN'T ANYONE LISTENING?

Using Active Listening Techniques

Listening is the process of becoming aware of all the cues that another party emits. It is the process of allowing another person to communicate the conscious and subconscious, both what the other person knows and what she or he may not yet understand.

Van Slyke, Listening to Conflict, *1999, pp. 98–99.*

One example of the dramatic impact poor listening behavior can have is a story told by a corporate executive with whom I have worked for a number of years. Peter and another vice president (Stan) usually worked closely on accounts and often consulted each other on issues related to clients. At one time, when their workload was particularly heavy, they each had to take primary responsibility for two clients. The client Stan was working with usually had contact with Peter, but Peter's attention was focused on a new larger contract. During a hectic day Stan asked Peter for advice about using the client's logo in some promotional material for Peter and Stan's firm. Peter said, "Sounds like a good idea but of course get approval from the client first." His colleague heard only, "Sounds like a good idea. . ." and proceeded to produce, and have mailed out, 20,000 pieces of literature using the client's logo to demonstrate credibility for Peter and Stan's firm. Now their company is the defendant in a multimillion-dollar lawsuit by the client for using its logo without permission. Peter has spent the last year trying to repair relations with this client. Poor listening can indeed be a costly mistake.

Harris (1997) describes listening as a "partnership in building rapport and relationship rather than simply receiving the speaker's words accurately" (p. 9). That is the message we are trying to communicate to our clients. Almost every time I enter an organization for the first time, I observe this one-directional communication where the receiver is not engaged in the communication process, usually because he or she is developing a response rather than actively listening. The notion of a partnership is a good one to promote. "Something about the management experience tends to hobble the listening skills of even the best-intentioned managers. Most managers are sincere in their desire to share ideas and information. Yet, in the end, their attempts at dialogues often turn into monologues" (Hiam, 1997, p. 92).

The word *listen* is derived from two Anglo-Saxon words: *hylstan,* meaning hearing, and *hlosnian,* meaning to wait in suspense. Listening is a combination of hearing sound and waiting in suspense for psychological involvement with the speaker or source generating the message. Consequently, it goes beyond simply hearing sound waves to include psychological involvement with the speaker and his or her message. "When we listen . . . we give the emotional mind a chance to breathe. We allow the slower rational mind to catch up and influence the perceptions generated by the rapid-firing emotional mind" (Van Slyke, 1999, p. 100).

Listening is defined as "a unitary-receptive communication process of hearing and selecting, assimilating and organizing, and retaining and covertly responding to oral and nonverbal stimuli" (Wolff, Marsnik, Tacey, & Nichols, 1983, p. 8). Each of those steps is critical to the process of listening. The listener first selects those stimuli to which he or she will pay attention (the first occasion for distortion to occur!). A story cited in Burley-Allen (1982) about two men's approach to listening suggests this.

> Two men were walking along a crowded sidewalk in a downtown business area. Suddenly one exclaimed, "listen to the lovely sound of that cricket." But the other could not hear. He asked his companion how he could detect the sound of a cricket amidst the din of people and traffic. The first man, who was a zoologist, had trained himself to listen to the voices of nature, but he did not explain. He simply took a coin out of his pocket and dropped it on the sidewalk whereupon a dozen people began to look around them. "We hear," he said, "what we listen for."

Then those stimuli must be arranged in such a way that the listener can make sense of them. Otherwise the listener can be overwhelmed with information that is too much to manage.

Some of the stimuli are then retained for future reference (another occasion for distortion, since we tend to remember things according to our biases). Finally, the listener, if actively involved in the communication process, responds verbally or nonverbally to the messages that have been heard. If any one of these steps is incomplete, the process fails.

One group I worked with had a great deal of difficulty with "collective memory." Each of them would remember ideas and decisions from meetings with a slight twist to them. Even when they had a recorder to write up summaries of the meetings, they still disagreed about the summary! As the meetings drew to a close, they would be so anxious to be "done with" a controversial issue that they didn't really listen to the summarizer, who tried to make sure they all heard the same decision. Only later would they then step forward and argue again about the issue.

The dialogue from these meetings would go something like this:

Summarizer: "So we all agree the new policy will require two signatures on requisitions before final approval can be granted."

Person who disagrees with policy: "Yes, we've agreed" (meaning: this will simply be a rubber stamp and any two signatures will do).

Person who agrees with policy: "Yes, I think we've debated this enough and we agree" (meaning: at last we will be firm about getting two supervisory signatures before any purchase is approved—we're finally cracking down!).

Only when the first requisition is presented for approval do they discover they don't really agree. Two things are happening: first, they are not willing to put energy into resolving their differences; and second, they are not listening carefully to the summarizer to make sure the "agreement" is spelled out in enough detail so that misunderstanding does not occur later.

Of all the skills of human communication, the one we take most for granted is listening. We assume that listening ability is acquired automatically as we grow older. Research reveals that we probably spend more time each day involved in listening than we do in using any other communication skill. We spend less time developing and refining that skill, however, than any of the other communication skills. The burden of making people listen has always rested on the sender of the message. That responsibility should be placed equally on the listener as well. As listeners, it is extremely important that we identify and improve our listening habits.

Why Is Listening Important?

In a recent study Sypher, Bostram, and Seibert (1989) concluded that "listening is related to other communication abilities and to success at work. Better listeners (as measured by a listening comprehension test) held higher level positions and were promoted more often than those with less-developed listening abilities" (p. 301).

Being a good listener is clearly identified with good management skills. A survey of personnel directors in 300 organizations found that effective listening was ranked highest among the skills defined as most important in becoming a manager (Robbins, 1989). Some of the most successful CEOs with whom I have worked made me feel they were carefully listening to each idea I raised.

Consultants understand the value of listening. In fact, it is probably the most important skill I use when assessing organizational needs. If you listen very carefully to what employees are telling you, the answers to their problems exist among all the verbiage. Solutions are all present, waiting to be discovered among the hidden agendas, the "fronts," and the language used to "position" themselves. Peters suggested:

> My correspondence occupies many a file cabinet after years of dealing with managers in turbulent conditions. The most moving letters by far are

the hundreds about "simple listening." In fact, if I had a file labeled "religious conversion"—that is, correspondence from those whose management practices have truly been transformed—I suspect that 50 percent of its contents would deal with just one narrow topic: going out anew, with a "naive" mind-set, and listening to customers (1988, p. 16).

Steil, Barker, and Watson (1983) reported that the majority of our time each day is spent listening: 14 percent of the day we spend in writing, 17 percent in reading, 16 percent speaking, and 53 percent in listening (p. 3). They go on to report, "Listening is a communication skill that we rarely receive formal training in; yet, listening is the skill we develop first and use most often. Instead of training, our listening behaviors are developed by watching and listening to others" (p. 5).

Types of Listening

One trainer reports on a workshop where participants are asked to draw a caricature of a successful leader. The more than 2,000 participants who have participated in this activity run the gamut from executive vice-presidents to maintenance workers and come from a diverse array of industries and locations. "What's noteworthy and very telling about this exercise is that 90 percent of the drawings depict effective leaders as having large ears, a big heart, or both. The message is clear: Effective leaders hear what others have to say and empathize with them. They walk in others' shoes by listening and caring. In a business environment often characterized by rapid change, these two critical, respected leadership characteristics are often missing for myriad reasons. We don't have time; we don't make time; we don't realize the importance; we don't know how" (Lucia, 1997, p. 25).

Wolvin and Coakley (1985) discussed several types of listening including discriminatory listening, comprehensive listening, therapeutic listening, critical listening, and appreciative listening. Each of these listening skills requires different techniques and focuses on a different form of communication.

Discriminatory listening is listening to distinguish the aural stimuli. This type of listening is basic to the other four. It is developed early in a person's life, and the importance of auditory discrimination is documented in research on the language acquisition of children.

Comprehensive listening is listening to understand. The comprehensive listener is successful if the message received is as close as possible to that which the sender intended. One variable directly related to comprehensive listening is memory. We cannot process information without bringing the memory into focus.

Wolvin and Coakley suggested that in order to improve comprehensive listening, a listener must capitalize on the amount of time difference between how quickly someone speaks and how quickly one can think and connect back to what is being said. They also make suggestions on listening for main ideas by paying attention to the transitions speakers use when they are introducing a main idea like "I want to make one impression on you and that is . . . , " or "Today we are going to discuss . . . ," or "Simply stated, the issue is . . . ." These transitions are signals that the speaker is about to present a main point.

Therapeutic listening is listening to provide a troubled sender with the opportunity to talk through a problem. The skills or techniques needed for therapeutic listening are focusing attention, demonstrating attending behaviors, developing a supportive communicative climate, and listening with empathy. The listener must be willing to enter the other person's world whole-heartedly, for a few moments.

Critical listening is listening to comprehend and then evaluate the message. The critical listener makes a decision to accept or reject the message on the basis of sound criteria. Particularly as consumers of the mass media, all people need to be critical listeners. Skills needed to be a critical listener include identifying the dimensions of source credibility, recognizing the influence of credibility, evaluating inductive and deductive arguments, detecting and evaluating reasoning fallacies, evaluating evidence, and recognizing emotional appeals.

Finally, **appreciative listening** is listening to obtain sensory stimulation or enjoyment through the words and experiences of others. Since appreciative listening is highly individualized, there are no criteria by which to draw a formula or list of skills.

Communication managers are engaged most often in comprehensive and therapeutic listening. When you are trying to solve people problems, you are listening most often for facts and feelings. You are also responding to individuals to let them know they have been heard and understood, even if you don't have a solution for them. Many times, they simply need a sounding board and once they have talked their way through the problem, without being interrupted with another person's problems, they can figure out the solution on their own!

Myths about Listening

As a consultant I begin almost every session with a client with a 15- to 20-minute lecturette and a short activity on listening. I begin by dispelling myths on listening.

Wolff, Marsnik, Tacey, and Nichols (1983) identified ten misconceptions about listening:

Listening is a matter of intelligence.

Good hearing and good listening are closely related.

Listening is an automatic reflex.

Daily practice eliminates the need for training in listening.

Learning to read will automatically improve listening.

Learning to read is more important than learning to listen.

The speaker is totally responsible for success in oral communication.

Listening is essentially a passive activity.

Listening means agreement.

Consequences of careless listening are minimal. (pp. 30–39)

First, listening in and of itself has no relationship to intelligence. Listening means paying attention to each point the speaker is making. If the listeners do not understand the language or the concept, then their careful involvement in the communication process will allow them to ask pertinent questions for understanding. The intelligent person may have the capacity to understand the concepts but not listen to them, while the active listener hears each point and if it is not understood, asks for clarification.

Second, good hearing simply means that the auditory signal has reached the listener's ear. There is no guarantee that the message got through. One may hear well but listen poorly.

Third, listening is not automatic. We think if we sit quietly we will simply "absorb" the message without effort. Good listening, like any other skill, must be activated. We can actually measure how involved a person is in the listening process. In an actively involved listener the heart rate increases, blood pressure rises slightly, and body temperature goes up.

Many people also think that because we listen each day, we are receiving daily training in this communication skill. I drive a car every day, but I don't get any better at following directions unless I make a conscious attempt to improve. As long as I play golf, I will continue to slice to the right until I get some lessons that will help me correct that swing. No amount of hitting the ball will change that unless I'm willing to pay attention to what I am doing wrong and try to correct it.

The next two misconceptions in the list both indicate the importance we have placed on reading as the most important communication skill. Yet in today's fast-paced world, we receive more messages orally than in written form. Reading and listening are two very different skills and require diverse styles of attending to stimuli.

The seventh and eighth items suggest that the listener plays a passive role in the communication process, and the speaker is totally responsible for the success of the communicative event. The listener does nothing and is not held accountable! These misconceptions make listening seem to be a much easier job than it really is. Obviously, communication is a cyclic, not linear, process.

Poor Listening

Unfortunately, most of us assume we are good listeners! Brownell (1990) asked subordinates to evaluate the listening ability of their managers. More than 50 percent placed their managers in the "poor" category. At the same time, "virtually all managers in this sample perceived themselves as 'very good' or 'good' listeners (a small percentage placed themselves in the 'fair' category) even though those managers received low ratings from their subordinates" (p. 412).

Ask managers how they interact with their subordinates and they will probably tell you they have an "open-door" policy, which implies they are ready to listen to whoever walks in. Ask the people who report directly to them and you will get a very different story: "My boss is constantly interrupted by the phone while we talk"; "My supervisor is distracted by what is on the desk during our conversations"; "My boss smiles, nods his head, gets a glazed look in his eyes, and then never responds to what I've just said to him." Our perceptions of our own listening ability are often inflated. We need to ask others if they feel they have been listened to after talking with us!

I tell clients (and myself!) that we must decide at the beginning of the communication process that we want to be involved in it. We "clear our minds" as if we were sweeping aside everything on the top of our desks. We should prepare to listen psychologically by placing ourselves in the other person's world for a few minutes. This means setting aside all our personal concerns and ideas for the time being, which is not an easy task. We also have to prepare to listen physically by maintaining eye contact, leaning forward, and positioning our bodies toward the person talking. This reminds both communicators that the focus is totally on the person talking.

One of the reasons individuals are hesitant to quit talking and listen is that they are afraid it will somehow convey agreement with what is being said. Silent listening, we are afraid, will be taken for silent support. We feel a desperate need to get our next point in, lest someone forget what our position really is! In other words, our focus is often on ourselves and "covering" our position rather than on the other person.

The final myth is that poor listening has minimal impact on the communication process. One has only to read case studies of poor listening to discover the depth of impact such communication behaviors can have: divorces, labor negotiations, missed directions costing companies hundreds of thousands of dollars. All point to the fact that the consequences of careless listening can be great.

One of our assumptions is that we are all good listeners. We are usually surprised when someone tells us we aren't listening! We heard the person but maybe we weren't really listening. The following section identifies some of the weak listening habits all of us have probably exhibited at one time or another.

Poor Listeners: Who Are They?

Poor listeners are you and I, anytime we haven't made the other person's thoughts our priority. Montgomery (1981) identified some of the most common poor listeners. Do any of these apply to you or your clients?

The unfocused listener is the person who is thinking of something else with wandering eyes and wandering head.

The fact-focused listener always has a mind full of little tidbits of information but may be completely lost as to what the facts prove or what the speaker is trying to get across.

The inattentive listener makes listening difficult if not impossible by slouching in his or her chair or over a table or on a counter as though lacking the energy to really pay attention.

A finicky listener calls the speaker or subject uninteresting and makes the burden of listening and understanding focus on the speaker. This person focuses on tiny details and misses what the person is trying to say.

An emotional listener highlights another bad habit of listening. This is a person who gets overly excited about things that are heard because of a word that has been misunderstood or some negative impact of the speaker.

The fake listener pretends to pay attention and to get the message, smiling, nodding, even looking intently at the speaker, but his listener's mind has detoured and may be a thousand miles away.

A note taker tries to write down every word the speaker is saying. Even with shorthand it would be difficult or impossible to do that. Good note takers sometimes miss the major message.

The unaware listener, instead of anticipating the points the speaker is making and mentally summarizing them, sits and lets the words go in one ear and come out the other. Unless you are working actively at listening, you aren't really listening. (pp. 30–60)

All of these types of listeners have attended my seminars and retreats. Often, there are several of them present at the same time! At one retreat I conducted for a large professional organization, one person made rather dramatic pleas for solidarity and then undermined consensus during the breaks. The fake listener sat in the front row, nodding and smiling, but, when asked by his supervisor, couldn't recall a single idea expressed that day. Another listener continually sidetracked the group with his off-the-cuff and off-the-topic comments! A communication specialist needs some techniques to handle these poor listeners in a group, some of which I have included at the end of this chapter under "Consultant's Tips on Listening."

Steil, Barker, and Watson (1983) identified the differences between bad listeners and good listeners:

- The bad listener tunes out dry subjects. The good listener looks for benefits and opportunities and asks what's in it for me.
- The bad listener tunes out if delivery is poor. The good listener judges content, skips over delivery errors.
- The bad listener tends to enter into an argument. The good listener doesn't judge until the message is complete.
- The bad listener listens for facts. The good listener listens for central themes.
- The bad listener shows no energy output and fakes attention, while the good listener's whole body works hard, actively exhibiting attention.
- The bad listener is distracted easily while the good listener fights to avoid distractions and knows how to concentrate.
- The bad listener resists difficult, expository materials and seeks light, recreational material while the good listener uses heavier material as an excuse to exercise the mind.
- The bad listener reacts to emotional words while the good listener does not get hung up on them.
- The bad listener tends to daydream with slow speakers while the good listener challenges, anticipates, summarizes, and listens between the lines. (pp. 72–73)

Communication specialists must not only guard against becoming poor listeners themselves but need to model effective listening behavior to train others as well. If you are interested in improving the communication process for the groups with whom you work, you need to develop techniques for helping others become better listeners.

Why Does Poor Listening Exist?

Every client I have ever worked with had some occasion in which poor listening was exhibited. Everyone is prone to poor listening habits for a variety of reasons. Burley-Allen (1982) discussed physical barriers to effective listening including the time of day and fatigue. There are moments in every day, and entire periods of time, when, because of your own physical or psychological condition, you are unable to tune into someone else's problem. If the environment does not provide privacy and freedom from distractions, it is very difficult to maintain the desired level of interaction.

Anxiety may also cause us to be poor listeners. If we are listening to defend ourselves against possible attack and are anxious about what may be said next, then we are not involved in active listening but rather are engaging in "defensive" listening. Defensive listening means we hear only those things we think are unfair or unjustified in order to respond to them. Kurtz (1990) talked about "chain reactions" involving an attack, a poor listener, and a reaction rather than listening to understand or clarify.

Timm (1986) also suggested that we are poor listeners because of self-centeredness and self-protection.

> Self-centeredness refers to the degree of "vested interest" we may have in our own point of view. When a difference of opinion arises among people, our vested interest in our ideas can create a listening barrier . . . . In other words, we are "listening" through a predetermined set of biases, looking for flaws in our "opponent's" views rather than seeking common understanding. We develop a mind like a steel trap—closed. (p. 251)

Self-centeredness is difficult to control. Listeners must be more interested in the other person than in themselves. That is something few of us are able to do on a regular basis. We can, however, enter another person's world temporarily, as an active listener.

Poor listening also becomes very obvious among groups as well. Groups who have a low level of listening show the following characteristics: dominance by a few members, cross-talk (several members talking at once), ideas lost (no mechanism for catching and retaining points), repetitive contributions, wordy inputs (individuals use much speaking time for little content), turned-off members, and inability to handle consensus decision making (Francis & Young, 1979, p. 87).

Active Listening: What Is It?

The term **active listening** means the ability to pick up, define, and respond accurately to the feelings expressed by the other person. When active listening is employed, speakers perceive that they are being understood. This perception allows them to explore and express their feelings, identify ideas as their own, and rely less on defensive behavior.

> Active listeners listen with their ears, their eyes, and their mind. They take in the objective information by listening to the literal words that are spoken. But every spoken message contains more than words. Speakers also communicate subjective information—their feelings and emotions—through other vocal sounds and nonverbal signals. These include verbal intonation like loudness, emphasis, hesitations, voice inflections, and the rate of speaking. Nonverbal signals encompass the speaker's eye movements, facial expressions, body posture, and hand gestures. By listening for feelings and emotions, as well as for literal words, you can grasp the

total meaning behind the speaker's message. Yet no matter how good you become at listening for total meaning, there still remains the potential for misunderstanding. (Robbins, 1989, p. 31)

Robbins is suggesting that even when a person uses active listening skills, the possibility of misunderstanding still exists. However, active listening significantly reduces this possibility. Active listening conveys trust and is one of the most effective ways for the listener to help the speaker feel comfortable with the interaction.

Dr. Thomas Gordon (1977), author of *Parent Effectiveness Training,* was one of the first authors to introduce the concept of active listening. An active listener is fully engaged in the communication process even when not talking. The active listener listens for unspoken words and ideas. Gordon also indicated the 12 most commonly expressed nonaccepting responses that defeat the active listening process:

1. ordering, directing, commanding ("You have to . . .")
2. warning, admonishing, threatening ("You better not . . . ")
3. moralizing, preaching, exhorting, imploring ("It's your duty.")
4. advising, giving suggestions, or solutions ("What you should do is . . .")
5. persuading with logic, lecturing, arguing, teaching ("Experience says that . . .")
6. judging, criticizing, disagreeing, blaming ("You'd be foolish to . . .")
7. praising, agreeing, evaluating positively, buttering up ("You're such a good . . .")
8. name calling, ridiculing, shaming ("How naive can you be?")
9. interpreting, analyzing, diagnosing ("Your problem is . . .")
10. reassuring, sympathizing, consoling, supporting ("Tomorrow will be better.")
11. probing, questioning, interrogating ("Why did you . . . ?")
12. distracting, diverting, kidding, avoiding, withdrawing, humoring ("Hey, have I told you . . .") (pp. 60–62)

These are the types of responses I work to have my clients recognize and stop using through role plays and practice.

It is very seductive to listen to someone else's problems and be asked for advice. We all think we can see so clearly what others ought to do with their lives. Often, however, the person is not really asking for advice but simply asking for empathy. The above responses tend to judge the other person's ideas as good or bad rather than simply accepting them. Gordon's list of nonaccepting responses is a good reminder of the type of responses that get in the way of active listening. Bite your tongue if you hear yourself using any of them! Avoiding use of the word *why* will eliminate a number of occasions when you appear to be challenging someone's feelings or ideas.

Ask questions that do not get the person off track but instead help focus on the issues rather than the "symptoms" of the problem. The active listener asks questions for clarification rather than explanation or justification. Those questions must come at appropriate times so that the listener is not interrupting. A variety of authors discuss at length the ability to ask such questions so that the listener can summarize the "whole picture" for the speaker (Montgomery, 1981; Robbins, 1989; Stiel, Barker, & Watson, 1983; Wolff et al., 1983).

Listening is a craft that must be developed. It is much easier *not* to develop that skill, so one has to be motivated to do so. Finally, people must create the most supportive climate in order to encourage effective listening.

Gibb (1961) identified the kind of supportive climate that a good listener wants to establish: a climate that is descriptive rather than evaluative and problem-oriented rather than controlling, one of spontaneity rather than strategy, empathy rather than neutrality, equality rather than superiority, and finally, one of provisionalism rather than certainty.

Tips on Listening

First, communication specialists must check their own psychological well-being before entering an active listening process. If you are unable, psychologically or physically, to listen to someone, you do that person a great disservice by pretending to listen. It would be much better to let the speaker know you are unable to help at that time but would be willing to assist in identifying someone who could. You could also make specific plans right then to meet with the client when you feel you will be better able to be an active listener.

Also, check on your general listening behavior. Ask others if you wait to hear someone out or if you tend to interrupt. Be prepared to accept their answers without feeling you must defend yourself. Ask others if you dominate small groups and how often you play the role of "interviewer" in a two-way conversation. If you don't like the answers you get, read this chapter again!

Second, move to a place that will provide some privacy and comfort for the person talking with you. In private conversation, people want to feel secure that the intended listener is the only listener. This may be something as simple as closing a door or moving to a quieter part of a large room. Ask the other person whether he or she is comfortable talking where you are or would prefer to move elsewhere.

Third, start by listening for feelings first. People who are upset about something initially need to let off steam before they are ready to talk about solutions. If you get the "yes but" response, you know they are not ready for answers. Besides, they need to come up with their own answer. If you give them the answer, then it will be your solution, not theirs; and if it doesn't work, guess who gets blamed?

Fourth, the communication specialist must have a vocabulary for listening. You must be ready to respond immediately and will need a variety of messages that indicate you have heard the other person and are trying hard to listen carefully. Francis and Young (1979, p. 87) identified a number of useful responses to establish active listening behavior.

Checking: "Can I repeat what you said in order to check my own understanding?"

Clarifying: "It seems to me that this is what you mean . . . ."

Showing support: "I hear you. Please carry on."

Building on: "Building on your last point, I would add. . . ."

Structuring: "Shall we look at the symptoms, try to define the problem, and then discuss possible solutions?"

Fifth, watch out for traps. For example, it is easy to get trapped by **cognitive dissonance,** which is the tendency to "dismiss or not allow into consciousness any information not consistent with what we believe or want to believe" (Kurtz, 1990, p. 7). If you are hearing something you do not want to believe, it is very difficult to maintain your active-listener role. For that moment, you need to set aside your opinions and listen only to support the other person.

Finally, listen with intensity, empathy, acceptance, and willingness to take responsibility for completeness (Robbins, 1989) rather than listen to argue a point of view that may or may not be consistent with your values. Empathy is not the same thing as sympathy. Rather than feeling sorry for someone, you are simply trying to place yourself in the other person's position—not to agree or disagree—but merely to understand his or her point of view.

You can transfer listening skills to your clients by providing descriptive feedback. Cite specific examples of when they have demonstrated those skills. Then ask clients to repeat information you have shared. This will put them in the habit of paraphrasing and listening closely. Some of the training techniques discussed in Chapter 6 could be used to develop a workshop on listening for your client.

Form 9.1, the listening quiz, is designed to help you pay more attention to your own attitude toward listening. Monitor your listening behavior for one day and ask others for feedback. How often during a typical work day are you an active listener? Are you like the person in the poem

"Conversation," wondering if the person listening to *you* is "missing"? As a hand-out it has powerful effects on clients and usually leads to discussions of occasions when poor listening has had serious consequences.

CONVERSATION

i have just
wandered back
into our conversation
and find
that you
are still
rattling on
about something
or other
i think i must
have been gone
at least
twenty minutes
and you
never missed me
now
this might say
something
about my acting ability
or it might say
something about
your sensitivity
one thing
troubles me tho
when it
is my turn
to rattle on
for twenty minutes
which I
have been known to do
have you
been missing too?

Source: Reprinted from *Dragonflies, Codfils & Frogs* by Ric Masten, p. 59. © 1977 Ric Masten.

LISTENING QUIZ

Directions: Mark each statement true or false (answers on p. 205).*

     _____ **1.** People tend to pay attention to what interests them.

     _____ **2.** People tend to expect or anticipate what they are familiar with.

     _____ **3.** Sometimes people distort things so they hear what they want to hear.

     _____ **4.** Listening is a natural process.

     _____ **5.** A person's training, experience, and knowledge affect what that person perceives.

     _____ **6.** Hearing and listening are the same.

     _____ **7.** Listening is a skill.

     _____ **8.** Most people have a short attention span and have difficulty concentrating on the same thing for too long.

     _____ **9.** Listening requires little energy; it is easy.

     _____ **10.** The speaker is totally responsible for the success of the communication.

     _____ **11.** An effective listener keeps an open, curious mind.

     _____ **12.** Speaking is a more important part of the communication process than listening.

     _____ **13.** When a listener's emotional level is high, he or she will be an effective listener.

     _____ **14.** When a person is involved with internal distractions, he or she will not be able to listen to what the speaker says.

     _____ **15.** Being critical and judging a speaker is not an effective listening skill.

The "Lessons Learned" story comes from Peter and Susan Glaser, a consulting team from Eugene, Oregon. I have watched these two individuals in action; they are extremely talented. Their style is highly interactive when they work with clients. The story they tell perfectly highlights the importance of listening. In this instance, one of their clients makes a dramatic statement about perceived ineffective listening.

LESSONS LEARNED

A Consulting Story from Susan and Peter Glaser

Susan and Peter Glaser are the co-owners of Glaser and Associates, a consulting firm in Eugene, Oregon. They focus their consulting activities in four areas: training in conflict resolution, team dynamics, and persuasion and influence; consulting intervention (crisis management); keynote addresses; and the production of media like the series of videotapes on "Mastery of Leadership Communication."

This experience concerns a training and intervention program done with the U.S. Forest Service (USFS), a state Department of Fish and Wildlife, a state Department of Recreation, county government officials, and a Native American nation. The Native Americans were outraged at the destruction caused by visitors to their lands. They felt tourists were desecrating their sacred grounds. They decided they must take steps to stop this destruction so they announced they would close to visitors the portion of the river that ran through their sacred grounds. The USFS officials said they could not close a river on public lands. The nation responded by posting signs along the river warning: "Go no further. You are trespassing on private Indian territory." All parties involved had been meeting for several months to try to resolve these issues but had been completely unsuccessful. We were asked to facilitate the conflict.

The first thing we did was to interview all parties to discover why they were unable to reach agreement. We then gave the entire group a report that was honest without being defeating. Third, we taught them a series of consensus-building skills from our video series that involve identifying issues without causing resistance, facilitating discussion, and crafting consensus from divergent points of view. They converted their oppositional positions into those interests and concerns they agreed on with extensive monitoring put in place.

At the end of the negotiations the Native American representative stood up and said, "We have once again decided to open our lands to any visitors who wish to enjoy it." There was a long pause while everyone looked at everyone else. We were afraid someone would say something that would destroy the entire session. Finally, one of the state representatives said to the tribal spokesperson, "I must ask you, what was it you heard today that got you to change your mind?" After another long pause, the tribal representative responded, "It was nothing that I heard today that got me to change my mind. . . . But today, for the first time, I believe you heard me."

You can reach the Glasers at <www.theglasers.com> or 541-343-7575.

Additional Resources

Nicholas, M. (1995). *The lost art of listening: How learning to listen can improve relationships.* New York: Guilford.

Timm, P. R. (1986). *Managerial communication: A finger on the pulse* (2nd ed.). Englewood Cliffs, NJ: Prentice-Hall.

Wolvin, A. D., & Coakley, C. G. (1988). *Listening.* Dubuque, IA: W. C. Brown.

Van Slyke, E. J. (1999). *Listening to conflict: Finding constructive solutions to workplace disputes.* New York: AMACOM.

*False— #6, #9, #10, #12, #13.

Chapter **10**

WHY ARE MEETINGS SO BORING AND UNPRODUCTIVE?

Managing Meetings

People can be motivated to be good not by telling them that hell is a place where they will burn, but by telling them that it is an unending commit-tee meeting. On judgment day, the Lord will divide people by telling those on his right hand to enter his kingdom and those on his left to break into small groups.

Author unknown

We all suffer from the same annoying tendencies during group meetings. One example is association board meetings, which Maron (1997) characterized in the following way:

- Discussion of controversial topics goes around in circles without resolution;
- Decisions you thought were made are constantly revisited;
- Personal rivalries erupt into bickering or spiteful behavior; and
- Committees complain about inconsistent guidance from the board. (p. 51)

Sound familiar? Most meetings involve some useless activity. In fact, meetings are usually thought of as time wasters. To help groups function more effectively the consultant can provide some ground rules for meeting management.

It has been reported that one corporation holds all its top-level meetings without chairs, requiring individuals to stand during the entire meeting. The goal is to force people to be quick with their comments, making the meeting more productive and efficient. This technique may not work with all groups; however, the goal is a noble one.

I recently worked with a group of individuals who scheduled a three-hour meeting every Wednesday morning, whether there was something to discuss or not. Every Tuesday afternoon, half of the staff met to plan what would be said in the Wednesday morning meeting. Consequently, the Wednesday meeting was a repetition for half of the attendees and for the other half it was a briefing on mostly routine information with no input from them. Two individuals in the group used a strategy to make the Wednesday meetings more productive. They requested that the meeting be moved to 11:15 because they had prior commitments earlier in the morning. Their strategy was to hold the meeting as close to the noon hour as possible so the meeting would only last 45 to 50 minutes. This strategy worked. There was less side conversation and less repetition of information. The important issues came up first and got dealt with, and the meeting was over before any unnecessary discussion could occur.

Why are meetings boring? One reason is that those who make up the agenda are often not in touch with the needs and interests of those who must attend the meeting! Frequently, I have discovered a staff spending 1 or 2 hours dreaming up items for an agenda the day before a meeting that others will attend. The meeting then turns into an information briefing, when most of the information could have been communicated in written form and saved everyone valuable time. This doesn't mean team briefings shouldn't occur. The team briefing can be very useful; however, when it occurs, meeting participants should know the intent of the meeting is to provide information, not to solicit opinions.

The other major reason meetings are boring is that a few people use meetings as an opportunity to promote their own agenda or issues, and the person in charge of the meeting does not limit the amount of time any one individual may control. These are just two of the issues this chapter addresses and for which it provides easy and simple solutions.

Why Meet?

Research suggests that most managers spend 2 to 3 days a week tied up in unproductive meetings. As much as 30 person days and millions of dollars are wasted each year on meetings that solve nothing (Mosvick & Nelson, 1987). As Barmash (1985) pointed out, many people have a very pessimistic view of the potential outcome of meetings. When people come to meetings with such negative expectations, they are bound to fail! If meetings are such a waste of time, why do people keep holding them?

To Announce Organizational Changes

We hold meetings when the rapid changes in the marketplace make it necessary for managers to keep employees informed on a regular basis. These environmental changes have also caused a great deal of reorganization, compelling individuals to meet to discuss and understand how reorganizing the system will affect their day-to-day jobs. In this highly technical environment changes in products, services, and marketing are so rapid it behooves the managers to keep employees constantly in touch with these changes.

Kanter (1983, 1989, 1997) and other writers who discuss future changes in corporate America (Naisbitt, 1982; Naisbitt & Aburdene, 1990) have indicated that the hierarchies of organizations are collapsing. Organizations are becoming more flat, with decision making at the lowest level of the hierarchy. An organization is described as flat when there are few hierarchical levels from the top of the organization to the bottom. With fewer hierarchical levels more people at each level are involved in decision making. Consequently, more meetings among those who must make decisions are necessary. The increase in *participative management* has encouraged group interaction and deliberation.

■ A NEW ECONOMIC INDICATOR

So much has been written about the decline in our nation's productivity and so many reasons advanced that one wonders why we haven't solved the problem.

But we haven't, and we won't unless we identify the real culprit. I, for one, know what it is; and it's as elusive as only the truly obvious can be.

Meetings.

It doesn't really matter where, be it government, business, or education, but meetings are held at the drop of a memo. They are wasteful, and mostly painful. I am reasonably certain that if there were an organization called the National Commission on the Study of Multiple Encounters, its findings would be devastating. It would discover, I am sure, that there were 3.8 trillion meetings held at American companies last year. Of that number, 70 percent lasted 45 minutes or more, and about 75 percent included 10 participants or more. If the NCSME pursued its research properly, it would also find that the growth trend of meetings has exceeded major economic indicators such as the gross national product, the rate of inflation, interest, unemployment—and productivity.

Meetings, I therefore suggest, have become our national pastime, yet one is hard put to see any advantage to them other than someone's decision to hold a meeting so the group can for a time avoid doing the job it is paid to do. In that sense, meetings are relaxing. The irony is that no one does.

The trouble with meetings is that too much is considered and too little is resolved. Meetings are self-perpetuating. They last twice as long as they should. They are an excuse and are often intended to impress others with the patent effort to induce employee participation. Meetings are a euphemism, a ploy really to evaluate the three P's—people, programs, and politics. Meetings are deceptive. Meetings aren't held to hear what everyone has to say, but for everyone to hear what one has to say.

Well, if the National Commission on the Study of Multiple Encounters could figure it out, the number of hours spent on meetings in the United States, based on the numbers I estimated earlier, is almost incalculable, as is the number of employees involved. It would come to trillions of man- or woman-hours annually that can be translated into lost productivity. So revealing would the findings be that they might be considered a new economic indicator—the American meetings rate, seasonally adjusted.

By Isadore Barmash. From *Newsweek*, September 9, 1985, p. 12. Reprinted by permission.

To Increase and Improve Solutions

Another reason to hold meetings is that individuals are able to identify more and better solutions to problems, although some individual creativity may be stifled. There is much research to suggest the advantages of several people contributing to the problem solving instead of developing solutions in isolation, particularly with complex tasks. There is greater motivation to perform well in a group setting because others are judging one's actions. A number of studies also suggest that groups consider more ideas than individuals operating in isolation, which is likely to improve the quality and originality of the decision (Schultz, 1989, p. 8). Since opportunities for communication have increased, the group's decision-making ability is enhanced as well (Gouran, 1982). In the introduction to their book, Poole and Hirokawa (1986) indicated:

> There is a world of difference between making a decision alone and making a group decision. The unique chemistry of social interaction can distill the best that each member has to offer, creating a resonance of ideas and a synthesis of viewpoints. A different chemistry can stop the reaction and contaminate the product with erratic reasoning or low commitment. Communication is the catalyst for this social chemistry and, as such, it is widely recognized as a key force in group decision making. (p. 15)

It is clear that group interaction changes the way in which solutions are generated and those solutions become more than just the sum of the individual efforts. In another research program, Hirokawa (1987) found four communication characteristics that distinguish the interaction in high- and low-quality decisions. First, high-quality decisions came from groups characterized by "vigilance" or careful, thoughtful, and systematic discussion of the pros and cons of solutions. Second, high-quality decisions were generated when the group practiced "second guessing" or challenging questionable information introduced by group members. Third, these groups participated in more accurate information processing, which means that group members actively rejected faulty information. Finally, the high-quality decisions came from groups characterized by the absence of what Hirokawa called "improbable fantasy chains." This refers to unrealistic hypothetical scenarios and stories. In short, low-quality decisions were made when the group relied on flawed information in arriving at their decisions. Thus, given the above conditions, groups have the ability to generate better solutions than individuals.

To Gain Acceptance of a Decision through Participation

Meetings also encourage a "buy-in" to solutions. We know the more individuals participate in the generation of the solution, the more likely they are to implement it. When individuals help determine the solution, they have already made a commitment to make sure it works. A great deal of the management literature points to the need to make employees a part of the process of decision making in corporations. "People are psychologically committed to ideas that they help generate in meetings, which goes beyond the product itself" (Napier & Gershenfeld, 1987, p. 421).

The CEO of one company formed a cross-sectional group to examine quality issues in the company. As a consultant, I was asked to facilitate the group's initial meetings and train them in effective decision-making processes. They were charged with eliminating procedures or policies that were blocking effective communication. At first, the committee members came into the group meetings defending their personal attachment to policies and subgroups. Over a period of several weeks, when the meeting facilitator continued to emphasize the goal of the group, they eventually "bought into" the idea that some policies and procedures may have been slowing down their ability to work together effectively. Eventually, the group recommended the elimination of 50 percent of the policy-making groups that had been formed over the years and dramatically streamlined procedures for approval of new services. When their recommendations were presented to the rest of the management teams, these teams were outraged. Since they had not been a part of the long discussions, they had no commitment to making such long-term changes. At that point, the total organization had to be brought into the decision-making process so that all members of the management team could experience some level of commitment to implement these new steps; otherwise the recommendations would fall on deaf ears. To the degree that individuals are involved in the decision making process, they will be willing to implement the final decision.

To Cultivate Members as Individuals

Group meetings also provide opportunities to display our skills to coworkers and superiors. This is often the time when our ability to solve problems can be recognized in front of others. It is important that the work team have a good sense of the skills of each individual so human resources are used appropriately. Often, meetings serve critical symbolic functions. Celebrating organizational members' successes and congratulating group achievements are important to the climate in the organization.

Finally, since our professional and personal lives are more blended today than ever before (see Chapter 19), meetings satisfy some of our personal and social needs as well. We do much more than work on tasks in the work environment. We form friendships, meet future mates, and have many of our social needs satisfied. While these are not the primary reasons for calling meetings, they are critical factors in our work life.

Although the preceding reasons for calling meetings are compelling, managers and consultants need to know when it is inappropriate to call a meeting because some other form of communication will work better.

When Should a Meeting Not Be Called?

The most effective leaders and group facilitators know when *not* to call a meeting as well as when one is necessary. Consider the following criteria for not calling a meeting:

- Information can be distributed in written form or by voice mail.
- A decision has already been made.
- Individual or programmed learning is best.
- Key people can't be there.
- There is no real agenda.
- Time and information are inadequate.

As you look down the list, can you recall meetings you have attended when one or more of these conditions existed? How did you feel during the meeting? Most individuals feel frustrated and angry that their time has been wasted. First, a meeting should not be called if information can be distributed more easily through written memos. This allows individuals to review that material at times most convenient to their schedule, which is much more effective than pulling everyone together at one time to listen to someone read information to them.

Second, if a manager tells a group that it has the power to make decisions, that manager can't later admit the decision has already been made. The meeting leader needs to make the intent of the meeting clear to the participants. That intent may be to advise the leader or supervisor, make recommendations, or actually decide an issue. The attitudes and actions of the group members vary greatly depending on the objective of the

Calvin and Hobbes   by Bill Watterson

FIGURE 10.1   *Calvin and Hobbes.* Copyright © 1991 Watterson. Reprinted with permission of Universal Press Syndicate. All rights reserved.

meeting. A leader gets into trouble when individuals come to a meeting expecting to have a role to play in a decision only to find out the leader does not want their advice after all! Don't ask others to make decisions if you aren't ready to accept a decision that may not be your choice!

Third, a meeting or training session should not be called when the topic can be covered in a more effective way. Sometimes people need different ways in which to learn. A training session is not always appropriate for the individuals or the subject matter. I have observed trainers attempt

■ THE USES OF MEETINGS

I learned not long ago of a meeting at a small plastics manufacturing firm. Present were a division manager, six department heads, and the heads of three sections. The topic: Should a replacement be hired for a recently injured secretary, or should a typist be secured from a temporaries service and kept on a week-to-week basis?

It took 50 minutes to reach a consensus on that question. Actually, the decision should have been made privately by the division manager or by the manager of the one office involved.

What was decided is not important. The effect of such meetings on the company is. Because of the length of the discussion about the secretarial replacement, time ran out before a second topic could be considered. A decision on it was not reached until another meeting weeks later. The topic: Should a new fluorescent lighting system for the plant be installed? Involved were not just one office but four departments—not to mention a $28,000 investment.

It should not be that way. First of all, meetings are expensive. When 12 people, each paid $15 to $25 per hour, meet for two or three hours, the cost for one session may easily exceed $500. Such a price is justified when it is necessary to bring representatives from engineering, production, finance, and marketing together to solve a legitimate problem. But when the session is held to get a consensus on whether coffee breaks should be taken at 10 A.M. and not at 10:30, or whether the copying machine should be moved 50 feet, blowing $500 worth of time on a meeting is unconscionable.

Second, when a manager calls meetings to decide on items that are inconsequential or that he should handle himself for other reasons, the importance of future meetings is diluted. People will find reasons not to attend whenever they can—a pity, because there will be some vital meetings that require input from everyone invited.

And third, when meetings are called by a manager who wishes to spread responsibility, a signal is given to his subordinates: "This is a policy you may wish to follow when you become a manager. Always cover yourself."

These situations tend to reduce initiative and harden the organizational arteries.

By Norman B. Sigband. Reprinted by permission, *Nation's Business*, February 1987, copyright © 1987, U.S. Chamber of Commerce.

to teach computer skills without giving participants the benefit of hands-on experience. You can't just talk about computers and expect others to learn how to use them. In addition, one-on-one training may be better than a room full of novice individuals all attempting to hit the same key on the keyboard at the same time. Consequently, a meeting called for the purpose of training must be the most appropriate way to deliver that skill.

Fourth, if the goal of a meeting is team building then the "team" must all be present or the meeting should not be called. You can't build a team when key players are not there. At the same time, individuals who are not going to be members of the team should not be present either. A client asked me to conduct a team-building session for one unit in the organization. When I asked who the team would be, I discovered they had planned for two individuals to come who were in the process of leaving the organization. One of these individuals had been a source of much conflict and everyone appeared to be relieved that he was leaving the organization. To have this individual attend a "team-building" meeting was inappropriate. I asked that anyone who was not a permanent member of the team be excused from the meeting.

Fifth, meeting participants seem most frustrated when no agenda is provided and no attempt is made to develop one at the beginning of the meeting. A meeting should not be called unless the meeting leader lets participants identify which items they feel need immediate attention. An "expectations check" is a system used to check on the needs of the group before the meeting begins. The leader simply asks, "Are there any items someone feels must be addressed before this meeting ends today?" This can be done ahead of time through written memos or orally at the beginning of the meeting. The leader must take responsibility for limiting the discussion and getting the group to agree quickly on top-priority items. The group decides which issues must wait until the next meeting and which must be discussed at this meeting. Finally, if the meeting leader has issues that must be addressed, all information relevant to those issues must be available to group members prior to the meeting.

Roadblocks to Effective Meetings

Once you have determined that a meeting is necessary, you need to be sure the purpose of the meeting is clearly articulated and that adequate information has been provided. As you think of things that can go wrong in the meeting itself, there are two major areas for concern: psychological issues relevant to the group process and procedural issues.

Groupthink

First, one needs to address group behavior. Janis (1972) writes about the phenomenon of "groupthink." This theory identifies some of the most difficult road blocks to effective group meetings and group decision making (see Chapter 12). Groups can fall into the trap of believing that they are invulnerable by discounting negative information, ignoring ethical considerations, pressuring dissenters into conforming with the group norm, believing unanimity exists when it doesn't, and appointing "mindguards" who watch for comments or ideas that seem out of the mainstream of the group's thinking. In short, these behaviors protect the group from attending to any information or ideas that contrast with its established views.

> I worked with one group who sent their "mindguards" to me as an "advance team" to make sure that I "got the picture" before I worked with the group. We sat in a cafeteria prior to the meeting I was to facilitate and I was surrounded by three individuals in the group who had been long-term members. These representatives wanted to be sure that I had an accurate history of the group to help me understand the issues they were now facing. One individual spoke first: "These young guys just don't understand how hard we have worked to establish a marketing strategy that will work. They come in with all these new ideas with no thought for our past efforts." The next fellow became agitated and, without realizing it, revealed their unwillingness to hear any idea different from their own when he said, "The next time one of these young kids tries to put something over on us I'm going to set him straight!" These individuals were completely unwilling to hear any idea that had not originated with them. Ultimately, the job of the facilitator was to make the group aware of their nonproductive behaviors. These groupthink behaviors are psychological blocks to productive meetings.

Procedural Issues

Procedural issues as well must be taken into account. Mosvick and Nelson (1987) surveyed over 1,000 managers to determine what goes wrong in meetings. They discovered the following actions topped the list of complaints:

1. getting off the subject (reported by 204 managers)
2. no goals or agenda (190)
3. too lengthy (187)
4. poor or inadequate preparation (94)
5. inconclusive (88)
6. disorganized (86)
7. ineffective leadership/lack of control (38)
8. irrelevance of information discussed (37)

   9. time wasted during meeting (37)
   10. starting late (36) (p. 19)

These complaints are not difficult issues to deal with. They don't indicate differences in philosophy or conflict as being the most obvious problems. Rather, the complaints of these managers have to do with procedures for running meetings. If leaders followed a few simple rules, they could eliminate most of these issues.

Techniques for Making Meetings More Productive

Given this variety of issues, the meeting facilitator needs to focus attention on what makes a meeting work. Five basic problems present themselves to the meeting facilitator. He or she must decide how to direct traffic, determine if the group is talking about how to discuss a topic or what topic to discuss, identify who does what during the meeting itself, develop strategies for handling information overload, and determine the goal of the meeting.

Directing Traffic

Directing traffic simply means that some system must be in place to ensure group members do not interrupt each other and all individuals are given a chance to speak. In large meetings (over 50), **parliamentary procedures** are necessary to control the flow of business. These procedures control how motions can be placed before the group and how discussion can be limited. The group must know how to deal effectively with matters brought before them. Consultants need to be familiar with these elementary principles to help facilitate extra-large meetings.

The following are the basic "survival steps" necessary to function according to parliamentary procedure. Parliamentary procedure is useful because it provides an orderly way to move through officer reports, and it allows every member an opportunity to present ideas in the form of motions for debate.

Four types of motions can be presented. A **privileged motion** takes priority over all other motions and is not debatable; thus an immediate vote is taken once the motion has been seconded. An example is a motion to adjourn, take a recess, or attend to the comfort of the group in some way.

Incidental motions deal with the procedures the group is using in the meeting. These must be voted on before main or subsidiary motions. Examples of incidental motions include suspension of the rules or a point of order.

Subsidiary motions apply to or amend main motions. They must be voted on before the main motion but are "outranked" by incidental or privileged motions. These types of motions include postponing the discussion or vote, amending a main motion, limiting debate on a main motion, and calling for the "previous question" (asking for a vote on the main motion).

Finally, the **main motion** is the statement of an item of business. These motions are actually the activity of the group but are voted on last, after any amendments or questions about procedures and privileges of the group have been decided.

If the group is using parliamentary procedure, then the chair must make sure these procedures are followed: no one makes a motion without being recognized, having the motion seconded, and having the floor opened for debate and discussion (no discussion takes place if the motion does not receive a second). The debate is controlled by not allowing interruptions, and the motion is reread when the discussion is finished. Only then does the chair call for the final vote.

Table 10.1 provides a brief summary of motions and their requirements. This can serve as a quick guide for large meetings. Knowing how to use these procedures will facilitate carrying out the business desired. The most likely place these procedures will be used is in large association meetings and democratic institutions. In business and industry, decision making does not take place on a scale so large as to require the use of parliamentary procedure.

In smaller groups, parliamentary procedure may get in the way of informal discussion, which can be carried out among 20 or fewer people. Still, the group leader needs to set some ground rules and ensure that all participants are heard. For example, one rule might be that everyone has a chance to present ideas only once before voting or deciding on an issue. Or the group could require a "first reading" prior to voting. In this case, the group hears about a suggestion or motion at one meeting but does not vote on it until the next meeting. This gives everyone a chance to think carefully about the idea before being asked to vote. The decision to use parliamentary procedure should be based on the following guidelines: the procedures should not get in the way of open discussion, should control debate, and should establish an efficient system for dealing with the work of the group. The ultimate goal is to avoid chaos!

Separating Topic from Procedure

Sometimes a group spends more time discussing how to proceed than discussing the topic itself. Obviously procedure is important; however, if the group gets too caught up in a procedural discussion, it is likely to accomplish very little. I have seen groups informally express agreement on an issue but then not be able to figure out how the process they were using would allow them to do what they wanted. *Procedures are useful only if they enhance a group's ability to get done what they want.* When the procedure becomes the issue, the group needs to be reminded of its basic goal or mission.

TABLE 10.1

PARLIAMENTARY PROCEDURE: TABLE OF MOTIONS

Motion	Vote Required	Debatable	Amendable	Needs Second	Interrupt Speaker
PRIVILEGED MOTIONS					
Fix time of next meeting	Majority	No	Yes	Yes	No
Adjourn	Majority	No	No	Yes	No
Recess	Majority	No	Yes	Yes	No
Question of privilege	Chair decides	No	No	No	Yes
Orders of the day	Chair decides	No	No	No	Yes
SUBSIDIARY MOTIONS					
Lay on table	Majority	No	No	Yes	No
Stop debate (previous motion)	$^2/_3$	No	No	Yes	No
Limit or extend debate	$^2/_3$	No	Yes	Yes	No
Postpone to definite time	Majority	Yes	Yes	Yes	No
Refer to committees	Majority	Yes	Yes	Yes	No
Amend	Majority	Yes	Yes	Yes	No
Postpone indefinitely	Majority	Yes	No	Yes	No
MAIN MOTIONS	Majority	Yes	Yes	Yes	No
INCIDENTAL MOTIONS					
Appeal	Majority	Yes	No	Yes	Yes
Division (for vote count)	Chair decides	No	No	No	No
Divide question	Majority	No	Yes	No	No
Withdraw motion	Majority	No	No	No	No
Point of order	Chair decides	No	No	No	Yes
Suspend rules	$^2/_3$	No	No	Yes	No
Object to consideration	$^2/_3$	No	No	No	Yes
Parliamentary inquiry	Chair decides	No	No	No	Yes
TO REOPEN AND BRING BACK BUSINESS					
Take from table	Majority	No	No	Yes	No
Reconsider	Majority	Yes	No	Yes	Yes
Rescind or repeal	$^2/_3$	Yes	Yes	Yes	No

Source: M. E. Doyle and D. Straus, 1986. *How to Make Meetings Work.* New York: Berkley Publishing Company.

Identifying Roles

Who does what? This question addresses the roles individuals play in the group. For example, there is usually one *historian* in every group who reminds the group of their history, who they are, and what they have done. Sometimes this behavior is very helpful in that it serves as a group conscience. Other times it can be blocking behavior because the person may constantly remind the group that a solution has been tried and did not work. While the historian's perception may be accurate, idea generation requires that the group not evaluate the idea until all ideas are expressed.

Other group roles include the *person who initiates* discussion. This person gets the discussion started and often serves as the sounding board for others. Usually someone is assigned to be the *recorder* for the group. Everyone needs to know who is *"in charge"* of the meeting. This person constantly tests the group's willingness to move on to another topic or make a final decision on the topic under discussion. These of course are not official roles but are personality traits that are manifest during the course of the meeting.

Schein (1988) identified a series of roles individuals play in the group process. Every meeting has a mixture of these various roles and member behaviors (see Chapter 12 for further discussion). **Task functions** are those behaviors that help the group concentrate on specific jobs. Someone gets the discussion started by making the first comments. Others provide and ask for information and opinions. Still others perform clarifying roles of pulling information together and testing to see if the group agrees on an issue. **Maintenance functions** are those behaviors that help the group stay together and deal with the interpersonal relationships of the group. These behaviors focus on resolving conflicts, being a "gatekeeper" or providing a way for all members to talk, giving encouragement to others, and setting the standards for the group. **Boundary management functions** are those activities that link the group to other groups. "Scouting" other groups or individuals for information and negotiating roles within the organization are important tasks for group members to perform.

There is also a series of blocking behaviors that prevent the group from moving forward. A person who is always negative no matter what the idea is, the dominator who has something to say on every topic, the person who constantly seeks attention, and individuals who remain silent can be some of the most difficult people to deal with. Chapter 14 discusses some techniques for dealing with these difficult people.

The role of group leader is a unique set of tasks. Besides learning to deal with these difficult personality types, the leader has a set of tasks for that role as well.

Group Leadership

Doyle and Straus (1986) suggested that the "meeting facilitator" is really a "meeting chauffeur." That analogy accurately suggests the major role for the meeting leader. The leader directs the group's activities and ensures that the group gets to its destination safely. If the group leader wants to participate in the discussion, then another individual should take over running the meeting for that period of time. The meeting leader must be the facilitator, not the dominant voice. In a sense, the meeting leader is more aware of the process the group uses to get its work done than the content of the discussion. Thus, the leader's primary jobs include (1) helping the group stick to the subject, (2) making sure everyone gets a chance to speak, (3) acting as a harmonizer and preventing others from being attacked, and (4) as Doyle and Straus suggest, monitoring "short-term memory" by placing ideas on a flip chart and "long-term memory" by making sure minutes are provided as a follow-up to the meeting.

The group leader must also decide *how much information is enough.* Sometimes a group leader, in an attempt to make sure everyone is fully informed, provides too much information. Individuals feel overloaded and unable to sort through the mass of data that has been presented. An advisory board can often help the group leader examine the information and condense it into easily consumed data so that individuals can make reasonable judgments.

The most important thing we have learned about leadership, after years of study, is that it is situational. **Situational leadership** means leaders must adapt to the environmental and individual needs of the moment. A person cannot change his or her basic personality; however, one can make slight modifications so that when the group needs a leader who is focused on task versus one who is focused on the relationships in the group, the leader can pay more attention to that issue. A "leader" is a person who is directing the activities of others, while "leadership" is a behavior that can be exhibited by anyone in the group. A group can be "leaderless" (without a designated leader) but will not function without "leadership" (behaviors exhibited by various group members that provide direction for the group). Therefore, leadership roles are important for everyone to understand.

Some authors refer to a leadership style as **transformational** (Tichy & Devanna, 1986). They defined it as a style of leadership that is "systematic, consisting of purposeful and organized searches for changes, systematic analysis, and the capacity to move resources from areas of lesser to greater productivity" (p. 27). This form of leadership is needed as corporations undergo dramatic change in markets and economic conditions in the United States.

Finally, the group leader must decide the goal of the meeting. If it is a decision-making meeting, then the suggestions given above will apply. If, on the other hand, it is a briefing, the leader needs to make the intent very clear. Briefings provide many useful services to the group including:

- Providing managers and supervisors with information they can share with employees
- Guaranteeing that supervisors, rather than the grapevine, are the primary source of information
- Building loyalty because employees are trusted and confided in
- Creating regularly scheduled occasions for work groups to get together to discuss business

- Increasing employees' understanding of business problems and concerns and their ability and desire to offer solutions
- Giving all employees permission to speak openly by structuring and institutionalizing face-to-face discussion
- Maximizing management's opportunities to deal with employee concerns before they cause morale problems and affect productivity (Johnson, 1990, pp. 55–56)

With the decision to hold a briefing or a problem-solving session the leader establishes a normative behavior for the group that will guide the interaction throughout the meeting. Rules that guide the "traffic," determined ahead of time, allow fewer interruptions.

Preparation for Meetings

The meeting facilitator needs to do a good deal of preparation for a meeting, even to the point of arranging the chairs. The first order of business is to find out about the participants so that the meeting can be planned to accomplish the goals they are assembling to address. By attending to logistics, the facilitator helps the participants focus on their business and avoid irritating distractions. The facilitator who knows how to prepare for a meeting can run an elaborate conference as effectively as a smaller gathering, but success requires systematic planning.

Learning about Participants

Napier and Gershenfeld (1987) suggested a list of questions the meeting leader ought to ask about the participants in order to be fully prepared to facilitate the discussions.

1. Whom does each of the participants represent within or outside of the organization?
2. Why have these individuals been chosen and not someone else?
3. What are each individual's organizational interest and needs? What does each of them want from the meeting? What hidden agendas might be influencing the life of the group?
4. What is known about each individual's personal goals and needs? Is his or her ego on the line? Do any have a stake in certain outcomes in addition to the organizational needs they represent?
5. Do the participants come with individual biases toward the leader, other members, the task at hand, or the general format of the meeting?

6. What are the personal skills and strengths available in the group that can be used if necessary?

7. What are the personal limitations and idiosyncrasies in the group that might block the task at hand?

History of the Group

1. How did the participants leave the last meeting? Were they pleased? Did they experience success? Or failure?

2. As a result, what are the expectations of this meeting?

3. What were the sources of pleasure, accomplishment, or other rewards experienced at the last meeting?

4. What were the sources of tension, frustration, or conflict?

Realistic Goals

1. What are the real task priorities of the members?

2. What is the best possible way to use the resources available in meeting these priorities?

3. What needs to be done to ready the group to work on the task so members can hear each other and focus on goals?

4. What do the individuals know when coming to the group?

5. What information do they not know but need to have in order to work effectively on the priorities at hand? (Napier & Gershenfeld, 1987, p. 428)

This type of detailed assessment of the group members and their past behaviors and expectations greatly enhances the likelihood for success at the meeting. A meeting planner who does not have access to this information is likely to repeat information the group has already covered, or raise or lower expectations unrealistically.

Attending to Logistics

Often it is the smallest of details that can make a meeting less than effective. The meeting leader should make sure the room is large enough, that the chairs and tables are arranged appropriately for the activity being conducted (e.g., conference tables if notes will be taken), and that all facilities are available to provide for the participants' needs (e.g., lunch arrangements, nearby bathrooms). One meeting leader who had failed to attend to these details found he had a disaster on his hands when the meeting started 35 minutes late because the audiovisual equipment had not been tested and did not work, the room got too hot, and a loud buzzing noise came from the lights throughout the meeting. In addition, two people sat on chairs in the hallway because the room was too small, the lunchroom was not prepared for as many participants as attended, and lunch took 1 hour and 45 minutes to serve! Busy people hate wasting time.

Following the meeting there are as many details as in the preparation stage. Minutes should be sent to all participants, follow-up actions must be taken as soon as possible, and the next meeting should be planned. Figure 10.1 visually represents the business meeting cycle. Note that the planning stages and follow-up stages are represented as a circle. The follow-up steps from one meeting affect organizational subunits, which in turn become the source of information for the next meeting.

The checklist provided in Form 10.1 will help the meeting planner review details to attend to not only prior to the meeting, but during and following the meeting as well. These are the kinds of details that will make participants eager or reluctant to come to the next meeting.

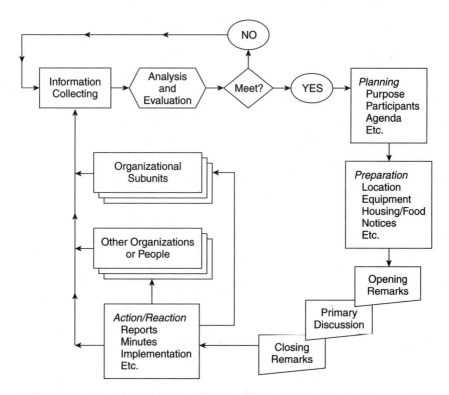

FIGURE 10.1   The Problem-Solving/Decision-Making Cycle   Reprinted by permission of Edward Baum. All rights reserved.

MEETING LEADER'S CHECKLIST

Preparing for the Meeting

_____ 1. Establish the reason for calling the meeting.

_____ 2. Develop the agenda.

_____ 3. Select the right people to attend.

_____ 4. Select the date and time.

_____ 5. Confirm date, time, and agenda with key people.

_____ 6. Notify all people who will be attending, and include starting and closing times.

_____ 7. Reserve a room.

_____ 8. Distribute agenda and materials for review, if needed.

_____ 9. Select person to chair the meeting, if appropriate.

_____ 10. Set up meeting room with needed equipment.

_____ 11. Prepare handout materials.

_____ 12. Request secretary to attend.

_____ 13. Arrange for refreshments, if desirable.

Opening the Meeting

_____ 14. Begin the meeting on time.

_____ 15. Introduce participants, if necessary.

_____ 16. Instruct recording secretary, if necessary.

_____ 17. Set the appropriate climate.

_____ 18. Review the agenda and announce the objective.

_____ 19. State any problems to be solved or decisions to be made during the meeting.

Conducting the Core of the Meeting

_____ 20. Encourage participation and orchestrate the roles of all group members.

_____ 21. Focus on subjects at hand.

_____ 22. Establish and follow an agreed-upon decision-making process.

_____ 23. Model appropriate roles and communication skills.

_____ 24. Listen for new ideas.

(Continued)

MEETING LEADER'S CHECKLIST *(Continued)*

_____ 25. Ask for information and clarification.

_____ 26. Seek others' advice.

_____ 27. Guide discussion toward the goals and objectives of the meeting.

_____ 28. Test for consensus.

_____ 29. Follow the agenda.

_____ 30. Remain flexible.

_____ 31. Do not allow any one person to dominate.

_____ 32. Control pace and keep to time frame.

_____ 33. Clarify decisions.

_____ 34. Record significant decisions.

_____ 35. Assign responsibilities and dates for implementing decisions.

_____ 36. Summarize steps needed to implement decisions.

_____ 37. Announce the next meeting, if appropriate.

_____ 38. Close the meeting on time.

After the Meeting

_____ 39. See that minutes are completed and distributed to all participants.

_____ 40. Follow up on implementation of decisions made during the meeting.

_____ 41. Announce and prepare for the next meeting, if necessary.

_____ 42. Evaluate the meeting, either formally or informally.

Planning a Conference or Convention

A conference or convention takes the same skills as running a business meeting, with the addition of 1,001 small details. Figure 10.2 lists some of those details and the amount of advance time needed to plan for each one. From determining a theme for the conference (see step 11, at 29 weeks) to mailing announcements (step 34 at 13 weeks) to last-minute details at the conference site, a conference planner must be extremely organized. The reactions of 500 (or more) participants who are "unhappy campers" because dinner took one and a half hours to be served, or room assignments got mixed up, or the key speaker was a dud, can be overwhelming! One excellent reference for checking every possible detail for a major conference is Nadler and Nadler's (1987) *The Comprehensive Guide to Successful Conferences and Meetings.* This book has more checklists than a meeting planner could ever possibly dream up on his or her own!

Another important resource is the professional organization Meeting Planners International. Its monthly publication, *The Meeting Planner,* gives extensive coverage to convention sites and materials, and its journal and national convention provide other opportunities for members' career development.

Besides the organizational details, the conference planner who adds something special to the conference will be rewarded with more requests to run meetings! I have worked with conferences where a laser light show was the finale, a nationally known star was a surprise speaker, and the closing session of the conference had the meeting facilitator interviewing attendees telling human interest stories about the conference in front of 1,000 people, Phil Donahue style. These are the conferences people remember.

Tips for Successful Meetings

- First, *those who are going to be involved in the meeting should always help build the agenda.* Either their input should be solicited before the meeting or at the very least they should be asked at the beginning of the meeting if there are items that need to be added. This can be done quickly and efficiently and still give all participants the sense that their ideas and needs are going to be addressed, if not at this meeting then at some future meeting. It is the task of the group leader to help the group determine how many of those items can be handled in any one meeting. The leader *must* ensure that items not addressed at this meeting are handled at the very next opportunity, or participants will soon learn it does no good to suggest items for discussion because they never come up again!

- Second, *a process observer should be assigned* for every meeting. A **process observer** is someone who agrees to refrain from being involved in the discussion in order to observe the process. For example, it is the job of the process observer to remind the group of the time they have left, when they have strayed from the topic

FIGURE 10.2   Forty-Nine Steps to a Successful Conference   From *How to Market Training Programs, Seminars, & Instructional Materials* by Don M. Schrello. Copyright © 1988. Reprinted with permission of The Marketing Federation, 109 58th Ave., St. Petersburg Beach, FL 33706. 813/367-4934.

under discussion, and when individuals have been interrupted and have not been allowed to complete a thought. They also could be put in charge of maintaining talk time by reminding individuals of the limit the group has agreed they will allow any individual. Forms 10.2 and 10.3 present sample observation sheets to help direct the observers' attention to important variables. (See the section of Chapter 12 called "Schein's Categories" for help in using Form 10.3.) These forms could be used by the chair of the meeting or another individual. After the process observers have experience with the technique, they will no longer need forms to remind them of behaviors on which to focus their attention. A consultant often serves in this role, at least initially.

One group asked me to facilitate a series of meetings designed to develop better communication among group members. In particular, complaints from female employees had the all-male management team worried. Women complained their ideas were not taken seriously, among other issues. We began the retreat by asking how individuals demonstrated respect for one another. A lively discussion was generated about people's strong belief that everyone should be respected! About 40 minutes into a rather intellectualized discussion of what respect means, the process observer made one simple observation about the level of participation in the group. "For the last 40 minutes the males have been actively involved in the discussion. Have any of you noticed that none of the women have commented? What do you think is happening here?" What followed was the beginning of an open discussion on the interaction style of the people in that room.

The process observer has to have a keen sense of timing, make objective statements about observed behavior, and be prepared to facilitate intense discussion that may follow. It is then possible that the process observer can make the group aware of procedural problems as well as dramatically increase group members' awareness of interpersonal issues. This can change the direction of the entire meeting and increase the potential for positive meeting outcomes.

- Third, as much as possible the *leader should remain neutral.* You cannot express your opinions and still fairly run the meeting allowing all points of view to be heard. When the leader feels compelled to express personal feelings, opinions, or expert advice, then a temporary leader should take over while the meeting leader assumes the role of a group member. If the roles of chair and advocate get confused, the meeting will quickly disintegrate into a briefing by the chair of decisions that have already been made. Those types of meetings are sometimes necessary; however, they

PROCESS OBSERVER FORM

Observee: _____

When I respond to each question, I will mark (√) next to the appropriate letter and then record the exact words used by my Observee to support my data.

   I.   How does project director select a co-worker?

      A. ( ) Asking.

      B. ( ) Inviting.

      C. ( ) Demanding.

      D. ( ) Sending an "I" message ("I need help," etc.).

      E. ( ) Sending a "You" message ("Will you help?" etc.).

      Words or statement used by observee: _____

      _____

  II. How does the team project get chosen?

      A. ( ) Imposed by one member.

      B. ( ) Shared decision.

      C. ( ) Suggestion followed by agreement.

      Words or statement used by observee: _____

      _____

 III. How do the plans develop?

      A. ( ) Mutual sharing of ideas.

      B. ( ) One person informs the others to do certain things.

      C. ( ) Another way (specify).

      Words or statement used by observee: _____

      _____

 IV. How does observee communicate?

      A. ( ) Uses "Yes, but" phrases.

      B. ( ) Uses "No, that won't work" phrases.

      C. ( ) Uses "I've got a better idea" phrases.

      D. ( ) Uses descriptive phrases. ("Will you clarify for me?")

      E. ( ) Uses supportive phrases. ("I like your idea . . .")

      F. ( ) Interrupts others.

      G. ( ) Listens and doesn't interrupt.

      H. ( ) Answers questions which others ask of him or her.

(Continued)

229

PROCESS OBSERVER FORM *(Continued)*

I. ( ) Does not answer questions directed to him or her by others.

Words or statement used by observee: _____

_____

Observer Question

V. How did I communicate my feedback to observee?

A. ( ) Sent "I" messages.

B. ( ) Gave accurate, observable data.

C. ( ) Gave process observation feedback.

D. ( ) Gave process interpretation feedback.

Personal comment: _____

_____

PROCESS OBSERVER ROLE FORM

Directions: Write each person's name in the column marked Observee. Process observe each member for role behaviors. Indicate the primary roles each member functions within by selecting the letter next to the role title. [Explanations of the role titles follow.] Write the letter in the column marked Code. Write the exact words and/or give an accurate description of the action in the column marked Behavior. Try to be precise, accurate, and clear in your observations.

MAINTENANCE ROLES	TASK ROLES	INDIVIDUAL/ BLOCKING ROLES
A. Harmonizer	E. Information Seeker	I. Silent One
B. Helper	F. Information Giver	J. Negativist
C. Quality Controller	G. Clarifier	K. Dominator
D. Follower	H. Summarizer	L. Judge
		M. Attention Seeker
		N. Quibbler

Observee Name	Code—Letters	Behavior—Exact Words/Describe Actions
1. _____	_____	_____
2. _____	_____	_____
3. _____	_____	_____
4. _____	_____	_____
5. _____	_____	_____

(Continued)

PROCESS OBSERVER ROLE FORM *(Continued)*

6. _____   _____   _____
_____   _____
_____   _____

Explanations of Roles

Maintenance Roles

A. Harmonizer
 1. Attempts to clear up disagreements.
 2. Deals with conflict in a nonthreatening manner.

B. Helper
 1. Encourages others to speak and share ideas.
 2. Shows warm and friendly attitude toward each member by making genuine, supportive statements such as, "I'd like to support you."

C. Quality Controller
 1. Analyzes the data and tries to help group understand information presented.
 2. Applies standards to data to evaluate.
 3. Suggests ways of keeping group on target by checking progress toward goal.

D. Follower
 1. Listens to another's ideas and nonverbally decides to accept them.
 2. May have own ideas but is willing to accept another way of achieving goals.
 3. Willing to follow to keep group active and moving toward solution.
 4. At times, firmly supports another's idea verbally.

(Continued)

PROCESS OBSERVER ROLE FORM *(Continued)*

Task Roles

E. Information Seeker

    1. Asks for facts/opinions/suggestions.

    2. Seeks information on the issue/topic/agenda point.

F. Information Giver

    1. Offers facts/suggestions.

    2. Responds to questions asked by other members.

G. Clarifier

    1. Interprets facts and clears up confusing statements.

    2. Asks questions for better understanding.

    3. Checks to see that questions are answered satisfactorily.

    4. Keeps one point on the agenda at a time.

H. Summarizer

    1. Pulls together related ideas.

    2. Calls for discussion after suggestions.

    3. At times, writes facts on newsprint.

    4. Makes closure on agenda points. Example: "I'd like to summarize. . . ."

Individual/Blocking Roles

I. Silent One

    1. Usually shy; answers questions with a Yes or No.

    2. Not inclined to enter discussion.

    3. Sometimes uses specific nonverbal messages to control group.

J. Negativist

    1. Usually replies to comments with "Yes, but . . ." or "It won't work."

    2. Makes comments on every topic.

    3. Uses nonverbals to reinforce verbal message (facial and body gestures).

K. Dominator

    1. Interrupts others to talk.

    2. Talks at great length on every topic.

    3. Attempts to control group by asserting an authoritative tone.

(Continued)

PROCESS OBSERVER ROLE FORM *(Continued)*

L. Judge

    1. Evaluates every comment in absolute terms.

    2. Gives advice even though it is not solicited.

    3. Uses phrases: "That's correct" or "I think you should do it this way."

M. Attention Seeker

    1. Monopolizes the discussion by "showing off."

    2. Uses nonverbals to attract attention.

    3. Interrupts others to gain center focus.

N. Quibbler

    1. Argues about small details. Example: "The bill was $2.97 and not $2.95."

    2. Corrects speech imperfections: "You didn't pronounce the *g* at the end of the word *going*."

should be called "briefings" and group members should understand they will not be coming to a meeting in order to express their ideas. Nothing is more frustrating than to attend a meeting expecting your ideas will be heard only to discover the intent of the meeting is for you to listen and not be heard.

A search committee was charged with hiring a new school administrator. The behavior of the chair was neutral and aided the discussion of other members until one particular name came up for discussion. Even though he admitted he knew the candidate personally (the candidate was a special friend of his son's), the chair continued to lead the discussion. Interspersed in his procedural statements controlling the discussion were expressions of opinion about the candidate. For example, he stated: "I think the comment on this candidate's lack of experience is unfair given the record of our other finalists." He then proceeded to attack each candidate making statements like, "Since she's not married, who would do the entertaining for her position?" and "This individual already holds this type of position, so why would he want to make a lateral move? We would be better off with our final candidate who is looking to move up." Finally he said, "I think we have an excellent candidate here; are there other comments?" It was clear he had already made up his mind and was going to control the discussion to ensure that his preferred candidate was selected.

A meeting leader should never become an advocate. If the meeting leader wants to voice an opinion, someone else should take over during that discussion, thus separating the role of meeting facilitator from advocate of one particular viewpoint. Otherwise, leaders have an unfair advantage because they can control the discussion while making their own statement.

- Fourth, *use a system that allows everyone to win.* "Loss aversion theory" suggests that the negative impact of losing is much more significant than the positive influence of winning. People are more concerned with negative consequences than potential advantages (Mosvick & Nelson, 1987, p. 59). An individual may receive much praise but what is remembered is one negative comment. Consequently, the leader needs to use descriptive feedback (see Chapter 13) so that individuals do not feel they are being attacked. Descriptive feedback simply describes a behavior or event without evaluating or attempting to interpret its meaning. I may say, "You were 15 minutes late to the last meeting and were 30 minutes late today. I get frustrated when I know you have missed important information." This is very different than saying, "You are always late. It shows you have no concern for others." Or saying, "I think you are always late because you simply don't plan ahead." The first alternative gets the message across without evaluating the person and lets the listener know how the behavior is affecting him or her as well. The second and third alternatives evaluate, blame, and interpret, encouraging greater defensiveness on the part of the listener.

- Fifth, don't forget that *meetings should be fun.* Introducing humor into a meeting may be just the thing to release some of the tension surrounding decision making. Sheila Feigelson's delightful text (1998) includes some great suggestions.

- Finally, in the decision-making process, *separate ideas from the people.* This allows the ideas to be assessed critically without individuals feeling they are being evaluated personally. A simple technique is to have all ideas expressed first and then, after the ideas are no longer associated with any individual, evaluate each idea. The use of these simple brainstorming techniques will go a long way toward ensuring protection of individual egos!

Essentially, the meeting leader must decide the goal of the meeting and act accordingly. If you want ideas, *really* want people to express their views, then you need to set up meeting perimeters that allow that to happen. If, on the other hand, you have already made up your mind and feel there are no alternatives, at least do your participants the courtesy of telling them ahead of time that you will be briefing them on your decision. Don't insult their intelligence by inviting their ideas and then making it perfectly clear that you do not want to hear them! And be prepared for "Murphy's Laws of Meetings."

■ MURPHY'S LAWS OF MEETINGS

- Rooms inspected in advance of your meeting will diminish in size by one-half between selection and use.
- A request for a "U-shape" table arrangement will be modified to a "W" to take into account the large columns that appeared overnight.
- The phrase "comfortable, stackable chairs" is a contradiction in terms.
- Material essential for premeeting preparation will not reach the participants. When it does arrive, it will not be read.
- By the time you arrive at your meeting with all necessary materials, prepunched holes will heal, clear printing will fade, collated materials will regroup, and felt pens will cast off their caps.
- Handouts will be 10% to 20% short, or enough will be left over to wallpaper a medium-sized ballroom.

- Ventilation and temperature controls will be part of the room decor and not intended to be functional.

- Guest speakers will bring a presentation prepared for a completely different group.

- When refreshments are served, one-half of the group will complain that there is not enough. The other half will observe that there is too much. All will complain about gaining weight.

- The PA system in use in an adjoining room will be piped into your meeting room as a convenience.

- For any equipment you bring, the extension cord will be 2 feet too short.

- For any situation not listed above, simply assume that your worst nightmare will be proven true.

P.S. This is the third time I had to type this sheet. The copy machine ate the first two!!!!!!!

Author Unknown.

The following story is from a long-time colleague and friend, Anita James. She has conducted hundreds (probably thousands) of training programs and worked with a wide variety of clients. The story she recounts of a meeting she was asked to facilitate for a university executive staff points out the problems a consultant can have when too many people think they are in charge of the meeting.

———— **LESSONS LEARNED** ————

A Consulting Story from Anita C. James:
Clarifying Who's in Charge

Anita C. James is an associate professor at Ohio University who teaches in the areas of organizational communication, training and development, and field research techniques. She conducts training programs and consults with business, government, and academic institutions in the areas of communication skills, management and supervisory skills, team development, and time management.

On Thursday, September 16th, 1999, I received the following email:

Anita: We have planned a "President's Retreat" for VPs and deans off-site on Sept. 29–30, beginning with lunch on the 29th and concluding with lunch on the 30th. I am writing to ask your help in facilitating that retreat. The principal subject will be "University Communication" and if you can do this I'd like to meet to get your thoughts on some of the organizational details.

Thus began a one-week planning process because we could not meet until the following week. I thought the first meeting would be with the president; instead, I received an email on the 20th that said, "I have scheduled Tues. Sept. 21st for this meeting with you and four top-level administrators [none of whom was the president] to discuss the 'president's retreat.' " This message was sent to me by a secretary.

At the first meeting, it became apparent that these four administrators wanted to control both the outcome of the retreat and the president (in terms of structuring his response), much as you would "handle" the president of the United States. The goal was to "develop a unified communications plan for the university." The specific goal for these four individuals, however, was to "get the president on board with our script." The entire schedule was laid out for me and I was asked to work around what they had already planned. I requested the following:

1. Sufficient time for groups to make decisions during their break-out times.

2. Time for me to produce a summary of the break-out groups' discussions because that summary would structure the groups' activities the next day.

3. I also insisted that I would randomly assign people to groups and they agreed. (I believed that if the top-level administrators had defined the groups, it would have been seen as one more indication of top-level attempts to manipulate the outcomes of the retreat.)

4. Finally, I requested that the total group remain just the top-level vice presidents and deans (about 20 people).

Two days later (less than a week prior to the retreat), I received via email a list of the break-out groups, which contrary to my recommendation had been assigned by the top-level administrators. I also noticed that this list had grown to a total of 39 people. I responded to this latest information with the following email to the president:

I have received and reviewed the list of participants for this week's retreat. As the facilitator, I have the following concerns:

1. The number of participants on my list is 39. This is a very large number to include as a "group of the whole" for critical decision-making activity.

2. The number of departments represented appears to number more than 18. This creates a situation where there are so many perceived competing agendas that achieving the goal of this retreat is very difficult.

While I recognize that it is difficult to "uninvite" anyone, the goal of the retreat is likely to be best achieved with the top-level administrators and deans in attendance. Those individuals would, when clear about the goals, communicate the information to their staff.

Respectfully, Anita

His response was:

Anita:

Understood, and I won't disagree. But we're committed to this now. We allowed the inclusion of a number of communication people because we wanted them involved, and I can't uninvite any VPs, deans, or faculty senate folks. We'll have to do the best we can.

The day before the retreat I received a list of groups and facilitators. I immediately sent the following message to the administrator in charge:

I just received a copy of the distribution of participants among the breakout groups. I note that facilitators have been appointed. It was my understanding upon leaving the meeting with you last Tuesday that the facilitators would not be determined in advance. Why was this agreement changed?

I realize I am the facilitator for the retreat and not in the policy-making group. If, however, we have agreed to something that, as a facilitator, I know makes a difference, then it is changed without consultation, and it makes my job more difficult.

Anita

The administrator claimed she forgot and simply acted on what the administrative assistant gave her. She ended her memo by saying, "My advice is to forgive and go forward as is. We're all working hard and running fast."

When it was time for the groups to begin their discussions, I was able to randomly assign facilitators by birthdays because the president intervened and requested that my instructions be followed. The person with the most recent birthday was the facilitator and the one with the next most recent birthday became the recorder. The retreat was actually quite successful. The top-level administrator wrote: "Thanks so much for being such an excellent facilitator. You really helped us move the conversation along, and we were, therefore, able to make significant progress on this very, very important topic. Thanks again for all your help."

Here are the lessons I learned from this experience:

1. If you're going to facilitate a retreat, being brought in after most of the planning has occurred is not a recipe for success.

2. If you believe strongly enough that a particular procedure is counterproductive, then you should insist on changing it.

3. Despite the rather abrupt tone of my message about the facilitators, the experience was ultimately a worthwhile one for the organization. Had I not maintained my position, I believe there would have been lingering suspicions in the minds of some participants about the validity of the process by which the outcomes were achieved.

You can reach Anita James at <james@ohio.edu> or by phone at 740-593-4840.

Additional Resources

Feigelson, S. (1998). *Energize your meetings with laughter.* Alexandria, VA: Association for Supervision and Curriculum Development.

Janis, I. L. (1972). *Victims of groupthink* (2nd ed.). Boston: Houghton Mifflin.

Lippincott, S. M. (1994). *Meetings: Do's, don'ts, and donuts.* Pittsburgh: Lighthouse Point Press.

Mosvick, R. K., & Nelson, R. B. (1987). *We've got to start the meeting like this.* Glenview, IL: Scott, Foresman.

Nadler, L., & Nadler, Z. (1987). *The comprehensive guide to successful conferences and meetings.* San Francisco: Jossey-Bass.

Chapter *11*

WHEN YOUR CLIENT ASKS: "HOW CAN I FACE THIS AUDIENCE?"

■ **WHEN WILL I EVER HAVE TO GIVE A SPEECH?**
Speaking Internally
Speaking Externally

■ **KNOWING AND UNDERSTANDING YOUR AUDIENCE**
How Will They React to the Content?
What Form of Presentation Will Deliver the Message?
What Is the Audience's Attitude toward You and the Event?
How Long Should the Presentation Be?

■ **STRUCTURE**
First Impressions
Opening Remarks
    Startling Statement
    Poignant Example
    Joke
    Impressive Statistics
Organization
    Cause-to-Effect Pattern
    Chronological Order
    Topical Approach
    Problem-Solution Pattern
Closing the Sale

■ **STRATEGIES**
Credibility
Reasoning and Supportive Material
Persuasion
Emotional Appeal

■ **DELIVERY**
Obstacles to Effective Delivery
Extra Pizzazz

■ **TIPS ON PUBLIC PERFORMANCE**

Lessons Learned: A Consulting Story from Sue DeWine

ADDITIONAL RESOURCES

242

The number one fear of Americans, above snakes and fear of death, is fear of giving a public speech.

From the Book of Lists

The capacity for oral expression, whether in conversation or in more formal contexts of communication, is a skill needed for both the clarity and pleasure of communication. Our neglect of the spoken word sharply distinguishes our society from that of ancient Athens, where elegance was the rule.

Joseph Katz,
Chronicle of Higher Education, 1982

The one universal skill of successful consultants is the ability to organize and express ideas.

T. J. O'Shea,
Presentation of Results, 1986

A leader must be able to handle a public moment of failure and embarrassment. Consider the following example from Gail Fairhurst and Robert Sarr's (1996) book on reframing messages and situations:

> City officials had planned an elaborate public ceremony around the implosion of a very tall structure in a major city. Government officials, employees, nearby residents, and members of the aggressive citizens' watchdog groups monitoring the cleanup process all gathered for the celebration. The moment all had waited for finally came. A series of loud pop-pop-pops sounded as fifty explosive devices went off in close succession. A cloud of mist and smoke swirled from the ground only to reveal that the 120-foot structure had dropped 45 feet—and then tilted at a fifteen-degree angle to the northwest. The crowd was silenced. Officials on the podium were stunned and embarrassed. One official had joked in her early remarks that she had two speeches prepared, one in case the demolition worked and one in case it didn't. But she hurriedly left the stage after the failed demolition and canceled her press conference. The Maryland construction firm on board to conduct the implosion had never had

one fail before. This was small consolation. The best that any of the officials at the podium could come up with was a remark from one, who said, "This is a credit to the construction workers of the forties." (p. 57)

In the days that followed, the building finally did come down, and the management teams took control of the "message" and communicated their commitment to a fast cleanup, reassuring people that the cleanup was proceeding safely. The authors end the story with this comment: "Whatever your position, whether you are in public affairs or not, if you lead people, your job is to manage meaning through framing. You cannot always control what happens in your environment, but you can influence how it is seen. If you do not manage meaning, others will step forward to do so—and they will not always be kind" (p. 199).

Most business leaders you will work with realize that presentation skills are critical to the success of any manager and yet few actually have those skills or demonstrate them on a regular basis. In the business world many people view themselves as highly competent individuals in a number of areas but do not tend to see themselves as effective speakers. "I received a pilot's license at the age of 40; I jumped from a plane as a sky diver a year later; I've tried many dangerous challenges, but I just cannot face an audience" (Makay & Fetzer, 1984, p. 35). The reason so many of us fear public speaking is we are afraid we will make fools of ourselves in front of a group.

As a consultant you may be asked to help a client improve his or her presentation skills. At the same time you must constantly be improving your own style since you will often be judged by your presentations. I have probably given hundreds of speeches during my career, and on those occasions when I was *not* nervous about it, I gave a less than stellar performance. Being nervous is an indication that you are excited about the occasion and want to do well. The trick is to learn how to turn that nervousness into positive energy and dynamic performances. I once had a colleague who was a theater major; she was backstage throwing up before every performance, and yet on stage she was brilliant! Overcoming stage fright begins by anticipating occasions when you will probably be called on to give a public presentation.

When Will I Ever Have to Give a Speech?

Most speaking occasions fall into two broad categories: internal presentations and company speeches to the public. Both can be critical to a manager's career. It is your job as a communication specialist to assist the manager with this communication task. You can offer your clients the following suggestions, as well as implement them when you make presentations yourself.

Speaking Internally

The 30-minute presentation you have been asked to give to corporate leaders could be the most important 30 minutes of your career. In those 30 minutes you can demonstrate you are self-confident, articulate, knowledgeable, and persuasive, or you can demonstrate you are nervous, unsure of yourself, and not clear about what you want your audience to do. Consultants must sell their services and present findings in a clear and uncluttered way. They must also help corporate leaders do the same thing.

Organization members are constantly asked to make internal presentations to colleagues, supervisors, and subordinates. In all cases, these speakers are being asked to sell themselves. If the speaker wants acceptance of a new policy, listeners have to trust the speaker before they will believe the policy is in their best interest. When the speaker is giving directions, listeners have to believe the speaker is knowledgeable enough to provide the details they need. If the speaker wants the boss to try out a new idea, the speaker must convince the boss that it is worth listening to.

One new manager with whom I worked was asked to brief his subordinates on a new product line. His anxiety increased as the day came closer; however, he was well prepared and had practiced some techniques to make his presentation effective. He found out later his superiors were using this occasion to help determine his potential to move into an upper-management position. On the day of his talk, he checked on the overhead and found out it had a burned-out bulb, which he replaced. He practiced presenting his talk in the room where it would occur and discovered he could not see his notes easily, so he had a small light placed on the lectern. Finally, as people filed into the room before his presentation, he greeted them at the door and learned five people were in the wrong session. Consequently, he avoided three disasters because he thought ahead and was prepared for potential problems. A good speech alone will not get a person a promotion, but a bad one can prevent upper management from selecting that person to play a more important role as an official company representative.

Speaking Externally

Corporate leaders are asked repeatedly to represent their organization in the public arena. Although current managers are more independent than the typical "organization man" of the 1950s, they still must understand the "party line." As Osborn (1991) suggested in reporting on Leingerger and Tucker's *The New Individualists*, the "organization man," with his faith in hierarchy and bureaucracy, no longer exists in this generation. Employees are more committed to what they do, to their professions, and to their work, but not to their company (p. 2). It will be even more important that corporate leaders, and the consultants working with them, understand the public relations nature of their talks.

Thrash, Shelby, and Tarver (1984) provided six strategies for external talks with an advocacy focus for the company. How a company responds to attacks and what it does to turn negative publicity around may very well spell success or failure for that corporation. The following six strategies can be used effectively for corporate advocacy.

1. *Withdrawal from confrontation* is used specifically to stop the escalation of the debate. The "no comment" is typical of this approach. You use it when it would be worse to respond to attacks than to try to answer them. It should be used carefully because it can easily have more negative consequences than positive. For example, the "attacker" gets to present the case without the opposite position being heard.

2. *Sleight of hand* focuses the audience's attention on something else, just as do the magic tricks from which this term was derived. This allows the company spokesperson to obscure a controversial issue. It may be viewed as ethically questionable because when the tricks are over, the objections still stand.

3. *Challenging opposing facts and arguments* is a strong position when you are able to refute the arguments as presented. You can weaken the attackers' position by proving their evidence is flawed, but the attacks may still have done their damage even if you are able to refute all issues.

4. *Redefining the issues* may be necessary if the facts presented by the attacker are true. You may need to point out the issues are not relevant or are misdirected. Sometimes this means identifying questionable assumptions about the facts made by the attackers.

5. *Presenting the company position* adds an important dimension to a presentation that has already exposed the opponent's arguments as invalid. It is important the audience understand fully what the company's stance is on the issues raised. You will need to identify the company position specifically, back it up with facts, explain the reason for the position, and explore the advantages and disadvantages of it. It is always better to identify the disadvantages yourself rather than have the opposing side state them in exaggerated terms.

6. Finally, you can adopt a *proactive approach* that anticipates the public's reactions and tries to resolve them before they are presented in a negative framework. Answering arguments before they become points of contention will result in fewer public relations problems for the company to handle. (Thrash, Shelby, & Tarver, 1984, pp. 156–157)

While internal and external speaking have different goals, the speaking techniques may be the same. Whether you are speaking internally or externally, a simultaneous first step with defining your purpose is knowing your audience.

Knowing and Understanding Your Audience

According to Mark Twain, "It takes three weeks to prepare a good ad-lib speech." Very few people can speak elegantly on the spur of the moment. Preparing yourself with information about the people to whom you will be speaking is essential. As Howell and Bormann (1988) suggested, communication events are joint ventures. "In a sense, people may say to one another, 'shall we communicate?' in much the same way that they might ask 'shall we dance?' " (p. 19)

How Will They React to the Content?

Before making a presentation speakers need to think about the audience and adapt the content and delivery of what they are going to say to the needs and interests of the audience members.

What are your goals for the presentation? What do you want your audience to know, believe in, or do as a result of your speech? Like readers of office memos, listeners to a speech need to know exactly what you want them to do as a result of receiving the message. How many memos bury the action step requested at the end of several paragraphs of background information? Often, people stop listening or reading long before they figure out what you are trying to communicate to them.

Do your audience members have the same background and level of experience as your own? The use of jargon and technical language can be an effective shorthand way of communicating to an audience, all of whom share a common understanding of the language. Complex, technical information may be essential as well for a highly trained and select audience. For an audience who may not have the same training or background as you do, the use of jargon, technical language, or complex information is not impressive; it is frustrating.

How much information do they already have on your topic? It is good to provide a short, simple summary of background information to make sure everyone has at least some common ground from which to understand your points. This background material, however, must be short, short, and shorter!

How were they selected to attend the presentation, or have they volunteered? A volunteer audience is very different from a group who is required to be there. If your audience did not select on their own to listen to you, you must develop an extended "need" step. This is your justification for why they need to listen. How will these ideas influence their daily lives? For example, if the topic is "teamwork," the audience may resent being told they must listen. Maybe they think they already function as teams! The speaker must convince them, early in the presentation, that information they are about to hear will make their jobs, or work lives, more pleasurable in some way.

What Form of Presentation Will Deliver the Message?

The size and composition of the audience and the physical facility determine the suitability of the form of presentation. Ask yourself the following questions:

Has the audience attended presentations similar to yours? How have they responded to such presentations? In other words, is this audience used to sitting and listening to formal presentations? Do they do this frequently? And do they seem to enjoy it? If they are "action-oriented" individuals who are *not* used to listening, you must provide some entertainment and high motivation for them to stay with you. Find out how they have reacted in similar situations. Are they likely to ask questions after the presentation, or, if you ask for questions, are you more likely to be met with a resounding silence?

How many people will be in the audience? Whether you choose to use a microphone, stand behind a podium, or move among the audience members will be determined by the size of the audience. Your nonverbal gestures have to be exaggerated with a larger audience. You can deal with 40 to 50 people as if they are still a small group, but any group approaching 100 might as well be 1,000! Once you are unable to see every face, and the audience is unable to hear you without amplification, then it doesn't matter how much larger the group gets because you will be using mass audience techniques anyway.

Will they be able to see visual aids clearly? Are there obstructions in the room that will prevent audience members from seeing anything you may display? It is always helpful to have some sense of how the audience may respond to certain types of visual aids. Using visual aids may be critical to your presentation. In Chapter 6 the advantages and disadvantages of various visual aids are discussed. This would be useful information to review for a public presentation. The items listed in the "emergency kit" have been absolutely vital to speakers in the past and will be quite useful to you.

■ EMERGENCY KIT FOR PRESENTATIONS

Paper towels
Small box of pushpins
Plug adapter (3-prong to 2-prong converter)
Extension cord(s)
Extension for slide projector remote control
Roll of masking tape
Small roll of transparent tape on dispenser
One box of assorted markers
12 manila file folders (when open to 19 by 12" they make a good emergency chart)
Transparency pens for writing on viewgraphs
1 box of transparencies (black on yellow)
Soft chalk (white and colored)
Eraser
Hand towel
Wet napkins
2 collapsible pointers
4 night-lights (for rooms having only off/on lighting)
1 8½ by 11" meeting pad
1 pocket-sized memo pad
2 pens
1 pack of 3 by 5" index cards
Calendar
Assortment of stomachache, headache, and/or cold medications
Box of throat lozenges
Various sizes of company logos
Corporate telephone directory
Small slide viewer or magnifying glass
6 translucent sheets with pockets for slides (in case major rearrangement or sorting is required)
White-out (for whiting out errors)
Single-edge razor blade
Scissors
Pocket knife
2 large clips (to hold charts in case easel is broken)
12 blank black slides
12 clear slides
Dime (for removing jammed slide trays)
Tweezers (for removing jammed slides)
Cricket (for slide change where no other signal is available)
Pocket flashlight
12 envelopes with stamps
Express mail or package service envelope and form
30 pieces of 8½ by 11" white card stock to fold in half for name tents
Stick-on name badges
Small American flag (in case you are accused of "flag-waving")

Source: Adapted from T. C. Smith, *Making Successful Presentations: A Self Teaching Guide* (New York: John Wiley & Sons, 1984).

Do some of the participants have special learning needs? For example, does anyone have visual, hearing, or mobility difficulties, and how can you accommodate these learners?

> I once conducted an entire seminar using flip charts posted around the room, only to discover two of the participants were legally blind and could not see a single word I wrote! A simple question before the presentation would have saved them, and me, the embarrassment of having to prepare transcripts of my presentation.

How much time will you have for the presentation, and will you include a question-and-answer period? Absolutely the worst thing you can do is go overtime. Even if you have given only half of your speech, once you are over the amount of time the audience has agreed to stay, you have lost them anyway! It is very tempting to squeeze in just a few final thoughts at the end. DON'T DO IT! Your audience will thank you. Err on the side of brevity.

These questions form a good checklist for the speaker prior to facing the audience. Insist on getting the answers before preparing your presentation. If you are unable to secure the information you want about the audience, you can ask a few questions in the beginning of your presentation and request a show of hands that will give you some general information about who is in the audience. In that way you can at least make some minor adaptations based on the information you get. For example, you can quickly access the number of males and females, number of supervisors and nonsupervisors, and so on.

What Is the Audience's Attitude toward You and the Event?

Finally, you need to have a sense of your audience's attitude toward you and the event. Margaret Bedrosian (1987) identified some of the audience you might be facing:

The audience might want you to win. This audience represents about 98 percent of the people you will be talking with. They don't want to waste their time and they are hopeful you will do a good job. The "halo effect" is the phenomenon that allows us to give a person extra chances to succeed initially. If you do not succeed, they will be disappointed too. However, there is that other 2 percent!

The audience might want you to fail. There is that other 2 percent of the people who would like to see you fail. Who knows why, nor is it important. For some perverse reason, their image of themselves improves as your credibility goes down. If you try to satisfy this small portion of the people listening, you will lose the rest of the group. Forget them! They have their own motivations to deal with.

The audience expects polish. Remember, we have significantly increased our expectations for presentations. Our audiences have been raised on MTV. They expect "flash." They will no longer accept a person's apology for not being a public speaker. They demand a polished performance. They expect you to be graceful, articulate, funny, timely, relevant, knowledgeable, and unbiased against any of the demographic groups represented among them. They expect you to be able to handle hostile questions without taking out your emotions on them. In short, they expect a lot!

The audience is easily bored. As Bedrosian pointed out, we are victims of a "million-dollar minute" mentality. Advertisers bombard us with short, dynamic messages. Audiences want to get the message in the shortest amount of time possible. Their attention span has shortened by about 90 percent in the last 20 years! You might as well assume they will start out bored and that your job is to wake them up so they will listen to a few short points.

The audience wants specifics. People respond best to human-interest stories that connect them to the presentation. I once talked about my father and his determination to succeed in this country and then connected it to a challenge facing the audience. Telling a personal story about my family did two things: made me more "human" and suggested how they might connect to the point I was trying to make. Remember that your audience is less involved in your topic than you are. Your job is to give them enough specific information and examples to make them want to learn more.

The audience will want to know what to do next. Unless you are giving an after-dinner speech for the sole purpose of entertaining, you will need to give your audience some specific actions to take. Do not expect them to figure it out on their own. Be clear about wanting them to vote, adopt your proposal, change their behavior, write to their legislators, or consider your new program.

> Tell them what to do, and if possible, link that recommendation to something they are likely to do in the next 24 hours. This helps create in them a "timed-release" reminder of their intention to act. Use phrases such as "Tomorrow morning when you face yourself in the mirror as you brush your teeth, say to yourself, 'This is the day I . . .' " or "The next time you set foot in an automobile ask yourself if you should . . ." or "Tonight when you take off your shoes and your feet revel in having their delicious freedom back, say to yourself. . . ." (Bedrosian, 1987, p. 58)

How Long Should the Presentation Be?

The title of one article says it all, "Less Talk Is More Convincing" (Whalen, 1990). How often have you heard people complain that a speech or presentation was too short? More often, their reaction is like that of the individual in the cartoon below: If the speaker says one more thing, we may scream! We have already learned more than we ever wanted to know about a particular topic! If you can't say it in 15 minutes or less, write it.

> My most difficult public speaking situation was the time I faced 8,000 parents and college students in a large convocation center made to hold 15,000. These graduation ceremonies were for M.A.s and Ph.D.s. Everyone is there to celebrate this moment of achievement for loved ones and no one wants to listen to a commencement speaker. The best thing you can do for them is be brief. I said that at the beginning of my speech and received applause. I also said if they would stick with me, hear only three points I wanted to make, I would promise to be brief. I actually had strangers coming up to me for years afterwards telling me they remembered those three points!

Structure

After analyzing your audience, you must begin to develop the structure of the speech. The organization of the presentation begins with the first impressions the audience has of the speaker.

First Impressions

The impression the group will have of you and your presentation starts with information they are given prior to your appearance. Usually, in a formal speech, this means the introduction. The introducer can do you a favor by providing a brief, but impressive, review of your accomplishments and credentials. Or, the introducer can inadvertently destroy your credibility by trying and failing to be funny, by identifying you with the wrong organization or project, or by misrepresenting your accomplishments.

The choices you then have are correcting (and embarrassing) the introducer, joking about yourself, or ignoring the bad introduction and depending on the introduction to your speech to set things straight. I usually ignore all but the most blatant mistakes. I also try to poke fun at myself in the beginning to try to balance the more elaborate introduction I have just received. You can avoid this problem altogether by writing your own introductions. Program planners will thank you and you will be sure the correct information is presented!

The audience's first impression of you continues as you approach them. What you wear, how you walk, the formality of the situation (which you may not have any control over), and the first words out of your mouth have great impact on the audience's willingness to listen. In a smaller audience, even your handshake leaves an impression.

Opening Remarks

The beginning of the presentation must capture the audience's interest, convince them to listen, overview for them what will follow, and connect you to the topic. If one of these elements is missing, then you have given the audience an excuse *not* to listen. There are a variety of ways to capture the audience's attention. The following describe some of those strategies used to open a speech.

STARTLING STATEMENT

"If we decide today to implement the following new policy, we can save the company $500,000 by the end of the month."

Such a statement is designed to make the listeners want to hear more. You have "teased" them with just enough information to suggest the rest of the presentation may be of particular interest to them.

POIGNANT EXAMPLE

"A customer in northern Ohio called the office yesterday to thank us for our new voice-activated dialing system. She has a 12-year-old son who is completely disabled and was unable to talk to his friends unless someone was there to dial and hold the phone for him. Until this new dialing system was installed, he could not have a private conversation with a friend. Imagine being 12 years old and having someone—especially your mother—listen in on all your conversations."

Here the speaker is trying to arouse the listeners' emotions. You want the example to remind them of the human side of an enterprise. In this case, it was designed to remind the listeners of the real value of developing new technology. Connecting an idea to everyday happenings helps to recognize the value of new products, services, or ideas.

JOKE

"With an introduction like that, how can I help but fail! *No one* can live up to such high expectations. Even God gets a day off every week!"

Jokes can easily backfire. Sometimes the most innocent comments can offend someone. The reference to God in the preceding example might be offensive to certain individuals. Plus, you cannot guarantee the joke is one people will laugh at. A "pregnant pause" following a joke is deadly. You must determine your success rate with humor prior to using it. I usually do not tell standard jokes, although I do use a lot of humor in my presentations. The form of humor I am best at is telling jokes about myself or teasing someone in the audience I am familiar with and know will not be offended by it. Use humor sparingly and when in doubt, *don't!*

IMPRESSIVE STATISTICS

"Cars that come off the assembly line on Fridays have twice as many problems as cars produced on any other day of the week. Each Friday, 14,500 workers are absent from work in our plants across the country and other workers must cover for their jobs. This means at least one in every 15 workers is unhappy on Fridays because they are having to cover for someone else. Unhappy people make mistakes."

To be used effectively, statistics must be impressive, rounded off to the next nearest whole number or round number, and applied to concepts that are easily understood. In the example above, the speaker took the 14,500 figure and made it more meaningful by pointing out how likely you would be to encounter these unhappy workers! After you have the audience's attention, your next task is to say something worthwhile in the body of the speech.

Organization

Any pattern can be an effective way to organize a speech. Some common structures are cause-to-effect, chronological, topical, and problem-solution.

CAUSE-TO-EFFECT PATTERN

First, a cause-to-effect pattern makes the audience aware of the relationship between some observed occurrence (the effect) and the event leading to that occurrence. For example, a window salesperson first demonstrates the loss of heat from a home and then claims the cause is air leakage around the windows.

CHRONOLOGICAL ORDER

A chronological pattern is especially useful when an executive is tracing the history of a problem or a product. When decisions are being made about the future of some project or product, everyone needs to have the same sense of history about the development of the project or product. A chronological approach creates a sense of joint ownership of the historical process.

TOPICAL APPROACH

Topical patterns are used when the general topic can be broken into smaller parts to be easily understood. For example, when a new benefits package is being introduced, the subtopics might include health, education, and retirement benefits. This helps the listeners organize their thinking and remember the main points.

PROBLEM-SOLUTION PATTERN

Problem-solution is my favorite structure for a speech. Answering these four questions can make the arguments clearer:

1. *What is the problem?* It is important that the audience understand early in your talk exactly what issue or problem is being addressed. Most people have a low tolerance for ambiguity.

2. *What are the implications of solving or not solving it?* The speaker must create a strong motivation on the part of the audience for solving the problem. There are many problems in the world we cannot solve or don't really care to solve. It is the speaker's job to convince the audience this is not one of those problems.

3. *How can it be solved?* Nothing is more frustrating than to listen to someone tell you about a crisis, get you interested in solving it, and then fail to provide any action for you to take. We have enough problems in our daily lives, so we don't want to hear about more of them and then not have any way to help solve them. That's simply too depressing!

4. *What's in it for the people listening if the solution is implemented?* The ultimate question the audience will ask is, what is the payoff for them if they get involved? There are very few, if any, truly selfless persons

in this world. We all need to feel we will benefit in some way. Perhaps it will make life more pleasant for our family, and thus ourselves. Perhaps it will make our job easier to do or will make us feel some pride in our affiliation with the company. In any case, it is the speaker's job to convince the audience members that they will benefit directly from the speaker's solution to the problem.

Closing the Sale

Recently, I have been actively involved in a university's $100 million campaign for private donations. I meet with alumni and corporate leaders around the country selling the university story. I am quite comfortable telling that story. As a consultant I have never had difficulty selling my services, but in consulting I am usually asked what my fees will be. In development work, if you don't *tell* prospects the amount you want from them, they will never ask. "Making the ask" is the equivalent of the salesperson's closing request for the order, and it is the final step in a persuasive appeal. Unfortunately, it is the very step many people shy away from. They stop their persuasive appeal right before the ask.

I found I had to relearn this principle for development work. In one case, the development officer and I had finished an elegant meal in New York City with an alumnus. We had talked all evening and reminisced about his time at the university, and I had taken an opportunity to detail future plans for the school with him and received good advice for our programs. I was ready to end the evening when the development officer expertly injected the ask into the conversation, which had been the primary goal of this trip. I almost missed making the ask altogether.

Quick (1988) told the story about the man who prays each week that God will let him win the lottery. After many months without winning, the man adds in desperation, the plea, "Lord, give me a break. Let me win the lottery!" From heaven comes a booming voice, "Give me a break, Sam. Buy a ticket." You won't get what you want by waiting for it to happen! You must initiate action.

Strategies

Three thousand years ago Aristotle identified the three basic forms of appeal to an audience: ethos, logos, and pathos. *Ethos* refers to the speaker's credibility or believability with the audience, *logos* refers to logical and factual appeals, and *pathos* refers to emotional appeals.

Credibility

We *want* to believe people we trust, like, or respect. Once the speaker's credibility is established, the audience is ready to listen and believe. How do you establish it? First, the way in which you are introduced to the audience will set the initial impression. As I mentioned earlier, I usually prepare my own introduction for someone to read. The presenters like this because it saves them the trouble of having to pick out the most notable points in your career. You will like it because you will be able to control what is said about you. I have been identified with the wrong organization, had my name mispronounced, had jokes told about me that were not funny, and had such a complete summary of my talk revealed that I wasn't sure there was anything new left to tell! Be prepared to counter a bad introduction.

Second, the beginning of your speech can indicate your level of training, education, or experience with the topic. You need to establish yourself as an expert without sounding like you are bragging. For example, by saying, "Although I have been a communication consultant for over 25 years, I am still amazed at how often major organizational problems are caused by poor human relationships." I have indicated the extent of my consulting experience in an indirect way.

Third, the detail with which you present material can convince the audience that you understand the subject and have something to share with them. It is critical that you find out how much they already know and that you have researched the topic thoroughly enough to be able to present new and interesting information to them.

Fourth, I always try to make personal contact with the audience before I begin so that they see me as a person like them. I may greet audience members at the door as they come in or walk among the audience before the speech begins and introduce myself to them. It is amazing how much friendlier the audience is to you if they have shaken your hand before you begin speaking.

Reasoning and Supportive Material

No matter how expert you are at the subject, you need *strong logic, expert testimony*, and *factual information* to back you up. The speaker presents the data and then makes a claim. The data must be reliable research findings, detailed examples, and information from other experts all taken from sources the audience trusts. The following questions will help you assess the quality of your information:

- Is the support accurate and reliable?
- Is the support directly related to the claims?
- Is the support the best available?
- Is the support information I can understand, accept, and believe?
- Is the support relevant to the needs of the audience?
- Is the support information the audience is likely to recognize, understand, and accept? (Makay & Fetzer, 1984)

Statistical data can be a form of support that is quite impressive or misleading and confusing. When using statistics make sure they are clearly understood by rounding them off, displaying them in graphs or charts, and giving them meaning by comparing them to some common example. I have colleagues who have made very effective use of visual aids to clarify statistical information; I have seen others receive snickers from the audience because the visual aid was poorly displayed, presented incorrect information, or was so confusing no one could translate it.

One speaker held up a 2-foot by 2-foot poster in a room with 75 people in it. Only those in the first few rows could read it. I observed another speaker read percentages from a written report that did not correspond to the percentages on the overhead. By the time she was finished, everyone was confused! I have also watched individuals try to explain a chart with vertical and horizontal axes and get the audience lost in meaningless graphics when the point could have been made simpler.

Reasoning from the data is even more important. If the speaker is not able to help the audience make the connection between the factual information and the actions they should take, then the facts are useless. *Cause-to-effect, either-or reasoning, generalizations,* and *problem-solution* can all be used effectively to make this connection between facts and desired outcomes.

Speakers need to be careful when using cause-to-effect reasoning that they are not simply connecting two effects and assuming that since one occurred before the other, it must have caused the second. The Food and Drug Administration is especially cautious about such reasoning by scientists. Either-or reasoning can be very effective if the speaker has been able to eliminate all other possibilities in the minds of the audience. Then the desired outcome is compared with a less desirable outcome to lead the audience to accept the speaker's solution. Generalizations, either inductively or deductively derived, are common uses of the reasoning process. Demonstrating for an audience that a large category has this characteristic, and since this item is in that category then it too has this characteristic, can be a very appealing deductive reasoning. Inductive reasoning, of course, would take the small examples, add them together, and form a major conclusion. Finally, in a problem-solution pattern the speaker must be careful to discuss how the solution would work, what its benefits would be (especially to audience members), its costs, and advantages.

Persuasion

In presentations of any kind you are essentially trying to persuade your audience of something. The goal may be to persuade them to adopt an idea or solution you are proposing or simply to accept you and your services. In any case, you are trying to get them to "move" in some direction even if it is only to retain certain kinds of information. Essentially the speaker wants to build the case based on "common ground" with the audience. What ideas and beliefs do they have in common with you? The speaker must build those ideas into the presentation and then slowly indicate where they might diverge.

Every client you work with will need to persuade individuals to adopt a viewpoint or support an organization-wide effort of some sort. "If there ever was a time for businesspeople to learn the fine art of persuasion, it is now. Gone are the command-and-control days of executives managing by decree. Today businesses are run largely by cross-functional teams of peers and populated by baby boomers and their Generation X offspring, who show little tolerance for unquestioned authority" (Conger, 1998, p. 84). Too often we think that public addresses and persuasion need to be only logical and rational. Yet we know that even successful corporate executives can be influenced by emotion. "Good persuaders are aware of the primacy of emotions and are responsive to them in two important ways. First, they show their own emotional commitment to the position they are advocating. Such expression is a delicate matter. If you act too emotional, people may doubt your clearheadedness. Second, persuaders must have a strong and accurate sense of their audience's emotional state, and they adjust the tone of their arguments accordingly" (p. 84). Helping a client do a complete audience analysis is probably the best support you could give. Not knowing the attitudes and interests of the audience may antagonize rather than gain support.

Gail Fairhurst and Robert Sarr (1996) identified one approach to managing leadership that would also suggest ways to help a client present a memorable message. They defined "framing" as "a quality of communication that causes others to accept one meaning over another" (p. xi) and they identified five tools for framing.

1. *Metaphors* describe your subject's likeness to something else. You use them when you want a subject to take on a new meaning but avoid using it when the metaphor will mask important alternative meanings.

2. *Jargon and catchphrases* frame your subject in familiar terms. Catchphrases can enhance meaning but they should not be used when a word or phrase is in danger of overuse, like "We've got to break the squares today."

3. *Contrast* illuminates your subject in terms of its opposite. It is sometimes easier to define what your subject is not than to state what it is. "This change process is not a slow-moving sailing boat but more like a speeding bullet."

4. *Spin* casts your subjects in a positive or negative light. A spin can reveal your subject's strengths and weaknesses but the spin cannot be excessively divergent from reality. "Which manager will show up?

The one who is cooperative and generous or the egotist who constantly reminds others of his successes and what is due him?"

5. *Stories* make your subject more real by way of example. Stories attract attention and can build rapport. But they can also mask important alternative meanings. "When I first came to this organization, I was young and inexperienced." (p. 100)

Emotional Appeal

We are not moved by logic alone. In fact, we often are more persuaded by our emotions, particularly when combined with factual information. Facts may convince us, but emotion will more likely make us take action. Among the emotional appeals that can be used successfully are empathy for a cause or a person, anger at some injustice, conviction of some value or moral principle, and excitement over some change. The ethical speaker, of course, uses emotional appeals along with sound reasoning and factual data. The unethical speaker may use emotional appeals that sidestep factual information.

Delivery

Unfortunately, sometimes the way you present something becomes more important than the content. Your goal is to ensure your delivery of the message does not "get in the way of," or distract from, your message. Your delivery will encourage or discourage the audience from listening.

Obstacles to Effective Delivery

Montgomery (1981) identified several characters that create a poor impression as public speakers. *Martha Mumbler* is a person who can easily be misunderstood. She swallows her words and speaks too softly. Her voice trails off at the end of sentences and she mumbles her words. *Roger Rambler* is a person who rambles on and on, never pausing for a reply. He never asks questions, just talks. *Slow-Speaking Sal* is a person who may put you to sleep with her monotone voice and her slow speaking. Your mind can work much faster than she can speak anyway.

Confidential Cal is a person who implies that everything is so important or so secretive that he speaks in a low, confidential tone, not so much hushed as it is muffled. *Nancy Nasal* constantly talks through her nose. It is such an easy, lazy way of speaking, it doesn't take much effort at all. *Shifty-Eyed Sam* is honest but his eyes cause others to doubt his sincerity. His eyes are always darting around, a glance at the side, eyes following any movement or sound. *Hesitating Herb* is never sure of himself. He verges on a stutter many times. It could be caused by a lack of confidence in one's own ability or vocabulary but it could also be a bad habit that gets worse with practice (pp. 30–60).

Practicing your speech with a video camera should make you aware of any annoying behaviors you have. In a recent presentation I watched, a speaker continually grabbed hold of the speaker's stand. This wouldn't have been so bad except the stand had a movable top and every time he grabbed it, it banged down on the top of the desk. Caught up as he was in his speech, he was completely unaware of the banging sound he was making throughout the speech.

Along with eliminating distracting mannerisms, the speaker must work to make the presentation interesting. You do this through the excitement in your voice, positive facial expressions, and gestures and movement that serve to enhance your speech.

You also need to check on the preparation of the room. The "Speaker's Checklist" will remind you of some of these details.

Once you have analyzed your audience and adapted to it, caught its attention in the introduction, organized your persuasive appeals into some logical sequence, and practiced effective delivery techniques, you are ready for a little "pizzazz."

Extra Pizzazz

There are techniques that, handled with finesse, add a clever twist to your presentation. Smith (1984) discussed a number of techniques that add "pizzazz" to your talks. Be careful they don't come off as "hokey." Here's one I've seen work.

Tell your audience that you will offer them a chance at a million dollars for their thoughts. Buy ten lottery tickets, tape them on a flip chart in the front of the room, and hand them out to the first ten ideas expressed by the group. It may just be the incentive you need to get discussion going.

Another technique I have seen work was used by a Professional Secretaries International group. Summarize your main points by providing each participant with a "survival kit" that contains representations of the points you are making. Their points were inspirational and included the following:

- a *toothpick* to remind you not to be too picky
- a *lollipop* to help you lick your problems
- a *rubber band* to help you be flexible
- a *paper clip* to help you hold things together
- a *caramel* to help you "chew the fat"
- a *stick of gum* to give you "stick-to-it-iveness"

■ THE SPEAKER'S CHECKLIST

Room

Reserved in advance.
Floor plan sent in advance.
Temperature and ventilation.
Coat racks in "secure" location.
Clean up in advance.
Six square feet per attendee?
Excess chairs removed.
Will corner seats in front row be
    able to see screen clearly?
Adequate clear space up front
    for you and equipment.
Divide large groups into smoking
    and nonsmoking.
Close blinds to eliminate distractions.
Must windows be blacked out?
Build speaker's platform with
    one-foot risers for larger groups.
Wastebasket, trash container.
Tape door latches for silence during
    late arrivals.
Table for hand-outs, etc.

Breaks

Refreshments scheduled.
Table for coffee, etc.
Wastebasket.
Restroom locations.
At least one break for every two
    hours (more frequently in
    afternoons).

Place Settings

Name tents, pencils, pads, water,
    ashtrays.
Broad felt-tipped markers for name
    tents (one for every three attendees).
Agenda for longer meetings.
Rolls of mints or candies.

Projector(s)

Who will supply projectors?
Tables or stands supplied.
Plugged in, aligned, and focused.
Any light fixtures in the way?

Lenses dust-free.
Spare bulbs on hand.
Take-up reel available for movie
    projector.
Extension cords taped to floor,
    outlets, and table legs.
Electrical circuits adequate to
    handle full load plus coffee urn,
    etc.
Remote control working properly.

Projectionist

Has marked script or cue sheet.
Has signal light or headphone
    buzzer.
If green, yellow, and red timing
    lights are used, agree on
    schedule.
Small light available for
    projectionist.

Sound

Mike and speakers working.
Practice putting lavaliere mike on.
Feedback problems?
Check levels and set if required.
Do you want talk recorded?

Screen

Large enough for readability.
High enough for visibility. (Bottom
    of screen should be $4^1/_2$ feet
    above floor.)
Fill screen with image.
Does image keystone?
Any hot spots from overhead
    lights?
Offset for viewgraphs.

Lighting

Adjustable?
Levels checked out and marked.
Who will work the lights?
Will auxiliary lights be required?
Windows adequately draped.

Signs

Room location sign in lobby or hall.

Meeting title on room door.

Message board for day-long sessions.

"Quiet Please—Meeting in Session."

Easel/Chalkboard

Fresh pad.

Fresh markers, varied colors.

Chalkboard cleaned.

Colored chalk.

Eraser.

Lectern

Light working?

Timer working? Noisy?

Water nearby.

Signal to projector/projectionist.

Pointer available.

Props hidden.

Script or cue sheet ready.

Height properly set.

Does it block anyone's view of screen?

Handouts

Arranged in order.

Conveniently located.

Evaluation forms or surveys.

Current reprints.

Where do you want hand-outs?

When will you distribute?

Visuals

In correct order.

All right-side up.

Extra blank viewgraph sheets.

Movies or videotapes advanced to proper start.

Source: Adapted from T. C. Smith, *Making Successful Presentations: A Self-Teaching Guide* (New York: John Wiley & Sons, 1984).

- a *piece of string* to help tie up the loose ends
- a *pin* to help you pinpoint problems
- a *penny* so that you will have enough "cents" to realize what a valuable asset you are to your profession!

All the italicized items were in a small bag. I adapted this technique to a speech on team building, but you could use it in a variety of ways. It was a great success and helped reinforce the points of my talk. The disadvantage is, it takes a good deal of time to prepare and only a very few minutes to present, but I thought it was worth it.

Another "jazzy" technique I have seen used is to have the audience visualize objects around the room. Walk around as if you are telling a story: "If I were in a home, over here might be the TV, next to the bookcase . . ." and so on. At the end have the audience repeat all the objects you identified and where they were located. The first letter of each object stands for a word you are trying to get them to remember. At the end, have them say the object as they visualize it, then the word it stands for, and in five minutes you can demonstrate how they can memorize a dozen or more concepts or ideas.

Tips on Public Performance

- Develop one standard presentation that you can always give on short notice. The topic should be a general "inspirational" topic. Here is the one I give. It is based on the "Four 'Cs' of life: Challenges, Commitment, Creativity, and Choices." The message is, accept challenges, do something with your life you are committed to, allow your creativity to flourish, and remember no one can make you feel a certain way or behave a certain way. We choose how we will react to any situation. Then I tell a story with each word.

   You can pick your own words to base your presentation on: "Success depends on *attitude, anticipation,* and *actions.*" Or, "Keep your sales presentations *short, simple,* and *sincere.*" Your stories may come from your own life. The key is the ideas and stories are so familiar to you that you are able to present them without warning. You will realize the advantage of having such a speech prepared the first time you're asked to "say a few words" on the spur of the moment.

- Start with developing the introduction and the ending. These are the most important steps and the most likely to be remembered. I always want to know exactly what the first and last words out of my mouth will be. I have seen too many speakers begin with a few worthless comments and end by mumbling, "I guess that's all I have to say for now." That is a poor way to leave the audience.

- Use examples relevant to the audience. Although your topic could be appropriate no matter what occupations or interests your audience may have, your examples must come from their daily lives. I recently gave a speech to 800 employees of an insurance company. Although I talked about listening carefully to customer needs, the talk was filled with investment product operations language, and their organizational values of service, integrity, adoption of change, accountability, and partnerships. The words used to express these values had been in print in a variety of organization publications and it was critical that my talk be tied to them.

- Practice using video cameras. You will be your own worst judge. Seeing yourself on camera, preferably on a large screen, will tell you better than any person can, what nonverbal distractions you may be incorporating in your speech. Remember that you will always look heavier and sound more nasal on tape than you appear to others (or let's hope so anyway!).

- Know your style and control the situation you get into. For example, if you are not normally a funny person, do not agree to be a stand-up comic after a banquet! If you are not good at extemporizing a speech, do not agree to deliver a speech away from a podium and have to fumble with your notes. Take the "Challenge Readiness Inventory" (Form 11.1) to help you determine what situations you'll be most comfortable with.

- In short, a public speech is like a sales pitch. "Know your product, know your prospect, involve the prospect, ask for action, and be prepared to handle opposition" (Quick, 1988).

- Try these techniques to control your nerves:

   Be prepared. The best defense against a nervous stomach is preparation and constant practice.

   Imagine what the speech will be like. Walk yourself through the speech in your mind, down to the last detail including what the audience will look like.

   Use stress reducers, which include relaxation techniques. Simply moving your shoulders up and down right before you speak will help. I find that 10 minutes of silence, sitting down by myself, does wonders for my concentration and poise.

   Focus on your message. If you really believe in what you are talking about, you will have a much easier time focusing on the message and not on the audience's reaction to you.

- Finally, keep your presentations *short, simple, and sincere!*

Check your readiness to give a presentation by completing Form 11.1, the "Challenge Readiness Inventory."

CHALLENGE READINESS INVENTORY

More than 100 business and professional leaders recently surveyed for The Synergy Group business newsletter named the following 16 challenges for today's well-rounded business presenter. Although you need not excel in all areas to succeed, the greater your versatility, the better prepared you are for success. You might want to take this test to rate your own readiness.

For the following 16 questions, rate your comfort level for the given challenges, and *circle the appropriate number* (0 = totally uncomfortable, 10 = totally comfortable). Then *put an asterisk next to the number you would like to reach in the future.*

1. Present a complete and concise briefing or report at a staff meeting.   0 1 2 3 4 5 6 7 8 9 10

2. Present a proposal or sales talk with appropriate documentation to a client group.   0 1 2 3 4 5 6 7 8 9 10

3. Meet one-on-one with colleagues, supervisors, employees, clients, community representatives, or reporters.   0 1 2 3 4 5 6 7 8 9 10

4. Deliver a 5- to 10-minute all-purpose, amusing, and motivating talk to groups from 3 to 3,000.   0 1 2 3 4 5 6 7 8 9 10

5. Deliver a 30- to 60-minute informative and persuasive talk to groups from 3 to 3,000.   0 1 2 3 4 5 6 7 8 9 10

6. Present 12 minutes of legislative testimony on a timely, specific industrial issue.   0 1 2 3 4 5 6 7 8 9 10

7. Participate in a panel discussion on some current controversy.   0 1 2 3 4 5 6 7 8 9 10

8. Participate in a friendly television interview lasting up to 15 minutes.   0 1 2 3 4 5 6 7 8 9 10

9. Participate in an aggressive interview during a crisis.   0 1 2 3 4 5 6 7 8 9 10

10. Introduce a major luminary in your field to 6,000 delegates at your international convention.   0 1 2 3 4 5 6 7 8 9 10

(Continued)

CHALLENGE READINESS INVENTORY *(Continued)*

11. Present a prepared speech from a text that your boss, delayed in flight, was supposed to deliver. 0 1 2 3 4 5 6 7 8 9 10

12. Work with a speechwriter to prepare and present a formal policy statement for your organization. 0 1 2 3 4 5 6 7 8 9 10

13. Present a one-minute television editorial on the benefits your industry brings to society. 0 1 2 3 4 5 6 7 8 9 10

14. Write and deliver three to five humorous comments for a "roast" of a boss, colleague, or friend to celebrate his or her recent accomplishments. 0 1 2 3 4 5 6 7 8 9 10

15. Participate in a lively question-and-answer session after one of your presentations. 0 1 2 3 4 5 6 7 8 9 10

16. Prepare and present a one- to three-hour training session with appropriate material for people just entering your field. 0 1 2 3 4 5 6 7 8 9 10

Now find the total of the numbers circled and the total of the numbers marked with an asterisk. Subtract the total of the circled numbers from the total of starred numbers, and read about your score below.

A score of 0 to 20 is Superb! You are close to your productive level of mastery in most areas. You may wish to keep reading to polish your skills and pick up pointers on how to help other people develop.

A score of 21 to 40 is Good. You are well on your way to full flexibility. A small investment of your time and energy can pay off handsomely.

A score of 41 to 60 is Average. You are sometimes at a disadvantage in a new presenting situation, but you recognize that you can overcome this handicap.

A score of 60+ is Challenging. You have a major project in front of you, one well worth the effort. Be sure to set small, achievable goals, work toward them regularly over time, and reward your successes along the way.

I have never wanted to be a speechwriter, and yet I often find my-self coaching someone through a public presentation. One of the most important skills a presenter can have is an ability to analyze the audience correctly. In this consulting story, the speaker was facing a potential "angry mob." My job was to help him be posi-tive and encouraging, and at the same time make an audience aware of great risks.

LESSONS LEARNED

A Consulting Story from Sue DeWine

Besides being the author of this book, Sue DeWine has run a consulting firm for over 25 years serving Fortune 500 companies, government agencies, education institutions, and professional associations. Currently she focuses on executive coaching (as illustrated by the following story) and strategic planning.

Recently I coached an executive through a public presentation where he was facing a rather hostile audience. It was his job to explain that the or-ganization was in financial troubles, would be replacing its top leader-ship, and for the time being was "leaderless," and to give them hope for the future all at the same time. Rumors were rampant. Coming into this session, people feared for their jobs. Creating a sense of hope was a huge challenge. At the same time it was critical that the audience understand the seriousness of the position the organization was in so they would all participate in cost-saving steps. Here are excerpts from the email I sent him providing some guidance for the development of the speech:

Tom:

Here are some basic ideas for us to talk through for your address.

1. "These are extraordinary times for _____ organization. We are facing challenges and opportunities unlike any in recent times."

2. "These challenges are financially based and necessitated the board putting in place processes and procedures that are outside what would be the nor-mal way to conduct business and make decisions at _____."

3. Causes for the financial problems:
   - *Income problem:* income is down 15 percent so we have made no progress toward meeting the growth projection.
   - *Spending problem:* we are spending too much relative to the new revenues we receive. Put another way, for the level of spending we do, we are not getting enough "bang for the bucks"—not enough return on investments.
   - The resulting deficit spending is being financed out of investments. It cannot continue. We're pulling out too much of the return we get on the invested endowment. In the current year we will have to draw out over $4 million to cover the deficit gap and pay for various special projects.

4. "Because our CEO and CFO are retiring at the end of this year, the board felt it was necessary to establish a strategic planning committee. This committee is made up of the president's staff and top-level officers. It is the charge of this committee to present a strategic plan to the board by the May meeting. This plan must establish a direction for the organization, identify our strengths, and address areas of weakness."

5. Then you need to provide some good news like:

   "This situation provides us with the unique opportunity to re-establish our pride in this organization, our long and illustrious history, and the strength of our employees. It also allows us to identify some unique opportunities."

6. Final statement should reinforce why you are addressing them and repeat how serious this is:

   "I was asked by the strategic planning committee to address you tonight because we wanted to be sure that everyone fully understood:
   - the seriousness of this situation;
   - the importance of the strategic planning process; and
   - how critical it is that we come together as a community to support efforts to protect our future.

   We know you have heard some of this message before. The board is now convinced that this is our last chance to turn the situation around.

   You will soon be asked to attend one of several open meetings to discuss the ideas developed by the strategic planning committee. I urge you to participate fully in these meetings. Please understand that this committee will need the best thinking represented in the organization and your full support once the plan is agreed to."

How should we then handle comments or questions? We need to try to control the specific questions because you don't want to get into details of any decisions the committee has already made. Perhaps you could end with a statement like the following:

"I am happy to answer general questions about the process; however, at this early stage I cannot address specific issues or decisions the committee has made or will make."

It's better to let them know what the boundaries are rather than get them thinking they'll get the answers to specific questions. In fact, it would be a good idea to put out this type of message in the invitation to the meeting. Nothing is worse than people thinking they are coming to a meeting where they will get a chance to challenge something and then be told at the time that those kinds of questions won't be entertained.

Let me know what you think. I'll try to reach you later today.

Over the next several days we crafted the final version of his message, which included much of what is listed above. It was critical that he communicate both messages at the same time. We did not want people to leave feeling hopeless; nor did we want them to ignore the seriousness of the situation.

The speech was as successful as possible, given the situation. This was not happy news he was reporting. However, a clear understanding of the situation is always better than what people imagine. The job of a coach for an executive presentation is to frame for the speaker the task he or she is facing, making him or her aware of probable obstacles in the minds of the audience. Audience analysis is key. You must know how the audience is thinking and what information is available to them prior to hearing the talk. The goal is for the audience to leave with a clear idea of what the speaker wants them to do or believe. And don't forget to coach them in delivery techniques! It is amazing to me how awkward some corporate leaders are in the public arena!

You can reach Sue DeWine at <dewines@marietta.edu> or by phone at 740-376-4741.

Additional Resources

Bedrosian, N. M. (1987). *Speak like a pro: In business and public speaking.* New York: Wiley.

Urech, E. (1998). *Speaking globally: Effective presentations across international and cultural boundaries.* Dover, NH: Kogan Page.

Walters, L. (1995). *What to say when . . . you're dying on the platform.* New York: McGraw-Hill.

Chapter **12**

CAN THIS GROUP WORK AS A TEAM?

Team-Building Techniques

The concept of synergy suggests that activities carried on by groups are more likely to produce higher levels of outcomes and higher quality output than activities carried on separately by individuals. There is, therefore, incremental value in team or group efforts which is missing in individual efforts.

J. *Hite*, Learning in Chaos, *1999, p. 174*

*F*rancis and Young (1979) defined a **team** as "an energetic group of people who are committed to achieving common objectives, who work well together and enjoy doing so, and who produce high quality results" (p. 8). The term *energetic* is important. A successful team looks forward to tackling difficult problems and identifying plausible solutions. From this definition, a team might seem to be the ideal approach to solving all of an organization's problems, but that is not always so.

Readiness for Team Building

One of the most important insights for any consultant or manager to have is to know when team building is not appropriate. One unit head recently solicited my assistance with developing a group of managers to work collaboratively and do a better job of decision making. One of these managers was in the process of being fired, a second was filing suit against the head of the unit, two others were assigned only part-time to that unit and had loyalties elsewhere. For the period of time in which two members were on their way out, it seemed obvious to me that this was not a time to build a team. In fact, this group *could not* become a team during that period of time. It is unreasonable to expect an individual who is in litigation against other members of a group to collaborate and sit around a table, helping to reach consensus or compromise on decisions facing that group. The unit head would be much better served to deal with the staff as individuals and avoid bringing them together as a group at all.

You can ask a client the following series of questions when a new group is being formed. This will help determine the likelihood of success for this new team or group. These questions, adapted from Harrison and

Shirom (1999), can be raised prior to the formation of the group or as the group moves through various stages.

1. What is the main task for this new group?

2. What are the critical task demands (e.g., effort, knowledge, skills)?

3. How much authority will the group need, and how much will be given? Are group members willing and able to operate under these conditions?

4. How will the leader of the group be chosen (e.g., manager-led vs. self-led)? What are the implications for the decisions based on leadership in the group?

5. How feasible is it to assign these tasks to a team? What are the benefits and liabilities of assigning them to a group?

6. How should group tasks be structured?

7. What material resources are needed, and can these be obtained? What organizational supports are needed and available?

8. How can the team be helped to work together effectively? How will members develop constructive norms and group processes?

9. How will group boundaries be defined?

10. How will members be assigned tasks and how will they renegotiate their tasks and assignments as they work on them? (p. 169)

When Not to Attempt Team Building

As the facilitator of team building, you will have the job of assessing the need for team building and determining its importance. In the preceding example the need for team building was not strong enough to overcome the barriers. In addition, the timing was the worst. You cannot build a team when other serious issues have to be resolved first.

In another example, a key executive in a group with whom I was working was the main reason for low morale and discontent. He would be gone in three months. This definitely was not a time to build a team with this executive and the rest of his staff.

A third reason for not using team building focuses on the degree to which the climate will support team building. In one organization, the mid-level managers were interested in working more closely together and yet at each step of the process, the unit head pitted them against each other and created a very competitive environment. Team building needs support from the top to be successful.

Do not use team building if teamwork is not necessary to achieve the work group's goals. For example, some projects require individual effort rather than team effort. Also, team building should not be used unless team members understand the purpose and requirements of team building and are committed to the process. The group must first recognize the need to work collaboratively as a team.

A colleague of mine at the vice presidential level in a financial institution was hired to be the quality control vice president and came into a group of top-level executives who did not perceive themselves to be a team but rather as independent and separate entrepreneurs. Often decisions were being made that benefited one unit but actually hurt the total effort of the organization. This group did not have a commitment to teamwork.

Additional times when team building seems unwise are when the company is undergoing extensive organizational change or when membership or leadership is about to change. Finally, when the particular team is working under an unusually great amount of pressure, team building should not be used. Wait until the crisis passes.

How to Determine Readiness

There are occasions when a large group of very diverse individuals have a common reason for wanting to work collaboratively. This was true of a group of medical affiliated individuals with whom I worked. One group was hospital administrators; the second group was the doctors; the third group was association members who served on the boards of directors of the hospitals. The history of these three groups was they were often in competition or direct opposition, and each felt they could survive on their own without the assistance of the others.

At the time I was asked to facilitate a large group setting, they were facing some problems and consequences that demanded they be collaborative. If the doctors, for example, did not send their patients to the hospitals, the hospitals' costs would soar and the institutions would not survive. If the hospitals, on the other hand, did not make the environment conducive and profitable for the doctors, then the doctors had no base of support. The association was interested in maintaining both the hospitals' and doctors' practices because that kept the association alive. These hospitals were facing patient shortages and had empty beds. As the meeting began, the historic relationship among these three groups surfaced, and they remained somewhat separate and antagonistic toward each other. It was critical that they understand the reality of their situation and figure out how they could build a team toward the common goal of success in the medical profession.

READINESS OF THE ORGANIZATION

In testing an organization's readiness for team building one should consider the following questions and use them as guidelines:

Do members of the work group in question need to work as a team?

Does the corporate climate support teamwork?

What problems and/or objectives does the work group have? Can the problems be solved and the objectives be met through team building or is some other intervention more likely to be successful?

Do the group manager and members believe team building is needed? Will they approach the activities positively and energetically or consider them a waste of time?

Will the group manager and members take responsibility for conflicts identified by the activities? Will the group be committed to conflict resolution?

Will the group manager and members be willing to change work methods and mind-sets, based on what they learn through team building?

Is now a good time to do team building? Can the company afford to let the group shift their efforts right now from regular work to team building? Are any changes in group membership or leadership expected in the near future?

Is there money in the budget for team building? (Spruell, 1987, p. 1)

These conditions, when met, provide a climate in which team building is most likely to occur. Assessing a group's readiness for team development is aided by such self-analyses as Shonk's (1982) (see Form 12.1).

TEAM DEVELOPMENT QUESTIONNAIRE

The following questions have been designed to *identify how* you feel *this team is functioning,* specifically, what *areas* you feel *need improvement.* The results will be compiled for discussion at an upcoming team-development meeting. You will have an opportunity to review a summary of question-naire results prior to the team meeting. You should be thinking about dis-cussing your responses and the responses of others at this meeting.

Where there are multiple choices, check only one answer. Please be as candid and specific as possible.

Key Issues

Goals

1. List the goals that require members of this team to work together.

_____

_____

_____

_____

_____

2. With regard to the goals of this team the people on this team are

_____ very committed.

_____ somewhat committed.

_____ somewhat resistant.

_____ very resistant.

Team goals that I feel have *low* commitments are:

_____

_____

_____

Team goals that I feel have *high* commitments are:

_____

_____

_____

(Continued)

TEAM DEVELOPMENT QUESTIONNAIRE *(Continued)*

3. To what extent do you know and understand each team member's goals?

   _____ very knowledgeable about team members' goals
   _____ fairly knowledgeable about team members' goals
   _____ somewhat vague knowledge of team members' goals
   _____ very vague knowledge of team members' goals

   Goals I would like to know more about are:

   _____

   _____

   _____

4. The goals of members of this team are

   _____ strongly in conflict.
   _____ somewhat in conflict.
   _____ a little in conflict.
   _____ not at all in conflict.

   The key conflicts I see are:

   _____

   _____

   _____

Roles

1. The roles of the members of the team are

   _____ very clear to me.
   _____ fairly clear to me.
   _____ somewhat unclear to me.
   _____ very unclear to me.

   Areas I would like to have clarified concerning my role are:

   _____

   _____

(Continued)

TEAM DEVELOPMENT QUESTIONNAIRE *(Continued)*

Areas in which I am unclear about what others expect of me are:

_____

_____

_____

Areas I would like to have clarified concerning others' roles are:

_____

_____

_____

2. Team members roles overlap

_____ very much.

_____ quite a bit.

_____ somewhat.

_____ not at all.

Roles that overlap are:

_____

_____

_____

3. Team members' roles that are in conflict are:

_____

_____

_____

Procedures

1. The decision-making process on matters that affect more than one member of the team is

_____ very clear.

_____ fairly clear.

_____ somewhat unclear.

_____ very unclear.

(Continued)

TEAM DEVELOPMENT QUESTIONNAIRE *(Continued)*

Decisions that need to be clarified are:

_____

_____

_____

2. Thinking of all the communications within this team, I would say they are

    _____ good with all members of the team.

    _____ good with some members of the team.

    _____ good with very few members of the team.

    _____ not very good with the majority of the team.

    Subjects that I feel need to be better communicated:

    _____

    _____

    _____

3. Team meetings

    _____ are very effective.

    _____ are fairly effective.

    _____ need some improvement.

    _____ need much improvement.

    I would like team meetings to be improved in these specific ways:

    _____

    _____

    _____

    _____

4. I believe the leadership of this team

    a. is helping the team's performance by:

    _____

    _____

    _____

(Continued)

TEAM DEVELOPMENT QUESTIONNAIRE *(Continued)*

    b. could improve the team's performance by:

_____

_____

_____

5. As teams work together, behavior patterns are established that help or hinder the team performance such as

   - following up or not following up on decisions.
   - raising or not raising sticky issues.
   - facilitating or delaying decisions.

   Do you feel that there are such patterns that inhibit this team's effectiveness?

   _____ Yes

   _____ No

   If yes, what are they?

_____

_____

_____

Relationships

1. Conflicts within the team are

   _____ openly discussed/resolved.

   _____ discussed somewhat.

   _____ very seldom mentioned.

   _____ not discussed at all.

   A conflict that needs to be resolved to improve the team's performance is:

_____

_____

_____

(Continued)

TEAM DEVELOPMENT QUESTIONNAIRE *(Continued)*

2. Relationships I would like to discuss are:

_____

_____

_____

3. What is causing stress for you and/or other members of the team?

_____

_____

_____

Environmental Influences

1. What constraints or influences outside of the team keep it from working more effectively? Please explain.

_____

_____

_____

General

1. What do you believe are the team's key strengths?

_____

_____

_____

2. If you could, what would you do to make this team more effective?

_____

_____

_____

Analysis of Key Issues

Please review the attached summary of responses to the team development questionnaire. Use this sheet to list what you believe are the major
issues for discussion/resolution and indicate their relative priority.
A = high, B = medium, C = low. These issues will provide the basis for
discussion at an upcoming team development meeting.

(Continued)

TEAM DEVELOPMENT QUESTIONNAIRE *(Continued)*

1. Environmental influences

_____
_____
_____
_____

2. Goals

_____
_____
_____
_____

3. Roles

_____
_____
_____
_____

4. Procedures

_____
_____
_____
_____

5. Relationships

_____
_____
_____
_____

6. Other

_____
_____
_____
_____

If a team is getting ready for team development, the members will have to find answers to these questions:

1. What are we here to do?
2. How shall we organize ourselves?
3. Who is in charge?
4. Who cares about our success?
5. How do we work through problems?
6. How do we fit in with other groups?
7. What benefits do team members need from the team? (Francis & Young, 1979, p. 8)

These organizing questions help get the group started. You might pose them at the first team-building meeting and ask the group to address them collectively.

MIND-SET OF THE GROUP READY FOR TEAM DEVELOPMENT

In order for any group effort to be successful, everyone connected to the group must have the same mind-set about groups in general. A belief system that assists a team-development program begins with the conviction that the group faces significant areas that need improvement and that the team has the power to do something about these issues. Team members must be willing to do a real diagnosis of the problems to identify tangible, achievable short-term results. The members must be committed to the team process. That means that they must accept the importance of feelings and attitudes; they must realize that the motivation for change comes from within; and they must recognize the interdependence of the teammates and be willing to risk new ways of working together (Shonk, 1982, pp. 24–26).

There are many reasons why an organization would want to develop a positive climate for team building. The following section lists a few of these advantages.

Advantages of Team Building

The 1990s saw the rise of a team focus in organizations. Total Quality Management (TQM) became a major contribution to organizational success. "TQM began in Japan just after WWII and transferred to the United States in the early 1980s, following American management's awakening to the fact that Japan was outperforming U.S. industry not only in costs but in quality and that Japan's superior performance was due, in no small measure, to its practice of continuous quality improvement based on Deming's theory and methods" (Argyris, 1999, p. 39).

In a meta-analysis of 63 studies, Nicholas (1982) found team-building interventions to be the second most effective intervention on measures of productivity and job behavior after structured laboratory training efforts. Team building had "an impact of 50 percent for every variable category measured" (p. 536). In another meta-analysis study of 126 studies, Neuman, Edwards, and Raju (1989) also found team building and lab training to be the most effective means of changing satisfaction and other attitudes. Clearly, team building generates a variety of positive results. "Team development in its best sense is creating the opportunity for people to come together to share their concerns, their ideas, and their experiences, and to begin to work together to solve their mutual problems and achieve common goals" (Dyer, 1987, p. 5).

Team building generates a variety of positive results for the group as a whole and for the individual members. The group benefits from the breadth of resources the individual members bring to the team. The combined talents and skills of the members allow them to manage complex issues creatively. Mature teams are capable of making better quality decisions than all but the most brilliant individuals. Hence, the use of a team should improve the overall quality of decisions. Furthermore, well-developed teams are capable of responding quickly and energetically.

For the individual member, the collective strength of the team may counteract the common concern that it is hard to influence organizations and make an impact outside the person's immediate area. The team changes this feeling as team members extend their viewpoint to see that they, together, can achieve a great deal. The team can feed the individual's need to have a sense of personal significance, and team processes motivate activity and achievement on the part of the members, together and individually (Francis & Young, 1979, p. 15).

Criteria for Evaluating Teams

These positive attitudes about teams on the part of members help make a team successful. There are other ways to determine a team's success. Responsibility for evaluating the efforts of the team may be the responsibility of the members themselves or the manager to whom they report. In either case, Francis and Young (1979, pp. 7–8, 60–61) offered the following characteristics as criteria for judging a team's effectiveness.

Output

The test of a team is its capacity to deliver the goods. A team is capable of achieving results that the individuals it comprises cannot do in isolation.

Objectives

A team needs a purpose that is understood, shared, and felt to be worthwhile by its members. This purpose can be described as the team's mission. The effective team is clear about its objectives. It sets targets of performance that are felt to be stretching but achievable. A goal should be within reach but should stretch the team's capabilities.

Structure

A mature team has dealt with thorny questions concerned with control, leadership, procedures, organization, and roles. The team structure is finely attuned to tasks being undertaken, and individual talents and contributions are used without confusion. With well-organized team procedures, roles are clearly defined, communication patterns are well-developed, and administrative procedures support a team approach.

Effective structure implies appropriate leadership. The team manager has the skills and intention to develop a team approach and allocate time to team-building activities. Being a team doesn't mean the group is leaderless. One group I worked with couldn't get past the "polite" stage where no one wanted to step forward and take charge. Statements like "I'd be happy for you to do it," "I think I'll let someone else take over this time," and "I don't want to step on anyone's toes" go beyond politeness and lead to useless activity. Every team needs leadership.

Every team also needs suitable membership. Team members must be individually qualified and capable of contributing the mix of skills and characteristics that provide an appropriate balance. Team members need to be well-developed individuals, and the team thrives on strong individual contributions. Each member offers something unique.

Energy

Team members need to take strength from one another. Collectively they feel more potent and find that team activities renew their vitality and enjoyment. Together, members develop effective work methods, including lively, systematic, and effective ways to solve problems together. Teamwork has to be fun and energizing.

Atmosphere

A team develops a distinctive spirit, a climate in which people feel relaxed, able to be direct and open, and prepared to take risks. This constructive climate allows for openness among members and for their support and simple enjoyment of one another. Team members feel a sense of individual commitment to the aims and purposes of the team. They are willing to devote energy to building the team and supporting each other. Team building cannot be done at the convenience of individual members.

A healthy atmosphere fosters the team's ability to create new ideas through the interactions of its members. Innovative risk taking is rewarded, and the team supports new ideas from members or from outside. Team and individual errors and weaknesses are examined without personal attack to enable the group to learn from its experience. The ability to provide critiques without rancor, to separate the person from the idea so that ideas, not people, can be criticized is a crucial skill for teams and their consultants and managers.

The team must have an open climate, where individuals feel free to raise problems and concerns without fear of being attacked. Individuals must be ready to accept feedback when it is freely given. The scale for rating team development (Form 12.2) can be a useful tool for determining the success of your team-building program.

TEAM DEVELOPMENT SCALE BY WILLIAM G. DYER

1. To what extent do I feel a real part of the team?

1	2	3	4	5
Completely a part all the time	A part most of the time	On the edge, sometimes in, sometimes out	Generally outside, except for one or two short periods	On the outside, not really a part of the team

2. How safe is it in this team to be at ease, relaxed, and myself?

1	2	3	4	5
I feel perfectly safe to be myself; they won't hold mistakes against me.	I feel most people would accept me if I were completely myself, but there are some I am not sure about.	Generally, you have to be careful what you say or do in this team.	I am quite fearful about being completely myself in this team.	A person would be a fool to be himself or herself in this team.

3. To what extent do I feel "under wraps," that is, have private thoughts, unspoken reservations, or unexpressed feelings and opinions that I have not felt comfortable bringing out into the open?

1	2	3	4	5
Almost completely under wraps	Under wraps many times	Slightly more free and expressive than under wraps	Quite free and expressive much of the time	Almost completely free and expressive

4. How effective are we, in our team, in getting out and using the ideas, opinions, and information of all team members in making decisions?

1	2	3	4	5
We don't really encourage everyone to share ideas, opinions, and information with the team in making decisions.	Only the ideas, opinions, and information of a few members are really known and used in making decisions.	Sometimes we hear the views of most members before making decisions and sometimes we disregard most members.	A few are sometimes hesitant about sharing their opinions, but we generally have good participation in making decisions.	Everyone feels his or her ideas, opinions, and information are given a fair hearing before decisions are made.

(Continued)

TEAM DEVELOPMENT SCALE BY WILLIAM G. DYER *(Continued)*

5. To what extent are the goals the team is working toward understood and to what extent do they have meaning for you?

1	2	3	4	5
I feel extremely good about goals of our team.	I feel fairly good, but some things are not too clear or meaningful.	A few things we are doing are clear and meaningful.	Much of the activity is not clear or meaningful to me.	I really do not understand or feel involved in the goals of the team.

6. How well does the team work at its tasks?

1	2	3	4	5
Coasts, loafs; makes no progress	Makes a little progress; most members loaf	Progress is slow; spurts of effective work	Above average in progress and pace of work	Works well; achieves definite progress

7. Our planning and the way we operate as a team is largely influenced by:

1	2	3	4	5
One or two team members	A clique	Shifts from one person or clique to another	Shared by most of the members, some left out	Shared by all members of the team

8. What is the level of responsibility for work in our team?

1	2	3	4	5
Each person assumes personal responsibility for getting work done.	A majority of the members assume responsibility for getting work done.	About half assume responsibility, about half do not.	Only a few assume responsibility for getting work done.	Nobody (except perhaps one) really assumes responsibility for getting work done.

9. How are differences or conflicts handled in our team?

1	2	3	4	5
Differences or conflicts are denied, suppressed, or avoided at all costs.	Differences or conflicts are recognized, but remain unresolved mostly.	Differences or conflicts are recognized and some attempts are made to work them through by some members, often outside the team meetings.	Differences or conflicts are recognized and some attempts are made to deal with them in our team.	Differences or conflicts are recognized and the team usually is working them through satisfactorily.

(Continued)

TEAM DEVELOPMENT SCALE BY WILLIAM G. DYER *(Continued)*

10. How do people relate to the team leader, chair, or "boss"?

1	2	3	4	5
The leader dominates the team and people are often fearful or passive.	The leader tends to control the team, although people generally agree with the leader's direction.	There is some give-and-take between the leader and the team members.	Team members relate easily to the leader and usually are able to influence the leader's decisions.	Team members respect the leader, but they work together as a unified team with everyone participating and no one dominant.

11. What suggestions do you have for improving our team functioning?

_____

_____

_____

_____

Group Roles

In order to pull a team together, the facilitator must be keenly aware of the variety of roles played out in most group settings. Some of these roles will render the group dysfunctional, while other roles are necessary for success.

Schein's Categories

Schein (1988) has identified group roles in three categories: task functions, building and maintenance functions, and boundary management functions, as Table 12.1 shows.

TABLE 12.1

SCHEIN'S GROUP ROLES

Task Functions	Building and Maintenance Functions	Boundary Management Functions
initiating	harmonizing	boundary defining
information seeking	compromising	scouting
information giving	date keeping	negotiating
opinion seeking	encouraging	translating
opinion giving	diagnosing	guarding
clarifying	standard setting	managing entry
elaborating	standard testing	managing exit
summarizing		
consensus testing		

Source: Schein, 1988, p. 50.

TASK FUNCTIONS

As you will recall from Chapter 10, *task functions* are those behaviors that help the group accomplish the job they have to do. For example, *someone* must initiate, or get the conversation started. Giving and receiving information and opinions ensure all group members share common information. Consensus testing is checking to see whether there is agreement among the group members.

MAINTENANCE FUNCTIONS

Maintenance functions are those that help hold the group together. Usually these actions deal with interpersonal relations and help members resolve and cope with conflict in the group. "Date keeping" makes group members aware of the difference between attitudes shaped by past experience and those based on current events.

BOUNDARY MANAGEMENT FUNCTIONS

Boundary management functions are those that link this group to others and the organization as a whole. For example, where do the responsibilities for this group begin and end and how can we find other groups to whom we might be related?

New Groups

Schein (1988) identified four problems of the individual entering a new group (pp. 41–42). First is identity: Who and what am I to be in this group? Second is control, power, and influence: Will I be able to control and influence others in this group? Third is needs and goals: Will the group goals include my own needs? Fourth is acceptance and intimacy: Will I be liked and accepted by the group; how close a group will we be? Those are individual challenges. There are also conditions that are not supportive of group activity. A new group may experience a series of conditions under which team building would *not* work such as the following:

- Team members have varied perceptions of overall team goals.
- There is confusion about the roles, responsibilities, and authority of each team member.
- The team lacks effective procedures for planning, problem solving, and decision making.
- Members frequently feel tense or bored and members lack commitment to the team.
- Members have poor interpersonal relationships and conflict is unmanageable.
- Communication is poor and criticism is abusive.
- Members feel overly dependent on or rebellious toward the team leader.
- Members do not feel of equal importance to the team.
- Members believe team authority is distributed unfairly.
- Members believe financial or other rewards are distributed unfairly.
- Evaluation of team progress is missing.
- Evaluation of team procedures is missing.

Any of these conditions can lead to the failure of the team development.

Types of Organizational Groups

There are many versions of teams in organizations today. One is the "self-managed" team. "**Self-managed teams** are small groups of co-workers (perhaps 8–15) who share tasks and responsibilities for a well-defined segment of work. At best they exhibit the principles of 'whole work'—planning, executing, and measuring whole operations, whether building whole components or providing one-stop shopping services for clients" (Jessup, 1990, p. 79).

Quality circles are another form of teams in organizations. **Quality circles** are groups of employees taken from various levels and units in the organization who meet with a facilitator to solve organization problems and make recommendations to upper management. Despite their initial praise, many report their lack of success. For example, Goddard (1988) reported that 57 percent of quality-circle programs fail because the work culture or management or both are unsupportive. There is no evidence that participative-type programs produce superior organizational performance if the company's overall management style is autocratic. In fact, in an operation where the job is well defined and managers and employees are comfortable with a directive approach, the costs of introducing a participative style may outweigh the benefits (p. 20). Employee-involvement programs must be tied to specific performance objectives (e.g., increased productivity and lower costs).

Bell and Rosenzweig (as reported in French & Bell, 1990) listed the essential ingredients for an effective work team:

> Get the *right people* together for a large block of *uninterrupted time* to work on *high-priority problems* or opportunities that they have identified and that are worked on in ways that are structured to enhance the likelihood of *realistic solutions and action plans* that are *implemented enthusiastically* and followed up to assess actual versus expected results. (p. 132)

Team-Building Session

A team-building session (seminar, workshop, retreat) must start with increasing the level of comfort with the group facilitator and with each other. If you are running the group as an outsider, then you will have to take extra time to bridge the gap between being a threatening stranger who may change people's lives for better or for worse and being a trusted guide who will lead this group through transformations resulting in more effective output.

One of the ways to increase the comfort level of the group is by establishing norms such as those described in the following sections.

Voluntary Participation

Anytime I have worked with a "mandatory attendance" group I have spent a great deal of time coping with their frustration. At the very least, I can make their participation voluntary once they are in the group. To the extent possible, you want the group to have chosen to participate in a group effort. Some people simply aren't "group" people and need the freedom and time to work independently.

Debriefing Time

However the facilitator designs activities and group work, there should always be more time devoted to discussing how an activity relates to their work world than to doing the activity itself. Every time I have tried to rush a group because I wanted to squeeze in one more activity or experience, I have regretted it.

Openness and Trust

The concept of reciprocity is acted out in terms of the openness of the relationship. If I am open with you, if I exhibit trust in you, you are much more likely to reciprocate than if I ask you to initiate trusting me first. The communication manager/consultant must maintain some distance and be careful with the type of information he or she reveals (see Chapter 19) because the overture may be misinterpreted and at the same time demonstrate the kind of openness that is *desired* about work-related issues.

Guidelines for Confidentiality

Participants have to have a sense of security before they can achieve co-operation. Basic needs must be met first. Therefore, the consultant/facilitator must talk about the importance of leaving what is said inside the session. He or she must also be overly cautious at first not to reveal inadvertently any information shared during early sessions until permission is given by the group and trust has been formed.

Conflict Resolution

Most groups have interpersonal conflicts of one kind or another. Working through those conflicts is a prerequisite for team work. This doesn't mean everyone present has to like or enjoy working with every other person in the team, but it does mean that every person present must have at least reached a level of comfort that they can work with every member of the team. Chapter 14 details more information on working with conflict and difficult situations as well as "difficult people"!

Much of the work in organizations is accomplished through the joint efforts of a team. Chapter 10 provided tips for running team meetings. This chapter has covered the importance and characteristics of building teams. Together, they should help you understand how groups function in organizations. The fact is, groups are used extensively, particularly with the implementation of participative decision making. It is not possible, therefore, to avoid participating in group action unless you lead a life of isolation.

Group Activities

The following are a few examples of team-building activities. For hundreds of others see *The Annual Handbook for Group Facilitators: Training and Consulting* published by Jossey-Bass/Pfeiffer, 1972–2000. These series of notebooks contain the best group activities I have ever seen. Each volume contains group activities, simulations, instruments, lectures on current human resource issues, and research material. I have used them for years and continue to get each new edition.

One of the easiest team activities takes no preparation on the part of the consultant and has never failed to help individuals experience almost immediate identity with the group. Here are the instructions you give to the group:

> "First, I'd like you to divide into groups according to the colors you are wearing today. Everyone with red on is in one group, and so on."

There are many variations of this procedure, like the type of shoes people are wearing, or giving them some characteristic to find out about others like common hobbies or sports. The advantage of this activity, rather than letting them find groups on their own, is that it avoids that childhood fear of not being selected to be in a group. It also provides a fun way to identify with others rather than just counting off groups.

> "Your group will have 10 minutes to determine the following:
>
> - the name of an animal that describes your group
> - a slogan for your team
> - a cheer with appropriate gestures to present to the rest of the group."

I have often used these identifiers throughout the rest of the workshop. Groups are very creative and immediately form a sense of team when they must present their "cheer" to everyone else.

Another one of my favorite activities, "Broken Squares" (Form 12.3), was first published in 1972. I have used it with children, college professors, and corporate executives. It has never failed me. The point of the activity is to demonstrate that in order for the group as a whole to succeed individuals sometimes must give up their personal goals. It's a hard lesson to learn in real life but this activity is a nonthreatening way to bring home the point.

BROKEN SQUARES

Goals

I. To analyze certain aspects of cooperation in solving a group problem.

II. To sensitize the participants to some of their own behaviors that may contribute toward or obstruct the solving of a group problem.

Group Size

Any number of groups of six participants each. There will be five participants and an observer/judge.

Time Required

Fifteen minutes for the exercise and fifteen minutes for discussion.

Materials

Chalkboard, chalk, eraser

Tables that will seat five participants each

One set of instructions for each group of five participants and one for the observer/judge

One set of broken squares for each group of five participants

Physical Setting

Tables should be spaced far enough apart so that the various groups cannot observe the activities of other groups.

Process

The facilitator may wish to begin with a discussion of the meaning of cooperation; this should lead to suggestions by the groups of what is essential in successful group cooperation. These may be listed on the board, and the facilitator may introduce the exercise by indicating that the groups will conduct an experiment to test their suggestions. Basic suggestions that the facilitator may want to bring out of the groups are as follows:

1. Each individual must understand the total problem.
2. Each individual should understand how he or she can contribute to solving the problem.
3. Each individual should be aware of the potential contributions of other individuals.

(Continued)

BROKEN SQUARES *(Continued)*

4. There is a need to recognize the problems of other individuals, in order to aid them in making their maximum contributions.

Instructions for the Facilitator

1. When the preliminary discussion is finished, the facilitator chooses an observer/judge for each group of five participants. These observers are each given a copy of their instructions. The facilitator then asks each group to distribute the envelopes from the prepared packets. The envelopes are to remain unopened until the signal to work is given.

2. The facilitator distributes to each group a prepared packet that consists of one copy of the instructions and a set of broken squares.

3. The facilitator then reads the instructions to the group, calling for questions or questioning groups as to their understanding of the instructions. It will be necessary for the facilitator or his or her assistants to monitor the tables during the exercise to enforce the rules that have been established in the instructions.

4. When all the groups have completed the task, the facilitator engages the groups in a discussion of the experience. Discussion should focus on feelings more than merely relating experiences and general observations. Observations are solicited from the observers/judges. The facilitator may want the groups to relate this experience with their "back home" situations.

Directions for Making a Set of Squares

A set of broken squares consists of five envelopes containing pieces of cardboard that have been cut into different patterns that, when properly arranged, will form five squares of equal size. One set should be provided for each group of five persons.

To prepare a set, cut out five cardboard squares of equal size, approximately 6 × 6". Place the squares in a row and mark them as shown, penciling the letters *a, b, c,* etc., lightly, so they can be erased later.

The lines should be so drawn that, when cut out, all pieces marked *a* will be of exactly the same size, all pieces marked *c* of the same size, and so forth. By using multiples of 3 inches, several combinations will be possible that will enable participants to form one or two squares, but only one combination is possible that will form five squares 6 × 6".

After drawing the lines on the 6 × 6" squares and labeling them with lowercase letters, cut each square as marked into smaller pieces to make the parts of the puzzle.

(Continued)

BROKEN SQUARES *(Continued)*

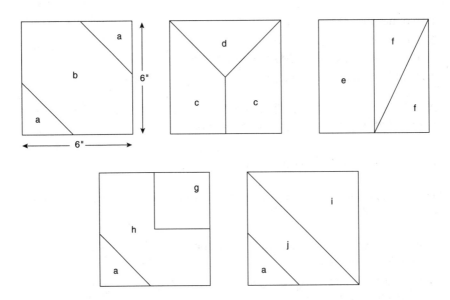

Mark the five envelopes A, B, C, D, and E. The cardboard pieces will be distributed in the five envelopes as follows:

Envelope	has	pieces
A		i, h, e
B		a, a, a, c
C		a, j
D		d, f
E		g, b, f, c

Erase the penciled letter from each piece and write, instead, the appropriate envelope letter. This will make it easy to return the pieces to the proper envelopes for subsequent use when a group has completed the task.

Instructions to the Group

In this packet there are five envelopes, each of which contains pieces of cardboard for forming squares. When the facilitator gives the signal to begin, the task of your group is to form *five squares of equal size*. The task will not be completed until each individual has before him or her a perfect square of the same size as that held by every other member of your group.

Specific limitations are imposed upon your group during this exercise:

(Continued)

299

BROKEN SQUARES *(Continued)*

1. No member may speak.
2. No member may ask another member for a card or in any way signal that another person is to give him or her a card.
3. Members may, however, give cards to other members.

Are the instructions clear? [Questions are answered.] Do not start until the facilitator gives the signal to begin working.

Instructions to the Observer/Judge

Your job is part observer and part judge. Make sure each participant observes the rules:

1. No talking, pointing, or other kind of communicating among the five people in your group.
2. Participants may give pieces to other participants but may *not* take pieces from other members.
3. Participants may not simply throw their pieces into the center for others to take; they have to give the pieces directly to one individual.
4. It is permissible for a member to give away all the pieces to his or her puzzle, even if he or she has already formed a square.

Do your best to strictly enforce these rules.

As an observer, you may want to look for some of the following:

1. Who is willing to give away pieces of the puzzle?
2. Did anyone finish the puzzle and then somewhat divorce himself or herself from the struggles of the rest of the group?
3. Is there anyone who continually struggles with his or her pieces but yet is unwilling to give any or all of them away?
4. How many people are actively engaged in mentally putting the pieces together?
5. Periodically check the level of frustration and anxiety—who's pulling their hair out?
6. Was there a critical turning point at which time the group began to cooperate?
7. Did anyone try to violate the rules by talking or pointing as a means of helping fellow members solve their puzzles?

The following story is one of my most memorable consulting experiences. Sandy Cheldelin and I have cofacilitated a number of times and I am always amazed by her skill. I have asked for her help with groups when I knew I could not do what was needed because I was an "insider"; and she has asked for my help in some situations when she felt she needed assistance. In this case, Sandy asked that I assist her and I have never been so thankful that I was not working with a group alone! Sandy was masterful in a very difficult situation.

LESSONS LEARNED

A Consulting Story from Sandra Cheldelin and Sue DeWine: Can This Group Ever Work Together Again?

Sandy Cheldelin is Director of the Institute for Conflict Analysis and Resolution at George Mason University. She has consulted with educational and industrial organizations for over 25 years. She and Sue have served as a consulting team on a number of occasions when one or the other of them felt the need for additional expertise or support.

Sandy had been working with a medium-size manufacturing organization for several months when the CEO asked her to facilitate an off-site retreat of the executive officers and the board of directors. The main topic to be discussed was a succession plan for replacing retired board members. Sandy asked Sue to cofacilitate the retreat, despite the fact that only ten participants would be present. Sue wondered at the time why there would need to be two facilitators for such a small group; however, Sandy proved to be psychic. Three to four facilitators would not have been too many given the direction the retreat took.

Sandy and Sue worked very hard the first day to report the results of one-on-one in-depth interviews they had conducted previously with each member of the team. Many issues about board membership, replacing members, and establishing goals for the board for the next five years were identified. By dinner time Sandy and Sue were feeling that most of the work had been completed and the following morning sessions would be an easy wrap-up of the decisions they had made. They relaxed and began to enjoy the elegant dinner that had been planned for the group.

Later Sandy and Sue learned that some of the team members had had several strong cocktails prior to the dinner and the group as a whole consumed a number of bottles of wine that evening. The private dining room was dimly lit and the group seemed quite mellow after such an intense day of discussions. Just as the group was finishing dessert, the chairman of the board, out of the blue, said to the CEO, "You know, Mike, your liberal ideas have often become a problem for this firm. Your Peace Corps radical left-wing approach to life is a little too much to take." Suddenly, the room was quiet and Sandy and Sue were immediately "awakened" out of their lulled sense of well-being. The CEO responded, "Edward, you're nothing more than an upper-class preppie." And they were off. As their voices became louder, you could physically feel the other members around the table shrinking into their chairs, hoping that no one would notice them witnessing this nasty attack by the group's two leaders.

There had always been tension between these two men. Edward was the retired leader of a successful industrial firm and served as a consultant to competitive firms. He was outspoken and not supportive of Mike. He felt Mike was "soft" and not a strong leader. Mike, the first non-family member to lead the firm, believed he was a participative manager but was more autocratic than he liked to admit.

The conversation didn't get better, despite Sandy's and Sue's interventions suggesting there might be a better place and time for this discussion. In fact, it turned even uglier. Mike said, "You know my life has not been as easy as you think. Did you know that my daughter won't even talk to me? That she's accusing me of attacking her?" At this point, Sandy and Sue wanted to disappear along with the rest of the team. No one wanted to hear this disclosure. Mike and Edward were sitting on opposite sides of the table, with Sandy by Edward and Sue by Mike. Both Sue and Sandy physically and psychologically tried to calm both men. We also attempted to paraphrase the feelings they were expressing without repeating the awful content of what they were saying to each other. At one point, Mike was on his feet pacing and Edward was half out of his seat. We both thought they could easily get into a physical match if we didn't stop the discussion immediately. During a pause, Sandy and Sue both jumped in and suggested the group leave. In ten seconds the room was cleared. No one could get out fast enough. We continued to talk with both men, then they left as well.

The most critical question was, "Could this team ever work together again?" The two leaders had said such ugly things to each other, witnessed by other team members, that it seemed impossible for them to move on. We both felt one of them would have to leave the organization. Thirty minutes after this confrontation we were in the meeting room trying to reconstruct what had happened when Mike walked in. He thanked us for being so supportive. This worried us because if it appeared that we had supported one of them over the other, then we had not maintained our neutrality. Naturally we were very relieved when Edward told us the same thing the next morning.

We stayed up late that night constructing a possible ending to this disastrous meeting. We thought some comic relief was in order, so I began the session with the following comment, "When Sandy asked me to help her facilitate this meeting, I wondered why you might want two facilitators for only ten participants. After last night I don't think three or four would have been too many." Laughter. "While the discussion between Mike and Edward was intense and awkward for all of us, to say the least, it did put on the table the conflict that exists. What we have to do now is talk about how the team can assist them in resolving some of the conflict between them." We then asked each team member to think about some action they could personally take to ease the tension, and to share that with the group. We ended with Mike and Edward's commitment to work on decreasing (they could not commit to eliminating) their conflict. All members told us we had been fair and neutral with the entire group and that this had helped them get through the experience.

So what's the ending to the story? Mike is still CEO and Edward has retired from the board. The answer to the question posed at the beginning is, "No, this group could not continue as a team." Sometimes too much damage has been done and it is not possible to hold the team together. A consultant's job sometimes is to help individuals survive until the team is recreated with new members. Sometimes the task is to help them cope until permanent resolution is possible.

You can reach Sandra Cheldelin at <scheldel@gmu.edu> and Sue DeWine at <dewines@marietta.edu>.

Additional Resources

Parker, G. M. (1998). *25 instruments for team building.* Amherst, MA: HRD Press.

Pfeiffer, J. W. (Ed.). (1991). *The encyclopedia of team-building activities.* San Diego: Pfeiffer.

Scholtes, P. R., Joiner, B. L., & Streibel, B. J. (1996). *The team handbook* (2nd ed.). Madison, WI: Joiner Assoc.

Torres, C., & Fairbanks, D. (1996). *The ASTD trainer's sourcebook: Teambuilding.* New York: McGraw-Hill.

Chapter **13**

HOW DO YOU TELL CLIENTS WHAT KIND OF JOB THEY ARE DOING?

Using Descriptive Feedback

■ **TYPES OF FEEDBACK**
■ **EFFECTIVE FEEDBACK**
 Useful Content
 Timeliness
 Clarity and Accuracy
■ **PERFORMANCE APPRAISAL**
■ **TIPS ON PROVIDING FEEDBACK**

Lessons Learned: A Consulting Story from Judith Sturnick

Additional Resources

304

Well, yes, you do have great big teeth; but, never mind that. You were great to at least grant me this interview.

Little Red Riding Hood
Quoted in What Color Is Your Parachute? *by R. N. Bolles, 1995*

*T*here are appropriate and inappropriate times when one should provide feedback to others. Probably when the wolf is staring intently at Little Red Riding Hood, it is not a good time to provide feedback about his big teeth! Knowing when to provide feedback, as well as the style and manner in which to do so, is a critical element for the communication specialist.

> The president of a state utility company came under heavy pressure from the parent corporate office to cut costs. He decided to issue a statement to all employees about the budget cuts and detail exactly what line items would be cut. Among a number of employee benefits that were slated for cuts, one item served as a catalyst for employee frustration at the arbitrary process used to make these cuts. "During the last fiscal year we spent a significant amount of money on donuts at departmental meetings. From this day on, no donuts will be served at company meetings." It seemed a trivial matter to warrant being listed among other more severe cuts and seemed to anger employees the most. Three days later, the president was pictured in the local newspaper with the CEO of the parent company who was on site visiting. And guess what the president had in his hand: a donut and a cup of coffee! This provided the fuel for a humorous form of feedback to him. One anonymous employee cut the picture out of the paper, attached it to the memo shown in Figure 13.1, and distributed it throughout the entire company, including, of course, the president's office. The memo was addressed to all employees, ostensibly from the office of the president.

This was a rather humorous way to provide feedback to the president about the perceived trivial criticism of donut distribution at departmental

Interoffice Memo

To: All of My Company Buddies

From: Your President

Date: 9/30/94

It has come to my attention that there was an alleged picture of me carrying an alleged donut in the alleged 9/29/94 city paper, Section F, Page 1. It is incumbent upon me to reply to these vicious rumors.

First, that was not me in the picture, but a person who looks exactly like me.

Second, I paid for the donut.

Third, I did not get the donut for me, but for my boss, for whom donuts are still legal.

Fourth, you will notice that there is a black mark on my forehead. This bruise came from the recent touch football game and resulted in temporary amnesia. My memory has since recovered and I now recall my donut policy.

Fifth, a close examination of the donut reveals that it is a peanut sprinkled donut, not my favorite chocolate-iced donut; therefore, I could not have even realized full pleasure from this alleged act. In fact, some experts even think that the item is a bagel.

In conclusion, there clearly was no violation of my donut policy indicated in the alleged picture. The "no donut" policy stands until we are through with this budget crunch.

Economically Yours,

Your President.

FIGURE 13.1

meetings! In this instance, the employee felt this humorous memo was a safer way to provide the boss with feedback than a face-to-face confrontation.

We all like to receive feedback but are afraid to ask for it. If I asked you "How am I doing?" you may really tell me and I may not like the answer! Feedback requires active listening and careful description of observed behavior. These two skills are the cornerstones to effective feedback and impactful interventions into human behaviors.

Schein (1988) suggests that most of what the process consultant does when he or she intervenes with individuals or groups is to manage the feedback process. The consultant makes observations that provide information, asks questions that direct the client's attention to the consequences of the individual's behavior, and provides suggestions that have implicit evaluations built into them (i.e., any given suggestion implies that other things that have not been suggested are less appropriate than what has been suggested) (p. 105).

Feedback comes in two forms: information on a person's behavior, and information on what impact that behavior can have on others. Remember that the overall purpose of feedback is to help, not attack. When giving feedback, make sure you can answer *yes* to these questions:

Timing: Have I checked with the receiver to determine the best time and place to give feedback?

Motivation: Am I being supportive while giving the feedback rather than ridiculing and hurting the receiver?

Language: Am I using positive or neutral rather than derogatory statements?

Tone: Am I using a friendly and caring tone of voice?

Value: Is the feedback useful to the receiver rather than an outlet for my feelings, frustrations, or anger?

Focus: Am I focusing on actions rather than attitudes or personalities?

Specificity: Am I using specific examples of observed behavior?

Information: Am I giving a manageable amount of helpful information rather than overloading the receiver with more information than is necessary?

Questions: Have I asked the receiver questions to ensure that my feedback was clear and helpful? (ASTD, 1988, p.3)

When receiving feedback, check for *yes* answers to these questions:

Timing: Have I agreed to the time and place for receiving feedback?

Trust: Do I trust the giver to accurately present information concerning my behavior?

Nondefensiveness: Am I prepared to listen to the feedback, rather than argue, refute, or justify my actions?

Specificity: If feedback is vague, am I requesting specific behavioral examples?

Tone: Am I using a neutral rather than a defensive tone of voice?

Questions: Have I asked questions that clarify the feedback?

Feedback is best when it is asked for and when there is a need for impartial knowledge. The client has to understand the difference between wisdom, which is a personal attribute of an individual, and knowledge, which is gained from books and facts. It is the consultant's job to be honest, direct, and nonthreatening.

Sometimes I am surprised at how willingly organizational members receive feedback. Just when I would expect defensiveness and denial, they admit the picture I am painting is on target.

> One illustration of this occurred with a colleague, Elizabeth Bernett, when we worked with a health-care organization. We conducted interviews and asked for written statements about what was preventing this group from moving forward and cooperating with each other.
>
> Participants told Elizabeth and me some very negative examples of how this group was dysfunctional. Some of the traits attributed to the group included being distrustful, deceitful, uncompromising, and overly critical of each other. We decided we would take the plunge and list all of the statements made by the group. We expected resistance and defensiveness. When we finished describing the list of attributes there was a long pause, and then someone spoke up and said, "Yep, that's us." Another said, "Sure sounds like us, doesn't it?" Nods of heads and general agreement indicated they accepted this feedback. Now our task was to find out if they were ready to change some of these behaviors or would they resist change because somehow these behaviors suited their individual agendas.

Types of Feedback

There are a variety of methods to provide feedback, many of which cause defensiveness. The function of feedback is to describe another person's observable behavior, disclose your thoughts and feelings about that behavior, interpret motives, and prescribe specific remedies. These may be our objectives; however, my experience has been that when people are evaluated they often feel attacked and begin to defend themselves.

Feedback is a way of helping another person to consider changing his or her behavior. It is communication to a person (or group) that gives that person information about how she or he affects others. As in a guided missile system, feedback helps an individual keep his or her behavior "on target" and thus achieve individual goals.

People give three kinds of feedback to others:

Evaluative: observing the other's behavior and responding with one's critique of it. "You are always late for everything. You are undependable."

Interpretive: observing the behavior and trying to analyze why the person is behaving that way. "You are late to meetings. I think you are spreading yourself too thin—trying to do too many things at the same time, and consequently you don't do anything really well."

Descriptive: observing the behavior and simply feeding back to the person specific observations without evaluating them, but sharing with the person how her or his behavior affects the speaker. "At the meeting last week you were 30 minutes late, on Monday you came when the meeting was half over, and today you missed the first 45 minutes of the meeting. I am concerned about the information you are missing by not being here."

In the first example, *always* and *undependable* are evaluative terms and create a climate of defensiveness on the part of the receiver. Chances are the person isn't *always* late, and using an all-inclusive term like *always* serves only to make the person angry. The receiver then naturally looks for ways to refute the statement. "I wasn't late to the staff meeting on Friday! You're being unfair."

In the second example the observer is playing dime-store psychologist and trying to figure out why someone is behaving a certain way. Unless you are a trained psychologist, your business is not to analyze and interpret someone else's behavior. You don't know why someone acts a particular way. All you can observe is behavior. You can't observe attitudes, nor should you be critiquing them.

In descriptive feedback we are describing, as specifically as possible, what we have actually observed the individual doing. We present that factual information, without judging the rightness or wrongness of the behavior and without trying to figure out why the person may have behaved that way.

Effective Feedback

Feedback should describe problematic behavior that the receiver can correct. Ideally, it is offered in response to the receiver's request, but whether or not it is solicited, effective feedback should be timely, clear, and accurate.

Useful Content

We have already discussed why feedback is more useful if it is descriptive rather than judgmental. Describing one's reaction to problematic behavior leaves the individual free to use the feedback or not, as the individual sees fit. Avoiding judgmental language reduces the need for the receiver to react defensively. Specific observations are more convincing than general ones. To be told that one is inattentive will probably not be as useful as to be told that: "Just now when we were deciding how to assimilate new employees, you were reading your mail. It made me feel that you were not interested or involved in the discussion."

Effective feedback takes into account the needs of both the receiver and the giver of the feedback. Feedback can be destructive when it serves only the giver's needs and fails to consider the needs of the person on the receiving end. For example, I may need to complain about the lateness of a report. The report writer may not need to hear my complaints because she is already aware of the deadline and cannot change the fact that some missing data from another department prevented her from finishing it earlier. It may make me feel better to "blow off steam" but in this instance it may actually impede the other person's ability to complete the task.

Effective feedback is directed toward behavior that the receiver can change. Frustration is only increased when a person is reminded of some shortcoming over which she or he has no control. One receptionist was criticized for her high-pitched voice over the phone. She had actually worked with a speech therapist and had improved it as much as possible. To continue to criticize her for something she could not change was not helpful; in fact, it was harmful. If the problem was severe enough, then her supervisor should have discussed other career options, but simply to continue to provide feedback that the problem existed could do nothing to bring about change.

Feedback is most useful when it is solicited rather than imposed and when the receiver has formulated the kinds of questions that people observing can answer. Unfortunately, people don't ask for feedback often enough. Therefore, we should take advantage of those rare opportunities when someone does ask us to take the time to provide it. It is easy to miss opportunities because one may dismiss a request as superficial.

> For example, someone recently asked me, "How are things going?" (referring to a project she was working on). I said, "Oh, just fine." Her response was, "No, I really mean, *how do you think things are going?*" Then I said, "Oh, you *really* want some feedback about your performance?" If the person had not persisted, I would have missed a very good opportunity to provide feedback about her work performance at a time when she was actually requesting it!

Timeliness

In general, feedback is most useful at the earliest opportunity after the given behavior has occurred (depending, of course, on the person's readiness to hear it and the support that is available from others). One of the most delayed examples of feedback I have witnessed occurred with two female trainers with whom I was working. We were designing a seminar and the two began discussing their earlier work together. Finally, one said, "Let's be sure we get straight what each person's role will be throughout the course of this seminar because we aren't always clear about how much we want someone to be involved." When she was asked to explain her point further, she described a workshop the two of them had designed in which she felt her talents were not fully used. In fact, she was unclear about the role she should take. I ended up being the mediator in this discussion, and I asked when this workshop had occurred only to discover it had been eight years earlier! Feedback that delayed is useless and unfair. It is unfair because the person who chose not to provide the feedback closer to the time the behavior occurred had been harboring resentment for a long time. Indirectly she may have been acting on that resentment in her behavior toward the other person, who could do nothing about it.

> Another example of poor timing would be if I asked my husband, during a formal banquet, how he liked my new outfit. To actually give me straightforward feedback, which may have been negative, at that time would have been inappropriate. What I really wanted him to say was, "You look great" whether I did or not! Why? Because there was nothing I could do to correct my appearance at that moment. The next time I was selecting an outfit to wear or buying a new one, when I could make a reasonable decision about how to use this information, would be a more appropriate time to tell me the outfit makes me look unattractive (if he dares to tell me that at all!). To provide such criticism in the middle of a social event could make both of us miserable!

Clarity and Accuracy

One way of checking to ensure clear communication is to ask the receiver to rephrase the feedback to see if it corresponds to what the sender had in mind. In this way too, the sender is training the other person to provide descriptive feedback.

Both giver and receiver should have an opportunity to check with others about the accuracy of the feedback. Is this one person's impression or an impression shared by others? A teacher knows that an entire classroom of students will not always be happy with the way in which the class is structured. The teacher must therefore check for themes that exist among most of the students. When you get disturbing or confusing feedback, be sure to check it with co-workers and colleagues. "Have you ever noticed me behaving in this way . . . ?"

Feedback, then, is a way of giving help; it is a corrective mechanism for the individual who wants to learn how well his or her behavior and intentions match and a means for establishing one's identity—for answering

"Who am I?" Feedback can be informal or a formal evaluation process, like performance appraisal.

Performance Appraisal

Performance appraisal programs are permanent parts of the organization's personnel function. Some organizations have very formalized systems that evaluate employees annually or semiannually. **Performance appraisal** systems are a formalized way of providing feedback to employees about their job performance. This feedback should include both positive and negative feedback. Documentation of the evaluation becomes a part of the employee's record and provides a basis for determining merit raises and career advancement.

Traditionally, performance appraisal has been a top-down activity. Employees' performances are evaluated by their supervisors. Many companies today are beginning the process of appraisal from the bottom up. Top-level executives are more uncomfortable about this approach because they have much to lose in the process. However, companies that have tried having employees evaluate their superiors report success with improving the general work climate. It runs out that senior-level managers are hungry for feedback about their performance. In fact, as a consultant, I am often asked by senior managers about their style of leading and managing. I find them extremely curious about how others perceive them. They know they have been "successful" because they have acquired a top-level job, but what they may be unaware of is how they come across to others on a one-to-one basis.

Whether the performance appraisal system is top-down or bottom-up, important issues need attention. Stroul (1987) suggested ten questions to be asked about a performance appraisal that will help focus the feedback on significant areas of management:

1. Are managers rewarded for developing subordinates? In many organizations, developing subordinates either is not rewarded or is inadvertently punished.

2. Do managers receive skill training and assistance in using the system and, specifically, in being helpers or counselors? Often, managers are given only the actual appraisal form and cursory instructions for completing the forms. Managers need training in rating performance objectively and in problem-solving and helping skills.

3. Are job descriptions or specific job-goal documents based on behavioral or job-relevant standards? Recent legal rulings suggest that performance appraisals are comparable to selection tests, and therefore must be demonstrably related to job content.

4. Are employees actively involved in the appraisal process? Generally, systems that incorporate end-user input function more effectively.

5. Does mutual goal setting take place? Research evidence suggests that joint goal setting is related to performance improvement and improved organizational climate.

6. Do appraisal sessions have a problem-solving focus? A problem-solving focus is essential for performance improvement.

7. Is the judge role clearly separated from the helper-counselor role? This is a gray issue that is often overlooked because of difficulty in implementation.

8. Do the paperwork and technical assistance required by the appraisal system place an unreasonable work load on the manager? This is often overlooked but is a key determinant of success or failure.

9. Are peer comparisons a central feature of the appraisal process? **Peer comparison** is a popular notion whereby an employee's work is compared to the performance of others in the work unit. This method must be handled carefully or competition is generated with devastating results.

10. Is information needed for administrative action accessible and effectively used? The person conducting the evaluation needs to understand what actions can be taken as a follow-up to the appraisal. This is another feature too often overlooked in designing a successful performance appraisal system.

These questions could be used to generate a performance appraisal system. However, an organization whose employees receive feedback only through this formal system once a year is in trouble!

Tips on Providing Feedback

Negative feedback is misunderstood much more readily than positive feedback. Consequently, go slowly and be descriptive. I prefer never to put negative feedback in a memo. There are too many opportunities to misinterpret the language. I use memos for good news and face-to-face meetings for bad news. I want to be sure people have a chance to ask any questions they might have when I am telling them something they may not want to hear. However, once the negative information has been communicated face-to-face, follow-up written documents are absolutely necessary to maintain a "paper trail."

Positive feedback that is too general has little impact. We shouldn't assume when we tell employees that they're doing a "good job" that the information will positively affect their performance. If they don't know exactly what it is they did well, it is unlikely they will know what to continue doing! In fact, if the feedback is perceived as too general, it might also be interpreted as insincere.

Keep feedback impersonal. It is important that the person and the person's actions be separated in discussions. I can like the person, respect the person, but find a particular behavior unacceptable. I love my children deeply, but I dislike intensely their tendency to squabble with each other. It is their behavior I find distasteful, not their person. Thus, when you provide feedback, make it impersonal and attach it to a specific behavior, not to the personality of the individual with whom you are talking.

Tailor the feedback to fit the person. Some people appreciate receiving straightforward, direct feedback about their efforts. Others cannot tolerate such directness and need positive reinforcement before they are prepared to handle negative information. Others learn best by example. Still others must hear new information several times before they really listen.

Use humor when appropriate. Sometimes it is easier to tease someone and indirectly provide feedback. This works when the relationship is a good one. The humorous memo in the beginning of this chapter was sent anonymously to the president of a company. It would be great if the president had a sense of humor, recognized the criticism as valid, and responded with his own humorous memo (I can imagine a variety of scenarios!). However, many top-level executives might not be able to handle such forms of feedback. In another organization, a short story written about the head of the unit satirized a recent series of decisions (or lack of them!). The story was never mentioned by the unit head in public. In private he expressed his inability to accept the feedback in that form.

Sometimes subtlety works best. There are times when direct confrontation over an issue is not the best approach. You may be calling too much attention to a problem others can then trivialize. For example, one woman who was constantly asked to take the minutes at executive meetings simply placed the memo pad in front of the senior member's chair at the next meeting, and then offered to provide him with a pen so he could take the minutes at that meeting. He got the message without her having to make a big deal out of the issue and began rotating this secretarial function among all present.

We know who we are by "bumping up against" other people. Their feedback helps shape our identity, self-esteem, and self-concept. The more feedback we provide for others, the better they are able to perform. The more we *ask* for feedback from others about ourselves, the clearer image we have of how others see us.

In the following story the consultant, Judith Sturnick, had to provide some negative feedback to clients and manage their negative feedback to each other. This takes great skill, which Judith has. She's been a university president and the former director of the Office for Women in Higher Education. The lessons she learned from this experience can be helpful to all of us.

━━━━ LESSONS LEARNED ━━━━

A Consulting Story from Judith Sturnick

Judith Sturnick is director of the Office for Women in Higher Education, the American Council on Education in Washington, D.C. She is former president of University of Maine at Farmington and Keene State College in New Hampshire. She frequently provides consultation services to university search committees. For five years she led a successful consulting business in San Francisco specializing in leadership and coaching for academic and private industry.

I was asked to work with the top-level management team of a large land grant institution in a multiyear leadership development program. I frequently led three-day leadership training sessions, which I preceded with in-depth interviews. In this situation I was working closely with the top eight executives of the university. The president of the university asked that I be candid in my assessment of their work toward prioritizing campus issues and building a sense of teamwork among the top-level administrators.

This campus had experienced a great deal of tension between faculty and administration, and between students and faculty. Issues of quality, access, and governance were heading the list of controversies they needed to address. Worst of all, the tension among the top-level administrators was as bad as or worse than elsewhere on campus. In particular, the president and the provost were at odds most of the time. The president was new to the campus and saw himself as a visionary and had an idealized picture of what a university should be like. He had been educated in a private, same-sex institution. The provost, on the other hand, was a former dean and a strong advocate of the faculty. She had been with this institution a long time and had seen four presidents come and go in a relatively short period of time. In short, she had learned not to depend on the president for stability. They could not communicate. It was as if they were speaking different languages when they talked to each other.

At one of my typical three-day training sessions, the president asked that I stay for a fourth day of private talks with him and the provost in an attempt to resolve some of their differences. I agreed, but that's not how it turned out. Late in the afternoon of the third day when the topic was how to deal with conflict on campus, suddenly the president made a switch in the plan and "took on" the provost in front of the group. I interrupted and said, "This is a very important conversation. I suggest we take it off line (meaning, not in front of the entire group) and continue it tomorrow in our meeting of the three of us." The president instead insisted that it be dealt with at that moment by saying, "No, we won't take it off line. I would prefer that everyone be a part of this. I want you to mediate this conversation. This will demonstrate that we can work together once we resolve our differences." The next three hours were like "peeling an onion." We uncovered layers of misunderstandings between these two people who were leading this institution.

I established the following guidelines for the conversation:

1. If one person was talking, no one else could talk.
2. Any response must refer directly to what has been said. "Old baggage" is not appropriate.
3. Each person was required to paraphrase what the other one said before he or she could respond. This served to reduce the "heat" of the conflict and allowed the speaker to make sure he or she was understood.
4. We would continue to bring the discussion back to common ground. "Why are we here? What is our goal for this meeting?"

At the end of a very intense discussion, there were long reflective pauses and the beginning of a dialogue. I then asked to do a "reality check" with the other team members; I asked them for their perceptions of the conversation and how they could contribute to resolving some of the conflict.

The next morning the whole team met for one final session. I asked each person to make a reflective comment about what the three days had meant. The rule was that no one could make a comment that did not help move the group forward. The provost and president were the last ones to make their comments. The provost said, "I understand some things I did not understand three days ago. I think we can work together." The president said, "I'm glad the team was here for the final discussion. I think it is very important to do this within the team. I sense great relief." My final comment was, "I think we've all worked hard, we're all exhausted . . . our work will continue and we don't want to lose ground. I'd like all of you to commit to a weekly staff meeting that allows each member of the team to say where his or her program is, and to bring back the concept of team."

I learned four lessons from this particular consulting intervention:

1. The consultant must have confidence in herself to handle any situation.
2. Nothing succeeds like good common sense.
3. You need many different tools to help a group and you never know which one will ultimately work with a particular group.
4. Consulting can be an exhausting activity.

Additional Resources

Cusella, L. P. (1987). Feedback, motivation, and performance. In F. M. Jablin, L. L. Putnam, K. H. Roberts, & L. W. Porter (Eds.), *Handbook of organizational communication* (pp. 624–678). Newbury Park, CA: Sage.

Downs, C. W., Johnson, K. M., & Barge, J. K. (1984). Communication feedback and task performance in organizations: A review of the literature. In H. Greenbaum, R. Falcione, & S. Hellweg (Eds.), *Organizational communication abstracts* (pp. 13–47). Beverly Hills, CA: Sage.

Edwards, M. R., & Ewen, A. J. (1996). *360 degree feedback: The powerful new model for employee assessment and performance improvement.* New York: AMACOM.

Laird, A., & Clampitt, P. G. (1985). Effective performance appraisal: Viewpoints from managers. *Journal of Business Communication, 22*(3), 49–57.

Chapter **14**

HOW DO I COPE WITH DIFFICULT PEOPLE?

Dealing with People and Conflict

If you can't do anything to improve on the silence, don't disturb it.

Author unknown

*F*or a manager, supervisor, consultant, or anyone responsible for the activities of others, there are times when silence is preferred to communication! Especially when you are dealing with difficult people or stressful events! My skills as a consultant are most often used when there is conflict or some "difficult" personalities with whom others must deal. One example of a "roomful" of difficult people is the following:

> I had been hired by a CEO to facilitate a top-level decision-making meeting between the budget committee of the organization and what served as the board of directors, who were external to the organization but had the final say in decision making for that group. I walked into the meeting and noted immediately that the two groups of people had lined themselves up on either side of a long, narrow table. An agenda had been given to me by the CEO prior to the meeting and ground rules were established early on for this to be a goal-setting and objective-writing session.
>
> Ten minutes into the meeting, a large, gray-haired, impressive individual on the right side of the table said to me and the assembled group, "When are we going to get *our* agenda?" When I asked what he meant, he pulled from his briefcase a second agenda that I had never seen and proceeded to explain that this agenda had been sent to the CEO prior to the meeting and he understood, as a member of the board of directors, that this would be the agenda discussed for this meeting. The first item on the agenda was misrepresentation of funds and distribution of funds by the chief financial officer (CFO) and his staff. At this point the CEO said, "Well, I am sure Sue DeWine will help the group address those issues, plus others you have raised. I want to turn this meeting over to her now" and he promptly left!
>
> It became clear very quickly, once other individuals jumped into the discussion, that this had been a land mine set for the CFO with the intention of dethroning him. I was supposed to facilitate a

collaborative discussion between these two groups in setting goals
for the future of this organization!

The board of directors was angry, arrogant, and belligerent. The
executive committee was stunned; and the CFO seemed to be walking blindly into this trap. How could a consultant help these individuals cope with a conflict-ridden agenda and two groups that
perceived each other to be difficult people? The only thing I could
do was plunge in and list the issues one by one, deal with them
matter-of-factly, and try to deflect the emotional response of individuals on the committee.

After a harrowing four hours' worth of negotiations, we came
out of this meeting for a break. I was told by individuals from both
sides of the table that they thought I had dealt with them fairly. For
the first time they felt their concerns were being heard and understood. I don't know if either side really understood the other, but at
least that's what they perceived to be happening.

(For more information on how to handle similar situations, see
the "Tips" section at the end of this chapter.)

Some people would describe certain members of that board as "difficult personalities." You can all think of a person in your life who is usually
negative, arrogant, or downright mean-spirited. *These are the 10 percent of
the workforce who cause 90 percent of the problems!* The American Psychiatric
Association (1980) identified such personalities as "difficult" to work with
in practically any setting.

Identifying the Difficult Personality

The American Psychiatric Association (1980) indicated that the **difficult
personality** is unable to adapt to the demands of interpersonal relationships or social roles. While everyone around them is changing, such people maintain constant, difficult patterns of behavior.

"This is the colleague or superior or subordinate with whom disagreement and strain seem almost inevitable, and who appears to obstruct operations which should proceed evenly and amicably" (Hollwitz,
Churchill, & Hollwitz, 1985, p. 1). These people cause distress for others
and are generally unresponsive to feedback.

Other authors suggest that difficult people have three things in common. First, their low self-esteem leads to views of the self as undeserving,
unloved, unappreciated, and unsupported. They tend to defend themselves by believing they do not have these needs. Second, they lack the
ability to cope with and resolve conflict. Instead they attempt to wear the

other down or use fear to control others. Third, they have a tendency to use the importance of the relationship as leverage to gain advantage. When they are denied the leverage, they tend to redefine the relationship (Brammer, 1993; Monroe & Borzi, 1987).

Other authors identify these individuals as "difficult employees" (Bissell, 1985), "unpleasant people" (Weiss, 1992), "difficult customers" (Deeprose, 1991), or "marginal employees" (Pfeiffer, Goodstein, & Noland, 1986a). They are further characterized as usually blaming someone other than themselves for problems; taking up a good deal of the manager's time; and overreacting to situations, thereby causing more distress for those around them.

Brammer (1993) developed an instrument to identify disruptive communication patterns often exhibited by difficult people. The characteristics of disruptive communication, identified by approximately 300 subjects in six types of organizations, were the following:

Characteristics of Disruptive Communication

---

aggressiveness
lack of clarity
poor listening
avoidance
not being approachable
complaining
negative verbal behaviors
apparent compliance, masked resistance
negative nonverbals
uncooperative behaviors
information strategies
conversation management
manipulative behaviors
lack of feedback
defensiveness
alibi
indecisiveness
gossiping

These characteristics are included in a questionnaire (Forms 14.1 and 14.2) that asks individuals to identify a person they consider difficult and respond to items about that person. We should first see how many might apply to ourselves! Some of the most difficult people I have encountered as a consultant include the following:

The Machiavellian Manipulator—This person has a serious problem with control. If manipulators aren't in charge, then they are angry and frustrated. Their major goal in any kind of group is to be the one that pulls the strings on the puppets.

The Bullheaded Blocker—No matter in what direction the group heads, no matter what ideas are suggested, this person's goal is to launch an offensive and to make clear why that idea won't work. Blockers must have played tackle in high school because every run seems to be countered by a block on their part.

The Conciliatory Crab—This person is disguised as being willing to go along with the group norm and the group idea but really becomes a crab outside the group setting or a complainer about what the group ends up doing. That's why I suggest that the conciliatory crab's true personality is disguised in the group meeting.

The Alert Analyst—The alert analyst sits back, remains silent most of the time, and tries to analyze the personality of the group. This person is a careful thinker. He or she sometimes comes up with good insights but most of the time does not contribute to the group process.

The Backseat Driver—This individual always wants to second-guess the leader or the group facilitator and without the same access to information believes he or she has a better solution. Backseat drivers don't trust others enough to allow them to use their skills.

The Knowing Know-It-All—This person appears to be the intellectual or the philosopher of the group. There's nothing you can tell this person that he or she hasn't thought of or read about before.

The Hidden Agenda Harry—I find the most difficult type of person to work with is the person who is not direct or obvious about his or her intent. You must always try to figure out in what direction such people are heading. They come under the guise of working on one problem when they really want something else—something unstated—to happen.

Actually, we have all encountered individuals we would describe as difficult people. However, we aren't as aware of when *we* are the difficult person! As a consequence, when I talk about defusing the difficult person, I am speaking to and about all of us!

COMMUNICATION QUESTIONNAIRE

Please read the following statements. Describe the typical communication behaviors of a person with whom you work, such as a superior, subordinate, or colleague/peer, by ranking each statement on a scale of 1 to 7. Think about the person's communication in general, rather than specific organizational communication situations.

Please circle the description of the subject.

Superior	Subordinate	Colleague/Peer
Male Female	Male Female	Male Female

7 = very strong agreement   3 = mild disagreement
6 = strong agreement   2 = strong disagreement
5 = mild agreement   1 = very strong disagreement
4 = neutral feelings or don't know

1. This person postpones things.
   7 6 5 4 3 2 1
2. This person procrastinates.
   7 6 5 4 3 2 1
3. This person is noncommittal when decisions need to be made.
   7 6 5 4 3 2 1
4. This person accepts responsibility.
   7 6 5 4 3 2 1
5. This person shifts responsibility to others.
   7 6 5 4 3 2 1
6. This person questions everything.
   7 6 5 4 3 2 1
7. This person does not play favorites.
   7 6 5 4 3 2 1
8. This person does not monopolize conversations.
   7 6 5 4 3 2 1
9. This person denies having had conversations.
   7 6 5 4 3 2 1
10. This person does not distort information.
   7 6 5 4 3 2 1

(Continued)

COMMUNICATION QUESTIONNAIRE *(Continued)*

11. This person acts in an authoritarian manner.

7 6 5 4 3 2 1

12. This person is dogmatic.

7 6 5 4 3 2 1

13. This person is autocratic.

7 6 5 4 3 2 1

14. This person is not conceited.

7 6 5 4 3 2 1

15. This person is never condescending.

7 6 5 4 3 2 1

16. This person always follows through.

7 6 5 4 3 2 1

17. This person harangues me and others.

7 6 5 4 3 2 1

18. This person is picky.

7 6 5 4 3 2 1

19. This person is cynical.

7 6 5 4 3 2 1

20. This person does not use sarcasm.

7 6 5 4 3 2 1

21. This person does not whine.

7 6 5 4 3 2 1

22. This person is approachable by me.

7 6 5 4 3 2 1

23. This person is inaccessible.

7 6 5 4 3 2 1

24. This person is very communicative.

7 6 5 4 3 2 1

25. This person communicates in a vague manner.

7 6 5 4 3 2 1

26. This person communicates antagonistically.

7 6 5 4 3 2 1

27. This person uses confrontational remarks.

7 6 5 4 3 2 1

Adapted from Brammer (1993).

SCORING FOR THE COMMUNICATION QUESTIONNAIRE

Write in your response to each item number:

AN	E	A	C
Item 6 ____	1 ____	*22 ____	7 ____
Item 11 ____	2 ____	23 ____	8 ____
Item 12 ____	3 ____	*24 ____	*10 ____
Item 13 ____	*4 ____		*14 ____
Item 17 ____	5 ____		*15 ____
Item 18 ____	9 ____		*20 ____
Item 19 ____	*16 ____		*21 ____
Item 26 ____	25 ____		
Item 27 ____			

*Reverse score. If you responded with a 1, change it to 7; a score of 2 = 6; a score of 3 = 5; a score of 4 = 4; a score of 5 = 3; a score of 6 = 2; and a score of 7 = 1.

Total:

(range 9–63)	(range 8–56)	(range 3–21)	(range 7–49)
average = 27	average = 24	average = 9	average = 21

AN = **Antagonism** is a measure of the degree to which the individual is confrontive, cynical, and authoritative.

E = **Evasiveness** identifies behaviors associated with not making decisions, postponing conversation, and not accepting responsibility.

A = **Accessibility** refers to the degree to which an individual is approachable.

C = **Conversation management** is associated with negative strategies to control conversations such as distorting information, condescending, and monopolizing talk time.

Adapted from Brammer (1993).

Dealing with the Difficult Person

One of the ways I deal with difficult people in my role as a consultant is by *cutting them off verbally*, saying: "Thanks, Jim, now let's turn to. . . ." I also use physical blocks by standing in front of, or next to, the person and physically cutting him or her off or out of the conversation. This technique can work well with individuals who are trying to dominate the conversation or manipulate relationships.

I have also turned to what I call *limited-impact techniques* whereby I attempt to isolate the person to minimize his or her impact on the group by having him or her do a single-person project or get involved in facilitating the group with me. This pulls the person out of the discussion. If all else fails, I ask the troublemaker to leave the group for a private discussion of the problems that he or she is causing. I use this technique with some of the worst cases listed above, like the blocker or the backseat driver.

It is important to *find a balance* between trying to ignore these people and spending a disproportional amount of time with them! Bissell (1985) suggested, "Avoid trying to ignore them. They will only chase you more, and raise the stakes. . . . If they set off a firecracker, which you act as if you did not hear, they will bring a bomb tomorrow!" (p. 30).

At the same time, they may overreact to minor situations and unless you are careful you will spend a great deal of time fighting fires with them! You need to *be direct and to the point.* Be sure to indicate what you can and cannot accomplish for them. You also have to let them fight their own battles. Don't become their "protector."

Deeprose (1991) suggested using *"six magic words to defuse anger:* 'I understand (that this is the problem); I agree (that it needs to be solved); I'm sorry (that this happened to you)'" (p. 6). This kind of direct language is used in the steps of assertiveness training techniques: describe the situation or behavior, indicate your reaction to it, outline the desired change in behavior, and finally, indicate actions you will take if the behavior does not change.

The best way to lower someone else's temperature is to *remain calm* yourself. The louder the other person gets, the quieter you should become. When a fire loses oxygen, it dies out. When anger has nothing to reflect off, it fades.

The assertiveness technique of the "broken record" works well with some difficult people. Repeating over and over the same statement about how you intend to respond to some request, rather than becoming upset that someone keeps making the same request, is an effective tool. Statements such as "I don't do any business over the telephone," "We do not deal with telemarketing programs," "I never buy any product by phone" are repeated several times until they end the conversation. In this situation, hanging up works well too!

Dealing with difficult people requires great patience and flexibility. These individuals test our skills in more ways than we imagine! They are often at the center of conflict situations, as discussed in the opening example between the CEO and the CFO.

Conflict and Stressful Events[1]

Besides having difficult people to deal with, we often negotiate stressful or conflict situations. When these conflicts occur between you and these difficult personalities, you will need a variety of techniques to help you manage this process!

J. W. Pfeiffer, a communication consultant, used an interesting analogy to explain why conflict so often occurs in an interpersonal relationship:

> In the late afternoon when you observe a sunset, the sun often appears to be a deep red, larger and less intense than it seems at midday. This is due to the phenomenon of refraction, the bending of light rays as they pass through the earth's atmosphere, and the higher density of dust in the air through which the light passes as the sun goes down. The sun has already moved below the horizon, but it is still in sight because its emissions are distorted by the conditions of the medium through which they must travel.
>
> In a similar way the messages which we send each other are often refracted by intrapersonal, interpersonal, and environmental conditions which contribute to the atmosphere in which we are relating. I may distort my messages to you by giving out mixed messages verbally and nonverbally, and you may distort what you hear because of your own needs and experiences. The two of us may be located in an environment, physical and psychological, which contributes to the difficulty in clearly sharing what we intend. In an atmosphere of suspicion, for example, we may both become unduly cautious in our communication. (Pfeiffer, 1973, p. 120)

While it is unlikely that total nonrefracted communication is possible, certainly we can improve our chances of meaningful dialogue by keeping in mind some of the principles of conflict management. This becomes particularly important in the organizational setting, where individuals often use up many hours attempting to resolve some interpersonal conflict.

Types of Conflict

There appear to be two types of conflict in the organizational setting: (1) **content conflict,** which is conflict over the goals of the organization, its structure, policies, or networks and (2) **personal conflict,** which takes the form of emotional and personal differences among the individuals in the organization. A conflict over content or issues might revolve around labor negotiations and pay increases; a personal conflict might focus on a group's inability to talk openly with a dictatorial, unfair supervisor.

Content conflict can be dealt with in rather routine, rational ways. Usually, the conflict does not get directed toward personalities. However, when a group discusses the organization's goals, often a subtext (unspoken dialogue) exists that deals with personalities. For example, one group was discussing a policy change in the way the sales force wrote up orders. On the surface, the conflict was over what type of procedure would work best but the underlying conflict had to do with a personal conflict between two individuals who had been "at war" for a long time. It did not really matter to either of them which procedure was adopted. All that mattered was that the other person's position be defeated.

Personal conflict is more difficult to cope with than content issues are. Once people start responding emotionally, then attention shifts from the issue to getting the emotions under control. Groups can be so uncomfortable with emotional outbursts that they allow them to sidetrack the discussion. People are so relieved when the yelling has stopped they are willing to live with an unresolved issue rather than risk "stirring things up" again!

CONFLICT-RESPONSE STYLES

Hall (1969, p. 6) identified five styles of dealing with interpersonal conflict, based on the responses of 387 managers. Individuals may use all five styles at one time or another. Think about which style you tend to use most often when you are in a conflict situation. Certainly there are times when we react to a situation before thinking about the consequences. What we are working toward, according to Hall, is the final style, synergistic.

The *win-lose* style is used when individuals associate winning with status and competence, and losing is seen as losing status. The result is an individual who is aggressive, dogmatic, and inflexible.

The *yield-lose* style is based on the assumption that human relationships are so fragile that they cannot withstand the process of working through differences. Here the person's need for affection and acceptance is most important and causes submissive behavior.

The *lose-leave* style views conflict as hopeless, and thus the individual simply strives for protection from a punishing experience by withdrawing from the situation entirely.

According to the *compromise* style, a little bit of winning and a little bit of losing are better than losing altogether. This strategy attempts to soften the effects of losing by limiting the gains of winning. Often this style results in a climate of suspicion for both parties because neither is completely satisfied with the results.

Finally, there is the *synergistic* style, which is the most desirable style. Here major importance is attached to the goals of the participants in the relationship and to the well-being of the relationship at the same time. The confrontation of differences in a problem-solving way and a tolerance for differences are key elements in this style.

The synergistic style assumes definite attitudes that may be helpful in managing conflict, such as:

Belief in the existence of a mutually acceptable solution

Belief in the desirability of such a solution

Belief in cooperation rather than competition

Belief that the other person is valuable and trustworthy

Belief that the other person can compete, but can choose to cooperate

A CONFLICT-STYLE INSTRUMENT

Rosanna Ross and I (Ross & DeWine, 1988) developed a conflict-style instrument that identifies the way in which individuals handle most conflict situations. The Ross-DeWine Conflict Management Message Style (CMMS) is a self-report instrument designed to assess conflict styles through messages used in interpersonal conflict (see Forms 14.3 and 14.4). CMMS identifies three message types: self-oriented, issue-oriented, and other-oriented.

The questionnaire is composed of 18 items, six that reflect each of the three styles. Each item uses a 5-point Likert scale from "never say things like this" to "usually say things like this." A respondent receives three subscale scores on this instrument, with scores ranging from 6 to 30. Mean scores on each subscale were determined ($n = 116$): *self*, 11.21; *issue*, 19.91; *other*, 18.16.

Respondents are directed to interpret their scores by (1) comparing their scale means with the normative data and with the means of their training group, (b) discussing how the styles apply to specific situations, and (c) determining how they would like to see their own subscale scores change.

A message with a focus on *self* reflects emphasis on the speaker's personal interests. An example of a self-focused item is: "You can't do (say) that to me—it's either my way or forget it!" A message that focuses on *issue* maintains that the problem can be solved without jeopardizing the relationship and emphasizes that both parties must deal with the problem. An example of an issue-focused item is: "This is something we have to work out; we're always arguing about it." A message that focuses on *other* emphasizes overlooking the problem and keeping the other party happy. An example of the other-focused item is: "That's OK . . . it wasn't important anyway."

The instrument is preceded by a cover page that directs subjects to recall and to describe in writing their most common behavior in conflict. This critical incident–recall is designed to encourage congruity between subjects' responses on the items and their actual behavior. On a second page, respondents are asked to consider each message separately and to decide how closely the message resembles comments that they have made in conflict situations. Respondents are told there are no right or wrong answers.

An individual's score on a given subscale indicates the frequency with which the respondent would select messages similar to those in that subscale. Although no interpretation section accompanies the instrument, the CMMS is designed for training purposes and includes an explanation of the three message styles and their mean scores. (See Ross & DeWine, 1988, for detailed statistical analysis of the instrument.)

This instrument can be used in training sessions, as you work with individuals in small groups, or on a one-to-one basis. It will provide insight for both you and the individual/group about how conflict is being handled. If you understand someone's style of resolving conflict, you are better prepared to negotiate.

CMMS: RECALL OF COMMUNICATION BEHAVIOR IN INTERPERSONAL CONFLICT

Instructions: Consider situations in which you find yourself in conflict with another person. How do you *usually* respond in this situation? (Please write the answers on this sheet.)

Below list some of the ways you often behave, comments you frequently make, and feelings you often have, when you are in a conflict situation:

_____

_____

_____

_____

_____

Instructions: Below you will find messages that have been delivered by persons in conflict situations. Consider each message separately and decide how closely this message resembles messages you have used in conflict settings.

The language may not be exactly the same as yours, but consider the messages in terms of similarity to your messages in conflict. There is no right or wrong answer to this test, nor are these messages designed to trick you. Answer in terms of responses *you make*, not what you think you should say.

Give each message a 1 to 5 rating on the answer sheet provided according to the following scale. Mark *one answer only.*

1	2	3	4	5
never say things like this	rarely say things like this	sometimes say things like this	often say things like this	usually say things like this

In conflict situations, I

1. ☐ "Can't you see how foolish that thinking is?"
2. ☐ "How can I make you feel better about this?"
3. ☐ "I'm really bothered by some things that are happening here; can we talk about these?"
4. ☐ "I really don't have any more to say on this . . . (silence) . . ."
5. ☐ "What possible solutions can we come up with?"
6. ☐ "I'm really sorry that your feelings are hurt—maybe you're right."
7. ☐ "Let's talk this thing out and see how we can deal with this hassle."
8. ☐ "Stop. I'm tired of arguing."

(Continued)

CMMS: RECALL OF COMMUNICATION BEHAVIOR IN
INTERPERSONAL CONFLICT *(Continued)*

9. ☐ "If I fail at this, don't expect help from me when *you're* in a spot."

10. ☐ "You can't do (say) that to me—support me or forget it!"

11. ☐ "Let's try finding an answer that will give us both some of what we want."

12. ☐ "This is something we have to work out; we're always arguing about it."

13. ☐ "Whatever makes you feel happiest is OK by me."

14. ☐ "Let's just leave well enough alone."

15. ☐ "That's OK . . . it wasn't important anyway. . . ."

16. ☐ "If you're not going to cooperate, I'll just talk to someone who will."

17. ☐ "I think we need to try to understand the problem."

18. ☐ "You might as well accept my decision; you can't do anything about it anyway."

Adapted from Ross, R., & DeWine, S. (1982). Interpersonal Conflict: Measurement and Validation. Presented at SCA, Louisville, KY.

SCORE SHEET FOR CMMS

Conflict Management Message Style Instrument

By each item number, list the rating (from 1 to 5) you gave that item on Form 14.3. When you have entered all ratings, add ratings for each column. Enter the resulting score in the space provided.

SELF (Items)	ISSUE (Items)	OTHER (Items)
1. ☐	3. ☐	2. ☐
8. ☐	5. ☐	4. ☐
9. ☐	7. ☐	6. ☐
10. ☐	11. ☐	13. ☐
16. ☐	12. ☐	14. ☐
18. ☐	17. ☐	15. ☐

Your Score	_____	_____	_____
Average Scores	(13.17)	(24.26)	(21.00)

The items that constitute the SELF focus deal with one's personal interests in the conflict situation. These messages suggest that one's primary concern is in resolving the conflict so that his or her view of the conflict is accepted by the other. This is a "win" approach to conflict resolution.

The items that constitute the ISSUE focus deal with an emphasis on both parties dealing with the problem. These message statements suggest an overriding concern with the content of the conflict rather than the personal relationship.

The items that constitute the OTHER focus deal with neither the conflict issues nor personal interests, but emphasize maintaining the relationship at a cost of resolving the conflict. These statements suggest that one would rather ignore the problem to maintain a good relationship with the other person.

All of us may use one of these styles in different settings and under different circumstances. People do tend to have a predominant style, which is evidenced by the kinds of messages sent during conflict situations. The intent of this instrument is to cause individuals to focus on what they are communicating in the messages they send during conflict and to make sure that what they are saying is what they intended to say.

The average scores reported on the CMMS instrument are based on research reported in Ross and DeWine (1983) and are an indication of scores one might expect to receive. Scores that are higher or lower than these averages indicate a higher or lower use of this message style than would normally be expected.

Ross, R., & DeWine, S. (1982). Interpersonal Conflict: Measurement and Validation. Presented at SCA, Louisville, KY.

Stages of Conflict

Pondy (1972) identified five distinct stages of conflict development:

1. *Latent conflict* deals with underlying sources of organizational conflict, like competition for scarce resources.
2. *Perceived conflict* can occur in either the absence or presence of latent conflict. Perceived conflict occurs if the individuals misunderstand each other's position.
3. *Felt conflict* may also be termed the *personalization of conflict* because it is at this stage that conflict affects the individual directly.
4. *Manifest conflict* is the actual occurrence of conflict, which may range from open aggression to apathy or even extremely rigid adherence to rules.
5. *Conflict aftermath* is a function of how well the entire episode or sequence of episodes has been resolved. Perhaps this stage will reveal the basis for a more cooperative relationship, or it might suggest how newly perceived problems might be handled, or it *may* foster more serious difficulties.

Causes of Conflict

Alan Filley (1975) identified some of the causes of conflict in the organization as follows: ambiguous responsibilities, conflict of interests, communication barriers, need for consensus, dependence of one person on another, suppression of disagreement, and personalization of the situation.

We know people would rather receive negative information than no information at all. Ambiguous situations and a vague understanding of job responsibilities lead to conflict. Many people are more frustrated by ambiguity than directions and instructions, even when they disagree with those instructions!

It is also evident that majority vote is a much simpler way to solve conflicts than reaching consensus. The criteria for selecting one method over the other is the degree to which commitment to the solution is needed. Consensus takes longer and generates more conflict initially. Majority vote, while quicker and easier, may simply delay the conflict until it is time to implement the decision. It is quite possible the conflict has merely been suppressed, only to be revealed later—like a disaster waiting for an unexpected moment to strike!

One of the difficulties in resolving or managing conflicts is that the real cause or issue often remains hidden behind symptoms. A careful analysis of the real cause is a crucial step toward managing the conflict situation.

Tips on Dealing with Conflict

The following steps will lead to assessment of the conflict situation in which you find yourself:

1. *Assess immediacy.* A relationship in conflict is an emotionally draining experience. One of the first things a person must decide is whether this relationship is important enough to him or her to warrant the amount of time and energy it will take to resolve the conflict. Once we are committed to the relationship and realize that it will require our energy and attention, we then seem more willing to try resolution techniques. You must answer these questions: How important is the relationship to me? How willing am I to devote time and energy, in order to cope with the emotional drain, in resolving this conflict?

2. *Identify the type of conflict. Intra*personal conflict exists within a person and may not involve others (e.g., making a decision between two choices). *Inter*personal conflict exists between two or more people. A relationship is not in conflict unless both persons involved are aware that the conflict exists. Conflict is either in the open and everyone knows it exists, or it is hidden and thus not everyone involved is aware of it.

3. *Decide on the basic coping strategy.* Initially, we must decide whether we can merely control the conflict (not let it get out of hand, cool it down but not really resolve it), or we actually are able to work at resolving the conflict. The conflict control strategy is characterized by statements such as, "I feel the conflict cannot be resolved at this time; however, I feel I must maintain the relationship so I choose to merely control the conflict, lower the emotional level, have a cooling-off period, etc."

   The decision to resolve the conflict assumes it can and must be resolved, with all issues out in the open and communication skills in use to achieve a solution.

4. *Distinguish symptoms from causes.* We often waste time trying to resolve symptoms instead of the real underlying cause of the conflict. (For example, when a girl complains that her boyfriend is always late for a date, it is possible that their disagreement over the time he arrives is only a symptom of a deeper conflict. They may each have different expectations for the relationship—she may want it to be permanent and he may regard her as just someone to date.) Symptoms let you know a conflict is present; causes of conflict are issues underlying the symptoms.

5. *Identify methods used so far.* We must be aware of our basic coping techniques for handling conflict. What have we already tried to do to resolve the conflict (e.g., ignore the problem, hope it will go away, try to win the argument through persuasion, compromise, give in and let the other person win)? Identify the methods used and the success of each technique.

6. *Brainstorm for alternatives.* When trying to arrive at solutions to an interpersonal conflict a person must be able to **brainstorm** ideas. He or she must be willing to list as many ideas as possible without evaluating them, no matter how wild or impossible they may seem. The strategy of brainstorming assumes that eventually some of these ideas may trigger a solution.

7. *Evaluate the likely outcome of each alternative.* Often it is difficult for us to imagine the best possible outcome of behavior. When a relationship is in conflict, we tend to see only the negative results. It is important that we evaluate each alternative negatively and positively, asking: "What is the worst possible outcome if this alternative is chosen?" and "What is the best possible outcome?"

8. *Select the alternative and communication skills needed to resolve the conflict.* Finally, we are ready to determine what communication skills are needed to resolve this interpersonal conflict and put into action all of the communication techniques outlined earlier. We ask ourselves, "What other techniques might I try to resolve this conflict? Where do I go from here?" Many people avoid conflict at all costs, and responding to these two questions helps uncover why they have such strong avoidance tendencies.

The preceding format allows the individual to carefully analyze the conflict situation before entering into a battle. These issues are of prime importance if interpersonal conflicts are to be resolved successfully. As a consultant I frequently use this format to help individuals analyze their fears about resolving conflicts. Describing for a client some of the conflict styles and using the conflict instrument will help your client (as well as yourself) identify the way in which conflict is normally handled and with what impact. Any of these ideas can be presented to the client as a form of analysis for their own particular setting. The most important step is to recognize that a conflict exists. Avoidance behavior permeates most work settings!

The longer individuals delay confronting a conflict, the larger and more pervasive it becomes. It is like the part of the iceberg that is under water. You cannot see it but it is there, waiting for you to run into it!

The main character in the following consulting story was clearly a difficult person with whom to work. David Seibold, a well-respected consultant in Santa Barbara, California, stood his ground even when the client changed and the entire focus of the consulting assignment changed. How he managed to survive this difficult person's influence is a great lesson for all of us.

Lessons Learned

A Consulting Story from David R. Seibold: The Admiral and the Loose Cannons

David R. Seibold is a professor and chair of the Department of Communication, University of California at Santa Barbara. His research focuses on organizational innovation and group decision processes. A former editor of the Journal of Applied Communication Research *and current chair of the Organizational Communication Division of the International Communication Association, he has published nearly one hundred papers and chapters and has received numerous research awards. He also has 20 years of consulting experience and has worked closely with business, government, and civic organizations.*

Another communication professor and I had been conducting training workshops for a regional utility company on an occasional basis for nearly a year. The company was struggling to stay competitive in the face of recent deregulation, alternative energy sources available to its customers, and the rocky road of incorporating nuclear energy into services heretofore limited to natural gas and turbine electricity. Inherent in these challenges were communication problems related to coordination, cooperation, climate, conflict, and control. Our training was offered through a specific and limited set of courses offered by our university's extended learning programs, but participants' positive reactions to the sessions had led to opportunities during the following year for more specialized work with a variety of units across the company. By the end of the second year, we were providing coaching consultations, facilitation, and team building with the company's senior executives.

Based on our growing familiarity with the organization and its managers' familiarity with us, the training and development coordinator contracted with us to conduct an organization-wide training needs assessment. We were to survey all supervisors, managers, and executives concerning their perceptions of their own and their employees' needs for communication skills training. We identified 25 areas with the help of human resources managers and focus group interviews with a cross-section of company employees. As needed, we could supplement the survey protocols with in-depth interviews of key individuals in the organization. We also were asked to draw upon our knowledge of the organization and to expand our report of the survey results into "a plan" for improving communication in the company in general. In turn, over the course of the following two years we would be responsible for the implementation of that plan: executive development, enhancing organizational climate, facilitating the flow of strategic information in the organization, delivery of skills training in the areas most needed, and coaching assignments. Indeed, we were trumpeted to the CEO by the vice president for human resources as "guys who can help us save this company."

One individual whom we wished to interview was the executive vice president (EVP) in charge of the company's planned nuclear facility. We had become aware of him, a corporate legend, from stories told to us by participants in our workshops. A retired naval admiral, his job included completing construction of the facility and "bringing it on line" within the next 18 months. "The fate of this company is in his hands," we had heard from the senior finance officer. He and his managers were under intense pressure, not only to create the organization's capability to provide nuclear energy profitably, but to do so in the face of construction delays, cost overruns, increasing governmental regulations, and the myriad problems of recruiting and training personnel to work in this specialized facility. The effect was an extraordinarily tense climate characterized by individualized action and strong task focus but little teamwork, interpersonal support, or information sharing.

The EVP's leadership style contributed to these dynamics and compounded them. Following the "command-and-control" orientation he had developed in the military, he closely monitored his direct reports (some said he micromanaged them), motivated through pressure (some suggested through fear), expressed himself frequently and forcibly (some added ferociously), and was quick to point out his employees' failings (some indicated publicly). He had single-handedly fired many employees and contractors on the building site. "The Admiral," as he was known, was cognizant of his approach. "I run a tight ship!" he told us during our interview with him.

We noted these dynamics in our report and intervention plan. Careful to avoid terms (and tone) like those above, we used established constructs in the social sciences. We referred to the EVP's leadership style, for example, as "overly directive," "autocratic," and "authoritarian." We should have been even more careful. Although we were aware in principle of the potential for miscommunication when technical language is used for non-technical audiences, our use of "autocratic" and "authoritarian" was (selectively?) interpreted by this WWII veteran as "fascist" and "dictatorial." And despite our awareness that organizations are also political systems subject to domination by managerial elites, our feedback challenged the established order and made us targets of the EVP's power. Our concerns with climate, esprit de corps, interpersonal trust, and motivation (and recommendations for enhancing same) were anathema to an executive focused on performance, productivity, loyalty, and—above all—discipline.

True to nautical form, the Admiral referred to us as "the loose cannons" to anyone who would listen. Our continued presence would threaten "to sink the ship," he told the CEO. He added an ultimatum: "Either they go or I do!" Faced with the loss of the only party who could "save the company," the CEO's directive to the vice president for human resources was clear and unequivocal: "Get rid of those loose cannons!"

Postscript

Within two years after our "departure," the Admiral retired from the nuclear facility he had brought on line in timely fashion but with lingering resentments from nearly all involved. The CEO also had retired and was succeeded by an executive with whom he had worked closely and successfully years before. His closest associate, the vice president for human resources, originally charged with dismissing us (but who had remained in contact with us) secured the new CEO's approval for our return to the company. Following another needs assessment and updating ourselves on developments in the organization, we rewrote our intervention plan (more carefully this time!) and proceeded as if little had happened in the interim. But apparently at least one thing had happened: we had become somewhat of a legend ourselves. As one manager enthused during one of our first training sessions after our return, "So you're the guys who took on the Admiral." Of course, after acknowledging the veridicality of that claim, we added "and lost!"

David R. Seibold can be reached at the Department of Communication, 4840 Ellison Hall, University of California, Santa Barbara, CA 93106-4020. (805) 893-4657 <seibold@alishaw.ucsb.edu>.

Note

1. Portions of this chapter were taken from Tortoriello, Blatt, and DeWine (1978).

Additional Resources

Axelrod, A. (1997). *201 ways to deal with difficult people*. New York: McGraw-Hill.

Bramson, R. N., & Bramson, M. (1988). *Coping with difficult people*. New York: Dell.

Brinkman, R., & Kirschner, R. (1994). *Dealing with people you can't stand*. New York: McGraw-Hill.

Monroe, C., Borzi, M., & DiSalvo, V. S. (1986). Conflict behaviors of difficult subordinates. *Southern Communication Journal, 53*, 311–329.

Ross, R., & DeWine, S. (1988). Assessing the Ross-DeWine conflict management message style. *Management Communication Quarterly, 1*(3), 389–413.

Tucker, R. K. (1987). *Fighting it out with difficult, if not impossible people*. Dubuque, IA: Kendall Hunt.

Chapter *15*

HOW CAN PEOPLE GET ORGANIZED WHEN THE RULES KEEP CHANGING?

Understanding Change Processes

René Fichant, the CEO of Michelin Tire, once told this story: Three men were shown a room with two doors. They were told that behind one door was wealth beyond their dreams—gold, silver, priceless jewels. Behind the other door was a hungry man-eating tiger. They were each given the option of entering the room and opening a door. The first man refused the choice and left. The second man—a good strategic planner—hauled out his computer, analyzed probability data, performed some risk analysis, plotted graphs, produced charts, created scenarios, and so on, and after much deliberation he opened a door and was eaten by a low-probability man-eating tiger. The third man (and of course, the third one is always the winner) spent his time learning to tame tigers.

I. *Cunningham*, The Wisdom of Strategic Learning, *1999, p. 3*

*C*hange is about predicting the future, adapting accordingly, and preparing for the unpredictable. However, you can't always predict how people will respond to change. One client I worked with attempted to signify how quickly goals may change by having the company goal statements handwritten on a legal pad and photocopied instead of being typed neatly. No one took him seriously.

On the other hand, I worked with a university committee for one and a half years developing a new plan for a required curriculum. The plan was to be presented to the university community for debate and discussion. The chair of the committee thought he should present this plan in the most professional manner possible so he had it printed in a small booklet. The faculty were outraged since it "looked" like the plan was too permanent and had already been adopted without their consent! They took that document *too* seriously.

Sometimes, as you attempt to deal with constant change, you feel you can't win! Charles Handy suggested in his book *The Age of Unreason* (1989) that the future only holds more change and uncertainty.

> The status quo will no longer be the best way forward. The best way will be less comfortable and less easy but, no doubt, more interesting, a word we often use to signal an uncertain mix of danger and opportunity. . . . While in Shaw's day, perhaps, most men and women were reasonable, we are now entering an Age of Unreason, when the future, in so many areas, is there to be shaped, by us and for us . . . for bold imaginings in private life as well as public, for thinking the unlikely and doing the unreasonable. (p. 4)

This chapter addresses the issues surrounding change, resistance to change, and strategic planning. Consultants are **change agents,** persons who enter a system and, by their very entrance, cause change to come about. Communication specialists (managers) who intervene into an ongoing relationship in the organization are change agents as well.

Types of Change

Watzlawick, Weakland, and Fisch (1974) identified two distinct types of changes that may occur in any organized system: "one that occurs within a given system which itself remains unchanged **(first-order change),** and one whose occurrence changes the system itself **(second-order change)**" (p. 10).

An example of first-order change is the addition of a department, such as a new product department, to the organization while the organization itself remains basically the same. However, when the addition of a department changes the very nature of the entire organization, like a "department" for quality control that affects the entire organization and changes the basic way its business is conducted, second-order change, wherein the system itself changes, occurs.

Second-order change is of much greater magnitude and more difficult to accomplish, and it is the type consultants and communication managers usually deal with. Watzlawick and colleagues described systems that are unable to create second-order change by saying,

> A system which may run through all its possible internal changes (no matter how many there are) without effecting a systematic change, i.e., second-order change, is said to be caught in a game without end. It cannot generate from within itself the conditions for its own change; it cannot produce the rules for the change of its own rules. (p. 22)

The consultant must help the client prepare for change because any type of change, even positive change, may be met with resistance. We tend to resist any disruption of our routines. The consultant must deal with this resistance before the group allows itself to move forward.

Resistance to Change

Resistance to change is experienced at almost every step. Moore and Gergen (1986) identified the fear of taking risks as a key factor in resistance to change "either in those managers who must decide whether to initiate change or those employees who are changed by its implementation" (p. 31). In their model (see Figure 15.1) they identified environmental factors likely to influence the individual risk taker.

They suggested how organizations can support risk taking:

- Organization expectations must be clear, and people at each level of the organization must be aware of what the expectations mean to their work groups.
- Reward systems, both formal and informal, must be identified and developed.

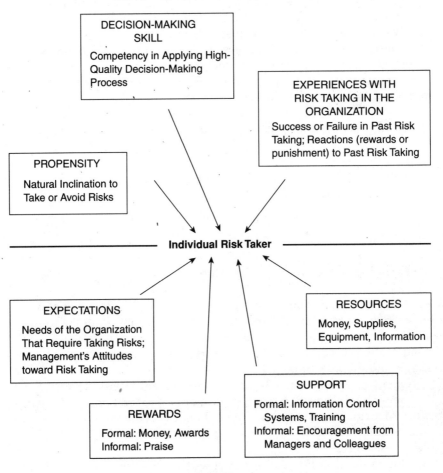

Internal Factors and Individual Tendencies

DECISION-MAKING SKILL
Competency in Applying High-Quality Decision-Making Process

EXPERIENCES WITH RISK TAKING IN THE ORGANIZATION
Success or Failure in Past Risk Taking; Reactions (rewards or punishment) to Past Risk Taking

PROPENSITY
Natural Inclination to Take or Avoid Risks

Individual Risk Taker

EXPECTATIONS
Needs of the Organization That Require Taking Risks; Management's Attitudes toward Risk Taking

RESOURCES
Money, Supplies, Equipment, Information

REWARDS
Formal: Money, Awards
Informal: Praise

SUPPORT
Formal: Information Control Systems, Training
Informal: Encouragement from Managers and Colleagues

**External Factors
Organizational Structure/Culture**

FIGURE 15.1   The individual risk taker's actions are influenced internally by individual tendencies and externally by organization structure/culture factors.   Based on Maggie Moore & P. Gergen, Risk Taking and Organization Change. In C. N. Jackson (Ed.), *Targeting Change: Organizational Development*. Alexandria, VA: American Society for Training and Development, 1986, p. 33.

- Support systems can take many forms, both formal and informal.
- Resources made available to employees can be a budget for a specific project, support staff, a mechanism through which to gather data, or equipment and supplies.

Once necessary risks are identified, employees themselves will be able to identify appropriate rewards and needed resources. Involvement of all employees in the discussion about risks to employees is critical to the success of any change effort.

Pasmore, Francis, and Haldeman (1982) suggested the following criteria for reducing employee resistance to change: (1) a well-defined, clearly articulated need for change; (2) support from top management; (3) support from the union leadership; (4) employee involvement and participation; and (5) careful management of expectations about the benefits to be gained from the intervention. Each of these criteria is explained through actual consulting examples.

Anderson (2000) has converted the readiness for a change into a formula. The change readiness formula is $C = abd > R$, where

C = change,

a = level of dissatisfaction with the status quo,

b = desired future state,

d = practical first steps toward desired state, and

R = costs of changing or resistance. (p. 37)

Explaining the Need for Change

"No amount of sophistication is going to allay the fact that all your knowledge is about the past and all your decisions are about the future," said Ian E. Wilson (quoted in Anderson, 2000, p. 91). Therefore, as indicated in the previous formula, it is important to think about potential change and prepare for it.

Often we assume it will be obvious to everyone why a change must be made. That assumption may lead to sloppy preparation of the change effort. Managers and consultants who do not take the time to explain the process and the reason why some change is necessary may be met with heavy resistance.

One communication audit project with a social service agency, with which some of my colleagues were involved, stands as a good example. The auditors started interviews without meeting with employees to describe in detail the goals and objectives of the project. First, they had a hard time scheduling interviews; it seemed everyone was too busy to fit a 30-minute interview into the work day. Then, of the few they did get scheduled, 80 percent did not show up. The researchers stopped the project and went back to square one.

They planned a meeting with union officials to describe the intent of the research and discovered something they should have found out in the beginning. Two years before, another team of "researchers" had conducted interviews on the apparently innocuous topic of "workplace communication," and jobs were redesigned and eliminated as a result. Many of the current employees' friends and relatives had lost their jobs in the last "purge" through information collected in interviews. No wonder the auditors were met with resistance to participate in yet another round of interviews! Don't assume individuals will understand the method or purpose of interventions into the organizations.

Gaining Support for Change

When middle management and/or line workers try to bring about change without support from top management, chaos is often the result. The same is true for union membership. One lighting manufacturing company hired me to conduct a series of team development workshops. The vice president for human resources was my contact person. I asked to meet with the president but never succeeded in establishing a meeting prior to the first workshop. It was a mistake for me to continue with the workshop when I had been unsuccessful in assuring top management's support. That is a mistake I have never forgotten.

On the Saturday morning when the first workshop was to begin, the president made a surprise visit. I was wondering where my "contact," the vice president, was when the president told me he had an announcement to make before the workshop was to begin. He stood up and announced that as of 5:00 the previous day the vice president, my contact, was no longer associated with the company. Then he proceeded to undermine any attempt on my part to make the series of workshops meaningful by saying, "We will continue with the workshops since we have already contracted for them, but the outcome of these discussions is very much in question until we hire a new vice president and get this company back on track." Thus, I began my first workshop on "team building" and the importance of everyone in the organization feeling that they are part of the decision-making process!

Dealing with Expectations for Change

Often the consultant is expected to have the answer that will immediately eliminate the problem. "In attempting to manage change in open social systems, systems which are driven by confusion and complexity, only the brave or foolish would claim to have the definitive answer to any particular problem" (Collins, 1998, p. 193).

At the other end of the continuum from having negative expectations of the intervention, employees can have expectations that are unrealistically positive. In working with another manufacturing company, the president asked me to intervene to discover why employee attitudes and morale appeared to be so low. I began a series of interviews and survey distribution. I received very positive encouragement from employees and had no difficulty getting them to talk with me. It became clear that this group of people saw me as a "savior," one who might be able to bring about the demise of the foreman of the plant. This individual was strongly disliked and feared. He used intimidation to get employees to work harder. He had recently implemented a punishment system on piecework for all employees. It is fair to say they hated him. They fully expected that I would be able to convince the president to fire this individual. Since I had no power to actually bring about any change in personnel but could only recommend, I had to carefully change their expectations for the outcome of this work. In fact, the president was unlikely to fire the foreman because of a relationship to his family. What I could do was recommend structural changes, provide some coping strategies for the employees, and suggest ways for the president to minimize the foreman's impact on the lives of the workers.

Implementing Change

In 1951 Kurt Lewin identified three steps in any change process that are still being applied today: initial "unfreezing" of behavior, "changing," and finally "refreezing" new behavior. During the first step, individuals must be made aware of damaging results from old ways of acting. The client must be stimulated to want to change; thus, results from data collections that reveal the lack of success with old patterns must be presented in a way to make individuals want to hear more.

In the second stage, new behaviors or changes are introduced, and in the final step, those new behaviors are reinforced and rewarded so that they get "frozen" in the individuals' minds as normal patterns.

Greiner and Metzger (1983) identified three other steps of change implementation: power reinforcement, leadership modeling, and re-education (p. 271). Power reinforcement speaks to the issue of top management's support for any change effort. If senior managers are not obviously supporting the change effort, then lower-level employees will see little reason to make changes in behaviors or systems.

Leadership modeling means having top management practice what it preaches. Employees watch management, and "if senior executives regard change as the responsibility of everyone but themselves, then the effort will falter" (p. 272).

Finally, re-education means unlearning old skills and acquiring new skills. This step combines the concepts of "unfreezing" and "refreezing," discussed in an earlier chapter. The final recommendations can then be reported to the appropriate people. Greiner and Metzger (1983) cited a case study that clearly demonstrates some of the pitfalls of the final report, which might document steps needed to implement change efforts.

> When one of the authors finished a particularly challenging assignment early in his career, he wrote a very incisive, well-documented report, which he felt included sufficient logic for a radical change. It was brilliant. He ordered 25 copies of the report to be printed. His consulting boss at the time stopped the printing and asked why so many copies had been ordered. The author replied that each member of senior management and the board of directors should have a copy. He could see clearly all the follow-up business to be sold as the client was impressed by a brilliant literary work that bordered on a doctoral dissertation.
>
> The author's boss was most understanding and agreed that the report was good. He then began to ask a few innocent questions. Had the client been consulted as to who should get a report? Which members of senior management might become alienated from the consultants if they chose to read the findings as an indictment of their previous management decisions? How much of the sensitive data in the report might be copied by someone and used for his or her own devices? What if someone left the company and took a copy to a competitor? How much damage would be done to the client?
>
> Needless to say, the author quickly contacted the client and asked for his opinion, explaining all the possible risks. The client felt that the report should not be distributed because of "potential sensitivities." The lesson was learned: always check with your client. There may be any number of reasons why the CEO or other key executives don't receive a copy, and a smart consultant won't overlook that. (p. 277)

In order for change to take place, both the consultant and the client must be ready to implement it. "The ability of the consultant to effect organizational change is in direct proportion to the client's ability to develop the climate for change and to provide the authority and support for the consultant to effect change" (Ferguson & Ferguson, 1988, p. 542). If the client isn't ready, even a Pulitzer Prize–winning essay won't have an impact.

The consultant acts as the client's conscience. As consultant, your role is to make sure the individuals see themselves as others see them. "The most useful tool in a consultant's kit to effect organizational change is not a sledge hammer, but a mirror" (Ferguson & Ferguson, 1988, p. 543). You must move at a speed with which the client can keep pace. Clients must see themselves in the mirror on their own, not have the mirror smashed over their heads!

Organizations must develop processes for dealing with dramatic changes as well as resistance to such change. Strategic planning is one approach for dealing with organizational change. Often consultants and internal managers are asked to facilitate the development of plans to cope with changing environments and change within the organization.

Strategic Planning

Strategic planning deals with the effects of constant change. "Change is not an episodic event in organizations but a normal, everyday occurrence, and both public and private organizations' survival will depend on the development of a capability to detect, analyze, and respond to constant change" (Sonnichsen, 2000, p. 103).

Pfeiffer, Goodstein, and Noland (1986a, b) defined **strategic planning** as "the process by which the guiding members of an organization envision its future and develop the necessary procedures and operations to achieve that future. 'Envisioning' involves a belief that aspects of the future can be influenced and changed by what we do now" (p. 1).

> Strategic planning is a reiterative process. Strategic planning and strategic management (which is the day-to-day implementation of the strategic plan) are never-ending tasks. The future, by definition, always faces us; thus, organizations must always be in the simultaneous process of planning and implementing their plans. (p. 3)

The fact that strategic planning has no time frame means organizations are like the painting crew on the Golden Gate Bridge in San Francisco. As soon as they reach the end of the bridge on one side, it is time to begin repainting on the other side. Painting the bridge and strategic planning never end.

Ernest (1985) suggested that "typically, planning within organizations focuses on the external environment alone, with little attention to organizational strengths and weaknesses" and calls for importance being placed on the "cultural dimension as a major component in organizational success. . . . There must be a fit between planning and the beliefs, values, and practices within the organization" (p. 49). In order to assess the organization's culture, we have to remember that the rules constantly change.

If we consider ourselves to be players of a game who know that the rules are real only to the extent that we have created or accepted them, then we can create a condition under which change can occur. This is an entirely different situation from one in which we feel like pawns in a game with rules we have no control over.

Greiner and Metzger (1983) graphically described the magnitude of the task for a change agent:

> In strategic planning, the consultant must be able to analyze all facts of a client's business from a financial, manufacturing, marketing, personnel, and organizational viewpoint, not to mention an in-depth understanding of the client's industry and competition. If that isn't enough, this comprehensive analysis must be performed in a way that crystallizes the key strategic issues and choices facing the client and then proposes realistic recommendations. To change the strategic direction of any corporation is a Herculean task, equivalent to turning a giant oil tanker in heavy seas. (p. 91)

Fortunately, in the role of consultant you do not have to know all the information. The client is the expert and in fact, if the plan is to succeed, clients must "own" it, rather than have it "handed" to them by a consultant who has done the analysis independently. The consultant acts as a facilitator of the process, keeping the group on task and making sure all planners have agreed with the analysis and plans.

If the client is prepared for planning, the consultant becomes rather unobtrusive. However, in most organizations with whom I have worked on developing planning documents, communication or interpersonal issues get in the way of decisions about the future. Unless those human interaction problems are dealt with first, the group will not move forward, but may actually move backward (see previous chapter on dealing with difficult people!).

Some recent practitioners have suggested that the change process must be increased to a rapid pace.

> In recent years business organizations have faced unprecedented challenges to grow revenue, reduce operating costs, and invest in new product development and new market opportunities. Global competition is fierce. Speed of execution is paramount. Business organizations do not have the luxury of time to set a strategic direction and engage all employees in achieving strategic business goals. As a result, businesses have reduced cycle time in many aspects of their operations with innovations such as simultaneous engineering, lean manufacturing, and just-in-time inventory. The mantra of "faster, better, cheaper" guides many decisions to improve business operations. It is now time to reduce the cycle time of designing and implementing organizational change. (Anderson, 2000, p. 3)

Goals, Objectives, and Action Plans

The goals of planning are to (1) determine the ability of the company to respond to demands by clients, (2) assess environmental factors external to the organization that will influence that company's success or failure, (3) set long-term goals and objectives, given company resources and probable or known changes in the environment, and (4) determine action steps necessary to attain company goals.

Determining the internal strengths and weaknesses of an organization must be a carefully thought-out process. If those strengths and weaknesses are constantly put in the customer's framework, they will look quite different from traits identified without the customer in mind. In one organization with which I worked, one department and the head of that department were perceived as very organized because reports were turned in on time and were complete and detailed. From the customer's viewpoint, however, their careful reporting habits sometimes got in the way of responding to customer requests in a timely fashion. The second goal of planning requires a sensitivity to the external environment. With the

■ THE SEA HORSE

Once upon a time a Sea Horse gathered up his seven pieces of eight and cantered out to find his fortune. Before he had traveled very far he met an Eel, who said,

"Psst. Hey, bud. Where 'ya goin'?"

"I'm going out to find my fortune," replied the Sea Horse, proudly.

"You're in luck," said the Eel. "For four pieces of eight you can have this speedy flipper, and then you'll be able to get there a lot faster."

"Gee, that's swell," said the Sea Horse, and paid the money and put on the flipper and slithered off at twice the speed. Soon he came upon a Sponge, who said,

"Psst. Hey, bud. Where 'ya goin'?"

"I'm going out to find my fortune," replied the Sea Horse.

"You're in luck," said the Sponge. "For a small fee I will let you have this jet-propelled scooter so that you will be able to travel a lot faster."

So the Sea Horse bought the scooter with his remaining money and went zooming thru the sea five times as fast. Soon he came upon a Shark, who said,

"Psst. Hey, bud. Where 'ya goin'?"

"I'm going out to find my fortune," replied the Sea Horse.

"You're in luck. If you'll take this short cut," said the Shark, pointing to his open mouth, "you'll save yourself a lot of time."

"Gee, thanks," said the Sea Horse, and zoomed off into the interior of the Shark, there to be devoured.

The moral of this fable is that if you're not sure where you're going, you're liable to end up someplace else.

Source: Robert Mager, *Preparing Objectives for Programmed Instruction* (San Francisco: Feron Publishers, 1984). Reprinted by permission.

constantly changing world environment, any organization is a candidate for obsolescence unless there's careful attention to environmental change.

Goals are long-term "directions" for the organization, while objectives are specific, measurable actions to be taken in order to reach the goals. **Objectives** must be *stated in clear language,* must *be measurable,* should *be obtainable* given current resources, and must have *a responsible party assigned* to them with a *time line.* Without these criteria, you do not have a plan, and without a plan, as the fable of the Sea Horse implies, you are likely to end up someplace you don't want to be!

Once broad goals have been set, and objectives identified, then action steps to take the group from "A" to "B" must be agreed upon. The sample outline in Figure 15.2 identifies the differences among goals, objectives, and action steps.

I worked with a medical association to set its objectives for a five-year period. I met with them in October and again in April of the following year. My first question was how many of the action steps had

While there are any number of ways to define goals, objectives, and action plans, they should include a clear indication of the major issues facing the group, what the group plans to do in response to those issues, and a brief outline of the specific actions they plan to take. These statements should be concise and to the point.

SAMPLE GOALS AND OBJECTIVES FOR THE ASSOCIATION OF COMMUNICATION CONSULTANTS

This hypothetical association recognizes the need to ensure that its members continue to be trained in communication theory so that their consulting practices will provide the most updated interventions to clients based on solid research results. Consequently, their first goal relates to member education:

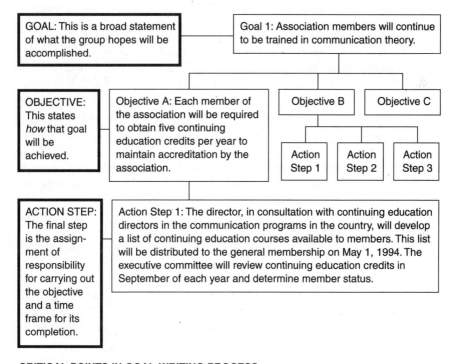

CRITICAL POINTS IN GOAL-WRITING PROCESS

1. Goals are broad statements of issues for the group.
2. Objectives must be measurable.
3. Action steps must assign responsibility and time lines.
4. Goals are not realized without specific objectives and action steps.
5. The group must attempt to reach consensus on all goals. This implies that each group member can "live with" that goal, not necessarily that each goal would be most important to every member.
6. This process takes time and extended discussion.

FIGURE 15.2   Goal Setting for Professional Associations   Developed by COMMUNI-CATION CONSULTANTS, 190 Longview Heights, Athens, Ohio.

been implemented. When I was met with blank stares, I knew that this time around, they had to agree to hold each other accountable or my time and theirs would be wasted. People naturally resist change of any kind.

Planning Model

Pfeiffer, Goodstein, and Noland (1986a, b) have developed as good a model as anyone that outlines the steps leading to strategic planning to handle change efforts (see Figure 15.3).

> To be successful, a strategic planning process should provide the criteria for making day-to-day organizational decisions and should provide a template against which all such decisions can be evaluated. . . .When a consultant asks managers about their organization's strategic plan, they frequently look pained or embarrassed and begin to search through their desk drawers or filing cabinets to find the plan, which is obviously non-functional. (p. 1)

Too often, plans are developed, placed in a file, and left there to collect dust. Thus the first question in the model by Pfeiffer and colleagues is, "How much commitment to the planning process is present?" If the answer is little or none, stop, do not pass Go, and cancel plans to move ahead into strategic planning steps! Step back and figure out how to get more commitment to the idea first.

The second step in their model is a **values audit,** which identifies the significant organizational values that cannot be "tampered with." This includes an assessment of the organizational culture and what type of change can be supported by that culture.

Step three is the **mission formulation.** Pfeiffer and colleagues suggest the organization answer these three questions: (1) What function does the organization serve? (2) For whom does the organization serve this function? and (3) How does the organization go about filling this function?

Strategic business modeling is the process by which the organization defines success and is the fourth step in this model. First the organization identifies a quantified business objective (e.g., increased profits) and then lists statements of how the quantified objectives will be achieved.

A **performance audit,** the next step, examines the recent performance of the organization on production, quality, service, profit, return on investment, cash flow, and so on. "The purpose of the performance audit is to provide the data through which the **gap analysis**—the determination of the degree to which the strategic business model is realistic and workable—can be conducted" (p. 13). The key question the audit must answer is whether the organization has the capability to implement its strategic business plan and achieve its mission.

The contingency plan identifies the major opportunities for and threats to the organization. Contingencies are considered because they will necessitate changes if they occur. Contingency planning is placed to the left of the linear phases of the model (see Figure 15.3) "because these contingencies are not based on highest probability events" (p. 15).

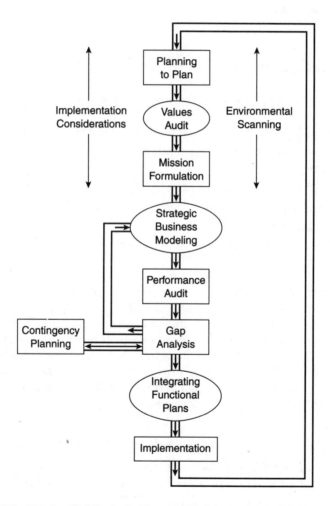

FIGURE 15.3   The Applied Strategic Planning Model   From J. W. Pfeiffer, L. D. Goodstein, & T. M. Noland. *Applied Strategic Planning: A How to Do It Guide.* San Diego, CA: University Associates, 1986. Reprinted by permission.

The final two steps are **integrating functional plans** and **implementation.** This is the place in which action steps are introduced and time lines assigned. The "final test of implementation is the degree to which managers and other members of the organization use the strategic plan in their everyday decisions on the job" (p. 17).

In the final analysis, each organization must apply the strategic planning process that suits its needs best. The applied strategic planning model is one example of a process that works with many, but not all, organizations. Everyone who is in a situation like that of Alice in the croquet game may have to develop a new age process to deal with such "unreasonable" change!

Tips on Change and Planning

What I have learned about change and the planning process includes:

- People tend to make great plans and then never implement them.
- The *process* of planning tends to help a group reach consensus about who they are.
- Without top management support, any change process is doomed.
- Resistance to change will occur even when the change is of benefit to the person resisting it!
- If you feel you have joined Alice in Wonderland, you probably have!

Strategic planning can be a long, involved process. In the following story Liane Gray Starner and I tell of one strategic planning process that lasted for nine months and was desperately needed by this organization. Liane is an excellent motivator for groups and often would activate the group to move forward when it seemed ready to get bogged down. The lessons we learned along the way, which are described in this story, we have put into practice with other planning processes.

—————————— **LESSONS LEARNED** ——————————

A Consulting Story from Sue DeWine and Liane Gray Starner: Can a Strategic Plan Save Our Organization?

Liane Gray Starner is a consultant for the Saturn Corporation. She also works with clients in education and government. She lives in Marietta, Ohio, but frequently travels across the country and in Asia and Europe to deliver training programs to Saturn employees.

In the fall of 1999 Liane called Sue and said: "How would you like to work with me on a long-term strategic planning process for a small manufacturing company? They need our help to keep them on task and identify who is the leader of this process, and our expertise in writing strategic plans."

Sue responded "I would enjoy working with you on any project, Liane. . . . I'm wondering why they have to identify who the leader is? What's up?"

Thus began a year-long assignment in which we met weekly with a group of the organizational leaders who had been charged by the organization's governing board with developing a strategic plan that would not only chart the future for the organization but get spending in line with the operating budget, increase profits, and unify what had been a conflicted group.

The organization was in trouble and had been for some time. Employees had been told that profit was declining but wouldn't listen or didn't believe the message. What made this time different? There was a leadership void. The top two posts were soon to be vacant but some board members claimed it had been over 15 years since the top leaders had shown strong leadership abilities. A combination of resignations, an increasingly bleak financial picture, and a limited marketplace had brought this organization to the brink of a crisis.

A strategic planning committee was appointed and a number of meetings had been held when members realized they needed some outside help with the planning process. An outside neutral person was sought and this led them to Liane, who then asked Sue to join her on this project. After meeting with key participants and attending several meetings, our concerns focused on the following questions:

1. Who is the leader of this strategic plan?
2. Was a "snowball" effect already in place?

What we determined was that the governing board of trustees had in effect become the "leader" of the organization and they had charged this committee and its chair with the development of a strategic plan that would cut costs to within their operating budget. There was a "snowball" effect in place since word had leaked that cuts were coming and task forces had been set up before our intervention. Some of the task forces were in direct opposition to the strategic planning committee and would no doubt clash unless they were brought into the process.

Early in the process one of our principal charges was to continue to challenge the committee to get the entire organization involved in this process. If they hoped for unification across the organization and support for the plan they would eventually come up with, they had to get unit heads involved in the initial discussions. We suggested the chairman of the board address the entire organization and alert them to the potential crisis as well as opportunities to come together and chart their future.

Another principle we supported from the beginning was to be careful not to have credit for taking positive steps in this process be attributed to us. Rather, our job was to make the client (the chair of the committee) look successful. It was critical to the success of the planning process that the committee and its leadership get all the credit when things went well because they would certainly need the memory of this praise when cuts had to be made later. At the same time we had to be prepared to take some blame if things did not go well. Consultants are often used as scapegoats and since our future does not depend on the success of this group—but the group's does—it is more important that the group be seen as successful, even if we have to take some unfair blame.

Another principle we followed was to continue to ask the group, "What is the desired outcome? How will you know when you have a successful plan? What should it look like?" In dozens of ways we were attempting to get them to establish criteria by which to measure their decisions and success. If they could agree on criteria to measure solutions, they would be much more successful at making very difficult decisions.

Finally, we carefully helped them plan a "rollout" of the plan that involved open meetings, public presentation to the board, visual reminders of the goals, and a reward system for innovative ideas contributed by employees. Our guiding principle during this stage was to recommend they not roll out a plan until they had a majority of the organization to "buy into" the plan.

No matter the outcome of the strategic plan, the process resulted in one very important outcome: the entire organization was fully aware of the crisis and had had ample opportunity to participate in setting the agenda. Of course not every idea was used; however, the committee worked hard to respond to all suggestions so the organizational members felt they had a chance to influence the process. Only the next five years will tell if their cost-saving measures and their strategic plan will save the company.

Will a strategic plan save an organization? Maybe not, but it certainly should highlight issues, help determine what an organization is and is not, and point the organization in a direction the group agrees is appropriate. Even so, that may not be enough to "save" the organization. Sometimes nothing you do as an outside consultant can help.

Liane Gray Starner can be reached at <jstarner@1st.net> or 740-896-3026.

Additional Resources

Conner, D. R. (1998). *Leading at the edge of chaos: How to create the nimble organization.* New York: Wiley.

Hite, J. (1999). *Learning in chaos.* Houston, TX: Gulf.

Kanter, R. M. (1997). *Frontiers of management.* Boston: Harvard Business School.

Morgan, G. (1997). *Images of organization.* Thousand Oaks, CA: Sage.

Chapter *16*

GLOBALIZATION AND INTERNATIONAL CONSULTING

by Mary M. Eicholtz

I praised one of my Korean trainees in a workshop today, and said that his work was very good. The trainee bowed his head, shied away with humility and modesty, and tried to deny the compliment. He said, "No, not all good." In the United States, a trainee would have said, "Thank you very much."

Adapted from Pamela Gale George, 1995

Today's global marketplace challenges organizations to communicate effectively with many different individuals. Within the organization, members of the workforce represent different ethnic, religious, and national groups and both sexes. Appreciation of difference is expected and sought in all types of organizations. Doing business in the global marketplace also requires a keen understanding of the distinctions among individuals from different cultures. Because of the emphasis on communication skills to facilitate multicultural interactions and understanding, consultants are asked to play an important role in bridging cultural gaps. Whether it's coaching an executive on how to communicate with international clients, developing a diversity and cultural sensitivity training program, or traveling to another country as a consultant, good intercultural communication skills and an understanding of the differences across cultures are valuable.

Understanding Culture within and beyond the Organization

Consultants are called by organizations to facilitate intercultural communication within the organization and beyond the organization with existing or potential clients in other regions of the world. Within the organization, identifying and accommodating cultural differences are important and a challenge to managers as employees with different cultural backgrounds learn to communicate with each other. Diversity in the workplace highlights the differences in race, ethnic origin, sex, ability/disability, and sexual orientation as well as country of origin. In the past, American companies believed that individuals who were different should assimilate into

359

the existing dominant culture. To assimilate into a culture often required the individuals to assume the values and beliefs of the organization as their own and give up characteristics that make them unique. In recognition and appreciation of difference in our society, we now believe that it is much more beneficial for an organization to accommodate difference. When we accommodate cultural differences, individuals retain their cultural identities and contribute that uniqueness to the organization.

Organizations also require information about successful intercultural communication when considering interactions with clients from different parts of the world. With the advances in technology and the emphasis on a global marketplace, these interactions are more commonplace and demand a new sensitivity to cultural issues. Effective communication with individuals who do not speak the same language or understand your cultural practices must be part of any strategic business plan. Traveling to other countries to do business or having clients travel to the main office often necessitates a comprehensive understanding of cultural practices.

Individualism or Collectivism

An important issue is whether a culture is oriented to achieving individual goals or collective goals. Cultures that espouse individual success tend to be more direct in their communication. Individuals seek and take credit for success. Likewise, blame is often attached to one individual. When individualism is part of the culture, it affects work, play, family life, achievement, and failure. The United States, Canada, and Australia are very individualist cultures. Because of this individualistic value, people in these cultures are not timid about asking for information that might help them achieve personal goals. In very direct language, they are more apt to use words like *you* and *I*. Rewards are given to individuals when targets are met, so everyone is motivated to communicate in a manner that will ensure success. Individualism makes working in groups and collaboration difficult.

Collectivism focuses on a concern for the success and welfare of the group to which one belongs. This group might be a work group, team, or extended family. Individuals in a group share both success and failure. They seek to identify how each member of the group can contribute to the group's overall goal. Communication in collectivist cultures is indirect and often ambiguous. It is more common to hear terms like *they* and *we*. Likewise, seeking information is less obvious and more collaborative. Discussion is valued as a method for determining group goals and procedures. Countries in Asia, South America, and Africa are more collectivist. Native Americans might also be considered collectivist. Team projects, discussion, and brainstorming would work well in these cultures.

High-Context and Low-Context Cultures

High-context and low-context cultures refer to the circumstances around which a message is delivered and received. Hall (1976) identified high-context cultures as those that rely on implicit messages in addition to the spoken word to understand what is being communicated. The sender assumes that the receiver(s) of his or her message have common cultural experiences. In a high-context culture, gestures, shortened words, nonverbal behavior, and social influences are used as frequently as language to convey a message. Japan, the Middle East, and South American countries tend to be high-context cultures.

Low-context cultures prefer explicit messages. Direct and honest communication is valued. The communicator does not rely on tradition, hidden messages, and cultural context. She or he does not assume the receiver(s) interpret the culture the same way she or he does. Therefore, individuals in a low-context culture might appear rude or abrupt to someone in a high-context culture. Likewise, someone in a high-context culture might seem shady or distrustful to an individual in a low-context culture. In general, individualistic cultures tend to be low-context cultures and collectivistic cultures are high-context cultures.

The Consultant's Role within the Organization

The consultant's role in promoting and facilitating intercultural communication within and beyond organizations can be demonstrated in many interactions, which are evident in two ways. First, the consultant can engage in actual intercultural communication training and development with employees. Furthermore, the consultant can demonstrate attention to intercultural communication by implementing the intercultural communication skills in all the interventions he or she employs with an organization.

Organizations often ask consultants to help improve the communication skills in a diverse workplace. Brislin and Yoshida (1994a) suggested that companies consider a four-part intercultural communication program for employees. These steps include awareness, knowledge, emotions, and skills. A thorough training program that includes all of these components could take several days, but the consultant should not overlook any area if the training is to be effective. Like any training program, a needs assessment should be conducted to ascertain the level of knowledge or skill the participants already possess. Awareness explores the realm of a person's consciousness toward difference and the values and biases that might influence his or her attitude toward diversity. The consultant's objective should be to make the individual comfortable with difference in intercultural situations. Once a person is aware of the impact of intercultural interactions, the consultant should provide knowledge about other cultures. This knowledge ranges from simple customs and traditions to more complex lifestyle considerations. One of the difficult challenges for consultants is helping people accept difference because so many of our emotions are connected to the ethnocentric belief that our culture is superior. Accepting other cultures, in a sense, invalidates our values and makes us feel that we are wrong. Consultants often neglect this aspect of intercultural communication training, but it can be an important element to success. Finally, after individuals are aware, knowledgeable, and emotionally ready, the consultant can proceed with various interventions.

■ CURES FOR CULTURE SHOCK

Americans tend to be direct. They strive for success and are unwilling to accept failure. Americans working with people of other cultures might find that their own values are not universally accepted. The clash of cultures can affect people's motivation and reduce their productivity, especially for a person who is working abroad.

To be successful in an unfamiliar culture, one must understand and adapt to the culture. Here are some proven strategies that can ease the impact of culture shock:

1. *Learn before you go.* Attend a training class or group discussion on the host culture. Experiment with food at ethnic restaurants, and contact businesspeople or students from the area to which you are going.

2. *Study the language.* It is important to learn the basic language for greeting others and shopping, even if business associates speak English. Also, learn significant gestures, customs, and expected courtesies.

3. *Socialize with host nationals.* Spend time both at home and abroad with people from the host nation.

4. *Be sensitive to cultural differences.* Be open to the new culture. Do not criticize local practices and customs. Relax and pick up the rhythm of the host nation. Realize that being direct can be interpreted as impolite or rude.

5. *Understand that co-cultures exist.* Complex cultures are made up of different religions and ethnic groups. Do not jump to simple conclusions based on limited knowledge. The host country might be a multicultural environment. Realize that your limited interactions might not be a representative sample.

6. *Accept your biased view.* Remember that you are observing the culture from your own frame of reference and filtering new experiences through your cultural biases.

7. *Be tolerant, patient, and open.* Be willing to live with inconveniences. Be patient with yourself and your hosts. Be curious and experimental. Keep an open mind; give the intercultural experience time to take hold.

Adapted from Hanson, J., and Fox, W. (1995). Communicating across cultures. *Training and Development, 49*(1), 56–58.

Consulting in Another Culture

As corporations assimilate into other cultures and become an integral part of the global society, they offer consultants opportunities to travel around the world and into multicultural situations. While the opportunities are exciting, the consultant must recognize the communication challenges. When one is communicating in other cultures, protocol, or the way things are done appropriately, is important. Protocol reflects customs and traditions. Greetings, appropriate gift giving, dress, proper language, and implicit messages are influenced by protocol. For example, in Japan people greet each other in a long low bow, in China a short bow is preferred, and in Hong Kong handshakes are the accepted greeting (Axtell, 1993). Several guidebooks contain this type of information, and a consultant expecting to work in a foreign culture must become knowledgeable about these protocol issues.

Cultural Impact on Specific Consulting Interventions

Consultants need to consider carefully the interventions they use with intercultural groups. While some interventions may be appropriate across cultures, others could cause frustration, embarrassment, or misunderstanding among the participants and for the consultant. Gibson (1998) suggested that consultants be able to adapt their attitudes and their interventions when consulting with intercultural clients. They need to be active listeners and flexible in their communication behaviors, always sensitive to differences. Most important, consultants need to know and be able to use a variety of consulting interventions. When one intervention is unsuccessful because of cultural difference, the consultant must be able to adjust the intervention or use a different approach to reach his or her objectives.

A consultant can do several things to avoid failures in intercultural consulting (Gibson, 1998). First, the consultant should do his or her research before approaching an intercultural assignment. Through the Internet, a wealth of current information is available to supplement the more traditional forms of knowledge. Second, the consultant should use his or her professional contacts to explore and discuss the experiences others have had in other cultures. This networking should include individuals such as professors, businesspersons, and international students and community members because they can offer insight and information not available elsewhere. A consultant can also conduct a mock intervention to test its acceptance with a small group of individuals from the target culture. Finally, a consultant should seek the client's advice, asking his or her opinion about the intervention before implementation.

■ WORKING WITH TRANSLATORS

In many international settings you will require the aid of a translator. It takes a great deal of skill on the trainer/consultant's part to make the translation become part of the training session rather than an interruption. In a recent training program I conducted in Prague, I had two translators for a week-long training session with bankers. This was a government contract and I did not participate in the selection of the translators. Fortunately, the two young women selected were excellent. One was a drama major and repeated my words with the same inflection and gestures I used! I discovered one very important technique: always look into the eyes of the trainee, even as the translator is speaking, to create the sense of communicating with each other. At first I would talk, pause, look at the translator and wait for her to finish before I turned back to the trainee. This broke my concentration and the trainee's as well. Once I got used to speaking slowly, pausing slightly, and maintaining eye contact with the trainees, it was almost as if we were ignoring the translator. It became very smooth—almost as if we could both understand English and Czech. However, I always wondered when I told a joke if the translator wasn't saying something like, "She just told a joke that wasn't very funny but laugh anyway just to make her feel better!" I also asked the translators to "sit in" on small group discussions. One would whisper in my ear what the group was saying, and from time to time, I would inject feedback with her help. By the end of the week, I felt comfortable enough to use any technique I would normally use with a group, but keeping in mind this culture. I recommend spending some time with the translators before the training to describe how you operate and exactly how you would like them to handle the group sessions.

From Sue DeWine, Communication Consultants.

Suggested Interventions in Different Cultures

The consultant should contemplate a culture's tendency toward high and low context, and individualist and collectivist societies when using the interventions outlined in this book. A chart like the one in Table 16.1 is very helpful. A consultant must examine the audience to determine how an intervention might be adapted. As with any presentation, relating to the audience is essential for success. If the goal is to change attitudes and behavior in a multicultural environment, it might be appropriate to present an intervention as it is intended so individuals feel slightly uncomfortable. For example, active listening is not a behavior that most individuals are comfortable with in individualistic or low-context cultures. However, if the goal of the session is to make them more aware of their inadequacies in listening, the intervention should be presented as intended.

TABLE 16.1

INTERVENTION APPROPRIATENESS CHART

Intervention	High Context	Low Context	Individualistic	Collectivist
Surveys/audits		X	X	
Strategic planning	X	X	X	X
Process observation	X	X	X	X
TQM	X	X	X	X
Team building	X	X	X	X
Re-engineering	X	X	X	X
Executive coaching		X	X	
NGT	X			X
Role plays		X	X	
Outdoor games		X	X	
Agenda setting	X	X	X	X
Norm setting	X	X	X	X
Active listening	X			X
Confrontation meeting		X	X	
Feedback	X	X	X	X
Focus groups	X	X	X	X
PERT		X	X	

Some interventions, however, are inappropriate for some cultures. A meeting confrontation would never work in a culture that deferred decisions to an authority figure. Pointing out displeasure or frustration would be considered rude and disrespectful. However, a variation of the intervention might work. If members of the group expressed their ideas anonymously, information could be exchanged in a collaborative spirit. Team building might be problematic in an individualistic culture where individual accomplishment is acknowledged; however, if within the team-building process, individuals can express their own ideas and goals, they might be more willing to work as a group.

In general, collaborative interventions work well in high-context, collectivist cultures where the good of the group is always put first. These interventions include strategic planning, process observation, TQM, team building, re-engineering, NGT, outdoor games, active listening, focus groups, and PERT. (These interventions are discussed in detail in Chapter 8.) The consultant must focus the energy on the group goal and accomplishment. In many of these interventions, nonverbal and assumed behaviors also play roles in their success. The consultant must be keenly aware of the group's communication behaviors, observing what is not said or expressed as well as what is said. Consultants can adapt these interventions by focusing on the individual's contribution to the group process and using the naturally competitive nature of individualistic cultures to accomplish the goal. Low-context cultures are also more direct in their communication and participation in these interventions.

In low-context, individualistic cultures, interventions that ask for direct communication by the participants or reward individual knowledge and contributions are particularly successful. These interventions include surveys and audits, strategic planning, process observation, re-engineering, executive coaching, role plays, confrontation meetings, feedback, and PERT. (These interventions are discussed in detail in Chapter 8.) These interventions allow individual input and direct communication. Additionally, outdoor games and TQM could appeal to the competitive nature of these cultures. Likewise, if the consultant modifies these interventions for anonymity and focuses on collaborative goals, they can be successful in more collectivist cultures.

Preparing Corporate Leaders for a Global Society

Communication can influence intercultural interactions beyond the boundaries of the organization. An executive who is well informed about a culture's protocols is more likely to succeed. Accommodating the values and beliefs of clients, customers, or suppliers in other cultures can ensure that business transactions will be conducted expeditiously. A consultant can coach and train organizational executives and managers about the most appropriate ways to communicate in other cultures. As companies move beyond the boundaries of their geographical home and do business in other countries and continents, managers, administrators, and technical workers need to understand how to interact with competitors, suppliers, and clients in other cultures. Odenwald (1993) reported on the definition of global training, agreed to at the 1991 ASTD annual conference, as containing three essential elements. These elements include

1. reaching commonly defined goals with people from cultures other than one's own while maintaining the integrity of the other culture,
2. facilitating the transfer of knowledge or skills so it can be used appropriately in the new culture, and
3. creating a climate in which changes in attitude, behavior, and perceptions are achieved through the sharing of knowledge and technology in a culturally appropriate way.

Keeping these goals in mind, global training can accomplish positive outcomes for the corporation including identifying business opportunities, giving an edge over other competitors, improving job satisfaction of overseas staff, and improving effectiveness in global business environments.

Similar to training for diversity within the organization, global training beyond the organization identifies three specific components of an intercultural curriculum (Odenwald, 1993). These elements include cultural awareness, intercultural communication training, and country-specific training. Cultural awareness focuses on the considerations individuals need to keep in mind when doing business in a multinational environment. Determining how multicultural communication might affect working relationships and how to establish personal interactions that promote teamwork and productivity is imperative in making employees culturally aware. The consultant can also cover the pitfalls of cultural taboos during this training. Intercultural communication skills assess and present the specific task and relationship skills necessary for communicating with individuals in other cultures. These topics can vary with the specific situation but might include language patterns, appropriate media for communicating, nonverbal communication, team building, negotiating, sales protocols, appropriate social behavior, and the use of a translator.

The final element is country-specific training. This training was one of the first recognized by corporations as necessary for employees who would be located overseas. It is equally important for family members and employees scheduled for short-term assignment in other cultures. Country-specific programs are similar to orientation programs that attempt to assimilate the employee to the new environment. They are specific to the culture and country where the employee will be located and include mundane details like where to shop and how to catch a cab, as well as complex interpersonal behaviors typical of the individuals from the culture. Country-specific programs need to be planned carefully with senior executives so expectations can be met.

In addition to understanding if a culture is individualistic or collectivist and a high-context or low-context society, the coaching of executives for intercultural interactions should cover several important concepts. These concepts include power distance, uncertainty avoidance, and masculinity. Power distance is the degree to which a society believes power is distributed unequally. This concept influences interactions between classes, superiors and subordinates, and individuals in official positions. Uncertainty avoidance refers to the rules a society provides so that ambiguous situations are avoided. Masculinity focuses on the degree to which a society embraces assertiveness and achievement over quality of life. These concepts can shape the way to do business in a particular culture.

Self-Assessment of Communication Behavior and Intercultural Communication Practices

One tool a consultant can use in coaching the corporate executive or international manager is a self-assessment questionnaire. Participants can complete the self-test to establish a quick evaluation of attitudes or to get participants thinking about intercultural communication attitudes. Used as an icebreaker to intercultural communication training sessions, the questionnaire can facilitate discussion about the topic. Zhao and Parks (1995) offered the questionnaire (Form 16.1) and its analysis (Form 16.2). They identified seven dimensions to intercultural communication behavior in their analysis. These dimensions include adaptation, display of respect, empathy, interaction management, interaction posture, orientation to knowledge, and role behavior.

INTERCULTURAL COMMUNICATION BEHAVIOR

Directions: This questionnaire is designed to help you identify your intercultural communication behavior. Each question has no correct or incorrect answer. Please read the whole question and then check the choice that most accurately describes your communication behavior. Work quickly; do not ponder.

1. When speaking with people from other cultures and nations, I usually _____ others' feelings, experiences, or potentials.

    ____ (1) ignore

    ____ (2) show little concern for

    ____ (3) show some concern for

    ____ (4) show concern for

    ____ (5) show deep concern for

2. While listening to people from other cultures and nations, I usually respond to them

    ____ (1) immediately in a highly evaluative manner based on my thoughts, beliefs, and values.

    ____ (2) in a highly evaluative manner based on my thoughts, beliefs, and values.

    ____ (3) in a descriptive and evaluative manner based on information, thoughts, and feelings gathered from the interaction and me.

    ____ (4) in a descriptive manner based on sufficient information, thoughts, and feelings from the interaction.

3. When explaining myself and the world around me, I usually use terms such as

    ____ (1) "It is human nature . . . ," "We've all experienced . . . ," and "What else could they have done . . . ?"

    ____ (2) "In my country . . . ," "We Americans find that . . . ," and "Japanese are generally . . . ."

    ____ (3) "My friends and I believe . . . ," "Most of you in the group know that . . . ," and "People in my profession all know that. . . ."

    ____ (4) "I believe that . . . ," "I feel that . . . ," and "My viewpoint is that. . . ."

4. In new or ambiguous situations overseas, I am _____ .

    ____ (1) very nervous and very slow to adapt to the situation.

    ____ (2) somewhat nervous and slow to adapt to the situation.

    ____ (3) a little nervous and adapt to the situation at normal speed.

(Continued)

INTERCULTURAL COMMUNICATION BEHAVIOR *(Continued)*

———— (4) comfortable and quick to adapt to the situation.

———— (5) very comfortable and very quick to adapt to the situation.

5. When interacting with people from other cultures and nations, I ———— "put myself in others' shoes."

———— (1) never

———— (2) seldom

———— (3) occasionally

———— (4) frequently

———— (5) always

6. In intercultural group activities, I ———— ask for *more facts* in order to accomplish our group task.

———— (1) always

———— (2) frequently

———— (3) occasionally

———— (4) seldom

———— (5) never

7. In intercultural group activities, I ———— initiate ideas in order to accomplish our group task.

———— (1) never

———— (2) seldom

———— (3) occasionally

———— (4) frequently

———— (5) always

8. In intercultural group activities, I ———— seek evaluation and clarification of our ideas in order to accomplish our group task.

———— (1) always

———— (2) frequently

———— (3) occasionally

———— (4) seldom

———— (5) never

9. In intercultural group activities, I ———— harmonize the relations of the group members.

———— (1) never

———— (2) seldom

———— (3) occasionally

———— (4) frequently

———— (5) always

(Continued)

INTERCULTURAL COMMUNICATION BEHAVIOR *(Continued)*

10. In intercultural group activities, I _____ mediate conflicts of the group members.

    _____ (1) always

    _____ (2) frequently

    _____ (3) occasionally

    _____ (4) seldom

    _____ (5) never

11. In intercultural group activities, I _____ regulate the evenness of participation of the group members.

    _____ (1) never

    _____ (2) seldom

    _____ (3) occasionally

    _____ (4) frequently

    _____ (5) always

12. In intercultural group activities, I _____ resist others' ideas.

    _____ (1) always

    _____ (2) frequently

    _____ (3) occasionally

    _____ (4) seldom

    _____ (5) never

13. In intercultural group activities, I _____ insist on my own views.

    _____ (1) never

    _____ (2) seldom

    _____ (3) occasionally

    _____ (4) frequently

    _____ (5) always

14. In intercultural group activities, I _____ attempt to manipulate the group by asserting my authority.

    _____ (1) always

    _____ (2) frequently

    _____ (3) occasionally

    _____ (4) seldom

    _____ (5) never

(Continued)

INTERCULTURAL COMMUNICATION BEHAVIOR *(Continued)*

15. As a member of an intercultural group, I _____ like taking turns in group discussion.

_____ (1) never

_____ (2) seldom

_____ (3) occasionally

_____ (4) frequently

_____ (5) always

SCORING YOUR INTERCULTURAL COMMUNICATION

Directions: To determine your score, adjust the numbers in the following questions: For Q6, Q8, and Q13, always = 1, frequently = 2, occasionally = 3, seldom = 2, and never = 1. For Q10, reverse the numbers: always = 5, frequently = 4, occasionally = 3, seldom = 2, and never = 1.

Now add the numbers you have chosen from the 15 questions. Your total score on this questionnaire should be between 15 and 67 (any score below 15 or above 67 means a miscalculation).

Above 57: You are likely to be successful in intercultural communication and management.

50 to 57: You are likely to be successful in intercultural communication and management.

40 to 49: You are likely to need some training in order to be successful in intercultural communication and management.

Below 49: You are likely to encounter many difficulties in intercultural communication. In order to be successful in intercultural communication and management, you need to adjust your attitude and behavior by participating in relevant training programs.

Communication Behavior and Intercultural Business Success

Communication behavior is important in managing an intercultural workforce and in handling international business. Numerous U.S. multinational corporations and Japanese companies in the United States report that the big problem in their organizations is difficult intercultural communication and its significant costs.

Ruben and Kealey's longitudinal study (1979) identified the following seven dimensions of communication competence as predictors of the success of international and intercultural business management. Other empirical studies (Kiechel, 1994; Kim, 1989; Zhao & Ober, 1991) confirmed these predictors.

1. *Adaptation* (related to question 4 in Form 16.1). Adaptation refers to the ability of individuals to learn to act appropriately in new or ambiguous situations. Those who are unwilling or slow to adapt to new situations may have many problems in intercultural interaction. Diplomats, missionaries, students, researchers, emigrants, employees of multinational corporations, and numerous others are going through the process of adapting when being abroad. Their survival and livelihood depend largely on their ability to acquire new knowledge and to perform according to the standards and practices of the host society (Kim, 1989).

2. *Display of respect* (related to question 1). This is the ability to show positive regard for another person in interpersonal and intercultural relations. Respect is conveyed in a variety of ways—through eye contact, body postures, voice tone and pitch, and general displays of interest (Ruben, 1976). International business managers perceive showing respect as a very important managerial skill for U.S.–international business success.

3. *Empathy* (related to question 5). Empathy is the ability to understand others' situations and feelings through giving and receiving feedback. Kiechel's (1994) study of managerial careers in the new economy pointed out that the new manager not only needs just as many analytical skills as the old one does, but he or she also must be empathetic. Empathy is one of the central communication skills. Empathy can be shown nonverbally through nodding, appropriate eye contact, and mirroring facial expressions. Listening actively and communicating (giving and receiving) feedback are perceived as important skills in international business (Zhao & Ober, 1991).

4. *Interaction management* (related to question 15). This is the ability to handle the process of human interaction. Interaction management

includes negotiation of topics discussed, taking turns, entering and exiting episodes, and handling topical development smoothly. Holding negotiations, conducting meetings, communicating decisions, and making presentations are important for international business management (Zhao & Ober, 1991).

5. *Interaction posture* (related to question 2). This refers to the ability to respond to others in a descriptive and nonjudgmental way. Judgment, evaluation, and appraisal are the major barriers to interpersonal communication. U.S. international business managers consider the skill of withholding judgment important in international business management (Zhao & Ober, 1991).

6. *Orientation to knowledge* (related to question 3). This means the flexibility with which individuals explain things to different people according to different situations in order to reach the same results. The research findings of Ruben and Kealey (1979) showed that orientation of knowledge predict cultural awareness and communication effectiveness in intercultural communication. Zhao and Ober's (1991) survey indicated that the vice presidents of international business in 78 Fortune 500 industrial corporations perceived maintaining flexibility as an important skill for international business success.

7. *Role behavior* (related to questions 6 through 14). Role behavior refers to the ability to perform both relationship and task roles and the ability to avoid self-centered roles. In intercultural interaction, developing a working relationship is the basis on which two parties can facilitate task roles. Without a good working relationship, two parties cannot conduct business (Alston, 1989; Fisher & Brown, 1988; LePoole, 1989).

Adapted from Zhao, J. J., and Parks, C. (1995). Self-assessment of communication behavior: An experiential learning exercise for intercultural business success. *Business Communication Quarterly, 58*(1), 20–26.

Managing Intercultural Communication

The global executive is faced with the challenge of managing communication in many different cultures. Achieving this formidable task requires skill and knowledge. A consultant can use the cross-cultural awareness exercise in Form 16.3 to measure the executive's strengths and weaknesses in knowledge about other countries and cultures.

CROSS-CULTURAL AWARENESS

Indicate the degree to which the questions listed below are true for you. Use the following scale.

1 = definitely no   2 = not likely   3 = not sure
4 = likely   5 = definitely yes

_____ 1. I can effectively conduct business in a language other than my native language.

_____ 2. I can read and write a language other than my native language with great ease.

_____ 3. I understand the proper protocol for conducting a business card exchange in at least two countries other than my own.

_____ 4. I understand the role of the Keiretsu in Japan and the Chaebol in Korea.

_____ 5. I understand the differences in manager-subordinate relationships in two countries other than my own.

_____ 6. I understand the differences in negotiation styles in two countries other than my own.

_____ 7. I understand the proper protocols for gift giving in at least three countries.

_____ 8. I understand how a country's characteristic preferences for individualism versus collectivism can affect business practice.

_____ 9. I understand the nature and importance of demographic diversity in at least three countries.

_____ 10. I understand my own country's laws regarding giving gifts or favors while on international assignments.

_____ 11. I understand the impact cultural factors have on the sales, marketing, and distribution systems of different countries.

_____ 12. I understand how differences in male-female relationships affect the business practices in at least three countries.

(Continued)

CROSS-CULTURAL AWARENESS *(Continued)*

_____ 13. I have studied and understand the history of a country other than my native country.

_____ 14. I can identify the countries of the European Community without looking them up.

_____ 15. I know which gestures to avoid using overseas because of their obscene meanings.

_____ 16. I understand the impact communication style practiced in specific countries can have on business practices.

_____ 17. I know in which countries I can use my first name with recent business acquaintances.

_____ 18. I understand the culture and business trends in major countries in which my organization conducts business.

_____ 19. I regularly receive and review news and information from and about overseas locations.

_____ 20. I have access to and use a cultural informant before conducting business at an overseas location.

Note to Consultants

This exercise can be used in a variety of ways. After participants identify their strengths and weaknesses, small groups can be assembled to discuss how to approach weak areas. The exercise can also be used to prompt the participants to discuss areas that the training session should focus on.

Using Case Studies to Evaluate Intercultural Consulting

Applying knowledge presented in intercultural interventions to case studies is an effective means to evaluate learning. These case studies can either be taken from the experiences of the participants or be hypothetical. Executives and managers can present case studies in writing at the beginning of the consulting period and then evaluate each other's situations at the conclusion of the coaching sessions. This process presents the reality of the international business world. Hypothetical case studies might also be appropriate for use in evaluation. Once the case study is presented, discussion in groups or one-on-one is beneficial. Participants can identify specific concepts presented to the executive or manager during the consulting period. The two case studies given here (Goodman, 1994) are typical of the stories that can enhance and evaluate learning and application.

■ CASE STUDY 1: **THAILAND**

John has recently been sent by his company to Bangkok to head up a staff of Thai account executives. After three months on site, he is beginning to settle in and become familiar with his Thai associates. One day after dictating a letter to his secretary, John is interrupted by a phone call from the United States. He excuses himself but not before asking his secretary to bring him the letter as soon as it is ready. During the phone conversation, the secretary knocks on the door and John motions for her to come in and give him the letter. He quickly scans it, puts it in the envelope, licks the envelope and stamp, and returns the letter to the secretary. The secretary appears to be upset but John cannot interrupt the conversation. Later in the day, John asks his secretary if everything is all right. She says yes, but John senses that there is something wrong.

What could John have done to upset his secretary? In many countries, the royal family is held in high esteem. Jokes about the royal family and provocative questions about royalty should be avoided. In Thailand, the king is regarded with great love and admiration. If properly coached before going to Thailand, John was probably well aware of the importance of the king in Thai society. What he failed to consider in this scenario was that given the high regard for the king, the king's picture appears in many places, including postage stamps. By licking the stamp that had a picture of the king on the reverse side, John was showing great disrespect for the king. This was very upsetting to the secretary. The secretary would not wish her boss to lose face by telling him of his disrespectful behavior, so he will probably continue to act in a disrespectful manner. This case study is an example of how power distance can influence a cultural norm. In high power distance societies, there is generally greater social distance between people of different statuses, greater use of titles, more respect for age, and a reduced likelihood that a subordinate would correct the behavior of a superior. (p. 38)

■ CASE STUDY 2: **UNITED STATES AND FRANCE**

A French tourist fell on a patch of ice in front of an exclusive store in New York City. After returning to France, he developed complications resulting from the fall. His condition worsened, so a few months later he wrote a letter to the American store asking for the name of the company's insurance carrier. Having no reply in three months, he sent a second letter via a private mail service. Two weeks later, he received a reply that said, in part, "We see no justice in your alleged claim since on the day you claimed to fall, 9/2/92, it was 90°F in New York and there was no possibility of there being ice on the sidewalk."

How do you explain this situation? In France, as in most of Europe, dates are written in the following sequence: day/month/year. The tourist wrote that he fell on 9/2/92, which was of course February 9, 1992, not September 2, 1992. (p. 37)

Consulting in a foreign culture requires that you understand basic norms of interaction. The following story describes Sue DeWine's experiences negotiating contracts in Asia, where the negotiations are quite different from those in the United States, as Sue quickly learned!

───────── LESSONS LEARNED ─────────

A Consulting Story from Sue DeWine

Most of my international negotiating experience has taken place in Asian cultures. On my first trip to Bangkok, Thailand, I was attempting to negotiate a contract for the university. I was staying a week and I had read enough to know that the first part of the week, maybe even most of the week, would be spent in getting to know the officials and attending formal receptions. So I wasn't surprised when no formal meetings were planned until late in the week. I spent most of my time meeting people and talking with officials and seeing the city. Over dinners, teas, receptions, and formal news events we talked casually about the university and what a strong relationship we would have with institutions in Bangkok. I was prepared to talk specifics but none were ever brought up. The day before I left, a formal meeting was planned for late afternoon. I was thinking this would finally be the negotiation session when we would talk finances and program details.

The meeting began with the usual tea and small sandwiches. Many officials were there and we began reviewing the week and how pleasant my visit had been. The officials talked about broad general topics and other projects they were involved with. Near the end of the meeting I tried to steer the conversation toward specific contract issues, but all I got were smiles. "Thailand is the land of smiles" is quite true. Individuals will rarely refuse any request. They will smile and simply not do it! When I returned to the United States, I thought I had not accomplished anything. Yet, within a week they had accepted the contract without change. What I had accomplished was building enough trust and a strong enough relationship that they were willing to enter into a contract, exactly as I outlined it, trusting me to be fair and accurate! I had been successful after all; I just didn't know it.

The most important thing I learned about negotiating in an Asian culture was not to expect to have a negotiating session at all! Negotiations actually take place while you are building relationships. Over tea or dinner, casual conversations may revolve around the promising relationship or program, but actual direct bargaining or negotiating "American style" simply does not occur. You spend a great deal of time building trust and friendships first.

I have had similar experiences in Hong Kong and Singapore. In Hong Kong I had a direct conflict with a hotel manager and instead of having a conversation with him about the conflict, I was advised by my Hong Kong colleagues to see him each morning, smile, and tell him that I was "working on the problem but did not yet have a solution." We were staying in a family suite at the hotel and according to hotel guidelines we had one too many people in the room. Later in the week my Hong Kong colleagues told me to change the message to the following: "Since we have two children with us we are trying to decide which one will have to stay somewhere else and we just haven't been able to decide." Because family is so important in this culture, and because I was not directly confronting him, they felt sure the manager would not bring up the issue again. He didn't, and we all stayed quite happily in the family suite.

Friendship, trust, and saving face are most important in this culture. Direct confrontation and conversation are often inappropriate and do not work as well as indirect suggestions and negotiations. This was a lesson I learned early and have tried to follow ever since that first contract was negotiated.

Additional Resources

Axtell, R. E. (1993). *Do's and taboos around the world*. New York: Wiley.

Brislin, R., & Yoshida, T. (1994). *Intercultural communication training: An introduction*. Thousand Oaks, CA: Sage.

Brislin, R. W., & Yoshida, T. (Eds.). (1994). *Improving intercultural interactions: Modules for cross-cultural training programs*. Thousand Oaks, CA: Sage.

Odenwald, S. B. (1993). *Global training: How to design a program for the multinational corporation*. Alexandria, VA: American Society of Training and Development.

Ting-Toomey, S. (1999). *Communicating across cultures*. New York: Guilford.

PART V

Evaluating Success

*E*valuating the success of a training or consulting intervention is a critical, but often neglected, aspect of the process. Chapters 17 and 18 outline steps that should be taken so that you and the client can determine the degree to which any approach has been successful. If you don't have a good understanding of what impact you have had in the past, you can't expect to be able to predict with any certainty how successful you will be in the future.

The argument made in these chapters is that evaluation should be a "front-end" activity, meaning it should be a part of the initial planning step, not tacked on after the intervention is completed. You may want to begin the evaluation with the very first introduction of some change in the system. You will need to determine from the beginning how you will measure your success.

Chapter *17*

EVALUATING THE IMPACT OF TRAINING

There is a decreasing willingness to spend money on faith and an increasing pressure to justify training costs. Therefore, it is necessary for those in the field to focus on training evaluation and to adequately demonstrate and communicate to management that training efforts are making worthwhile contributions.

Robert S. Dvorin,
ASTD Info-Line, 1986

Allocation of funds for training programs are based on an assumption that better trained employees will be greater assets to any organization. It is often difficult, however, to determine specific benefits to the organization as a result of training. Many training programs are not evaluated in any systematic way. A great deal of practical advice about the need for training evaluation has been written (Bakken & Bernstein, 1982; Deming, 1982; Denova, 1970; Dopyera & Pitone, 1983; Kearsley, 1982; Salinger & Deming, 1982; Zenger & Hargis, 1982), but few researchers have attempted to measure levels of training impact.

Wexley and Latham (1981) suggested:

> The typical approach to training and development is to review a program with one or two vice presidents at the corporate office, various managers in the field, and perhaps a group of prospective trainees. If the program looks good, the organization uses it. In fact, the program may be used again and again until it becomes all but institutionalized. It continues to be used until someone in a position of authority decides the program has outlived its usefulness. (p. 78)

This is a typical system for evaluating the impact of training in many organizations. Much of the evaluation is done on the basis of opinion and judgment. In the end, no one really has a good understanding of exactly what the training has accomplished.

Obstacles to Evaluation

In a survey distributed by *Personnel*, approximately 75 percent of the companies contacted had no formal methods of evaluating the effectiveness of their training programs, although approximately 30 percent of these companies either recognized the need for developing techniques for evaluation or were attempting to formulate a system (Wagel, 1977). In a more recent survey, nearly one-half of the large industrial corporations surveyed listed a lack of standards and yardsticks as the most pressing problem, weakness, or shortcoming with respect to evaluation of in-house management training programs (Clegg, 1987).

Besides the obvious reason why evaluating training is important, there is a more subtle one. A major new study finds that employees participating in company-sponsored training do, indeed, value it. Participants reported that training makes a difference not only on the job but in the way they view their employer and how inclined they might be to jump to another company. In general, the more training workers receive, the happier they are with that training and with their employer (Schaaf, 1998, p. 60). In short, an organization sends an underlying message by offering training and it affects the way employees view the organization as a whole. This message is almost as important as the content of the training.

Clearly many organizations still have not implemented formal evaluation procedures. A variety of myths surround the evaluation process, preventing this implementation.

Training Evaluation Myths

Often, individuals do not conduct formal evaluation programs because they believe it cannot be done. Phillips (1987, pp. 2–4) identified nine myths about evaluation of training that training directors must overcome:

Myth 1 I can't measure the results of my training efforts.

Myth 2 I don't know what information to collect.

Myth 3 If I can't calculate the return on investment, then it is useless to evaluate the program.

Myth 4 Measurement is only effective in the production and financial areas.

Myth 5 My chief executive officer does not require an evaluation, so why should I do it?

Myth 6 There are too many variables affecting behavior change for me to evaluate the impact of training.

Myth 7 Evaluation will lead to criticism.

Myth 8 I don't need to justify my existence; I have a proven track record.

Myth 9 The emphasis on evaluation should be the same in all organizations.

Myth 5 becomes a cover for many of the other excuses. If no one has asked for the information, why should I put myself through the extra trouble? Underlying myths 1, 2, 6, and 7 is a lack of confidence or ability to conduct such evaluation programs. Therefore, excuses are invented about the kind of information to collect and the way in which to collect it. Myths 3 and 4 suggest very limited uses of evaluation programs and thus provide an excuse for nonimplementation. Myth 8 may suggest a false sense of security. If the only reason someone can think of to conduct an evaluation is to justify his or her existence, then it probably does need to be justified!

Inadequate Evaluation Methods

In order to link training to bottom-line results, training directors must show outcome results from the training. The only way to prove the existence of any concrete results from training is to have an evaluation program in place from the beginning of the design process. Even when evaluation programs are put in place, they are often inadequate. Of all the methods that could be used for evaluation of training, companies still list the following as their most frequently used source of information: informal collection of passing comments, evaluation based on attendance records, student participation, end-of-course evaluation sheet, and end-of-course report by instructor. These evaluation methods are subjective and inaccurate. Many people have pointed out these shortcomings:

> With the field of human resource development getting attention from so many quarters, we see a growing need for the field itself to establish consistency and order in how it is counted and measured. The needs range from the evaluation of individual training programs to data development for national policy deliberation. Unfortunately, many decisions in allocation of resources for HRD . . . are being made with only the crudest kinds of information. (Craig, 1983, p. 1)

Bunker and Cohen (1977) also concluded that "training evaluation is one of the most under-researched and neglected areas of industrial/organizational psychology" (p. 525). Summary reviews of training evaluation literature have lamented the lack of organizational support for evaluating training programs (Goldstein, 1978; Grant, 1977). Thus, while there is a general sense of the positive impact of training on employees, sound evaluation methods have not been developed.

Many authors discuss the need for justifying training programs by "documenting bottom-line results . . . or on-the-job performance" of trainees after training (Cornwell, 1980, p. 289) as well as evaluating the direct cost/benefits of training (Deming, 1982). Types of evaluation devices suggested have been a repertory grid (Smith, 1990), a "pre-then-post" measurement where the participant is asked to rate prior knowledge *after* training, and an extended control group pretest design (Bunker

& Cohen, 1977). All of these methods identify different aspects of training. One way to organize an evaluation program is first to decide what aspect or level of training is to be evaluated and then develop the method to be used.

Criteria for Evaluation

Often missing in evaluation programs are the criteria or standards against which evaluators must compare the training. In an ASTD (1988) publication the following seven questions were posed in order to help evaluators determine what ought to be evaluated:

1. *What questions do you want to answer?* How did participants feel about the training? What did they learn? How did they learn? How did the training affect their attitudes and behavior? What were the organizational results?

2. *How will you measure the items addressed in your questions?* Will you administer paper-and-pencil test questionnaires and surveys? Will you require participants to demonstrate their new knowledge and skills in a role-play simulation?

3. *What are the objectives of your training program?* Are your evaluation criteria based on these objectives?

4. *Do the criteria indicate improvement between expected and actual performance* when measured against your needs analysis?

5. *What data sources are already available to help you measure results?*

6. *Are there alternative methods for generating these data* such as interviews and on-site observations?

7. *What are the best and most cost-effective methods for measuring the results of the training?*

Background Information

In addition to these typical questions, Sredl and Rothwell (1987) recommended the collection of background information on the program, including the following information.

The context of the program. To investigate this aspect, you might ask the following questions:
1. How many trainees annually attend the program?
2. On average, how many trainees attend each offering (session) of the program?
3. How long does the program last?
4. Where is the program usually held? In how many locations?

5. What do supervisors in the organization think about HRD gener-ally? The HRD department? This program?
6. What is the organization's culture like? Where along a continuum between authoritarian and democratic does it fall?
7. What is the history of this program? What led to its being offered?
8. What organizational policies and/or procedures are related to the program, if any?

Program participants. These questions should be asked:
1. What kinds of people attend the program? (Consider the job class, tenure with the organization, and attitudes.)
2. How are these people selected? Is attendance mandatory, volun-tary, or negotiated? Why are selection procedures handled this way?
3. When are attendees selected? Is there any special cycle of regis-tration? On what is that cycle based?

How the program is conducted. Ask these questions:
1. What are the instructional goals and objectives?
2. What needs assessment method was used? How was it used?
3. Was a front-end analysis performed?
4. How were the instructional objectives verified?
5. What is the purpose of the program?
6. How is the program structured?
7. How is instruction delivered? How were delivery methods selected?
8. What assumptions are made about entry-level skills of trainees? Are prerequisites specified? How are trainees' knowledge and skill levels screened?
9. How much planning precedes each program offering? To what extent is an attempt made to tailor each offering to needs of the group attending?
10. What exercises and media are used? How were they prepared? Tested?
11. By what methods is the program evaluated?
12. How are results of evaluation used?

Program outcomes. Ask these questions:
1. How well have learners liked the program? What accounts for these attitudes?
2. How well have learners performed in the program? What histori-cal information exists on any trends in test scores? How are demonstrations rated?
3. What evidence exists that the program has changed on-the-job performance in a desirable way? In any way?
4. What evidence exists that the program has contributed to higher productivity, higher morale, lower absenteeism, fewer mistakes?
5. What evidence exists to show that participation in the program increased the value of existing human resources? Contributed to

achievement of individual career plans? Contributed to achievement of organizational strategic and HR plans?

Levels of Evaluation: Kirkpatrick's Model

One author developed a theoretical model from which evaluation tools might be developed. Kirkpatrick's (1979) model for evaluation identified four levels of training impact. It includes the trainees' reactions or attitudes toward a training event (How well did the trainees like the program?), their learning of new knowledge, skills, or attitudes (What principles, facts, and techniques were understood and absorbed?), improvements in job behavior (What changes have occurred in the participants' behaviors?), and organizational results (How have turnover, absenteeism, reduction in grievances, and morale changed?).

Hamblin (1974) divided Kirkpatrick's fourth level into noneconomic organizational variables (e.g., quality, employee morale) and ultimate value or economic variables (e.g., sales, costs, profits). Hamblin explained that evaluation at each of the levels of the hierarchy will help to identify the reasons why successful training outcomes might occur at one level but not at the next higher level. For example, employees' general reaction to the training (Kirkpatrick's level 1) might be quite positive (e.g., the participants enjoyed the training, thought it was interesting), but they could still score low on a knowledge test (Kirkpatrick's level 2).

Unfortunately, many people attempt to measure only level 1, reaction. Rae (1997) pointed out the major problem with this one-shot approach to evaluation:

> It is often said that assessment or validations of training made at the end of a training event can suffer from a contamination which will cast serious doubts on any results. If the course has been a highly successful and enjoyable experience the learners can be so pleased with themselves and the event that they are in a state of euphoria. In this emotive state, particularly as they are saying goodbye to their fellow students with whom they may have formed particular relationships, views expressed on the training may be clouded. (Rae, 1997, p. 125)

Establishing the basic criteria that the training must match will help get past this basic level of "reaction." Once these criteria have been identified, then the task becomes one of developing methods to evaluate training events that match the criteria. The following is a fairly comprehensive review of evaluation methods for training programs.

Evaluation Methods

There are a variety of evaluation methods, including the following:

Paper-and-pencil tests: This method measures how well trainees learn program content. An instructor administers paper-and-pencil tests in class to measure participants' progress.

Attitude surveys: These question-and-answer surveys determine what changes in attitude have occurred as a result of training. Practitioners use these surveys to gather information about employees' perceptions, work habits, motivation, values, beliefs, working relations, and so on. Attitude surveys also reveal respondents' opinions about their jobs, the workplace, co-workers, supervisors, policies, procedures, and the organization. If you conduct a program to change attitudes, before and after surveys can assess improvement.

Simulation and on-site observation: Instructors or managers' observations of performance on the job or in a job simulation indicate whether a learner's skills have improved as a result of the training.

Productivity reports: Hard production data such as sales reports and manufacturing totals can help managers and instructors determine actual performance improvement on the job.

Post-training surveys: Progress and proficiency assessments by both managers and participants indicate perceived performance improvement on the job.

Needs/objectives/content comparison: Training managers, participants, and supervisors compare needs analysis results with course objectives and content to determine whether the program was relevant to participants' needs. Relevancy ratings at the end of the program also contribute to the comparison.

Evaluation forms: Participants' responses on end-of-program evaluation forms indicate what they liked and disliked about the training. While this is an inadequate form of evaluation if used by itself, it does at least give the program planners the participants' immediate holistic response to the training.

Professional opinion: Instructional designers critique and assess the quality of the program design.

Instructor evaluation: Professional trainers administer assessment sheets and evaluation forms to measure the instructor's competence, effectiveness, and instructional skills.

Cost analysis: The training manager compares costs of instructor's fees, materials, facilities, travel, training time, and the number of trainees to determine the hourly cost of training for each participant. (Taken from ASTD, 1988 Info-Line, p. 8)

A review of current evaluation forms reveals a lack of well-developed instruments to measure more than the immediate reaction of participants. As a result, I have developed an instrument to measure the impact of training on behavior changes and job performance in more detail.

Training Impact Questionnaire

Kirkpatrick's (1979) hierarchy appears to provide the clearest and most comprehensive assessment of training impact. Sredl and Rothwell (1987) developed a model demonstrating ways to evaluate each of Kirkpatrick's levels of assessment (see Figure 17.1). This model served as the basis for the development of the Training Impact Questionnaire (TIQ) included in this chapter. Most organizational training evaluation takes place at the first level, participants' overall reaction to the training program. The amount of knowledge acquired, the second level, can be measured fairly easily with objective tests. Level 4, impact on organizational variables, can be measured with organizational outcome data (e.g., turnover rate, absentee records, etc.)

Figure 17.1 identifies Kirkpatrick's four levels as well as the additional level recommended by Hamblin. I decided that level 3, behavioral changes and application to job tasks, would be the focus of this research. Kirkpatrick's level 3 is similar to Bloom's taxonomy (Bloom, Englehart, Faurst, Hill, & Krothwohl, 1956). The levels of knowledge that Bloom describes include knowledge, comprehension, application, analysis, synthesis, and evaluation.

The instrument described here addresses level 3, behavior. Redding (1984) suggested that an "organization has a right to expect that, as a result of being trained, all trainees will demonstrate at least three behavioral outcomes . . . cooperation . . . comprehension . . . and competence" (p. 9). Competence refers to the obvious fact that the trainees must be equipped with the techniques and the resources to function in their organizational role at an acceptable standard of expertise.

A systematic assessment of behavioral changes after training and the participants' ability to apply those changes to job tasks are a critical part of the evaluation process. At the same time, little evidence exists that this type of evaluation is conducted with any degree of confidence. The instrument described in this chapter is based on participants' perceptions of their ability to apply learned skills to the job compared to a supervisor's assessment of their job performance.

Newstrom (1978) discussed the need for all four levels of Kirkpatrick's model to be included in any evaluation of training. Consequently, while the TIQ is an attempt to go beyond the typical reaction questionnaire used in organizations, it also is designed to include both level 1 and level 3 of Kirkpatrick's model. These two levels must be evaluated by the participants and/or their superiors and subordinates, while level 2 (knowledge) must be developed for each unique training experience, and level 4 (organizational variables) must be measured with organizational outcome data. All four levels should be measured for a comprehensive assessment of training impact (see DeWine, 1987a, for details on instrument development and reliability and validity tests).

Training evaluation is critical to successful human resource development. Currently, organizations are evaluating the reactions of participants

Focus	Hierarchy of Evaluation	Ways of Measuring
How do results affect the organization or individual over time?	**Ultimate Value** Hamblin's Level 5	Evaluation of Organization Strategy; Career Progress
	(Kirkpatrick)	
What are the results produced by behavioral change?	**Results** Level 4	Experimental Research
How much participant change subsequently affected job behavior or performance?	**Behavior** Level 3	On-the-Job Demonstrations
How did participants change by the end of a program?	**Learning** Level 2	Tests
What did participants like or dislike?	**Reaction** Level 1	Participant Evaluations

FIGURE 17.1   Hierarchy of Evaluation Approaches   Based on H. J. Sredl & W. J. Rothwell, *The ASTD Reference Guide to Professional Training Roles and Competencies, 1 & 2*, New York: Random House, 1987.

but doing little to assess the impact of communication training on other levels of Kirkpatrick's hierarchy. The TIQ is an attempt to provide a tool with which to measure the application of the perceived level of skill learned on the job as well as the degree to which the participant perceived the skill has been mastered.

Strong internal reliability and validity tests suggest that this instrument can measure these factors successfully. The instrument should be administered two to four weeks following the training program so that impact and not reaction to training is measured. A specific skill taught during the training is identified and the respondent answers questions regarding that skill. Supervisors, as well as subordinates, are also asked to complete the questionnaire in order to measure observations of the training participants' skill performances (see Forms 17.1 and 17.2, participant's and supervisor's forms of the TIQ). A comparison of supervisors' and subordinates' perceptions of the participants' ability to apply the skill to the job helps to identify the extent to which self-perceptions conflict with others' observations of behavioral change.

This instrument, as well as the many other forms of evaluation listed earlier, can be used in several study designs. For example, the evaluator may need to have information about the participants' knowledge of a subject matter prior to the training to determine how much they have learned from the training itself; therefore a before-and-after design would be used. Another way to determine more precisely the impact of training is to compare a group of participants with nonparticipants, or a "control" group. The consultant or trainer might administer before-and-after tests of both the participants and the nonparticipants. In any case, the evaluator should plan carefully the evaluation method that will be used so that the data are the most meaningful.

Nadler (1982) has called for more research on human resource development programs as well as evaluation of the immediate impact of the training on individuals and the organization. With training programs increasing dramatically, organizations need valid tools by which to measure the impact of these training programs. The TIQ will provide an important mechanism by which to accomplish this task. One thing is quite clear: when no formal, well-developed evaluation of training is in place, the organization has little idea whether the training is helpful or harmful. When billions of dollars are being spent, it would certainly seem prudent to ensure those dollars are invested wisely.

PARTICIPANT'S TRAINING IMPACT QUESTIONNAIRE

Several weeks ago you participated in the _____
training program. The purpose of this survey is to show how much the
program has helped you on the job.

The survey consists of skills that were presented in the program. Feel
free to answer honestly. Your answers will be confidential and will be
used only for improving the program. Thank you for helping to improve
the program.

Instructions

You will be asked to evaluate each skill presented in the training program.
The survey lists a skill and then gives a series of statements about that
skill. Mark your reaction to each statement on the accompanying answer
sheets.

Mark your response as follows:

1—strongly disagree (statement never true)

2—disagree (statement rarely true)

3—sometimes agree and sometimes disagree

4—agree (statement usually true)

5—strongly agree (statement always true)

Please respond to all statements. Thank you.

Skill A: _____

_____

Please fill in the appropriate response for each item on the answer sheet.

1. I use this skill regularly on the job.
2. After this training program I would perform this skill without practicing.
3. I didn't learn this skill in the training program, so I had to learn it on
   the job.
4. I perform the skill differently on the job because work conditions
   don't permit me to perform it the way I learned in the training program.
5. I perform the skill differently on the job because the skill doesn't work
   the way I learned it in training.
6. I perform the skill differently on the job because my supervisor told
   me to do it differently.

(Continued)

PARTICIPANT'S TRAINING IMPACT QUESTIONNAIRE *(Continued)*

7. I never perform this skill on the job.

8. The skill isn't part of my job.

9. I get help to perform the skill because I didn't learn it in the training program.

10. I don't perform the skill on the job because the skill is too difficult for me.

11. I don't perform the skill on the job because the skill comes up so rarely that I forget how to do it.

12. I don't perform the skill because I was assigned a different job.

13. I learned to perform the task well in the training program because the program was effective.

14. The skill could be learned from a manual or an instruction sheet as easily as in a training program.

15. I had trouble learning the skill because the training program was confusing.

16. The skill would have been easier to learn with more reference materials.

17. Because of learning this skill, I feel more comfortable about doing my job.

18. Because of attending this training program, I feel better about the company.

19. After attending this training program, I am interested in attending other training programs.

20. I think my participation in this training program will help me to advance in the company.

Scoring

Reverse score these items: 3, 4, 5, 6, 7, 8, 9, 10, 11, 12, 14, 15, 16

Sum the items for two scores:
  1. Relationship of skill to the job: 1, 2, 3, 4, 10, 14, 20, 21, 22, 23
  2. Skill performance: 5, 6, 7, 8, 9, 11, 12, 13, 16, 19

SUPERVISOR'S TRAINING IMPACT QUESTIONNAIRE

Several weeks ago one of your employees participated in the _____ _____ training program. The purpose of this survey is to show how much the program has helped him or her on the job.

The survey consists of skills that were presented in the program. Feel free to answer honestly. Your answers will be confidential and will be used for improving the program.

Instructions

The survey lists a skill and then gives a series of statements about that skill. Mark your reaction to each statement on the accompanying answer sheets.

Mark your response as follows:

1—strongly disagree (statement never true)

2—disagree (statement rarely true)

3—sometimes agree and sometimes disagree

4—agree (statement usually true)

5—strongly agree (statement always true)

Please respond to all statements. Thank you.

Skill A: _____

_____

Please fill in the appropriate response for each item on the answer sheet.

1. My employee uses this skill regularly on the job.
2. After training, he or she has been able to perform this skill without practicing.
3. He or she didn't learn this skill in the training program, so he or she had to learn it on the job.
4. Work conditions don't allow him or her to perform the skill the way he or she learned it in training, so he or she does the task differently on the job.
5. He or she performs the skill differently on the job because I, as his or her supervisor, told him or her to do it differently.
6. He or she never performs this skill on the job.
7. The skill isn't part of his or her job.

(Continued)

SUPERVISOR'S TRAINING IMPACT QUESTIONNAIRE *(Continued)*

8. He or she doesn't perform the skill on the job because he or she didn't learn the skill in the training program, so he or she gets help to do the skill.

9. He or she performs the skill well on the job because the skill is easy for him or her.

10. He or she doesn't perform the skill on the job because the skill comes up so rarely that he or she forgets how to do it.

11. He or she doesn't perform the skill because he or she was assigned a different job.

12. He or she learned to perform the task well in the training program, but could have learned it just as easily from a manual or an instruction sheet.

13. Because of learning this skill, he or she feels more comfortable about doing his or her job.

---------------- **LESSONS LEARNED** ----------------

Did the Training Make a Difference in Performance?

Unfortunately, I think most of the time the answer to this question is no. If there is an impact on performance, we are not finding out about it often enough. Typically, there is not a follow-up evaluation of a training program to see just how these new skills have improved performance on the job. Most often the trainer hands out a form at the end of the session that basically asks, "Did you enjoy the training program?" Of course, they enjoyed it. They were away from the routine of the job and if the trainer was good at her job, she made it a pleasant experience. But did it actually change the way the participants perform their jobs? Despite all the discussion in the training literature about various forms of training evaluation, and my own contributions to this discussion through the development of instruments and methods to evaluate changes in performance, too few companies take the time and money necessary to evaluate the impact of such programs on the company's bottom line.

A training department that can show a direct relationship to increasing profits and decreasing expenses through training stands an excellent chance of never being eliminated. Otherwise, all too often when the budget gets tight, one of the first things to go is the training program. I do believe we can teach participants new skills that will help them do their jobs better. I also believe we need to do a much better job of documenting how those skills get used on the job. The following are lessons I have learned about evaluation:

1. Always hand out an evaluation immediately at the end of a training session, but do not stop there.

2. At least 50 percent of the time plan a follow-up evaluation to ask training participants if they are still using the skills they learned during the training program. I suggest 50 percent because you'll be lucky if the percentage of times you can do this is that high.

3. Do not depend just on the participant to determine if the new skills are being used. Employ some form of assessment by those who work with this employee: ideally you would ask a superior, subordinate, and co-worker for each participant. I did say "ideally"!

4. Translate the results into useful information for the organization. If you can connect training results to outcome data (number of absentee days, rate of turnover, etc.), your results will be much more meaningful.

5. Keep track of your own evaluations and use them to adjust your training program the next time. Look over the most recent ones right before you go into your next training session.

If we do not know the impact of our training programs, then we cannot claim much about how useful they are. All of us who conduct training programs either aid or hinder organizations' perceptions about the usefulness of these activities. Therefore, the way each of us handles our own evaluations affects perceptions of every other trainer.

Additional Resources

Arnold, W. E., & McClure, L. (1996). *Communication training and development* (2nd ed.). Prospect Heights, IL: Waveland Press.

Biech, E. (2000). *The 2000 annual: Vol. 1. Training.* San Francisco: Jossey-Bass/Pfeiffer.

DeWine, S. (1987). Evaluation of organizational communication competency: The development of the communication training impact questionnaire. *Journal of Applied Communication, 15,* 113–127.

Kirkpatrick, D. L. (1998). *Evaluation training programs: The four levels.* San Francisco: Berrett-Koehler.

Chapter *18*

STRATEGIES FOR EVALUATING A CONSULTATION

Once upon a time in the land of Fuzz, King Aling called in his cousin Ding and commanded, "Go ye out into all of Fuzzland and find me the goodest of men, whom I shall reward for his goodness."

"But how will I know one when I see one?" asked the Fuzzy.

"Why, he will be sincere,*" scoffed the king, and whacked off a leg for his impertinence.*

So, the Fuzzy limped out to find a good man. But soon he returned, confused and empty-handed.

"But how will I know one when I see one?" he asked again.

"Why, he will be dedicated,*" grumbled the king, and whacked off another leg for his impertinence.*

So the Fuzzy hobbled away once more to look for the goodest of men. But again he returned, confused and empty-handed.

"But how will I know one when I see one?" he pleaded.

"Why, he will have internalized his growing awareness,*" fumed the king, and whacked off another leg for his impertinence.*

So the Fuzzy, now on his last leg, hopped out to continue his search. In time, he returned with the wisest, most sincere and dedicated Fuzzy in all of Fuzzland, and stood him before the king.

"Why, this man won't do at all," roared the king. "He is much too thin to suit me." Whereupon, he whacked off the last leg of the Fuzzy, who fell to the floor with a squishy thump.

The moral of this fable is that . . . if you can't tell one when you see one, you may wind up without a leg to stand on.

Robert Mager, Goal Analysis, 1972

*I*f you don't know how to tell when you are successful at solving human communication problems, then you may not have a leg to stand on, or a platform from which to launch your activities! You need to be articulate about how the client will know when the problem has been solved.

The evaluation needs to assess the relationship between the consultants or communication manager and the client, the results of intervention into interpersonal relationships in the group, the progress the organization has made toward reaching its overall goals, and how much the group's activities have contributed to that achievement.

Information can be collected from the consultant/manager, the client system, outcome data like attitude surveys or turnover rates, and bottom-line figures. Standard data collecting methods discussed in Chapter 4 are used: observation, interviews, content analysis, questionnaires, personnel and demographic data, and company publications and documents. Using these approaches and methods, how does one go about organizing an evaluation program for consulting?

Criteria for Evaluating a Consultation

While there are a variety of methods for evaluating the success of a consultation, the following are the criteria I have found to be the most indicative of success: consultant effectiveness, consultant satisfaction, client satisfaction, and project outcome.

Evaluating the Consultant's Effectiveness

Lippitt and Lippitt (1986) posed the following organizing questions to evaluate the competency of the consultant:

Does the consultant's relationship with the client model interpersonal relations for the group? The consultant must be a role model for the kind of relationships that need to exist for the group to be successful. The way in which you interact with the client speaks volumes about your ability to train others to function as a team.

Does the consultant make sure contractual arrangements are clear from the outset? During the entry stage, the consultant and the client should establish exactly what each is willing to do, when it will be done, and how they will tell when they are done. Expectations of each party to the contract must be clearly identified.

Does the consultant really have the skills needed to help solve the client's problem? One of the worst things a consultant can do is claim talents and abilities that she or he does not possess. To raise expectations and not deliver is worse than doing nothing at all. You need to be very clear about what you can and cannot do.

Does the consultant gain influence in the client organization through appropriate means? The consultant usually does not have the power to change the organization but must convince others to make changes. For that reason, it is very important that the consultant have the ear of the decision makers. Employees must feel that what they tell the consultant will be listened to by top management. Often individuals feel the best way to get top management to hear their concerns is to say them through another voice.

Does the consultant track clients to apply what is learned independently rather then rely on the consultant? As an outside consultant, I always assume that my job is to work myself out of a job. If the client is depending on me on a permanent basis to continue to solve problems for the group, then I become an internal employee. It also indicates a lack of talent in the group. I am usually able to identify an individual who has at least some ability to solve human communication problems. I work at having that individual step into my role as an insider. This can also be true of internal consultants since they should not become permanently attached to one particular unit in the organization.

Does the consultant treat others nonjudgmentally and with respect? The consultant's greatest asset is objectivity. This means treating each person with respect. The consultant cannot afford the luxury of identifying the "good guys" and the "bad guys." People sense when you are looking out for your own welfare at the expense of theirs.

Does the consultant keep clients' information to himself or herself? If you want to find out what's going on, you have to be able to reassure people that what they tell you in confidence will not be individually attributed. If something they share with you in private comes back to them through other sources, they will know not to trust you. You must also be careful not to inadvertently pass along private information because even though your intentions may be good, the impact will be the same. People will try giving you less important bits of information to see what you do with it. You will be "on trial," so watch your step!

Can the consultant identify the problem and keep it in focus? Often the client does not know how to identify the problem. It may be disguised as something else. In one case the top manager trusted one assistant but not the other and yet the problem was described as "needing to have clearer job descriptions for the two assistants." It is the consultant's job to help the client articulate the problem and focus on it until some resolution is reached. Clients may try to sidetrack outside consultants because, although they know they need help, they may also like to avoid the problem, hope it goes away, and when it doesn't get solved, blame the consultant for not solving it!

Does the consultant explain the role the client is expected to play and the contribution the client is expected to make? I recently had a group ask me to interview all members of one unit and then plan a feedback session between top management and the unit members. When it was time for the retreat, unit members said they were afraid the head of the unit would not listen to them. They felt that all he did was talk *at* them about his goals and objectives but that he did not listen to their concerns. I had a meeting beforehand with the unit head and made it clear that during the retreat his role was to listen and if he began talking I would tap him on the shoulder and remind him to listen. I had to do it only twice during the retreat and he got the message. Clients want to know exactly what you expect of them. Their role should always be clearly defined.

Is the consultant willing to undergo an evaluation of his or her services? Good consultants and communication managers want to know how they are doing. Chapter 13 provides tips on giving feedback to others. The consultant may have to train the client in providing feedback, but it certainly should be welcomed.

Evaluating the Consultant's Satisfaction

Some of the questions you might ask yourself in an evaluation of your satisfaction with a particular consulting assignment include:

Did you fully accomplish what you promised in the initial proposal?

In addition to completing work objectives, did your efforts lead to the desired results?

Did the client benefit from your services?

Had you performed your duties differently, would the outcomes have changed?

Did the results occur even though you did not complete the work as promised?

Did the consulting expense exceed the possible benefits?

Were you pleased with the project's conduct and success?

Did you enjoy consulting on the project?

How do you feel about your relationship to the client?

Were you able to establish professional trust and rapport?

Would you consult with this client again? (Kelly, 1986)

You are not the only or necessarily the best source of assessment for your own success. However, these questions are a good place to begin the evaluation. A part of your success depends on your satisfaction with your work. Next, you must assess your client's satisfaction.

Evaluating the Client's Satisfaction

Holtz (1989) suggested to clients who are hiring consultants, six criteria to assess the impact of the consultant's work. First is *enthusiasm.* Enthusiasm indicates the depth and degree of a consultant's interest in the task. Second, *leadership.* In many cases consultants are called upon to lead the client's staff in writing or assembling a proposal, for example. Third, *presentation.* This may refer to a formal presentation to an assembled group or there may be occasions when it refers to instructions to a client's staff by the consultant. Fourth, *efficiency*. When you have a new employee, you may be able to permit that person a few weeks to become oriented and make a full contribution, but you cannot afford that luxury with a consultant. Fifth, *effectiveness*. This is closely related to efficiency and yet it is not the same thing. Effectiveness refers to the degree to which the desired end result is achieved. A consultant may be efficient, in other words finish whatever he or she does with great speed, and yet not produce the result desired. Finally, *openness*. It refers to the consultant's willingness to share what he or she knows with the client and the client's staff. It means honest and conscientious work and not holding back information (pp. 185–186).

Evaluating the Project Outcome

Fuchs (1975) suggested three broad areas in which to evaluate the success of the consulting project. First, compare the performance against the proposal. This includes an assessment of the objectives of the consultant's assignment; a clear understanding of the scope of the undertaking, what findings were to be expected, and results to be accomplished; schedule and starting date; project costs; and staff personnel. These are measurable outcome variables and can be clearly defined. There may be a need to identify some intervening variables that cannot be controlled. For example, even though the client and consultant agree on a starting date, it might be delayed because of external factors that neither the client nor the consultant can control.

Second, the consultant's contribution to the company's financial position is another area for evaluation. This includes a statement of income and expense less sales returns and allowances, cost of goods sold and manufactured, direct labor, selling costs, and accounts receivable. How did the consulting intervention affect these outcomes?

Third is long-term benefits. Rudolph and Johnson (1983) pointed to the problems involved in failing to recognize this criterion. They suggest:

> Many beginning communication consultants feel a postseminar/workshop form is adequate, but the form does not measure any end result or impact on the organization. All it measures is the seminar/workshop participants' reactions to the session leaders and the immediate reactions to items asked, such as the number of assignments, amount of interaction, adequacy of the meeting room, session content, quality of food, and the participants' perception of how useful the information covered in the session will be when they get back to the job. This information is invaluable when it comes to determining success and learning at the session but it does not answer the question about changes stemming from the sessions. (p. 53)

Long-term benefits may be the most important measurement of the consulting activity. While actively engaged, the consultant should materially raise the competence level of the people in the organization. This should be accomplished by demonstrating leadership ability that encourages project team managers to perform in a superior manner. The consultant should be the catalyst in making things happen and in reshaping the areas of the company in need of constructive change (pp. 140–141).

While all of the above suggestions provide guidance for the evaluation of a particular assignment, the consultant must judge himself or herself as well. Your own professional development program will identify standards by which to measure your success.

Professional Development

The consultants or communication specialists are often so busy helping other people improve their skills that they forget to work on their own development in a consistent fashion. You must practice what you profess to be good for others.

Phillips (1987) suggested that a trainer or consultant must have a personal development model that contains three essential elements: a sound grounding and working familiarity with a body of knowledge, research, and theory; a development of skills including listening, presenting, observing, sensing, supporting, challenging, and diagnosing; and the development of self or who one is: one's beliefs, values, and life experiences. Knowledge, skills, and self-confidence are the attributes needed to achieve success.

Bard and Stephen (1987) have produced a professional development checksheet for trainers to be filled out by the trainer and his or her manager. It asks respondents to list the priority of the performance statement as well as the degree of competency the individual has in that area. Form 18.1 lists those competencies. Bard and Stephen suggested,

> If your plan is to work in HRD [Human Resource Development] for a few years as part of your career path, the development of a learning plan can help you focus your professional growth while in the field. You will also find the expertise required in learning how to direct your development will be valuable when you move to other departments in the organization. If you have chosen HRD as your profession, the continued acquisition of new skills and knowledge is one of the essentials of becoming and remaining a competent professional. (p. 27)

Lippitt and Lippitt (1986) pointed out the need for all professionals to participate in a professional association, discipline, or education process to maintain competency. All professionals should be engaged in life-long development and learning. In order to bring the best techniques for working with others to the relationship, consultants and communication specialists must constantly be attending workshops and seminars and receiving higher education. Anyone not doing that is in jeopardy of bringing less than his or her best effort to the client system.

These evaluation methods generate data that must sometimes be statistically analyzed. Knowing when you have meaningful results is critical.

THE LEARNING NEEDS ASSESSMENT SCALE

Learning Needs

This assessment scale generates two kinds of data: your most important job functions and your present competency level for 37 areas within eight functions. When completing the scale, choose a number from 1 to 5 to rate each; 1 is the lowest rating, 5 the highest.

For the priority rating, use the following guide:

0   You do not perform that function.

1   You occasionally perform the function, but it is not critical to the organization now or in the near future.

2   You regularly perform the function, but it is not critical and is unlikely to become so in the near future.

3   You regularly perform the function, and it is necessary and may become more important in the near future.

4   You perform the function occasionally now but may perform it more frequently in the future, and it is critical to your job.

5   You perform the function frequently, and it is critical to your job.

For the competency rating use the following guide:

0   You are not able to perform the function.

1   You can perform the function partially or with difficulty and lack most of the skills and knowledge you require.

2   You can perform the function, but there are significant skills and knowledge you need to acquire.

3   You are competent in performing the function but still need to acquire more knowledge or experience to feel fully confident.

4   You are at mastery level but can still increase your performance by increasing your skills and knowledge.

5   You can perform at a level of excellence and don't need additional skills or knowledge at this time.

(Continued)

THE LEARNING NEEDS ASSESSMENT SCALE *(Continued)*

Ratings (0–5 scale)

Functions and Performance Statements	Priority		Competency	
	Mine	Manager's	Mine	Manager's
1. Learning Needs Assessment				
Use competency-based models, performance analysis, and other needs assessment techniques.				
Design and use various instruments, surveys, questionnaires, and other data collection methods.				
Analyze data and translate into program needs.				
2. Develop Learning Strategies and Designs				
Select best strategies to meet learning needs.				
Use adult learning theory and principles.				
Develop learning objectives and designs.				
Use diverse learning methods.				
3. Provide Learning Materials				
Research and collect information from print and nonprint sources.				
Develop multimedia materials.				
Write and produce case studies, exercises, manuals, and other print materials.				
Evaluate film, software, packaged programs, and other vendor materials for rental and purchase.				

(Continued)

THE LEARNING NEEDS ASSESSMENT SCALE *(Continued)*

Ratings (0–5 scale)

Functions and Performance Statements	Priority		Competency	
	Mine	Manager's	Mine	Manager's
4. Facilitate Group Learning Activities				
Use effective presentation methods.				
Use group interaction methods.				
Use full range of learning methods.				
Use audiovisual equipment and materials.				
Use computer-based instruction.				
5. Evaluate Learning Results				
Design and use methods and instruments to collect learning-related data.				
Formulate recommendations for program redesign.				
6. Internal Consulting				
Conduct data collection and problem analysis.				
Formulate strategies and develop plans to solve learning-related problems.				
Contract with in-house clients regarding problem analysis as well as strategies and resources required to solve learning problems.				
Prepare organizational climate for change.				
Work with a wide variety of personalities and styles to implement plans.				
Evaluate effectiveness of strategies and plans.				

(Continued)

THE LEARNING NEEDS ASSESSMENT SCALE *(Continued)*

Ratings (0–5 scale)

Functions and Performance Statements	Priority		Competency	
	Mine	Manager's	Mine	Manager's
7. Individual Counseling				
Assist individuals to assess learning needs and develop learning plans.				
Provide learning-related information and resources.				
8. Management				
Develop and maintain a positive working relationship with line and upper management.				
Communicate the importance of human resource development to line management and upper management.				
Develop yearly and multiyear training and development plans.				
Develop yearly and multiyear budgets.				
Select competent staff.				
Develop positive work environment for staff.				
Effectively supervise and motivate staff.				
Contract with, manage, and evaluate consultants.				
Schedule and coordinate staff, facilities, materials, and equipment to meet program goals.				
Develop and maintain an information system providing performance data to staff, management, and other departments.				
Evaluate individual staff and program performance.				

Interpreting the Meaning of Statistics

In Chapter 5, I identified a number of statistical tests that can be applied to organizational data. Statistical tests will tell you if you have a significant result, but they cannot tell you if that result is meaningful.

For example, I worked with a client who wanted to measure the impact of the training program on employee attitudes about the company. We administered pre- and post-tests on employee satisfaction with the company. There were statistically significant differences in participants' scores after the training session. However, the meaningfulness of those results was less clear since the turnover rate and absenteeism did not decrease. Is a 3.4 on a 5.0 scale meaningful? What does it mean when someone checks the midpoint? The respondent may not have an opinion, be undecided, feel both a little positive and a little negative, or simply not have any basis for judgment. Thus, I believe statistical results must always be accompanied with more "rich" data that help explain the statistical analysis and make it meaningful.

Choosing Evaluation Techniques

Figure 18.1 identifies a variety of techniques for evaluation. It compares the evaluation methods most appropriate for consulting with those appropriate for teaching, training, and counseling. For example, if the client wants only an immediate reaction to how well the consulting went, then determining whether the "band-aid" stopped the "bleeding" is all that is necessary. In other words, did the brief intervention provide immediate relief? Or if we want to examine the degree to which knowledge has increased, an internal consultant test could be developed to measure the knowledge base acquired by the internal consultant about the client.

On the other hand, consulting often deals with changing behavior, and a Management By Objectives (MBO) system would help track this. If a change in behavior is the goal, then the manager and the employee would need to identify the change and agree on a way to measure whether it has in fact changed.

Finally, evaluating the success of the consulting intervention in terms of organizational outcomes can be accomplished by determining when the problem is solved and is no longer an issue. The client and the consultant need to agree on the indicators of its resolution.

The techniques listed for training evaluation were discussed in the previous chapter. Teaching and consulting are also listed since these helping professions have many things in common with consulting (see Chapters 2 and 3). Since teaching is a more long-term relationship, the evaluation methods can be more long term as well. The counseling evaluation

Kirkpatrick's four levels of training evaluation	Consult	Train	Teach	Counsel
Reaction	band-aid stops bleeding	"happy-gram"	teacher evaluations	reduced stress test
Knowledge	internal consultant	objective tests	objective essay/test	self-awareness questionnaire
Behavior	MBO system	DeWine's TIQ	behavioral objectives	client is more competent
Organizational outcomes	problem is solved	turnover rate is decreased	job place-ment is successful	positive impact on family

FIGURE 18.1   Evaluation Methods

methods are much more personal. For example, to measure the success of consulting on a "reaction" level, one might measure the amount of reduction in stress an individual experiences, with pre-and post-intervention measurements.

LESSONS LEARNED

Did the Consultant Earn His Salary?

Evaluation is a critical, but often neglected, area of consulting. Usually it is not thought about until the intervention is practically completed. The consultant should select the method of evaluation during the first step of designing the entire intervention. In other words, evaluation is a front-end activity as well as a terminating ritual. The following are the lessons I have learned from my own experiences, as well as those of my colleagues.

- Do *some* kind of evaluation, even if it is only on the reaction level. Use whatever is available until you are able to infuse the system with a more comprehensive program.
- *Ask the right questions.* Several lists of potential questions have been provided in this chapter. Some you must ask of yourself and some must be asked of others. It is always good to check your perception of yourself and your activities with the perceptions of those you are helping.

- *Be responsive to feedback.* If your consulting activities are going to be evaluated then you must be open to suggestions for change or else there is no reason to conduct the evaluation.

- Others will be watching you for guidance as you *handle negative feedback.* As a role model you need to show how action can be taken on suggestions for improvement.

We cannot determine where we should head next if we don't understand where we have been. Evaluation must be a planned activity from the beginning of the intervention or one cannot hope to move the group forward.

Additional Resources

Biech, E. (2000). *The 2000 annual: Vol. 2. Consulting.* San Francisco: Jossey-Bass/Pfeiffer.

Lippitt, G., & Lippitt, R. (1986). *The consulting process in action* (2nd ed.). San Diego, CA: University Associates.

Schein, E. H. (1999). *Process consultation revisited: Building a helping relationship.* Reading, MA: Addison-Wesley.

PART VI

Professional Development for the Consultant

The last section of the book focuses on personal issues for the consultant or communication manager. Chapter 19 addresses issues related to forming friendships and romances in the organization. Since people spend a great deal of time at work, personal relationships will develop. The consultant needs to be aware of the impact of such relationships for two reasons: it may affect the group with whom you are working, and it may affect your own relationships with individuals. I hope this chapter is thought provoking and provides some insights about how undisclosed relationships can make situations worse.

Chapter 20 deals with professional development topics as well as issues related to starting your own firm: taxes, legal forms, marketing your services, and maintaining clients. This is a very practical chapter that will give you some clear guidance for beginning the job of being a consultant. Much of this information relates specifically to an outside consultant rather than an inside employee.

Chapter *19*

HELPING CLIENTS MANAGE PERSONAL AND PROFESSIONAL RELATIONSHIPS AT WORK

Women are far more likely to form close relationships with one another (at work) than their male counterparts with whom they engage in intimate and sympathetic conversation. Their greater needs for affiliation lead women to open up with a rapport and honesty unprecedented in relationships between male colleagues.

L. B. Rubin,
Just Friends: The Role of Friendship in Our Lives, *1985*

*F*riendships are formed, romantic liaisons are established, and marriages are born—all at work. Men and women working together on challenging, exciting projects are attracted to the work and to each other. They also react differently to friendships formed at work. Consultants and managers who are not aware of the importance of these relationships to the organization and to the work are likely to be caught off guard when they occur.

In particular, the consultants' greatest advantage is their objectivity. When consultants place themselves in a position of friendship or special relationship to anyone in the organization, then their effectiveness is greatly jeopardized. At the same time, the consultant is often attempting to establish teams without knowledge of the personal relationships existing among team members. Not taking these relationships into account may hurt that process. Kanter (1983) suggested,

> It is in the post-entrepreneurial corporation's interest for its members to have a generalized team feeling and emotional absorption in the work itself, but not to center feelings on particular people. Any strong attachment to something or someone other than the task at hand is likely to pose a threat to the openness, inclusion, collaboration, and trust essential to post-entrepreneurial organizations. It limits the flexibility to redeploy people. It is distracting to both those participating in it and those observing. (pp. 284–285)

This belief is shared by many in the organization, and yet to believe we can disallow personal relationships is certainly naive. In fact, recent research suggests that employees are more tolerant of romantic relationships at work than is commonly believed (DeWine, Pearson, & Yost, 1993). What we can do is learn to identify these natural links within the group, help individuals understand when their relationship is hurting effectiveness of the group, and work with them for some resolution. In this chapter, professional relationships, friendships, and romantic pairs are explored in the context of improving the general climate of the organization.

Professional Relationships

Schindler-Raiman (1987) described a cluster of value changes that influence attitudes toward work, including personal relationships in the workplace. The rapidity of change in the modern world has created an environment of uncertainty. This uncertainty has resulted in an acceptance of temporary bonds and multiple loyalties in one's personal and professional life rather than the emphasis on permanent commitments and single loyalties. Respect for authority has changed to confrontation and questioning of authority figures.

The effect of the work environment on individual workers has gained more attention from management as employees have demanded an improved quality of work life and a healthy environment. Instead of conforming to established patterns of time, employees are developing new ways of organizing time to their personal advantage.

All these changes suggest greater recognition of employees as individuals who relate to each other on a personal basis rather than as interchangeable functionaries whose relationships can be predicted according to job title. For the consultant or communication manager, recognition of the uniqueness of interpersonal work relationships affects both the way one structures organizational communication and the way one interacts with co-workers.

Gender and Professional Relationships

Although women have attacked the "good old boy" system for its discrimination against women, it has provided men with natural links to other professionals who can help them get their jobs done. Women recognize the value of such professional relationships and resent the fact that they have been denied access to valuable networks that would support their careers and jobs.

When one of my colleagues accepted a top-level executive position in a corporation, she soon learned how difficult it would be to train the previously all-male group of executives to give her access to the same networks they enjoyed. Within the first month of the job, the CEO informed her that he and the other six top-level executives of the company would be taking their annual fishing trip and staying in his condo at Hilton Head. He explained that this "retreat" always helped them work out problems that needed the support of all members to resolve. He apologized that it was too bad she couldn't go. He didn't realize that he had hired an individual who wasn't about to accept things as they had always been.

Her first task was to convince the CEO of the great disadvantage to his organization as well as to her if she was left out of this important informal communication. Her second, and perhaps more difficult, task was to assure him that it would not lead to suspicions by the spouses that there would be any suggestion of inappropriate behavior since this would now be a co-ed group. She recommended a talented consultant to work with the group on establishing team behavior and the impact of a female on their all-male retreat. They decided to rent two condos, bring the consultant (who was also a female) along and make their previously all-male "bonding" trip a high-level team-building session instead.

Knowing that informal settings are important for team-building activities, the consultant suggested developing various activities that all members could participate in. Since the new female executive did not particularly enjoy fishing, she worked toward a compromise.

"John, isn't it true that Roy doesn't like fishing?" Well, yes, the CEO agreed that Roy usually found some other activity to participate in by himself on the afternoons they went fishing. "And isn't it true that most of the other executives also play golf?" Yes, that was true. "So why not," she asked, "play golf on one afternoon and go fishing on another afternoon so that all of the group could participate in at least one of the activities they enjoyed?" and have an opportunity to spend time with the CEO in an informal setting. In the end, he agreed. For the first time this group enjoyed the retreat in an informal setting, where team members could appreciate each other as individuals in a "mixed" group.

Relationships with Bosses and Clients

We all know that more deals get cut on the golf course than in the boardroom. Those informal relationships make negotiating easier. You work harder to reach a compromise with someone you know and like. While you are negotiating on Friday, it is difficult to turn down your golfing partner whom you expect to see on the course again Sunday morning. It is much easier to turn away a stranger to whom you have no personal commitment.

At the same time, I believe that sometimes only a fine line separates professional relationships, platonic friendships, and romance. The consultant or manager who socializes with only some of the staff, to the exclusion of others, will pay the price of supposed favoritism. No matter how fair the individual may attempt to be, others' perceptions of that fairness will always be tarnished by their observation of those close, personal conversations that are likely to occur in informal surroundings.

It is difficult to draw that line especially since we are spending so much time at work that it naturally becomes the place where friendships are formed. Joseph Straub (1992) suggested to new executives,

> Keep your distance without losing rapport . . . . As a supervisor, you have to relinquish some of the easygoing relationships you enjoyed before you left the rank and file to join management. When you need a sympathetic ear, try talking to your spouse, friends outside of work, or co-workers at your own level—but not subordinates. (p. 3)

I think this is especially true for the consultant. By the very nature of your position, you are an outsider hired to provide an objective view of life in an organization. Once you lose that objectivity, you are less useful to the organization. At the same time, individuals must feel they can talk informally with you about problems and concerns and that they would not have to come to your office to do so.

Socializing with your boss or client can be an aid to developing trust but it can also backfire. I suggest the following guidelines for conversation with clients or your boss in social settings (DeWine, 1987b):

> *Take cues from your boss or client.* If your boss or client keeps business out of the conversation, it is risky for you to mention office matters. If you are unsure whether something is appropriate, refer to it briefly and watch the reaction. Nonverbal behavior (sitting back, looking away) can be a clue that your boss or client doesn't feel comfortable talking about the subject.
>
> *Drink in moderation or not at all.* Even if a few drinks don't normally affect you, it's smart to stick to a wine spritzer or a beer if you feel that drinking is appropriate because your boss or client is drinking. Drinking more isn't worth the risk of saying or doing something you'll later regret.
>
> *Avoid revealing personal information.* No matter what your boss or client chooses to tell you about his or her personal affairs, it is not smart to talk about your marital, family, financial, or health problems. Nor is it advisable to betray any lack of confidence about your professional abilities, your career choice, or your job.
>
> *Be cautious in your comments about other staff members.* If you are asked your opinion of other employees or what you know about them personally, don't be overly critical. Instead, try to address your boss's or client's concern and offer suggestions on how the problem situation could be remedied. If, for example, you are asked whether you have noticed that a colleague has a drinking problem, talk about ways the

person might be helped rather than focusing on the times he or she has been late or has botched an assignment.

Keep the socializing professional if your boss is of the opposite sex. The more relaxed the setting, the more opportunity there is for misinterpretation of language and behavior. Individuals who suspect that their boss's or client's intention may be romantic or sexual are smart to bring up their spouses, "significant others," or family in the conversation.

Don't confuse your role as a colleague with your role as friend. If your boss or client invites you out more often than your colleagues, don't advertise that fact. Your colleagues may be reluctant to share information or work closely with you if they feel you have access to the boss or client that they don't.

Mentoring[1]

One type of relationship that bridges the gap between strictly professional relationships and those that are more personal is a **mentoring** relationship. Mentoring relationships can be formalized programs established by the organization to assimilate new employees or can occur naturally between colleagues who develop a close relationship as well.

Ever since the Greek poet Homer's "faithful and wise" Mentor first advised Odysseus, wise individuals have counseled, coached, and taught the young. When Odysseus was away from home for many years, he entrusted his son, Telemachus, to his friend and advisor, Mentor. While Odysseus was gone, Mentor served as guardian, teacher, and father figure to his young protégé. Since those ancient times there have been mentors and protégés in virtually every discipline and career area.

Organizations pay close attention to the relationships developing between experienced employees and their subordinates. These relationships are often credited with adding to the success and satisfaction of an individual's work life. One corporate executive described for me the unique way in which he was hired. It points to both the advantages and challenges of mentoring. An executive in another company had given Ray advice for several years on his career and served as a mentor to him. One evening, at a social event, this mentor told him about a top-level position in his company. As they talked about the position and Ray's abilities and experiences, the executive became convinced that Ray was the right person for the job and he offered it to him on the spot. Ray was thrilled and accepted immediately. This is a good example of how mentoring can work at its best. When Ray started at the company, however, the story of his hiring was already circulating around the corporate offices and rather than enhance his credibility it forced him to overcome suspicions that he wasn't qualified for the position but had received it only as a favor. He had no "honeymoon" period and had to work extra hard at convincing others he was capable and ready to handle a significant increase in responsibility. So, networking can help you, but it can sometimes serve to reinforce others' misperceptions.

Facilitated Mentoring

Many organizations recognize the value of mentors to newer and younger employees. Wilson and Elman (1990) suggested the principal benefits of organizational mentoring as the transmission of corporate culture and the provision of a "deep sensing" apparatus for top management.

> Mentoring can contribute to employee motivation, job performance, and retention rates . . . mentoring provides a structured system for strengthening and assuring the continuity of organizational culture. The existence of a strong corporate culture that provides members with a common value base, and with implicit knowledge of what is expected of them and what they in turn can expect from the organization, can be vital to organizational success and effectiveness. (pp. 88–89)

Murray (1991) defined **facilitated mentoring** as "a deliberate pairing of a more skilled or experienced person with a lesser skilled or experienced one, with the agreed-upon goal of having the lesser skilled person grow and develop specific competences" (p. 19). At the same time, other authors acknowledge that mentoring relationships can involve peers (rather than superior and subordinate) and can be designed to accomplish organizational assimilation.

Benefits of Mentoring

In a study of critical incidents of mentoring relationships, we (DeWine, James, & Hale, 1991) discovered that most subjects remembered the mentoring relationship as extremely positive. The most frequently mentioned positive outcome was enhancement of career development. For example, subjects said, "I was able to gain more money and freedom to exert more influence over my position," "My mentor gave me advice on going to conferences as an equal," and "After two years of a mentor's guiding my career in insurance and benefits and assisting me with my resume, I obtained a management position" (p. 5). They also reported skill development and increased self-esteem as related benefits.

The mentors reported positive outcomes as well, for example: "When my protégé is successful in something encouraged by me, there is some 'reflected glory' involved and the possibility of a sense of accomplishment on my part" (p. 5).

Types of Mentors

In another study of mentoring relationships of women (DeWine, Casbolt, & Bentley, 1983), we identified the following profiles of these relationships:

Parent—By far the most prevalent theme described by protégés is a relationship similar to a father/daughter relationship, where there is great respect for this "older and wiser" person who influences the protégé's life and career significantly. Interestingly, this parental relationship did not seem to exist in the female-female relationship. Women did not tend to see mentors in "mother" roles in this sample of subjects.

White Knight—Many protégés described their mentors in glowing terms as if they were above human error. Usually, there was a point in the relationship when the protégé discovered the mentor had made a mistake and at that point the "white knight falls off his horse." Their respect for the mentor was not necessarily diminished but their awe of this individual was. One subject said, "I thought he had all the answers at first until I saw him caught short by one of his own managers once. This just made me realize how human he was."

Mentor-to-Friend Transformation—A large number of mentoring relationships undergo a change from mentor-protégé to friend-friend and vice-versa. Often the mentor starts out as a person who sponsors the protégé's entrance into an organization, and then once the protégé is firmly established, this relationship, which was built on "socialization," is no longer a critical part of the protégé's environment. Consequently, the two individuals change their relationship to friendship. This transformation can occur in the other direction, for example, one subject indicated that "we started out as friends but she moved more quickly than I through the organization and soon become my mentor."

The Badger—Some mentors activate their protégés' motivation by "badgering" their charges. This constant challenge and demand for excellence forces some to achieve more than they thought they could. One subject described this type of relationship when she said, "He pushed me into things, he delegated to the extreme and forced me into succeeding. I didn't dare let him down."

The Seductive Manipulator—While the "badger" tries fairly openly to push or shove the protégé into positions of responsibility, the seductive manipulator does so without the protégé's really being aware of these activities on her behalf. The mentor merely places opportunities in the protégé's path and indirectly points them out. In some ways it's the old "bait-and-switch" game. One entry-level manager described this type of interaction in the following way: "She used to offer me increased opportunities for visibility in the corporation as if they had happened by chance. It was only later that I learned that these were all carefully planned for my benefit as well as hers. I didn't really know that I was being prepared for a managerial position until my replacement had already been trained by me!" While there were no examples of sexual harassment in this sample, this type of interaction could be conducive to it.

The Guilt Trip Producer—Often managers felt guilt whenever they let their mentor down by not performing to her or his standards or expectations. The theme of "you can be more than you are" was repeated over and over so that to fail that mandate was to admit that you were only as good as your mentor originally found you. "I felt terrible when the first long report I had done under his guidance was not successful. It was as if he had failed too and it was my fault" is typical of this interaction.

The King/Queen—This theme describes an interaction in which the mentor is very dictatorial and authoritarian. Here the interaction is more one of action by decree. "He manipulated me. I ended up watching his kids for him and even became the go-between for him and his wife." In this situation the protégé is told how to go about the business of becoming successful.

The Self-Promoter—This mentor clearly sees advantages to surrounding herself or himself with some of the "best and brightest." In this case the mentor understands the advantage of having successful protégés. In one case, a woman described a male mentor who was extremely negative toward professional women, with the exception of his female protégés. In those instances he clearly saw the advantage of working with the best, "even if they were female."

Cheerleader—Many protégés described their mentors as individuals who either "watched from the sidelines" or "followed from behind," encouraging and cheering them on as they continued to advance. "She told me I could do anything," "He inspired me; I always could turn to him for encouragement even when we were no longer in the same discipline" are examples of this type of interaction. In a "cheerleading" relationship the mentor seems to derive pleasure in watching the success of the protégé.

Groom—Mentors who are in positions of power and have the ability to move a protégé into a position of greater responsibility often are seen as "grooming" their protégés for a particular position. Many protégés indicate that their mentors groomed them for special assignments, in many cases for the mentor's own job so that the mentor was able to move up.

Overwhelmingly, the women in this study saw their mentor relationships as positive and viewed them with great nostalgia. Even when some of the more negative themes were developed, women saw these relationships as useful to their careers. A small percentage of subjects had had some experiences they saw as being used and manipulated. In all cases, the termination or even some change in the relationship was difficult to manage.

Termination of Mentoring Relationships

Many of the mentoring relationships described by these subjects continued beyond the study. Others went through normal terminations due to one or the other person's moving from the area, moving out of the organization, or moving out of the profession, so the mentor and protégé were no longer in close contact. The most difficult change was when the participants remained in contact but the nature of the relationship was influenced somehow, and one or both individuals had a difficult time accepting their new roles.

Many protégés described the difficulty they had in "breaking away" from a mentor who was still seeing them in the role they played in their initial interactions. Several mentioned teachers who still saw them as students. One said, "I am 40 years old now and am a peer and colleague to one of my mentors, but she still insists on introducing me as one of her former students. I have never been able to change her perception of me as one who is basically still 'learning the ropes.' "

When the advice of the mentor is no longer needed, it is particularly difficult for the mentor to accept this change in the relationship. Even after the mentor-protégé relationship ends, there is likely to be a great loyalty in the once strongly committed relationship between two previous partners, unless there is a serious falling out between them. According to the norm of reciprocity, two demands are expected in relationships. This concept suggests that (1) one helps those from whom one receives help; and (2) one does not injure those who have helped him or her (Swenson, 1973).

Very few people ever make it alone. We all need someone to lead the way, show us the ropes, tell us the norms, encourage and support us, and make it a little easier for us. Whether that someone is a mentor, friend, supervisor, or colleague, there is an element of friendship in each case. How you, as the communication manager or consultant, manage that relationship can enhance or hinder your effectiveness in solving communication problems in the organization. The challenge in being a communication specialist is that everyone expects you to model the most effective type of communication on all occasions!

Friendships at Work

Can co-workers be friends? Or must you maintain some distance in your working relationships? By opening up your private life to examination by those you must supervise, be supervised by, or with whom you compete for scarce resources, are you making yourself too vulnerable? Obviously, there is no easy answer. In fact, each person must decide individually the extent to which he or she will consent to be vulnerable.

We do know that there are differences in the ways in which men and women typically handle personal friendships and work. Rubin (1985) summarized these differences:

> Women, even aspiring women, find themselves enmeshed in the struggle between achievement and affiliation. . . . The working world may be dominated by men, but the issues that are at the forefront when women work together are women's issues: affiliation vs. professionalism, jealousy and role confusion, nurturing and autonomy. Men's concerns are professional—getting the job done, being competent, moving up. Many women share these concerns, but they are interlaced with more relational desires—that of liking and being liked, sharing and not sharing, inclusion and isolation. In the nine-to-five of a man's world, we are wrapped up in the female sphere still. (p. 56)

Rubin went on to identify how she perceives women cope with friendship on the job:

> Given the fact that most working environments are patriarchally structured and not particularly nurturing, how do women cope? In large part, by bringing the mountain to Mohammed. That is, by doing men's work in a woman's way. Women are far more likely to form close relationships with one another than their male counterparts with whom they engage in intimate and sympathetic conversation. (p. 67)

If we agree with Rubin's assessment, males and females handle friends at work quite differently. The problem I have with Rubin's observations is that they are based on biological differences rather than psychological differences. A person's characteristics may be closer to what is considered typically masculine or feminine, *regardless* of his or her sex or sexual preference. We know that for some people in the organization (males *and* females), interpersonal relationships are of prime importance, while to others, work always comes first. Neither approach is right or wrong, simply different. Communication managers and consultants must understand and appreciate the differences. There are also differences in peoples' reactions to romance in the office.

Romance at Work[2]

> People with whom one is working are the people who excite. A day spent launching a project, writing a paper, or running a seminar is more likely to stimulate intellectually and sexually than an evening spent sharing TV, discussing the lawn problems, or going over the kids' report cards. (Jamison, 1983, p. 45)

With women moving into more powerful organizational positions, and men and women working as partners on exciting and stimulating projects, love in the office is more prevalent than ever before. The thrill of achievement and the pleasure of working side by side with bright, competent people can stimulate seductive feelings. Additionally, an office affair is more intense since the individuals see each other not just evenings and weekends but all day, every day. The couple thus develop an intimate understanding of each other's work world (Quinn & Lees, 1984).

Beliefs about Office Romances

Much has been written in the popular press about this topic, with authors suggesting a variety of coping strategies. This advice ranges from "dealing with the culprit privately" (Gray, 1984) to "saying no to office romances" (Handley, 1986), to hiring professional consultants to run "gender-awareness" sessions focusing on sexual tensions (Collins, 1983, 1987). One author suggested breaking up office romances by practicing "proactive crisis management instead of reactive damage control" (Braiker, 1988).

Corporate executives' assessment of the impact of office romances in the workplace varies as well. Helen Gurley Brown, editor of *Cosmopolitan* magazine, champions acceptance of affairs on the job and has been quoted as saying, "You can be sure that the more committed people are to their work, the more likely they are to fall for someone they meet on the job." Chester Wright, chief of the Work Force Effectiveness and Development Division for the U.S. Office of Personnel Management concluded, "Sexual attraction is inevitable" (Spruell, 1985, p. 21). Another executive advises, "The best approach is to set in place a policy that restricts that specific situation" (Plax, 1989, p. 16). The outcome can vary from "heading to the altar or [to] the unemployment line" (Luckert, 1989, p. 12). If the individuals involved are "single, not too powerful, and work in areas that don't overlap," then some suggest these relationships may be "tolerated quite well" (McLaughlin, 1988, p. 153). These conditions, however, are infrequently met.

Despite wide talk and increasing impact, few academic studies have examined intimate work relationships. Instead, conclusions have been drawn from case studies, anecdotal evidence, and questionable survey methods. For instance, Jamison (1983) concluded from a single case study, "Careers are damaged, perhaps irreparably" (p. 42). A survey asked college students whether they believed sexual intimacy in the workplace would foster better communication between the workers, create a more harmonious work environment, and enhance creativity (Powell, 1986). Individuals who are not caught up in the drama or the consequences of such behavior have little experience on which to base such predictions.

Other surveys asked people to indicate how much of a problem they think romance may be in the office. For example, a study by Mishra and

Harell (1989) revealed that managers in Michigan believed workplace romances were a problem in their companies. However, the survey questions were not precise; thus, the reader does not know the exact nature of the problems subjects thought office romances presented. Some researchers have drawn conclusions from "conversations with professional men and women" (Crary, 1987, p. 27) without reporting exactly how many conversations were conducted. Books have been written about the subject (Horn & Horn, 1982; Westhoff, 1986) but none of these texts reviews the impact of office romances on the communication structure in the organization. Rather they deal with the pervasiveness of the problem, raise questions for managers who must supervise the romantic couple, and describe how these relationships may turn into sexual harassment cases.

Studies of the Effects of Office Romances

Mainiero's (1986) lament that research on organizational romances suffers from a lack of methodological rigor and that most of it is an analysis of anecdotal material and/or case studies is not unwarranted. Her comprehensive review of 19 previous studies, starting in 1975, indicates that a number of research questions revolving around the organizational climate need to be asked.

Quinn's 1977 study was one of the first serious attempts to examine intimate relationships at work. One hundred thirty-two descriptive case studies were analyzed to develop a questionnaire that was administered to 211 individuals. Behavioral changes brought about by office romances ranged from romantic partners being easier to get along with and being more productive to the negative results of gossip, hostility, and loss of productivity. Unfortunately, this study is nearly 25 years old, and the office environment, as well as the increase in romantic relationships at work, has significantly changed individuals' perceptions of office romance. Quinn's early research led the way for later researchers to examine this issue more closely.

In the field of communication, several scholars have examined romantic relationships at work. Dillard and his associates have conducted a series of studies looking at the impact of office romance (Dillard, 1987; Dillard & Broetzmann, 1989; Dillard & Witteman, 1985). Dillard's research is based on data collected through phone interviews and focuses primarily on motives for intimate relationships and the impact of those motives on romantic involvement, organizational participativeness, and job performance. This research lays the groundwork for a more intense look at the impact intimate relationships have on co-worker communication patterns as well as superior-subordinate communication networks.

A second communication focus on office romance comes from Miller and Ellis (1986), who looked at romantic relationships and the effect of gender, status, and attractiveness of the participants on the attributions of motives. This research was conducted with undergraduates and their perceptions of how these relationships might affect organizational climates. Subjects were given vignettes and asked to assume the degree to which the individuals in the vignettes would do less work, assume more power, lose the respect of co-workers, and become inaccessible. Using undergraduate students plus hypothetical cases resulted in severe limitations on the conclusions.

In spite of this research activity, many issues dealing with the impact of romantic relationships on co-worker communication behavior remain to be explored. While Dillard and Broetzmann's research (1989) measured the impact on the organization in terms of absenteeism, tardiness, enthusiasm, complaints, and general job performance, we were interested specifically in the change in interoffice communication as a result of the office romance. Communication behaviors were examined from the point of view of the co-worker as well as participant. Miller and Ellis (1986) suggested that observers of office romance are affected by their biases and thus their observations are less valid. However, if we are studying the impact of office romance *on co-workers,* then the only way we can understand this phenomenon is to study it from their perspectives.

Subjects in one study (DeWine, Pearson, & Yost, 1993) were asked about changes in their ability to trust, get along with, share information with, influence, and communicate with romantic partners. Besides surveying co-workers' perceptions, those subjects who had participated in an office romance themselves completed additional survey instruments and were separated out for comparison.

We found that the majority of people who completed our survey tolerated, and in most cases accepted, office romance. It did not appear to affect co-worker relationships negatively, but rather, people were fairly neutral toward romantic partners. Office affairs do occur. It's not likely they can be ruled out; thus, we must figure out how to cope with them and limit their negative impact.

Dealing with human beings in an organization means dealing with relationships. Many of the problems organizations face are caused by dysfunctional relationships among those who must make decisions about the organization's future.

When I asked one vice president to allow a team of researchers to study friendships in his organization, his answer was, "We don't have anything like that going on around here. We're here to work." I suspected he thought we would be researching more intimate relationships, but whether he actually thought we would research friendships or romances, they definitely *were* "going on there" and to believe otherwise was to ignore half the activity in the organization! We live much of our lives at work and we need to be sensitive to all the relationship issues that exist. Not to do so results in ignoring a major portion of our lives and significant influences on our productivity, to say nothing of our general well-being!

LESSONS LEARNED

Maintaining Friendships at Work

Maintaining friendships and working relationships without creating confusion takes skill. I have counseled many people who found themselves in difficult situations when they tried to separate a personal friendship from a romantic attraction from a working relationship. The following suggestions come from those conversations and many peoples' experiences:

- *Develop your closest friendships outside client systems.* Everyone needs someone in whom to confide. Those confidences must not affect the work relationships that already exist. Consequently, they should be shared with individuals not in the immediate work environment (e.g., spouses, close friends not in the organization). Of course you must restrain yourself from betraying the confidentiality entrusted to you. Information shared with friends at work should be very general and should not name specific individuals.

- *Don't start an intimate relationship unless you are prepared to cope with the consequences.* Those consequences may include one of the partners leaving the company if the relationship interferes with people's ability to work together. Other consequences, such as lack of trust by co-workers, perceived favoritism leading to resentment, and breakdown in relationships among co-workers, may not be so obvious.

- *Become a mentor to someone else; it will be rewarding to both of you.* As a consultant, I often have taken "consultants in training" with me to observe and cofacilitate. One of the best ways to learn how to handle conflict in a group is to observe it; the process is difficult to describe in detail. At the same time, I benefit by having another person to act as a process observer who may pick up things I have missed. The mentor benefits as much as, or more than, the protégé.

- *Recognize that males and females cope with friendships at work differently.* This difference may not have as much to do with biological sex as psychological sex. One individual will approach the office secretary with friendly overtures, maintaining the relationship first and asking for help second. Others will think first of the work to be done, and only when it is completed will then turn to maintaining the relationship with "small talk." Understanding this difference allows us to be more tolerant of them rather than reject one approach or the other.

Notes

1. Parts of this section are taken from DeWine, Casbolt, and Bentley (May, 1983) and DeWine, James, and Hale (May, 1991).
2. Parts of this section are taken from DeWine, Pearson, and Yost (1993).

Additional Resources

Berryman-Fink, C., Ballard-Reisch, D., & Newman, L. (1993). *Communication and sex-role socialization.* New York: Garland Press.

Horn, P. D., & Horn, J. (1982). *Sex in the office.* Reading, MA: Addison-Wesley.

Rubin, L. B. (1985). *Just friends: The role of friendship in our lives.* New York: Harper and Row.

Chapter 20

THE BUSINESS OF CONSULTING

Entrepreneurship, Marketing, Ethics, and Career Development

434

A lawyer who defends himself has a fool for a client!

Author unknown

So you made it to the end of this book and you are still interested in becoming a consultant or communication specialist? This means you want to be your own boss, maybe practice what you preach on clients and your own employees and colleagues. But just because you are able to help large groups of people establish effective work climates doesn't mean you will be able to do it for yourself. You may be an outstanding facilitator with groups who must make decisions; however, you may know little about how to establish a group of your own! This final chapter provides some practical suggestions about actually starting a consulting business.

A colleague and I taught a small-business class in a community filled with creative, talented, and highly educated individuals. Because few large businesses were located in this small community, many people had chosen to start their own businesses. We were teaching a ten-week course covering financial, legal, and personnel issues related to small businesses.

On the first night of class we discussed why individuals might want to own their own business and the advantages and disadvantages of doing so. One member of the class said he was looking for something new to challenge himself. We cautioned him to think about this carefully before making any big decisions. One week later, at the second class, Jake walked into class all smiles. "I quit my job on Tuesday and bought a restaurant on Wednesday!" In the stunned silence that followed this announcement, my colleague covered her disbelief and asked, "Jake, have you ever owned or even worked in a restaurant before?" "No, but I eat in them a lot and I figured I would learn quickly!"

We hadn't even covered getting a bank loan yet! As the evening went on Jake learned the importance of developing a business plan. We discussed how a business plan outlines potential problems with the new business. Later that week, Jake discovered he had bought the restaurant only, not the parking lot attached to it! In fact, he learned the previous owners had rented the parking lot. One of the reasons they had decided to sell the restaurant was that the owner of the parking lot had not renewed their lease because he planned to build an office building on it. Jake had bought a restaurant without a parking lot! That's a hard way to learn the importance of a business plan.

This chapter is for readers who are now, or want to be some time in the future, independent consultants, external to any organization. External consulting means being a small-business owner. The first step in establishing a small business is the development of a business plan.

The Business Plan[1]

It is a fact that nine out of ten small businesses fail in the first five years. If you are thinking of becoming an independent consultant, be prepared for five years of low, or no, profit. In my experience, identifying clients and business are not the most important problem: cash flow is.

The owner of a small business must be aware of legal ramifications, tax benefits, insurance options, liability issues, and financial plans, as well as maintain a high-quality product or service. According to estimates by the U.S. Department of Commerce[2] there are some 10 million small businesses in the United States, not counting about 2-1/2 million family-owned farms. These 10 million small businesses make up 90 percent of U.S. businesses. They account for 55 percent of the domestic employment and 43 percent of the gross national product.

One of the primary factors determining the success or failure of any small business is the "business sense" of its owner or operator. Many people become small-business owners because they have a creative idea, a talent, or a craft that they want to market, but they have little information or experience with business concerns.

Consultants might fall into the same category; a lot of talent but little knowledge of what it takes to run a successful small business. They may have the talent and skill to be a consultant but not have the knowledge or the experience necessary to set up a consulting firm. The development of a business plan could prove quite useful to any individual considering consulting as a full-time job. Such a business plan would include an analysis of the following types of information.

Parts of a Business Plan

Part one of a business plan should be a *brief statement* or *definition of the services or products* one intends to market. In the case of a consulting firm, the consultant must be able to describe in simple language the skills and techniques that can be delivered to an organization. Consultants must be able to state in a sentence or two exactly what they could deliver to an organization as a consulting firm.

The second part of the business plan should *define the target market.* By target market I mean who the customers will be, the size of the market, trends in that market, and a description of the competition. One might be wise to target a particular population with which one wishes to work, especially as a start-up business. For example, one consulting firm works entirely with hospital administrations, another works with political campaigns, and yet another communication consulting agency works with industrial top-level management to perfect their public speaking skills. In any case, it is important that you have a specific target in mind when developing your firm and your marketing strategies.

You might want to focus your consulting firm in a particular location, in which case the analysis of your competition will be easier to manage. It is important that you find out what kind of consulting is already going on within the organizations with whom you want to work, who is conducting that training or consulting, the prices they are charging, and how they are marketing themselves. Nothing is less successful than approaching an organization with a consulting contract that has already been completed by some other firm. *Know your territory.*

The third part of the business plan is to *develop strategies for new services or product improvement.* This might mean completing training yourself to learn new skills and new strategies or it might mean developing packaged programs that could be modified to serve a variety of organizations.

The next area outlined in the business plan is the *overall marketing strategy.* Marketing strategies are discussed in greater detail later in the chapter and must be a part of the plan. Some consulting firms take a broad-base approach to advertising through some sort of mass-mailing campaign. Others prefer a more personalized strategy in which hundreds of contacts and interviews are made with potential clients and personal letters are sent to targeted clients in organizations.

The fifth section of the business plan should be an *outline of the organizational structure.* Who will own the firm, who will participate in its activities besides yourself, and what will the make-up and structure be in the organization? Even though you are running a small business, it is just as important for you to determine how that business will operate as it is for the larger organizations with which you may be consulting.

The sixth area to be analyzed as part of the business plan is the *financial procedure* used to support this activity. The potential owner should outline a profit/loss forecast of potential income as well as potential loss for a given period of time. All too often people assume that a consulting firm that operates out of a home will have little, if any, cash flow problems. One incurs overhead costs with a home business just as any small-business owner might encounter. There are administrative expenses, staff development costs, secretarial fees, and insurance, just to name a few.

All too often the firms with which a consulting agency might deal have long periods of time between delivery of service and payment for service. The consultant must be prepared to cope with this time span. As a part of your financial program, you need to develop a break-even chart where you consider fixed and variable costs. Examples of fixed costs are rent or mortgage payments and insurance premiums. Variable costs include material to be used for each client, which would vary according to a particular situation. You might want to prepare a packet of hand-outs for each participant, for example, or slides and overhead transparencies for a talk to a large group.

These six areas are critical steps toward making some important decisions about establishing a consulting firm. Wolfe (1984) also suggested identifying if there is a seasonal or cyclical factor in your business. Do clients need your services more at any particular time of the year or at certain stages in their growth? This could help you narrow the focus of your marketing campaign.

Forms of Ownership

Probably one of the most important initial decisions is which type of legal form your consulting firm will follow. There are three basic types of forms that any small business may use. One may establish a sole ownership or proprietorship, a partnership, or a corporation.[3]

SOLE OWNERSHIP

Sole ownership, or proprietorship, businesses make up 78.6 percent of the business concerns in the United States but only 11.3 percent of the sales. In a **sole ownership** legal form, the business is owned and operated by a single person. The advantages are (1) this is probably the easiest form of business to establish, thus incurring low start-up costs; (2) fees to register a sole ownership are minimal; (3) there are few legal restrictions or regulations, and as sole owner you receive all of the profits from the small business; (4) the sole owner has complete control over decision making and management policy; and (5) this type of legal form is flexible, which lets you respond to specific situations.

There are a number of disadvantages incurred with sole ownership. First, assets and liabilities of the proprietorship are merged into the assets and liabilities of the owner. This means that the debts of the proprietorship are the debts of its owner.

Second, income is taxed as income to the individual. You cannot hire yourself as an employee; thus, money taken from the company cannot be deducted as wages to an employee and/or a business expense. Additionally, it is extremely difficult to raise capital, especially long-term financing from banks.

Third, it may create an unstable business life. For example, if the owner dies, the business dies. This is especially important if the owner's goodwill and personal contact with clients have built the business.

Finally, it does provide you with a limited viewpoint since you have only one person's ideas, views, and knowledge as input into decision making for the firm. You must acquire appropriate licenses and permits, open and manage a company checking account, and be responsible for all the functions of your small business, from major financial decisions to janitorial duties.

PARTNERSHIP

The second type of legal form is a partnership. Partnerships make up 7.7 percent of the businesses in the United States and only 4.4 percent of sales. A **partnership** is an association of two or more people who carry on as co-owners of a business concern.

The financial advantages of a partnership legal form are low start-up costs and additional sources of money that may be available through one's partner or partners. Each partner brings personal skills and experience to the business, thus providing a broader management base than a sole proprietor can achieve. However, many new consultants cite the flexibility to make business decisions as one of their primary reasons for establishing a consulting firm of their own. The more partners the business has, the less flexibility any individual may have.

A major disadvantage to a general partnership is that each partner is personally liable for wrongful acts by any of his or her partners in the operation of the partnership; in essence, you are your brother's keeper. Personal assets of the partners may be used to satisfy liabilities of partnerships but not vice versa. Like proprietorships, representative partners cannot be employees, and wages are not business expenses. Partnerships may create an unstable business life in that the elimination of any partner constitutes automatic dissolution of the partnership.

In order to establish a partnership, a written partnership agreement should be developed, although one may develop out of an oral agreement or business practice. Specifically, the following are indicated: what the business is and what its goals are; how much each partner will contribute in cash; how each partner shares in profits and losses; procedures for withdrawal of funds and payment of transfers; provisions for continuing the business if a partner dies; and specification of the financial, legal, and managerial powers of each partner.

INCORPORATION

The third legal form is the establishment of a corporation. Corporations make up 13.7 percent of the businesses but 84.3 percent of the sales (see Figure 20.1). A **corporation** is a legal entity that exists separately and distinctly from its owners.

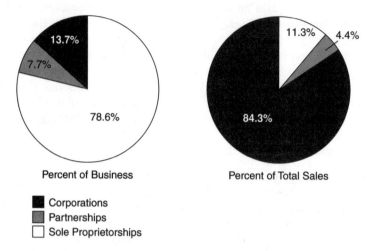

FIGURE 20.1 Forms of Ownership Most businesses in the United States are sole propri-etorships, but they account for only 11.3 percent of sales. Although only 13.7 percent of U.S. businesses are incorporated, corporations bring in 84.3 percent of sales. Partnerships are the least used form of business and bring in the smallest contribution to sales.

The advantages of a corporation are that liability of the owners is equal to their investment, and ownership is easily transferred; thus, the organiza-tion exists beyond the life of its owners. In addition, certain tax advantages are incurred, such as the salary of the owner(s) being deductible as a busi-ness expense and the owner being treated as an employee for benefit of re-tirement. Plus, it is much easier to raise capital from lending institutions. Finally, you have the ability to draw on expertise and skills of more than one person.

The disadvantages of a corporation legal form include double taxa-tion of dividend profits as well as corporate taxes and end taxes. Closely regulated by government agencies, the corporation becomes the most ex-pensive form of business to organize, and maintaining the necessary recordkeeping information is costly and complicated.

To incorporate one must develop articles of incorporation that include the nature or purpose of the business to be conducted, description of cap-ital structure, and names and addresses of other corporations similar to your own. There are special types of corporations such as a closely held corporation, in which stock is not available to the public through the sale on any stock exchange, and professional corporations, wherein an indi-vidual or group's profession is licensed.

Finally, one could develop a subchapter S. Some of the requirements for this special type of corporation are that it may have no more than 15 shareholders; no shares may be owned by other corporations or nonresi-dent aliens; no more than 20 percent of the income may come from passive sources (i.e., rent, royalty, dividends); and finally, no more than 80 percent of the sales income can be generated outside the United States.

The advantages to this special type of corporation are that there is no double taxation to both the individual and the company, business losses can be carried back to prior years of the owner's income, and the control of the organization is similar to a partnership.

The disadvantages are that it may be confusing and costly to set up and follow necessary rules. Also the IRS may watch the formation of these special corporations very carefully. The incorporation of your firm establishes its credibility to some extent and protects you in terms of any liability to clients for promised services.

Table 20.1 summarizes the advantages and disadvantages of the three basic legal forms of business. One of these legal forms will work best for your circumstances. An attorney should be consulted to make certain you comply with local, state, and federal laws. Once you have established your firm legally, you next have to let people know you exist!

Many good books outline these options (Bagley & Dauchy, 1998) and include forms with which you can establish your own business entity (Friedman, 1998).

TABLE 20.1

ADVANTAGES AND DISADVANTAGES OF FORMS OF OWNERSHIP

	Sole Proprietorship	*Partnership*	*Corporation*
Simplicity	+ Easiest to start + Low start-up costs + Few legal restrictions	+ Easy to start + Low start-up costs	− Most regulated
Authority	+ Complete authority	± Divided by agreement	− Rests with stockholders
Liability	− Personal assets/debts not separate from business assets/debts	− Each liable for actions of all	+ Limited
Taxes	± Taxed as individual	± Taxed as individuals	− Taxed as employees; business taxed separately
Financing	− May be difficult to get	± More resources than individual, fewer than corporation	+ Most likely to attract
Stability	− Dies with owner	− Dissolves with elimination of any partner	+ Has separate life from any of owners

Marketing

Greiner and Metzger (1983) suggested,

> To the surprise and frustration of most consultants, marketing is the lifeblood of the industry. Consultants would rather consult than sell; after all, that is what drew them to the field. It is natural for them to assume that effective consulting skills, combined with a few satisfied clients, should lead to an endless stream of new clients. Therein lies the marketing failure of most consultants and consulting firms. (p. 41)

Consultants think of themselves as professionals in some rather narrow definition of the field. People in the business of consulting have to think of themselves as small-business owners who must market their services.

Identifying Your Market Niche

It is important that the consulting firm identify the type of firm it is and market itself correctly. Suryanarayanan (1989) identified five basic types of consulting firms:

1. *Pure strategy advisors* may be small firms such as the Boston Consulting Group that provide high-cost advice mainly to chief executives.

2. *Traditional management consultants* are firms such as McKinsey and Co., Booz Allen & Hamilton, and Arthur D. Little that combine strategy consulting with advice in functional areas such as marketing, manufacturing, and logistics or industry-specific advice in such industries as automotive or consumer electronics. These firms are much more diversified and larger than the pure strategy firms.

3. *Accounting firms* are relatively recent entrants into consultation in a purposeful organized manner, although they have engaged in general counsel for many years. Until recently they marketed themselves as computer experts, but soon learned there were ways to serve other needs of the client. With consulting revenues rising at a faster pace than auditing and tax-practice fees, many accounting firms will soon find their earnings from consulting overtaking all other earnings. Examples include Andersen Consulting, Coopers and Lybrand, and Price Waterhouse.

4. *Human resources firms* may specialize in developing compensation packages. Most work closely with a client's personnel director or the CEO to develop a strategic human resource policy. Companies in this category include Hay Group, acquired by Saatchi and Saatchi in 1984, and Sibson and Co., a Johnson and Higgins company.

5. *Specialized firms* offer advice on specific markets or skills. They are hired by their counterparts in client businesses. Examples include

Oliver Wyman and Co., specializing in the financial services industry, and Symmetriz in systems development for operations management. This category also includes university professors and sole practitioners offering specialized services. Competition in this category is fierce.

Once you have identified the type of firm you have developed or will develop, you must advertise what you have.

Getting the Word Out

There are many ways to make contact with clients and market the service of your company when you want to increase the client pool. Smith (1990) suggested the consulting company can get its message out through its own staff, present and past clients, professional associations, associates in other businesses, suppliers or subcontractors, and other consultants who may not have the same services to offer. The range of tools covers press advertising and articles; talks on radio and television; conferences; teaching institutions; special seminars; research projects; receptions with or without presentations; pamphlets; letters; web pages and ads; telephone calls; and personal calls. The client may be reached through his or her staff, the general public, the government, trade unions, shareholders, professional associations, associates, suppliers, and educational institutions. In short, you use every possible contact to get the word out. Marketing is indirect or direct.

INDIRECT MARKETING

Most service professionals believe it is easier to keep an old client than attract a new one. Businesspeople who take client retention for granted while they constantly seek new business may experience serious losses. Most consultants I have worked with, including my own firm, have depended heavily on referrals from satisfied clients. That means that the first principle of marketing for consultants is to satisfy current customers. Begin by getting one client and making that client very happy with your work.

White and Mindiole (1986) suggested the following steps to ensure your clients stay with you:

1. Develop client satisfaction letters, surveys, or meetings in which evaluations of your firm's performance can be gathered.

2. Ensure that more than one key professional from your firm maintains regular contact with significant clients.

3. Implement a client service planning program in which detailed plans for providing additional services to key clients are developed.

> Often, I receive consulting contracts by word of mouth. Someone is looking for outside help, mentions it to a colleague, who, it turns out, has worked with me directly or has heard me speak, or read an article I've written and passes my name along. In one case, I conducted a workshop for alumni returning to the university for a weekend. Two days later I received a phone call from a corporate lawyer who was in charge of setting up an in-house employee development program for 1,500 employees of a national insurance company. When I asked how she had acquired my name she replied, "Actually, my parents called me and raved about your workshop they had attended and insisted I must hear you talk. Since I rarely hear them give such glowing compliments, I decided I would follow their advice!"

No matter the size of the consulting firm, the best marketing strategy remains referral. Richard Ziehm (1989), president of Precision Extrusions, Inc., suggested the following criteria for hiring consultants:

> I've picked management consultants almost strictly through referrals. I read at least part of most direct-mail pieces, but rarely accept phone calls. I discuss our needs with friends in the basic organizations to which I belong. . . . Even my accountants, attorneys, and competitors are good sources of referrals. If I were selling consulting services, having consulted with Precision Extrusions previously, I would hunt for business by selling to the competition of my recent successes. For example, I would send direct mail to other extrusion companies and mention that I had a recent project at Precision Extrusions. This piques interest, arouses curiosity, and appeals to a CEO's sense of insecurity. Can I afford not to learn what this guy taught so and so? (p. 26)

Greiner and Metzger (1983) call this indirect marketing, claiming that

> indirect marketing is largely the domain of the biggest and longest established consulting firms. . . . These elitist consulting firms perceive little need to advertise or make "cold calls" on clients. They want their quality image to be so pervasive in the market's consciousness that key decision makers in client organizations naturally select them before considering an unknown, though perhaps equally qualified consultant. Above all, the indirect approach is low-key and subtle, to the point where the client does not realize that he or she is the "victim" of hidden persuasion. (p. 43)

All of these indirect marketing techniques introduce your services in fairly informal ways. Direct marketing techniques are more formal, more obvious advertising strategies.

DIRECT MARKETING

Direct marketing can be quite costly. In consulting, the direct approach recognizes that you are marketing an intangible personal service, much the same as life insurance. Direct sales requires contacting by mail or distributing some form of advertising to large numbers of people. "For every 20 people contacted, five executives' doors are opened. For every five doors opened, one sale is consummated" (Greiner & Metzger, 1983, p. 46).

Once you get into the CEO's office, you should ask three questions in the initial interview:

1. What are you especially proud of about your organization in the past several years?
2. What things would you like to change?
3. If you could wave a magic wand, what things would you do that you haven't been able to do because of lack of time or expertise?

These three questions allow you to identify possible problems and how you may be able to help. Question 1 identifies the organization's strengths, question 2 identifies its weaknesses, and question 3 helps you determine what has been keeping organization members from solving the problem.

Greiner and Metzger (1983) remind us of the proverb: "Listen and you may learn something new; keep talking and you only espouse what you already know." That is a good principle to remember in that initial and subsequent interviews.

Schrello (1988) suggested the following tips for individuals who are attempting to market seminars or consulting activities. For direct marketing copy he advises:

1. Capture the readers' interest.
2. Describe a need you know they have.
3. Show how your product or service can meet that need.
4. Establish your credibility to do what you claim.
5. Request action now.
6. Add a clincher of some kind: a bonus, premium, or added reason to act now. (p. 5)

He also recommends that you set up a problem the customer recognizes, show how your product or service can solve that problem, then prove your solution. Written or broadcast promotional materials should talk to your readers personally and involve them just as you would face to face. Writing as if for an individual, rather than a group or an organization, is a proven technique.

Speak to emotional and intellectual needs of your readers. Always use "you," never "we." For example, "You will get . . ." rather than "We will give you. . . ." Schrello (1988) also suggested that, based on studies of persuasive words by the Yale Psychology Department and an analysis of what works best, the 15 words that spell direct marketing success are

Discovery	Easy	Free
Guaranteed	Help	Introducing
Money	New	Now
Proven	Results	Save
Today	Win	You

In consulting you must continually market your services (see Figure 20.2). Since your skills are the product you are promoting, your attitude toward yourself and what you can provide are critical. Tepper (1987) identified the most important ingredient for a successful consultant: a positive attitude.

> Attitude is critical to the consultant because regardless of your chosen field, you risk rejection more than any other professional. Consultants run an even higher risk of rejection than salespeople. In sales you sell the client a product and/or service. It is delivered, you receive your commission check, and you are on to the next person. In consulting, you sell the prospect on a service, then you have to keep selling the client on your value and ability, on the program, and on the approach you have developed. (p. 311)

Marketing your services is more difficult than marketing some inanimate object. Because you cannot present this service objectively, you must develop ethical guidelines to direct your behavior.

Ethics

One of my students reported on the following historical event:

> Dora, an 18-year-old, was sent to Sigmund Freud for therapy (Freud, 1901). Her father was a close friend of Freud and wanted him to "bring Dora to reason." She was having hysterical attacks that annoyed her father. After several weeks of therapy, Freud learned that Dora's father wanted her to have a romantic interlude with his friend so that he could enjoy the company of the friend's young wife. Dora's hysterical outbursts were a direct result of being faced with the dilemma of not wanting to obey her father. The outbursts increased with his persistence.
>
> Considering the father as the client, Freud proceeded to try to convince Dora that the request was not unreasonable. Although Freud acknowledged the validity of her perceptions, he decided not to tell her this because he was working in the best interests of her father. Luckily, Dora deduced that Freud was acting on her father's behalf and subsequently dropped out of therapy.

SUE DEWINE
Midwest Associate

Communication Consultants, Inc.
154 Martha Avenue
Centerville, Ohio 45459
(513) 866-7524
or
(513) 433-7804

Specializing in Optimizing
Human Potential in
Industry and Education

Using this picture business card early in my career reminded people who I was.

COMMUNICATION
CONSULTANTS,
INCORPORATED   8 York Drive
Athens, Ohio 45701
(614) 594-7539

SUE DeWINE
MIDWEST ASSOCIATE

ORGANIZATIONAL COMMUNICATION
SCHOOL OF INTERPERSONAL COMMUNICATION
OHIO UNIVERSITY
ATHENS, OHIO 45701

I used for some years this standard business card with my firm's logo imprinted on it. I included my university address because I am often making contacts for the university at the same time.

STEPS I WILL TAKE IN
ESTABLISHING MY
PROFESSIONAL NETWORK

(names & contacts)

1. _____

2. _____

3. _____

4. _____

(over)

5. _____

6. _____

Communication Consultants
8 York Dr., Athens, OH 45701
(614) 593-7539

This is a card I use as part of a networking exercise. I ask participants to fill out the card at the end of a session, listing the names of individuals or goals they want to set for themselves in the next six months. Then I ask them to place the card in their wallet so that they remember these goals every time they reach for their money. They will also be reminded of my firm's name whenever they see the back of the card.

SUE DeWINE

COMMUNICATION
CONSULTANTS

190 LONGVIEW HTS.
ATHENS, OHIO 45701
740-593-7539
DEWINE@EUREKANET.COM

SPECIALIZING IN.....

¥ TEAM BUILDING

¥ CHANGE MANAGEMENT

¥ STRATEGIC PLANNING

¥ COMMUNICATION SKILLS
     TRAINING

¥ CONFLICT MANAGEMENT

¥ MEETING/RETREAT
     FACILITATION

This is the business card I have used in recent years.

FIGURE 20.2 A business card keeps the consultant's name and service in the client's mind.

Obligations to the Client

This anecdote raises a serious ethical question: What are the consultant's obligations to the client? Few would deny that the consultant has an obligation to exercise honesty, objectivity, and diligence in the performance of his or her duties and responsibilities or that the consultant owes the client respect, including maintenance of confidentiality. As with most homilies, it is far easier to preach an ethical consultant-client relationship than to practice it.

One must ask, "Who is my client and what interventions are in the client's best interest?" Deetz (1992) would respond that the consultant "should represent the various stakeholders, the total corporation, and any report should be publicly available" (p. 347). In this view, the consultant must be working for the good of the whole, not for a single individual to the detriment of others. Ethical concerns include, but are not limited to, the following issues:

- We should consider whether our response to a situation will compromise our personal dignity and integrity or that of our organization and profession. We have an obligation to "give back" to the profession, and thus we should not leave an organization worse off than we found it.

- It is unethical to be a "hit-and-run" consultant who leaves behind injured victims.

- Failing to recognize one's professional limitations and exaggerating one's qualifications are clearly unethical and dangerous practices.

- The roles of "yes man," a "hatchet," or "dime-store psychologist" can also be viewed as unethical roles for a consultant. The consultant is responsible for helping the client identify and resolve a problem by bringing professional expertise and objectivity to the situation.

- No consultant should consent to intervene unless there is a commitment to follow-up activities. Otherwise employees will not only mistrust that consultant but are likely to mistrust all interventions in the future and they will resist the implementation of beneficial changes in their organizations.

Consultants must maintain strict standards of confidentiality. Information about the client gained during the course of the consultation relationship cannot be communicated to others unless the client has specifically agreed to such disclosure. This restriction also applies to any research efforts on the part of the consultant. The consultant must keep any results from consulting practices anonymous to protect the consultant as well as the client.

The American Psychology Association suggests that "information received in confidence is revealed only after most careful deliberation and when there is clear and imminent danger to an individual or to society and then only to appropriate professional workers or public authorities" (as cited in DeWine & James, 1978). Every effort must be made to protect the client's right to privacy, not only on ethical grounds but for legal considerations as well.

Ethics and Professional Behavior

Lippitt and Lippitt (1986) identified as **normative ethics** those basic areas of conduct controlled by the industry: qualifications, contracts, fees, objectivity, and confidentiality. They also recognize that a consultant must develop a personal code of **situational ethics,** that is, behavior guided by each unique situation encountered in professional practice.

Although the professional associations can provide guidelines for appropriate behavior, consultants basically stand alone when faced with ethical dilemmas. We must be able to live with our decisions, and standards must be thought out ahead of time if we are to be prepared to make on-the-spot decisions about our behavior.

Wexley and Latham (1981) identified major categories of behaviors considered improper or unethical for training and development professionals. They include lack of professional development, violation of confidences, use of cure-all programs, dishonest evaluation of program outcomes, failure to give credit, and abusive treatment of trainees.

It is easy for a consultant to assume that his or her training (in communication, management, personnel, psychology, etc.) enables him or her to diagnose the corporate ailment before consulting with the client. This is as foolhardy as the physician who makes a diagnosis over the telephone and then prescribes medication without seeing the patient. True, it is faster and cheaper, and presents the consultant in an omnipotent pose, but it is neither objective nor unbiased. We do not always possess the remedy for the ills of an organization at our fingertips.

As long as we remember that we are responsible for the decisions we make, the recommendations we advance, and the changes we instigate, and that the responsibility is a lighter burden if we have been as objective and straightforward with the client as possible, then we are effective models of our profession.

Consultants must accept moral responsibility for the consequences of their consulting practices. Consultants need not only ethical standards to govern the effect of outcomes generated by their interventions, but legal protection as well. While it is important that clients take ownership for their part in the problem, consultants must accept responsibility for possibly making the problem worse.

An internal consultant, by virtue of having to live with any actions taken, will be more aware of the result of such action than will an external consultant who can leave the situation. A consultant must be ready to terminate a consulting relationship when it is reasonably clear that the client is not benefiting from it. Finally, consultants need to take their own advice: if it is appropriate for clients to be constantly improving their product, then that must be true for the consultant as well.

The following list of ethical guidelines developed for internal consultants certainly applies to external consultants as well:

1. *Independence:* Both internal and external consultants must be able to collect information and analyze it without interference or influence by senior managers. What the managers do with the analysis once it is presented is up to them; however, I require that an executive summary be distributed to all participants. I also encourage clients to immediately (within 2 or 3 days of the report being distributed) take some action as a result of the input from organizational members. This can be something as simple as a memo announcing the formation of a task force to study some issue raised as a result of the intervention. In one case employees recommended a one-page flyer listing key leaders and their phone numbers and email addresses. Compared to other recommendations that included issues related to reorganization, this was a simple suggestion that could be implemented quickly. Taking some first steps shows employees that their suggestions have been heard. Even though some steps will take much longer to implement and some may never be implemented, these initial first steps send an important message about the value of participants' input.

2. *Confidentiality:* There must be an understanding that contact with personnel during data collection will be confidential and that respondents will be treated fairly and will understand the purpose of the data collection. Participants must be guaranteed anonymity.

3. *Competency:* Consultants have the responsibility to decline any contract for which they are unqualified. Your credibility will suffer if you do not understand the limits of your abilities.

4. *Respect for clients:* All clients should be treated with respect and dignity. They deserve full disclosure about the purpose of the data collection and how the information will be used.

5. *Integrity:* You achieve integrity when you are viewed as honest and fair. Fairness can best be interpreted as balancing both the positive and negative sides of an issue and reporting findings accurately and in noninflammatory language (adapted from Sonnichsen, 2000, pp. 156–157).

A consultant who does not follow these guidelines can be perceived as a spy, a "hatchet man/dragon lady," or a number cruncher.

Authors warn novice consultants of the perils of signing contracts without clear guidelines on ethical issues of compensation, disclosure of confidential material, and rights of ownership of consultant materials (Hirsch & Shwom, 1995). These issues, which we discussed in Chapter 1, will haunt you if there is no clear guideline established. Who really owns the information collected? Unless your client has agreed that you can use the information, usually the organization feels it owns all information and material used during your consulting activity and would consider it highly unethical if you used it elsewhere.

The overriding guide for you should be the answer to this question, "Will my action be in the best interest of the client?" Take the action only when the answer to this question is yes.

Career Development

In a particularly poignant article, Greiner and Metzger (1983) described "Stepping Back: How to Stay Sane and Avoid Burnout." It is true that consultants are often least likely to follow their own advice.

> There are hours and hours of sedentary life in planes, airports, cars, client meetings, restaurants, and report writing. Your once youthful figure sinks rapidly to the bottom. To top it off, there are long flights, rough flights, close connections, lost luggage, poorly maintained rental cars, high-sodium and high-cholesterol food, filthy hotel rooms, and extreme climate changes that play Handel's *Messiah* on your sinus cavities.
>
> **Warning: Consulting may be harmful to your health!**
> **Suggestions: Stay away from booze, dancing, junk food, and commuter airplanes!**
>
> Never take yourself or your client too seriously. A sane consultant will maintain perspective, recognizing that all humans, including consultants, are not omnipotent; in fact, that aura of fallibility is what makes the consulting game so interesting and challenging. Clients, just like spouses, lovers, relatives, and friends, often do things for their own selfish reasons, not yours. (pp. 328–329)

One colleague arrived at a training program with two different shoes on, one brown and one black. He was very embarrassed and decided to point it out himself before someone else did. He discovered that the audience warmed up to him very quickly after his admission! The consultant has to be human too. I always point out my poor spelling before someone else points it out to me. "By the way," I say at the beginning of writing ideas on newsprint, "I believe Mark Twain's philosophy that people who can spell words only one way are not very creative. I want you to know, you are looking at a very creative person!"

If I take myself less seriously, somehow that allows me to present my self more honestly.

Career Paths for Consultants

A career as a consultant, particularly an outside consultant, can be extremely taxing. Most people do not remain in the field for an entire career. Greiner and Metzger (1983) suggested:

> The vast majority [of consultants] perhaps as high as 60 percent, remain as consultants for only three to six years to gain the necessary experience, expertise, and exposure before moving on to that choice job of planning director at International Widgets. Another 30 percent realize that they are doing better financially than in private industry and stick it out for up to ten years until they too, leave for International Widgets as vice president for personnel. The remaining 10 percent are either faculty at universities who consult part-time forever, or they are senior partners in consulting firms who find that they are consulting less, administrating more, and earning in excess of $150,000 per year. (p. 332)

These are the kinds of career choices one must make. At the same time, all of us need to achieve balance in our lives.

Bellman (1990) discussed criteria by which a consultant might evaluate the balance in his or her practice. He suggested that the consultant consider such questions as the following: "What is my work schedule?" "How much work do I want to do?" "How effective can one person be, balancing all the parts of the consulting practice?" "How often do I say no to work?" "What should my travel schedule be?" "How long does it take me to work?" "Where should I live and where should I work?" "How should I establish administrative efficiency?" You must be content with your answers in order to stay in the profession.

Financial Rewards of Consulting

The Northeast and Pacific coast regions tend to offer the highest salaries with the Southeast and West Central regions offering the lowest. However, salaries vary more by type of industry than by geographical location. The best paying industries are manufacturing, transportation, communications, and public utilities. The worst paying industries are health services, finance, insurance, and banking. By position, training managers and specialists in management and in career and organization development tend to earn the highest salaries, while classroom instructors and instructional designers earn the lowest salaries.

Independent consultants can earn anywhere from $1,000 per day to what I would consider an average of $1,500 to $2,000 per day to $20,000 per half-day lecture for some of the most well-known consultants in the country. The fee depends on what the market will bear, the desire of the consultant, and the consultant's experience level. My fee varies depending on the ability of the client to pay (e.g., I will occasionally work with school systems at a significantly reduced rate because I want to help them) and the inconvenience caused to my life. If it requires travel and extended time away from my home, I charge more per day than I would if the consulting is within driving distance. New consultants look at those amounts and figure they could be making a six-digit salary immediately. However, they fail to recognize that consultants do not work every day of the week, every week of the year and that independent consultants have significant overhead charges such as office space, secretarial services, and paying for their own insurance and health care.

Future Directions

Since consultants often act as role models for the desired behavior of others, they must have a well-defined professional development program for themselves. The future of the field depends on their ability to adapt to new, innovative ideas and a changing environment and to bring an up-to-date approach to client systems that are also facing change.

Schindler-Raiman (1987) suggested a number of challenges and changes that consultants had to deal with in the 1990s and that will continue in the 2000s. They include (1) doing more with less, (2) the fluctuating national mood (fluctuating between pessimism and optimism and based on the value of the dollar, election results, various world crises, etc.), which affects the people with whom we work, and (3) the speed and complexity of changes (speed of change has led to an overload of information and the constant development of new techniques, knowledge, and technology).

The set of changes that consultants will have to deal with include demographic and population changes. The increasing mobility of the population will require more training of new employees and helping them adjust to a new organization. The aging of the population means fewer young employees and increased competition for jobs by employable persons. This situation will require the consultant to be able to decrease stress for those working in highly competitive systems. As the workforce becomes increasingly multicultural, consultants will be called on to help workers understand and use human resources representing different ages, life stages, and ethnic and racial groups. Keeping individuals abreast of population demographic changes and helping older workers accept and work with younger managers and vice versa will be challenges for the consultant in the contemporary workplace.

Complex communications technology and systems change present whole new series of challenges for consultants. There will be more emphasis on creative leadership than ever before, which means consultants will have to help long-time leaders change their styles, understand the necessity for such changes, learn to detect conflict and use it as a resource, and become more sensitive to the many realities of their systems. Schindler-Raiman (1987) suggested that trainers and consultants do the following:

- Increase our knowledge and skills with respect to future trends.
- Increase our training methodology tool kits by inventing new, creative training designs.
- Employ the inside/outside team concept and risk teaming with someone else inside or outside the system to increase one's skills and visibility.
- Admit when we do not know something and be able to recruit additional trainers and consultants as resources.
- Enhance what we already know about data collection and the use of resources.
- Understand and learn all about new technologies.
- Be selective in our choices about new technology.
- Learn more effective ways of involving potential participants.
- Find ways to use our time more effectively.
- Learn to confront clients more skillfully when they have legitimate differences of opinion.
- Introduce the possibility of using volunteers in systems.
- Help clients learn modern participative, productive ways of holding meetings, and support clients in recognizing that committing errors is a component of managing and that one can learn and grow from analysis of both success and mistakes. (p. 25)

If you can accomplish all of the above, you will definitely need to incorporate—you will have so much business that only that legal form can handle it! Attempting to follow these guidelines, and knowing how to lead a balanced personal life without becoming an 18-hour-a-day, 7-day-a-week consultant, will require your most intense concentration!

Criteria for Evaluating One's Consulting Business

The eight criteria by which Peters and Waterman (1984) identify excellent companies can also identify outstanding consultants. These attributes of excellence provide goals for practicing consultants. They are characterized by eight phrases (pp. 13–15):

A bias for action, for getting on with it

Close to the customer

Being entrepreneurial

Productivity through people

Hands-on, value-driven

Stick to the knitting

Simple form, lean stuff

Simultaneous loose-tight properties

A "bias for action" means being analytical in one's approach to decision making but not paralyzed by that fact. A consultant must take action and demonstrate to the client that the climate can change. Just like an organization, a consultant can end up analyzing a situation longer than necessary, until it's too late to take action.

"Close to the customer" suggests keeping in touch with clients and understanding their needs. Organizations that lose sight of their target population will produce products no one wants. A consultant who loses sight of clients' needs by getting wrapped up in his or her own goals and motivations will not have that client for long.

"Being entrepreneurial" means being innovative and taking risks. Outside consultants must be especially high risk takers because they are on their own, without a parent organization.

"Productivity through people" can occur only if management regards human beings as the most important investment for the corporation. Believing that human resource development ensures the future of the organization is an attitude that successful consultants embrace themselves and foster in their clients.

"Hands-on, value-driven" is explained by Peters and Waterman as "the basic philosophy of an organization has far more to do with its achievements than do technological or economic resources, organizational structure, innovation, and timing" (p. 15). A consultant needs to identify the philosophy that drives his or her activities and interventions. This philosophy should define how one believes people are motivated and what techniques will persuade others.

If you "stick to your knitting," you will "never acquire a business you don't know how to run" (p. 15). A consultant should stick to what he or she knows best. Do not expand into product innovation if that is not your expertise.

"Simple form, lean stuff" implies simple but eloquent designs for the system and for operating the organization. I have found that some of the most simple and direct designs for intervening into an organization work best. When I try to design a complex, highly structured innovation, it usually misses the target.

In communication management "simultaneous loose-tight properties" implies an approach to interacting in the organization that includes both centralized and decentralized activities. Some decision-making practices need to be centralized in the hands of a few while others need broad-based support and involvement. The consultant's job is to help the organization distinguish which approach is needed for different decisions.

Just as Peters and Waterman use these criteria to identify excellent companies, we can use them to point out an outstanding consultant. These basic principles about working with customers relate quite well to the client-consultant relationship.

W. Edwards Deming, the father of "quality" in organizations, has indicated that managers and executives are least prepared to deal with human problems. Many managers come from technical training and experiences where a problem can be fixed by replacing a part or a process. With human beings we are constantly molding and shaping and rarely replacing with a small part! I hope this book has helped in some small way to assist you in dealing with the complex human interactions we find not only at work, but also at home.

LESSONS LEARNED

Surviving the Consulting Business

The first decision you will make, which will affect every other decision, is whether you will be working full-time as a consultant or part-time with a full-time job somewhere else. The skills and techniques discussed in this book can be used by full-time or part-time outside consultants, as well as internal managers. All these techniques, instruments, activities, and practices will help individuals make better business decisions. But the decisions about how you will operate as a consultant all stem from the amount of dependence you have on your consulting income. Here are the lessons I have learned from starting my own firm:

- At least initially, don't give up your "day job." We know that nine out of ten small businesses fail in the first five years because of cash flow problems. Unless you have signed on with a large consulting firm, you could have large overhead charges and long waiting periods for cash to flow into the business. You will need additional income until the company is solvent.

- Identify a niche for your practice. If you have a unique specialty, begin your practice working in that area only. You can branch out after you have "cornered the market" in your niche area.

- Have colleagues you can call on if the assignment requires skills beyond your expertise. Rather than turn down a job, hire colleagues to help you out. They will return the favor. This means you need to network with consultants who operate in very different areas from your own.

- Establish some kind of identity so clients will believe your claims of expertise. This may mean affiliating with a more well-established consultant or firm, affiliating with a university as a faculty member, or joining a consulting association and obtaining its credentials. Anyone with a business card can call himself or herself a consultant. You want to be a person who has something to offer, based on legitimate experience and training.

Consulting with human beings on human issues has been some of the most rewarding work in my career. It can also be frustrating and downright demoralizing. It is always the most exhausting work I do. You must have enough confidence in your ability to walk away from the assignment knowing you have accurately represented yourself and done the best job you are capable of doing. Your reward, besides the income, is the satisfaction that comes when a difficult problem has been solved, or when a group has overcome differences and conflict to produce high-quality services or products. When I have a participant or client tell me that I made the difference in the success of a project or some organizationwide program, or that I had an impact on their personal life, it makes all my frustrations and expended energy worthwhile. I hope you have that same experience!

Notes

1. The section on legal forms is adapted from DeWine, S. (1987a, November). *Firming up your own communication consulting firm.* Paper presented at the Speech Communication Association Convention, Chicago, IL.
2. Unless otherwise indicated, all statistics are from the U.S. Department of Commerce, Washington, D.C.
3. For additional information on various legal forms, consult one of the following references: Baumback, C., & Lawyer, K., *How to organize and operate a small business,* Englewood Cliffs, NJ: Prentice-Hall, 1979; Mancuso, J. R., *How to start, finance, and manage your own small business,* Englewood Cliffs, NJ: Prentice-Hall, 1978; Siropolic, N., *How to start your own business, and how to make money,* Boston: Houghton Mifflin, 1977.

Additional Resources

Bagley, C. E., & Dauchy, C. E. (1998). *The entrepreneur's guide to business law.* New York: West Educational Publishing.

Biech, E., & Swindling, L. B. (2000). *The consultant's legal guide: A business of consulting resource guide.* San Francisco: Jossey-Bass/Pfeiffer.

Block, P. (2000). *Flawless consulting: Guide to getting your expertise used* (2nd ed.). San Francisco: Jossey-Bass.

Friedman, R. (1998). *The upstart small business legal guide* (2nd ed.). Chicago: Dearborn Financial Publishing.

REFERENCES

Adams, S. (1996). *The Dilbert principle*. New York: Harper Business.

Alonzo, V. (1998, September). Don't lecture them. *Incentive, 172*, 55–57.

Alston, J. P. (1989). Wa, Guanexi, and Inhwa: Managerial principles in Japan, China, and Korea. *Business Horizons, 32*(1), 26–31.

American Management Association. (1978). *Executive skills*. New York: Author.

American Psychiatric Association. (1980). *Diagnostic and statistical manual of mental disorders*. Washington, DC: Author.

American Society for Training and Development (ASTD). (1988). *Practical guide for technical and skills trainers: Vols. 1 & 2*. Alexandria, VA: Author.

Anderson, M. C. (2000). *Fast cycle: Organizational development: A fieldbook for organization transformation*. Cincinnati: South-Western.

Anderson, R. L., & Terborg, J. R. (1988). Employee beliefs and support for a work redesign intervention. *Journal of Management, 14*, 493–503.

Anonymous. (1997). How can you use online chat rooms to enhance distance learning? *Training, 34*(3), S6.

Anonymous. (1998). The set-up-to-fail syndrome. *Harvard Business Review, 76*(2), 104–105.

Argyris, C. (1999). *On organizational learning*. Oxford: Blackwell Business Publishing.

Arnold, W. E., & McClure, L. (1996). *Communication training and development* (2nd ed.). Prospect Heights, IL: Waveland Press.

Atwater, E. (1992). *I hear you* (Rev. ed.). New York: Walker.

Auerbach, C. (1997). *The 1997 McGraw-Hill training and performance sourcebook*. New York: McGraw-Hill.

Austin, N. K. (1995). The enneagram: Management's new numbers game. *Working Woman, 20*, 16–21.

Axelrod, A. (1997). *201 ways to deal with difficult people*. New York: McGraw-Hill.

Axtell, R. E. (1993). *Do's and taboos around the world*. New York: Wiley.

Bagley, C. E., & Dauchy, C. E. (1998). *The entrepreneur's guide to business law*. New York: West.

Baird, L. S., Schneier, C. E., & Laird, D. (1983). *The training and development sourcebook*. Amherst, MA: Human Resource Development Press.

Bakken, D., & Bernstein, A. (1982). A systematic approach to evaluation. *Training and Development Journal, 36*, 44–51.

Barcus, S. W., & Wilkinson, J. W. (1986). *Management consulting services*. New York: McGraw-Hill.

Bard, R., Bell, C. R., Stephen, L., & Webster, L. (Eds.). (1987). *The trainer's professional development handbook*. San Francisco: Jossey-Bass.

Bard, R., & Stephen, L. (1987). Developing your learning plan. In R. Bard, C. R. Bell, L. Stephen, & L. Webster (Eds.), *The trainer's professional development handbook* (pp. 27–40). San Francisco: Jossey-Bass.

Barmash, I. (1985, September 9). A new economic indicator. *Newsweek*, p. 12.

Bates, R. (1998, June). The virtual classroom. *Insurance and Technology, 23*, 23–25.

Baum, E. (1991). *Meeting leader's checklist.* Adapted from Higher Education Management Institute, 1979. Unpublished manuscript. Ohio University, Athens, OH.

Baumback, C., & Lawyer, K. (1978). *How to organize and operate a small business.* Englewood Cliffs, NJ: Prentice-Hall.

Bazerman, M. H., & Lewicki, R. J. (1983). *Negotiating in organizations.* Beverly Hills, CA: Sage.

Beckhand, R. (1967). *Organizational development: Strategies and models.* Reading, MA: Addison-Wesley.

Bedrosian, N. M. (1987). *Speak like a pro: In business and public speaking.* New York: Wiley.

Bell, C. R. (1985). Diagnosis: Frameworks for consultants and clients. In C. R. Bell & L. Nadler (Eds.), *Clients and consultants: Meeting and exceeding expectations* (pp. 152–164). Houston, TX: Gulf.

Bell, C. R., & Nadler, L. (Eds.). (1985). *Clients and consultants: Meeting and exceeding expectations* (2nd ed.). Houston, TX: Gulf.

Bellman, G. M. (1990, December). Balancing your work in your life. *Training and Development Journal, 50–58.*

Bergquist, W., Merritt, K., & Phillips, S. (1999). *Executive coaching: An appreciative approach.* Sacramento, CA: Pacific Soundings.

Berryman-Fink, C., Ballard-Reisch, D., & Newman, L. (Eds.). (1993). *Communication and sex-role socialization.* New York: Garland.

Biech, E. (1999). *The business of consulting.* San Francisco: Jossey-Bass/Pfeiffer.

Biech, E. (2000). *The 2000 annual: Vol. 1. Training.* San Francisco: Jossey-Bass/Pfeiffer.

Biech, E. (2000). *The 2000 annual: Vol. 2. Consulting.* San Francisco: Jossey-Bass/Pfeiffer.

Biech, E., & Swindling, L. B. (2000). *The consultant's legal guide: A business of consulting resource guide.* San Francisco: Jossey-Bass/Pfeiffer.

Bissell, C. B. (1985). Defusing the difficult employee: How to handle problem people. *Management World, 14*(2), 30–31.

Blake, R. R., & Mouton, J. S. (1989). *Consultation* (2nd ed.). Reading, MA: Addison-Wesley.

Blake, R. R., Mouton, J. S., & McCanse, A. A. (1989). *Change by design.* Reading, MA: Addison-Wesley.

Block, P. (2000). *Flawless consulting: Guide to getting your expertise used* (2nd ed.). San Francisco: Jossey-Bass.

Blodgett, P. C. (1997). Six ways to be a better listener. *Training and Development, 51*(7), 11–12.

Bloom, B. S., Englehart, M. D., Furst, E. J., Hill, W. H., & Krathwohl, D. R. (1956). *Taxonomy of educational objectives: The classification of educational goals, by a committee of college and university examiners. Handbook 1. Cognitive domain.* New York: David McKay.

Boland, A. (1996, February). Multimedia fortifies learning. *Advertising Age's Business Marketing, 81,* 20.

Bolles, R. N. (1995). *What color is your parachute?* Berkeley, CA: Ten Speed Press.

Bowers, D. G., & Stambaugh, L. K. (1986). Making organizational surveys pay off. In C. N. Jackson (Ed.), *Targeting change: Organizational development* (pp. 41–47). Alexandria, VA: American Society for Training and Development.

Boyer, R. K. (1987). *Developing consultation skills: A simulation approach.* In W. B. Reddy & C. C. Henderson (Eds.), *Training, theory, and practice* (pp. 58–77). San Diego: University Associates.

Braiker, H. B. (1988). The etiquette of office romance. *Working Woman, 13,* 148–152.

Brammer, C. (1993). *Identification of disruptive communication behaviors and instrument development.* Doctoral dissertation, Ohio University, Athens, OH.

Bramson, R. N., & Bramson, M. (1988). *Coping with difficult people.* New York: Dell.

Brinkman, R., & Kirschner, R. (1994). *Dealing with people you can't stand.* New York: McGraw-Hill.

Brislin, R., & Yoshida, T. (1994a). *Intercultural communication training: An introduction.* Thousand Oaks, CA: Sage.

Brislin, R. W., & Yoshida, T. (Eds.). (1994b). *Improving intercultural interactions: Modules for cross-cultural training programs.* Thousand Oaks, CA: Sage.

Brown, F. W., & Dodd, N. G. (1998). An approach to organizational intervention. *Journal of Management Consulting, 10*(1), 46–49.

Brown, R. (2000, January 26). *Corporate Leaders Seminar.* Presentation at Ohio University, Athens, OH.

Brownell, J. (1990). Perceptions of effective listeners: A management study. *Journal of Business Communication, 27,* 401–415.

Bucalo, J. P. (1984, December). An operational approach to training needs analysis. *Training and Development Journal,* 80–84.

Buller, P. F., Craqun, J. R., & McEvoy, G. M. (1991). Getting the most out of outdoor training. *Training and Development Journal, 45,* 58–61.

Bunker, B. B., Nochajski, T., McGillicuddy, N., & Bennett, D. (1987). Designing and running training events: Rules of thumb for trainers. In W. B. Reddy and C. C. Henderson (Eds.), *Training, theory, and practice* (pp. 225–239). San Diego: University Associates.

Bunker, K. A., & Cohen, S. L. (1977). The rigors of training evaluation: A discussion and field demonstration. *Personnel Psychology, 30,* 525–541.

Burley-Allen, M. (1982). *Listening: The forgotten skill.* New York: Wiley.

Business Week. (1984, September 10). A consulting maverick goes straight, 95.

Caplan, R. E., & Darth, W. H. (1987). Realistic simulations: An alternative vehicle for laboratory education. In W. B. Reddy & C. C. Henderson (Eds.), *Training, theory, and practice* (pp. 137–147). La Jolla, CA: University Associates.

Carr, N. (1998). The politics of e-mail. *Harvard Business Review, 76*(2), 12–13.

Chenault, J. (1989). Training for changing consultant roles. *Management Consulting, 5,* 48–54.

Christensen, C. R. (1987). *Teaching in the case method: Text, cases, and readings.* Boston: Harvard Business School.

Clampitt, P. G. (1991). *Communicating for managerial effectiveness.* Newbury Park, CA: Sage.

Clegg, W. H. (1987). Management training evaluation: An update. *Training and Development Journal, 41*(2), 65–71.

Coghlan, D. (1988). In defense of process consultation. *Leadership and Organization Development Journal, 9,* 27–31.

Collins, D. (1998). *Organizational change.* New York: Routledge.

Collins, G. (1983). Managers and lovers. *Harvard Business Review, 61,* 142–153.

Collins, G. (1987, February 1). Men vs. women in the office. *The New York Times.*

Conger, J. A. (1998). The necessary art of persuasion. *Harvard Business Review, 76*(3), 84–95.

Conner, D. R. (1998). *Leading at the edge of chaos: How to create the nimble organization.* New York: Wiley.

Consalvo, C. M. (1993). *Training with outdoor activities.* Aldershot, Hampshire, England: Connaught Training.

Cornwell, J. B. (1980, August). Measuring back-on-the-job performance. *Training,* 289–292.

Craig, R. L. (1983). *Measuring human resource development.* Paper presented at the Senior HRD Management Forum, ASTD National Issues Committee, Washington, DC.

Crane, T. G. (1998). *The heart of coaching.* San Diego: FTA Press.

Crary, M. (1987). Managing attraction and intimacy at work. *Organizational Dynamics, 15,* 26–40.

Crescenzo, S. (1998). The best of times. *Communication World, 15*(3), 11–15.

Culnan, M. J., & Markus, M. L. (1987). Information technology. In F. M. Jablin, L. L. Putnam, K. H. Roberts, & L. W. Porter (Eds.), *Handbook of organizational communication* (pp. 420–444). Newbury Park, CA: Sage.

Cunningham, I. (1999). *The wisdom of strategic learning: The self-managed learning solution.* New York: McGraw-Hill.

Cusella, L. P. (1987). Feedback, motivation, and performance. In F. M. Jablin, L. L. Putnam, K. H. Roberts, & L. W. Porter (Eds.), *Handbook of organizational communication* (pp. 624–678). Newbury Park, CA: Sage.

Cypher, B. D., Bostrom, R. N., & Seibert, J. H. (1989). Listening, communication abilities, and success at work. *Journal of Business Communication, 26,* 293–303.

Daniels, T. D., & DeWine, S. (1991). Communication process as target and tool for consultancy intervention: Rethinking a hackneyed theme. *Journal of Education and Psychological Consultation, 2*(4), 303–322.

Daniels, T. D., & Spiker, B. (1991). *Perspectives on organizational communication* (2nd ed.). Dubuque, IA: W. C. Brown.

Davis, M. E. (1986). Problem definition. In S. Barcus & J. Wilkinson (Eds.), *Handbook of management consulting services.* New York: McGraw-Hill.

Deeprose, D. (1991, September). Helping employees handle difficult customers. *Supervisory Management, 6.*

Deetz, S. (1992). *Democracy in an age of corporate colonization: Developments in communication and the politics of everyday life.* Albany: State University of New York Press.

Deming, B. S. (1982). *Evaluating job-related training: A guide for training the trainer.* Englewood Cliffs, NJ: Prentice-Hall.

Dennis, H., Goldhaber, G., & Yates, M. (1978). Review of research systems and procedures in organizational communication research. In B. Ruben (Ed.), *Communication Yearbook 2* (pp. 243–269). New Brunswick, NJ: Transaction Books.

Denova, C. C. (1979). *Test construction for training evaluation.* New York: Van Nostrand Reinhold.

Dent, H. S. (1995). *Job shock: Four new principles transforming our work and business.* New York: St. Martin's.

DeWine, S. (1980). *Firming up your own communication consulting firm.* Paper presented to the Speech Communication Association, New York, NY.

DeWine, S. (1987a). Evaluation of organizational communication competency: The development of the communication training impact questionnaire. *Journal of Applied Communication Research, 15,* 113–127.

DeWine, S. (1987b, June). Socializing with your boss. *Personal Report,* p. 8.

DeWine, S., Casbolt, D., & Bentley, N. (1983, May). *Moving through the organization: A field study assessment of the patron system.* Paper presented at the International Communication Association, Dallas, TX.

DeWine, S., & Daniels, T. (1993). Beyond the snapshot: Setting a research agenda in organizational communication. In S. Deetz (Ed.), *Communication Yearbook 16* (pp. 331–346). Newbury Park, CA: Sage

DeWine, S., & Eicholtz, M. (2000). Managing after the merger: Feedback at BAS CASE ANALYSIS. *Management Communication Quarterly, 13,* 679–684.

DeWine, S., & James, A. C. (1978). *The Hippocratic oath and standards for organizational communication consultants.* Paper presented to the Speech Communication Association, Minneapolis, MN.

DeWine, S., & James, A. C. (1988). Examining the communication audit: Assessment and modification. *Management Communication Quarterly, 2,* 144–169.

DeWine, S., James, A., & Hale, C. (1991, May). *Organizational maintenance: Successful assimilation through mentoring relationships*. Paper presented at the International Communication Association, Chicago, IL.

DeWine, S., James, A., & Walence, W. (1983, May). *Validation of organizational communication audit instruments*. Presented at the International Communication Association, Hawaii.

DeWine, S., & Modaff, D. (in press). *Misunderstandings and the communicative organization*. Los Angeles: Roxbury.

DeWine, S., Pearson, J. C., & Yost, C. (1993). Intimate office relationships and their impact on work group communication. In C. Berryman-Fink, D. Ballard-Reisch, & L. Newman (Eds.), *Communication and sex-role socialization* (pp. 139–166). New York: Garland.

Diamond, M. A. (1986). Resistance to change: A psychoanalytic critique of Argyris and Schon's contributions to organization theory and intervention. *Journal of Management, 23*(5), 543–562.

Dillard, J. P. (1987). Close relationships at work: Perceptions of the motives and performance of relational participants. *Journal of Social and Personal Relationships, 4,* 179–193.

Dillard, J. P., & Broetzmann, S. M. (1989). Romantic relationships at work: Perceived changes in job-related behaviors as a function of participant's motive, partner's motive, and gender. *Journal of Applied Social Psychology, 19,* 93–110.

Dillard, J. P., & Witteman, H. (1985). Romantic relationships at work: Organizational and personal influences. *Human Communication Research, 12,* 99–116.

Donaldson, L. (1999). *Performance-driven organizational change.* Thousand Oaks, CA: Sage.

Dopyera, J., & Pitone, L. (1983, May). Decision points in planning the evaluation of training. *Training and Development Journal,* 66–71.

Downs, C. (1988). *Communication audits.* Glenview, IL: Scott, Foresman.

Downs, C., DeWine, S., & Greenbaum, H. (1994). Organizational communication instrumentation. In R. Rubin & H. Sypher (Eds.), *Instrumentation in communication.* New York: Longman.

Downs, C. W., Johnson, K. M., & Barge, J. K. (1984). Communication feedback and task performance in organizations: A review of the literature. In H. Greenbaum, R. Falcione, & S. Hellweg (Eds.), *Organizational communication abstracts* (pp. 13–47). Beverly Hills, CA: Sage.

Doyle, M., & Straus, D. (1986). *How to make meetings work.* New York: Berkeley.

Dryden, G., & Vos, J. (1997). *The learning revolution.* Auckland, New Zealand: The Learning Web.

Dyer, W. G. (1987). *Team building: Issues and alternatives.* Reading, MA: Addison-Wesley.

Earley, P. C., Connolly, T., & Lee, C. (1989). Task strategy interventions in goal setting: The importance of search in strategy development. *Journal of Management, 15*(4), 589–602.

Edwards, M. R., & Ewen, A. J. (1996). *360 degree feedback: The powerful new model for employee assessment and performance improvement.* New York: AMACOM.

Eisenberg, E. M., & Goodall, H. L. (1997). *Organizational communication: Balancing creativity and constraint.* New York: St. Martin's.

Ellis, S. K. (1988). *How to survive a training assignment: A practical guide for the new, part-time or temporary trainer.* Reading, MA: Addison-Wesley.

Ernest, R. C. (1985, March). Corporate culture and defective planning. *Personnel Administrator,* 49–60.

Facilitation skills. (1998). Phoenix, MD: Brainstorm Dynamics.

Fairhurst, G. T., & Sarr, R. A. (1996). *The art of framing.* San Francisco: Jossey-Bass.

Falcione, R., Goldhaber, G., Porter, T., & Rogers, D. (1979, November). *The future of the ICA communication audit.* Paper presented at the meeting of the International Communication Association, Philadelphia, PA.

Farace, R., Monge, P., & Russell, H. (1977). *Communicating and organizing.* Reading, MA: Addison-Wesley.

Feigelson, S. (1998). *Energize your meetings with laughter.* Alexandria, VA: Association for Supervision and Curriculum Development.

Ferguson, S. D., & Ferguson, S. (1988). *Organizational communication.* New Brunswick, NJ: Transaction Books.

Filley, A. C. (1975). *Interpersonal conflict resolution.* Palo Alto, CA: Scott, Foresman.

Fish (video). (1998). Burnsville, MN: ChartHouse International.

Fisher, A. B. (1989, April 24). The ever-bigger boom in consulting. *Fortune,* pp. 113–134.

Fisher, R., & Brown, S. (1988). *Getting together: Building a relationship that gets to yes.* Boston: Houghton Mifflin.

Flores, L. G., & Fadden, J. (2000, January). How to have a successful strategic planning meeting. *Training and Development Journal,* 31–34.

Francis, D., & Young, D. (1979). *Improving work groups: A practical manual for team building.* San Diego: University Associates.

French, W. L., & Bell, C. H. (1990). *Organization development: Behavioral science interventions for organization improvement.* Englewood Cliffs, NJ: Prentice-Hall.

Freud, S. (1901). Fragment of an analysis of a case of hysteria. In J. Strachey and A. Freud (Eds.), *The standard edition of the complete works of Sigmund Freud,* 7 (pp. 7–122). London: Hogarth Press.

Frey, L. R., Botan, C. H., Freidman, P. G., & Kreps, G. (1991). *Investigating communication: An introduction to research methods.* Englewood Cliffs, NJ: Prentice-Hall.

Friedman, P. G., & Yarbrough, E. A. (1985). *Training strategies from start to finish.* Englewood Cliffs, NJ: Prentice-Hall.

Friedman, R. (1998). *The upstart small business legal guide* (2nd ed.). Chicago: Dearborn Financial.

Fuchs, J. H. (1975). *Making the most of management consulting services.* New York: AMACOM.

Furr, R. M. (1985). Surviving as a messenger: Client-consultant relationship during diagnosis. In C. R. Bell & L. Nadler (Eds.), *Clients and consultants: Meeting and exceeding expectations* (2nd ed.). Houston, TX: Gulf.

Gabarro, J. J., & Harlan, A. (1976). Note on process observation. *Teaching.* President and Fellows of Harvard College.

Gephart, M. A., Marsick, V. J., VanBuren, M. E., & Spiro, M. S. (1996). Learning organizations come alive. *Training and Development, 50*(12), 34–45.

Gerwig, K. (1991, October 9). Insurer's videoconferencing cuts travel time, boasts training. *Imaging News,* pp. 6–7.

Gibb, J. R. (1961). Defensive communication. *Journal of Communication, 11,* 142.

Gibson, M. K. (1998). Avoiding intervention pitfalls in international consulting. *Journal of Management Consulting, 10*(2), 59–65.

Glenn, E. C., & Podd, E. A. (1989, January). Listening self inventory. *Supervisory Management,* 13–15.

Goddard, R. W. (1988, May). Gathering a great team. *Management Weekly,* 20–22.

Goldhaber, G. (1986). *Organizational communication* (4th ed.). Dubuque, IA: W. C. Brown.

Goldhaber, G., Dennis, H., Richetto, G., & Wiio, O. (1979). *Information strategies: New pathways to corporate power.* Englewood Cliffs, NJ: Prentice-Hall.

Goldhaber, G., & Rogers, D. (1979). *Auditing organization communication systems: The ICA communication audit.* Dubuque, IA: Kendall/Hunt.

Goldhaber, G., Yates, M., Porter, T., & Lesniak, R. (1978). Organizational communication: 1978. *Human Communication Research, 5,* 76–96.

Goldstein, I. L. (1978). The pursuit of validity in the evaluation of training programs. *Human Factors, 20,* 131–144.

Goldstein, L. L. (1989). *Training and development in organizations.* San Francisco: Jossey-Bass.

Goodall, H. L. (1989). *Casing the promised land: The autobiography of an organization detective as cultural ethnographer.* Carbondale, IL: Southern Illinois Press.

Goodman, N. R. (1994). Cross-cultural training for the global executive. In Brislin, R. W., & Yoshida, T. (Eds.), *Improving intercultural interactions: Modules for cross-cultural training programs* (pp. 36–39) Thousand Oaks, CA: Sage.

Gordon, T. (1977). *Parent effectiveness training.* New York: P. H. Wyden.

Gordon, W. J. (1961). *Synectics: The development of creative capacity.* New York: Harper & Row.

Gouran, D. S. (1982). *Making decisions in groups: Choices and consequences.* Glenview, IL: Scott, Foresman.

Grant, D. L. (1977). Issues in the evaluation of training. *Professional Psychology, 8,* 659–673.

Gray, S. (1984, June 18). Romance in the workplace: Corporate rules for the game of love. *Business Week,* pp. 70–71.

Greenbaum, H., De Wine, S., & Downs, C. (1987). Organizational communication measurement: A call for review and evaluation. *Communication Management Quarterly, 1,* 129–144.

Greenbaum, J. (1999, February). Shifting to accelerated learning. *HRFocus,* S5–S6.

Greiner, L. E., & Metzger, R. O. (1983). *Consulting to management.* Englewood Cliffs, NJ: Prentice-Hall.

Grodin, D., & Lindlof, T. R. (Eds.). (1996). *Constructing the self in a mediated world.* Thousand Oaks, CA: Sage.

Gutek, B. A. (1985). *Sex and the workplace: The impact of sexual behavior and harassment of women, men, and organizations.* San Francisco: Jossey-Bass.

Hale, C. L., Cooks, L., & DeWine, S. (1992, November). *Anita Hill on trial: A dialectical analysis of a persuasive interrogation.* Presented at the Speech Communication Association, Chicago, IL.

Hall, B. (1997). *Web-based training cookbook.* New York: Wiley.

Hall, E. T. (1976). *Beyond culture.* New York: Doubleday.

Hall, J. (1969). *Conflict management survey.* Conroe, TX: Telemetrics International.

Hallowell, E. M. (1999). The human moment. *Harvard Business Review, 77*(1), 58–66.

Hamblin, A. C. (1974). *Evolution and control of training.* London: McGraw-Hill.

Hampton, D. R., Summer, C. E., & Weber, R. E. (1973). *Organizational behavior and the practice of management.* Glenview, IL: Scott, Foresman.

Handley, E. (1986). Saying no to office romances. *Bureaucrat, 14,* 35–38.

Handy, C. (1989). *The age of unreason.* Boston: Harvard Business School.

Hanson, J., & Fox, W. (1995). Communicating across cultures. *Training and Development Journal, 49*(1), 56–58.

Hanson, P. G., & Lubin, B. (1987). Assessment of trainer skills by self, peers, and supervisors. In W. B. Reddy & C. C. Henderson (Eds.), *Training, theory, and practice* (pp. 47–58). La Jolla, CA: University Associates.

Harris, R. M. (1997). Turn listening into a powerful presence. *Training and Development, 51*(7), 9–11.

Harrison, M. I. (1990). Hard choices in diagnosing organizations. *Journal of Management Consulting, 6,* 13–21.

Harrison, M. I., & Shirom, A. (1999). *Organizational diagnosis and assessment: Bridging theory and practice.* Thousand Oaks, CA: Sage.

Hesselbein, F., Goldsmith, M., & Beckhard, R. (1997). *The organization of the future.* San Francisco: Jossey-Bass.

Hiam, A. (1997). Is anybody listening? *Training, 34*(8), 92.

Hirokawa, R. Y. (1987). Why informed groups make faulty decisions: An investigation of possible interaction-based explanations. *Small Group Behavior, 18,* 3–29.

Hirsch, P., & Shwom, B. (1995). Case 2: When communication consulting becomes political. *Business Communication Quarterly, 58*(3), 28–29.

Hite, J. (1999). *Learning in chaos.* Houston, TX: Gulf.

Hollwitz, J., Churchill, R., & Hollwitz, T. (1985, November). *Communication with the difficult personality: Adaptive responses in organizational settings.* Paper presented at the annual meeting of the Speech Communication Association, Washington, DC.

Holtz, H. (1989). *Choosing and using a consultant: A manager's guide to consulting services.* New York: Wiley.

Horn, P. D., & Horn, J. (1982). *Sex in the office.* Reading, MA: Addison-Wesley.

Howell, W. S., & Bormann, E. G. (1988). *The process of presentational speaking* (2nd ed.). New York: Harper & Row.

Huse, E. (1985). *Organization development and change* (2nd ed.). St. Paul, MN: West.

Iacocca, L. (1984). *Iacocca: An autobiography.* New York: Bantam Books.

Jablin, F. M. (1990). Organizational communication. In G. L. Dahnke & G. W. Clatterback (Eds.), *Human communication: Theory and research* (pp. 156–182). Belmont, CA: Wadsworth.

Jablin, F. M., Putnam, L. L., Roberts, K. H., & Porter, L. W. (1987). *Handbook of organizational communication: An interdisciplinary perspective.* Newbury Park, CA: Sage.

Jackson, C. N. (Ed.). (1986). *Targeting change: Organizational development.* Alexandria, VA: American Society for Training and Development.

James, A. C. (2000). *Rules of thumb when using PowerPoint.* Personal correspondence, Athens, Ohio.

James, A. C., & DeWine, S. (1990). Shoot out at Midwest Manufacturing. In B. D. Sypher (Ed.), *Case studies in organizational communication* (pp. 177–189). New York: Guilford.

Jamison, K. (1983, August). Managing sexual attraction in the workplace. *Personnel Administrator,* 45–51.

Janis, I. L. (1972). *Victims of groupthink* (2nd ed.). Boston: Houghton Mifflin.

Jennings, C. (1997). So far, yet so near. *People Management, 3*(18), 42–45.

Jessup, H. R. (1990, November). New roles and team leadership. *Training and Development Journal,* 79–83.

Johnson, P. M. (1990, August). Communicating for commitment and productivity. *Training and Development Journal,* 55–57.

Jones, J. E., & Pfeiffer, J. W. (1979). Role playing. *The 1979 annual handbook for group facilitators.* San Diego: University Associates.

Kanter, R. M. (1983). *The changemasters.* New York: Simon & Schuster.

Kanter, R. M. (1989). *When giants learn to dance.* New York: Simon & Schuster.

Kanter, R. M. (1997). *Frontiers of management.* Boston: Harvard Business School Press.

Katz, D., & Kahn, R. (1978). *The social psychology of organizations.* New York: Wiley.

Katz, J. (1982, July 21). It's time to reverse our retreat from reality in teaching college students. *Chronicle of Higher Education,* 40.

Kearsley, G. (1982). *Costs, benefits, and productivity in training systems.* Reading, MA: Addison-Wesley.

Kelley, R. E. (1986). *Consulting: The complete guide to a profitable career.* New York: Charles Scribner.

Keltner, J. W. (1987). *Mediation.* Annandale, VA: Speech Communication Association.

Kiechel, W. I. (1994, April). A manager's career in the new economy. *Fortune, 129,* 68–72.

Kim, Y. Y. (1989). Intercultural adaptation. In M. K. Asante & W. B. Gudykunst (Eds.), *Handbook of international and intercultural communication* (pp. 275–294). Beverly Hills, CA: Sage.

Kirkpatrick, D. L. (1967). Evaluation of training. In R. L. Craig & L. R. Bittel (Eds.), *Training and development handbook.* New York: McGraw-Hill.

Kirkpatrick, D. L. (1987). *More evaluating training programs: A collection of articles from* Training and Development Journal. Alexandria, VA: American Society for Training and Development.

Kirkpatrick, D. L. (1998). *Evaluation training programs: The four levels.* San Francisco: Berrett-Koehler.

Kreps, G. L. (1989). A therapeutic model of organizational communication consultation: Application of interpretive field methods. *Southern Communication Journal, 55,* 1–21.

Kurpius, D. (1978). Consultation theory and process: An integrated model. *Personnel and Guidance Journal, 56,* 18–21.

Kurtz, T. (1990, September). Dynamic listening: Unlocking your communication potential. *Supervisory Management, 7.*

Laird, A., & Clampitt, P. G. (1985). Effective performance appraisal: Viewpoints from managers. *Journal of Business Communication, 22*(3), 49–57.

Langdon-Dahm, M. (1986). *Trade secrets: 25 proven success tools for working, dealing, and winning with people.* Dayton, OH: Learning Development Systems.

Lauer, L. D. (1996). Eleven ways to renew your effectiveness: Communication keys that will change the way you lead. *Nonprofit World, 14*(2), 48–50.

LePoole, S. (1989). Negotiating with Clint Eastwood in Brussels. *Management Review, 78,* 58–60.

Lewin, K. (1951). *Field theory in social science.* New York: Harper & Row.

Linestone, H., & Turoff, M. (1975). *The Delphi method: Techniques and applications.* London: Addison-Wesley.

Lippincott, S. M. (1994). *Meetings: Do's, don'ts, and donuts.* Pittsburgh, PA: Lighthouse Point Press.

Lippitt, G., & Lippitt, R. (1986). *The consulting process in action* (2nd ed.). San Diego: University Associates.

Lippitt, G., Lippitt, R., & Lafferty, C. (1984). Cutting edge trends in organization development. *Training and Development Journal, 38*(7), 59–62.

London, M. (1989). *Managing the training enterprise: High quality, cost effective employee training in organizations.* San Francisco: Jossey-Bass.

Lucia, A. (1997). Leaders know how to listen. *HR Focus, 74*(4), 25.

Luckert, L. M. (1989). Love at the office. *Women in Business, 41,* 12–13.

Ludlow, P. (Ed.). (1996). *High noon on the electronic frontier: Conceptual issues in cyberspace.* Cambridge, MA: MIT Press.

Mack, T., & Summers, M. (1999, January). Danger: Stealth attack. *Forbes,* 88–92.

Mager, R. S. (1984). *Preparing instructional objectives* (2nd ed.). Belmont, CA: Lake Publishing.

Maier, M. R., Solem, A. R., & Maier, A. A. (1975). *The role play technique: A handbook for management and leadership practice.* San Diego: University Associates.

Maiorca, J. J. (1991). Basic statistics for the HRD practitioner. In W. Pfeiffer & W. Jones (Eds.), *The 1991 annual: Developing human resources* (pp. 245–265). San Diego: University Associates.

Makay, J. J., & Fetzer, R. C. (1984). *Business communication skills: Principles and practice* (2nd ed.). Englewood Cliffs, NJ: Prentice-Hall.

Maniero, L. A. (1986). A review and analysis of power dynamics in organizational romances. *Academy of Management Review, 11,* 750–762.

Manzoni, J. F., & Barsoux, J.-L. (1998). The set-up-to-fail syndrome. *Harvard Business Review, 76*(2), 101–113.

Maron, R. M. (1997, January). Self-assessment: A remedy for dysfunctional board behaviors. *Association Management, 49,* 51–53.

Marsh, S. C. (1992). *Harvard Business School career guide: Management consulting.* Boston: Harvard University Press.

Masoner, M. (1988). *An audit of the case study method.* New York: Praeger.

Massy, J. (2000, January). Is technology-supported training different in Europe? *Training and Development Journal,* 26–30.

Masten, R. (1991). *I know it isn't funny but I love to make you laugh.* Carmel, CA: Sunflower.

May, L. S., Moore, C. A., & Zarnmit, S. J. (1987). *Evaluating business and industry training.* Boston: Kluwer.

Mayo, G. D., & DuBois, P. H. (1987). *The complete book of training: Theories, principles, and techniques.* San Diego: University Associates.

McArdle, G. E. (1999). *Training design and delivery.* Alexandria, VA: American Society for Training and Development.

McCain, M. (1999, July). Scaling the great wall. *Training and Development Journal,* 38–42.

McCall, M. W., Jr., & Lombardo, M. M. (1979). *Looking Glass, Inc.: The first three years* (Tech. Rep. 13). Greensboro, NC: Center for Creative Leadership.

McClelland, D. C. (1987). *Human motivation.* New York: Cambridge University Press.

McLagan, P. A. (1983). *Models for excellence: The conclusions and recommendations of the ASTD training and development competence study.* Washington, DC: American Society for Training and Development.

McLaughlin, P. (1988). An affair to dismember. *Canadian Business, 61,* 153–155.

McMurrer, D. P., Van Buren, M. E., & Woodwell, W. H. (2000). Making the commitment. *Training and Development Journal, 54*(1), 41–48.

McNair, M. P. (Ed.). (1954). *The case method at the Harvard Business School.* New York: McGraw-Hill.

Meador, B. D., & Rogers, C. R. (1973). Client-centered therapy. In R. Corsini (Ed.), *Current psychotherapies* (pp. 119–165). Itaska, IL: F. E. Peacock.

Messmer, M. (1998). Improving your listening skills. *Management Accounting, 79* (9), 9.

Metzger, R. O. (1989). *Profitable consulting: Guiding America's managers into the next century.* Reading, MA: Addison-Wesley.

Miller, K., & Ellis, K. (1986, November). *Romantic relationships in the workplace: Stereotypes and attributions.* Paper presented at the annual meeting of Speech Communication Association, Chicago, IL.

Miller, K. & Medved, K. (2000). Managing the merger. *Management Communication Quarterly, 13,* 659–667.

Mills, G. E., Pace, R. W., & Veterson, B. D. (1989). *Analysis in human resource training and organization development.* Reading, MA: Addison-Wesley.

Mintzberg, H. (1998). Covert leadership: Notes on managing professionals. *Harvard Business Review, 76*(6), 14–147.

Mishra, J. M., & Harell, R. (1989). Managing today's hot workplace issues (drug testing, smoking, AIDS, and office romance). *Management World, 18,* 26–29.

Mitchell, G. (1987). *The trainer's handbook: The AMA guide to effective training.* New York: American Management Association.

Moline, T. (1990). Upgrading the consultant. *Journal of Management Consulting, 6,* 17–22.

Monroe, C., & Borzi, M. (1987, April). *The difficult personality: Analytic and strategic concerns.* Paper presented at the annual meeting of the Eastern Communication Association, Syracuse, NY.

Monroe, C., Borzi, M., & DiSalvo, V. S. (1986). Conflict behaviors of difficult subordinates. *Southern Communication Journal, 53,* 311–329.

Montgomery, R. L. (1981). *Listening made easy: How to improve listening on the job, at home, and in the community.* New York: AMACOM.

Moore, M., & Gergen, P. (1986). Risk taking and organization change. In C. N. Jackson (Ed.), *Targeting change: Organizational development.* Alexandria, VA: American Society for Training and Development.

Morand, D. A. (1996). Politeness as a universal variable in cross-cultural managerial communication. *International Journal of Organizational Analysis, 4*(1), 52–74.

Morgan, G. (1997). *Images of organization.* Thousand Oaks, CA: Sage.

Mosak, H. H., & Dreikurs, R. (1973). Adlerian psychotherapy. In R. Corsini (Ed.), *Current psychotherapies* (pp. 1–34). Itasca, IL: F. E. Peacock.

Mosvick, R. K., & Nelson, R. B. (1987). *We've got to start meeting like this.* Glenview, IL: Scott, Foresman.

Muir, C. (1996). Using consulting projects to teach critical thinking skills in business communication. *Business Communication Quarterly, 59*(4), 77–87.

Murray, M. (1991). *Beyond the myths and magic of mentoring.* San Francisco: Jossey-Bass.

Nadler, L. (1982). *Designing training programs: The critical events model.* Reading, MA: Addison-Wesley.

Nadler, L., & Nadler, Z. (1987). *The comprehensive guide to successful conferences and meetings.* San Francisco: Jossey-Bass

Nagata, A. L. (1995). Less lecture, more training. *Training and Development, 49*(4), 7–8.

Naisbitt, J. (1982). *Megatrends.* New York: Warner Books.

Naisbitt, J. (1994). *Global paradox: The bigger the world economy the more powerful its smallest players.* New York: W. Morrow.

Naisbitt, J., & Aburdene, P. (1990). *Megatrends 2000: Ten new directions for the 1990s.* New York: W. Morrow.

Napier, R. W., & Gershenfeld, N. K. (1987). *Groups: Theory and experience* (4th ed.). Boston: Houghton Mifflin.

Neuman, G. A., Edwards, J. E., & Raju, N. S. (1989). Organizational development interventions: A meta-analysis of their effects on satisfaction and other attitudes. *Personnel Psychology, 42,* 461–489.

"New Wired World" (1999, September 20). *Newsweek,* online <http://www.cs.cmu.edu/afs/cs.cmu.edu/user/bam/www/numbers.html>.

Newman, A., & Smith. M. (1999, July). How to create a virtual learning community. *Training and Development Journal,* 44–48.

Newstrom, J. W. (1978). Catch-22: The programs of incomplete evaluation of training. *Training and Development Journal, 32*(11), 22–24.

Nicholas, J. M. (1982). The comparative impact of organization development interventions on hard criteria measures. *Academy of Management Review, 7,* 531–542.

Nicholas, M. P. (1995). *The lost art of listening.* New York: Guilford.

Nowack, K. M. (1991, April). A true training needs analysis. *Training and Development Journal,* 69–73.

Nunn, N. (1998). *Harvard Business School career guide for management consulting 1999.* Boston: Harvard Business School Press.

O'Brien, M. (1997). Executive coaching. *Supervision, 58*(4), 6–8.

Odenwald, S. B. (1993). *Global training: How to design a program for the multinational corporation.* Alexandria, VA: American Society for Training and Development.

Orsburn, J. D. (2000). *The new self-directed work teams: Mastering the challenge.* New York: McGraw-Hill.

Osborn, M. (1991, September 17). '90's workers turning page on loyalty. *USA Today,* p. 1B.

O'Shea, T. J. (1986). Presentation of results. In S. W. Barcus and J. W. Wilkinson (Eds.), *Management consulting services* (pp. 235–252). New York: McGraw-Hill.

Pace, R. W., & Faules, D. F. (1989). The design, conduct, and evaluation of human resource training. In R. W. Pace & D. F. Faules, *Organizational communication* (2nd ed.). Englewood Cliffs, NJ: Prentice-Hall.

Parker, G. M. (1998). *25 instruments for team building.* Amherst, MA: HRD Press.

Pasmore, W., Francis, C., & Haldeman, J. (1982). Sociotechnical system: A North American reflection of empirical studies of the seventies. *Human Relations, 35,* 1179–1204.

Peoples, D. A. (1988). *Presentations plus.* New York: Wiley.

Peters, T. (1988). *Thriving on chaos: Handbook for a management revolution.* London: Macmillan.

Peters, T. (1993). *Liberation management: Necessary disorganization for the nanosecond nineties.* London: Pan/Macmillan.

Peters, T., & Waterman, R. H. (1984). *In search of excellence: Lessons from America's best run companies.* New York: Warner Communications.

Peterson, G. L. (2000). *Communicating in organizations* (2nd ed.). Boston: Allyn & Bacon.

Pfeffer, J., & Salancik, G. (1978). *The external control of organizations.* New York: Harper & Row.

Pfeiffer, J. W. (1973). Conditions which hinder effective communication. In *The 1973 Annual Handbook for Group Facilitators* (p. 120). La Jolla, CA: University Associates.

Pfeiffer, J. W. (1986a). *Strategic planning: Selected readings.* San Diego: University Associates.

Pfeiffer, J. W. (1986b). Encouraging managers to deal with marginal employees. In W. Pfeiffer, L. D. Goodstein, & T. M. Noland (Eds.), *Understanding applied strategic planning: A manager's guide* (pp. 4.17–4.25). San Diego: University Associates.

Pfeiffer, J. W. (Ed.). (1991). *The encyclopedia of team-building activities.* San Diego: Pfeiffer.

Pfeiffer, J. W., Goodstein, L. D., & Noland, T. M. (1986a). *Understanding applied strategic planning: A manager's guide.* San Diego: University Associates.

Pfeiffer, J. W., Goodstein, L. D., & Noland, T. M. (1986b). *Applied strategic planning: A how to do it guide.* San Diego: University Associates.

Pfeiffer, J. W., & Jones, J. E. (1973). Design considerations in laboratory education. In J. E. Jones & J. W. Pfeiffer (Eds.), *The 1973 annual handbook for group facilitators* (pp. 177–194). La Jolla, CA: University Associates.

Pfeiffer, J. W., & Jones, J. E. (1972–2000). *The 1972–2000 annual handbooks for group facilitators.* San Diego: University Associates.

Phillips, C. (1987). The trainer as person: On the importance of developing your best intervention. In W. B. Reddy & C. C. Henderson (Eds.), *Training, theory, and practice* (pp. 29–35). La Jolla, CA: University Associates.

Phillips, J. J. (1997). *Handbook of training evaluation and measurement methods.* Houston, TX: Gulf.

Pincus, J. D. (1997). To get an MBA or an MA in communication? *Communication World, 14*(3), 31–34.

Plax, T. G. (1991). Understanding applied communication inquiry: Researchers as organizational consultant. *Journal of Applied Communication, 19*(1 & 2), 55–70.

Pondy, L. R. (1972). Organizational conflict: Concepts and models. In J. M. Thomas & W. G. Bennis (Eds.), *Management of change and conflict* (p. 100). Middlesex, England: Penguin.

Poole, N. S., & Hirokawa, R. Y. (1986). Communication and group decision making. In R. Y. Hirokawa & N. S. Poole (Eds.), *Communication and group decision making* (pp. 15–34). Newbury Park, CA: Sage.

Porter, L. C. (1987). Game, schmame! What have I learned? In W. B. Reddy & C. C. Henderson (Eds.), *Training, theory, and practice* (pp. 67–74). La Jolla, CA: University Associates.

Powell, G. N. (1986). What do tomorrow's managers think about sexual intimacy in the workplace? *Business Horizons, 29,* 30–35.

Powers, D. M. (2000). *The office romance: Playing with fire without getting burned.* New York: American Management Association.

Prince, G. M. (1970). *The practice of creativity.* New York: Harper & Row.

Putnam, L. L., Phillips, N., & Chapman, P. (1996). Metaphors of communication and organizations. In S. Clegg, C. Hardy, & W. Nord (Eds.), *Handbook of organizational studies* (pp. 375–408). Thousand Oaks, CA: Sage.

Quick, T. L. (1988). *Power, influence, and your effectiveness in human resources.* Reading, MA: Addison-Wesley.

Quinn, R. E. (1977). Coping with Cupid: The formation, impact, and management of romantic relationships in organizations. *Administrative Science Quarterly, 22,* 30–45.

Quinn, R. E., & Lees, P. O. (1984). Attraction and harassment: Dynamics of sexual politics in the workplace. *Organizational Dynamics, 13,* 35–46.

Rae, L. (1997). *How to measure training effectiveness* (3rd ed.). Aldershot, Hampshire, England: Gower.

Redding, W. C. (1979). Graduate education and the communication consultant: Playing God for a fee. *Communication Education, 28,* 346–352.

Redding, W. C. (1984). *Professionalism in training: Guidelines for a code of ethics.* Paper presented at Speech Communication Association, Chicago, IL.

Reddy, W. B. (1995). *Intervention skills: Process consultation for small groups and teams.* San Diego: Pfeiffer.

Reddy, W. B., & Henderson, C. C. (Eds.). (1987). *Training, theory, and practice.* San Diego: University Associates.

Reinard, J. C. (1994). *Introduction to communication research.* Madison, WI: Brown & Benchmark.

Riblen, R. I. (1983). *Training development guide.* Reston, VA: Reston.

Richards, D. (2000). The coaching roundabout: A personal narrative about helping executives lead change. In M. Anderson, *Fast cycle organizational development.* Cincinnati: South-Western.

Robbins, S. P. (1989). *Training in interpersonal skills: Tips for managing people at work.* Englewood Cliffs, NJ: Prentice-Hall.

Robinson, D. G., & Robinson, J. C. (1995). *Performance consulting.* San Francisco: Berrett-Koehler.

Roebuck, D. B., Sightler, K. W., & Brush, C. C. (1995). Organizational size, company type, and position effects on the perceived importance of oral and written communication skills. *Journal of Mathematical Economics, 27*(1), 99–115.

Rogers, E. (1988). Information technologies: How organizations are changing. In G. Goldhaber & G. Barnett (Eds.), *Handbook of organizational communication* (pp. 437–452). Norwood, NJ: Ablex.

Romiszowski, A. J., & deHaas, J. A. (1989, October). Computer-mediated communication for instruction: Using email as a seminar. *Education Technology,* 7–8.

Ronstadt, R. (1980). *The art of case analysis: A guide to the diagnosis of business situations.* Dover, MA: Lord.

Rosenberg, M. J. (1987). Evaluating training programs for decision making. In L. May, C. Moore, & S. Zammit (Eds.), *Evaluating business and industry training* (pp. 57–74). Boston: Kluwer.

Rosow, J. M., & Zager, R. (1988). *Training. The competitive edge: Introducing new technology into the workplace.* San Francisco: Jossey-Bass.

Ross, R., & DeWine, S. (1988). Assessing the Ross-DeWine conflict management message style. *Management Communication Quarterly, 1*(3), 389–413.

Rossett, A., & Arwady, J. W. (1987). *Training needs assessment.* Englewood Cliffs, NJ: Educational Technology Publications.

Rothwell, W. J., Sander, E. S., & Soper, J. G. (1999). *ASTD models for workplace learning and performance: Roles, competencies, and outputs.* Alexandria, VA: American Society for Training and Development.

Ruben, B. D., & Kealey, D. J. (1979). Behavioral assessment of communication competency and the prediction of cross-cultural adaptation. *International Journal of Intercultural Relations, 3*, 15–47.

Rubin, L. B. (1985). *Just friends: The role of friendship in our lives.* New York: Harper & Row.

Rudolph, E. E., & Johnson, B. R. (1983). *Communication consulting: Another teaching option.* Annandale, VA: Speech Communication Association.

Sackman, H. (1975). *Delphi critique: Expert opinion, forecasting and group process.* Lexington, MA: Lexington Books.

Salinger, R., & Deming, B. (1982). Practical strategies for evaluating training. *Training and Development, 36*, 20–29.

Schaaf, D. (1998). What workers really think about training. *Training, 35* (9), 59–66.

Schein, E. H. (1985). *Organizing culture and leadership.* San Francisco: Jossey-Bass.

Schein, E. H. (1987). *Process consultation: Vol. 2. Lessons for managers and consultants.* Reading, MA: Addison-Wesley.

Schein, E. H. (1988). *Process consultation: Vol. 1. Its role in organizational development* (2nd ed.). Reading, MA: Addison-Wesley.

Schein E. H. (1999). *Process consultation revisited: Building a helping relationship.* Reading, MA: Addison-Wesley.

Scherer, P. S. (1989). The turnaround consultant steers corporate renewal. *Journal of Management Consulting, 5*(1), 17–24.

Schindler-Raiman, E. (1987). Risks we must take: Changes, challenges, and choices for consultants and trainers in 1987 and beyond. In W. B. Reddy & C. C. Henderson (Eds.), *Training, theory, and practice* (pp. 17–26). La Jolla, CA: University Associates.

Scholtes, P. R. , Joiner, B. L., & Streibel, B. J. (1996). *The team handbook* (2nd ed.). Madison, WI: Joiner Associates.

Schrello, D. M. (1988). *How to market training programs, seminars, and instructional materials.* Long Beach, CA: Schrello Direct Marketing.

Schultz, B. G. (1989). *Communicating in the small group: Theory and practice.* New York: Harper & Row.

Sheppard, B. H., & Bazern-tan, M. H. (1986). *Research on negotiation in organizations, 1.* Greenwich, CT: JAI Press.

Sherwood, J. (1981). Essential differences between traditional approaches to consulting and a collaborative approach. *Consultation, 1* (1), 52–55.

Shonk, J. H. (1982). *Working in teams: A practical manual for improving work groups.* New York: AMACOM.

Shuster, H. D. (1990). *Teaming for quality improvement: A process for innovation and consensus.* Englewood Cliffs, NJ: Prentice-Hall.

Sigband, N. B. (1987, February). The uses of meetings. *Nation's Business,* 11.

Signorovitch, D. (1995, April). The search for focus and flexibility. *Communication World, 12,* 20–23.

Smith, B. J., & Delahaye, B. L. (1987). *How to be an effective trainer: Skills for managers and new trainers* (2nd ed.). New York: Wiley.

Smith, B. P. (1990). Marketing of management consulting. *Journal of Management Consulting, 6,* 34–40.

Smith, T. C. (1984). *Making successful presentations: A self-teaching guide.* New York: Wiley.

Snyder, A. (1995). Executive coaching: The new solution. *Management Review, 34*(3), 29–32.

Sonnichsen, R. C. (2000). *High-impact internal evaluation: A practitioner's guide to evaluating and consulting inside organizations.* Thousand Oaks, CA: Sage.

Spaid, O. A. (1989). *The consummate trainer: A practitioner's perspective.* Englewood Cliffs, NJ: Prentice-Hall.

Spechler, J., & Wicker, J. (1980). Internal consulting groups: Catalysts for organizational change. *Management Review, 69*(11), 24–28.

Spruell, G. R. (1985). Daytime drama: Love in the office. *Training & Development Journal, 39,* 21–23.

Spruell, G. R. (1987). First-rate technical skills training. *ASTD Info Line* (p. 1). Alexandria, VA: American Society for Training and Development.

Sredl, H. J., & Rothwell, W. J. (1987). *The ASTD reference guide to professional training roles and competencies, 1 & 2.* New York: Random House.

Steele, F. (1985). Consultants and detectives. In C. R. Bell & L. Nadler (Eds.), *Clients and consultants: Meeting and exceeding expectations.* Houston, TX: Gulf.

Steil, L. K., Barker, L. L., & Watson, K. W. (1983). *Effective listening: Key to your success.* Reading, MA: Addison-Wesley.

Steiner, G. A. (1979). *Strategic planning: What every manager must know.* New York: Free Press.

Straub, J. (1992, April). Keeping your distance without losing rapport. *Supervisory Management, 3.*

Sullivan. R. L., Wircenski, J. L., Arnold, S. S., & Sarkees, M. D. (1990). *The trainer's guide: A practical manual for the design, delivery, and evaluation of training.* Rockville, MD: Aspen.

Suryanarayanan, S. (1989). Trends and outlooks for U. S. consulting. *Journal of Management Consulting, 5,* 3–9.

Swenson, C. (1973). *Introduction to interpersonal relationships.* Glenview, IL: Scott, Foresman.

Sypher, B. D. (1990). *Case studies in organizational communication.* New York: Guilford.

Sypher, B. D. (1997). *Case studies in organizational communication: Perspectives on contemporary work life.* New York: Guilford.

Sypher, B. D., Bostram, R. N., & Seibert, J. H. (1989). Listening, communication abilities, and success at work. *Journal of Business Communication, 26,* 293–303.

Tepper, R. (1987). *The consultant's problem-solving workbook.* New York: Wiley.

Tevlin, J. (1999, December 10). So you want to talk on the phone to a real live person? Sorry, you can't. *Athens Messenger,* p. 4.

Thach, L., & Woodman, R. W. (1995). Organizational change and information technology: Managing on the edge of cyberspace. In W. W. Burke (Ed.), *Managing organizational change.* New York: American Management Association.

Thrash, A. A., Shelby, A. X., & Tarver, J. L. (1984). *Communication and business in the professions: Speaking up successfully.* New York: Holt, Rinehart, & Winston.

Tichy, N. M., & Devanna, M. A. (1986, July). The transformational leader. *Training and Development Journal,* 27–32.

Timm, P. R. (1986). *Managerial communication: A finger on the pulse* (2nd ed.). Englewood Cliffs, NJ: Prentice-Hall.

Ting-Toomey, S. (1999). *Communicating across cultures.* New York: Guilford.

Tompkins, P. K. (1992). *Organizational imperatives: Lessons of the space program.* Los Angeles: Roxbury.

Torres, C., & Fairbanks, D. (1996). *The ASTD trainer's sourcebook: Teambuilding.* New York: McGraw-Hill.

Tracey, W. R. (1989). *Designing training and development systems.* New York: American Management Association.

Training Directors' Forum E-Net (2000, January 12). *How not to get swamped, 1*(43), <lakewood2 @mail.Omm.com>.

Tucker, R. K. (1987). *Fighting it out with difficult, if not impossible people.* Dubuque, IA: Kendall/Hunt.

Urech, E. (1998). *Speaking globally: Effective presentations across international and cultural boundaries.* Dover, NH: Kogan Page.

Van de Ven, A., & Delbecq, A. L. (1971). Nominal versus interacting group processes for committee decision-making effectiveness. *Academy of Management Journal, 14,* 203–212.

Van de Ven, A., & Delbecq, A. L. (1974). The effectiveness of nominal, Delphi, and interacting group decision-making processes. *Academy of Management Journal, 17*(4), 605–621.

Van Slyke, E. J. (1999). *Listening to conflict: Finding constructive solutions to workplace disputes.* New York: AMACOM.

Van Warner, R. (1995, February 13). Opening lines of communication critical to overall performance. *Nation's Restaurant News,* 35.

Vergara, G. H. (1999, January/February). Finding a compatible corporate culture. *Healthcare Executive, 14,* 46–47.

Waldmen, L. E. (1998). *The power of 360 feedback: How to leverage performance evaluations for top productivity.* Houston, TX: Gulf.

Walters, L. (1995). What to say when . . . you're dying on the platform. New York: McGraw-Hill.

Warshauer, S. (1988). *Inside training and development: Creating effective programs.* San Diego: University Associates.

Watzlawick, P., Weakland, J., & Fisch, R. (1974). *Change: Principles of problem formation and problem.* New York: Norton.

Weaver, M. J. (1999). Beyond the ropes: Guidelines for selecting experimental training. *Corporate University Review, 7*(1), 34–37.

Weaver, T. (1971, January). The Delphi forecasting method. *Phi Delta Kappan,* 267–271.

Webster, L., & Henderson, S. C. (1987). Charting your HRD career. *The trainer's professional development handbook.* San Francisco: Jossey-Bass.

Weider-Hatfield, D., & Hatfield, J. D. (1996). Superior's conflict management strategies and subordinate outcomes. *Management Communication Quarterly, 10*(2), 189–208.

Weiner, B. (1985). *Human motivation.* New York: Springer-Verlag.

Weiss, D. H. (1992, March). How to deal with unpleasant people problems. *Supervisory Management,* 1–2.

Weitz, A. J. (1995). Change: How to remove the fear, resentment, and resistance. *Hospital Management Quarterly, 17*(2), 75–79.

Westhoff, L. A. (1986). What to do about corporate romance. *Management Review, 75,* 50–55.

Wexley, K. N., & Latham, G. P. (1981). *Developing and training human resources in organizations.* Glenview, IL: Scott, Foresman.

Whalen, J. (1990, October). Winning presentations: Less talk is more convincing. *Supervisory Management,* 1–10.

White, L., & Mindiole, C. (1986). Marketing professional services. In S. Barcus and J. Wilkinson (Eds.), *Handbook of management consulting services.* New York: McGraw-Hill.

Wilson, J. A., & Elman, N. S. (1990). Organizational benefits of mentoring. *Academy of Management Executives, 4,* 88–94.

Wolf, W. B. (1990). A parable: The consultant as detective. *Consultation, 9,* 93–94.

Wolfe, L. D. (1984, June). Minding the business of consulting. *Training and Development Journal,* 45–47.

Wolff, F. I., Marsnik, N. C., Tacey, W. S., & Nichols, R. G. (1983). *Perceptive listening.* New York: Holt, Rinehart & Winston.

Wolvin, A. D. , & Coakley, C. G. (1985). *Listening.* Dubuque, IA: W. C. Brown.

Wolvin, A. D., & Coakley, C. G. (1991). A survey of the status of listening and training in some Fortune 500 corporations. *Communication Education, 40,* 152–164.

Woodman, R. W. (1989). Evaluation research on organizational change: Arguments for a Combined Paradigm approach. In R. W. Woodman & W. A. Pasmore (Eds.), *Research in organizational change and development* (pp. 161–180). Greenwich, CT: JAI Press.

Woodman, R. W., & Wayne, S. J. (1985). An investigation of positive findings bias in evaluation of organization development interventions. *Academy of Management Journal, 28*(4), 889–913.

Zemke, R., & Armstrong, J. (1997). How long does it take? (The sequel). *Training, 34*(5), 69–79.

Zemke, R., & Kramlinger, T. (1989). *Figuring things out: A trainer's guide to needs and task analysis.* Reading, MA: Addison-Wesley.

Zenger, J. H., & Hargis, K. (1982). Assessing training results: It's time to take the plunge. *Training and Development, 36*(1), 10–16.

Zhao, J. J. (1996). Using case studies for international business communication training. *Business Communication Quarterly, 59*(4), 11–24.

Zhao, J. J. , & Ober, S. (1991). Communication skills needed by U.S. international businesspersons. *Delta Pi Epsilon Journal, 33,* 52–60.

Zhao, J. J., & Parks, C. (1995). Self-assessment of communication behavior: An experimental learning exercise for intercultural business success. *Business Communication Quarterly, 58*(1), 20–26.

Ziehm, R. (1989). How I use management consultants. *Journal of Management Consulting, 5*(1), 25–27.

Figure 10.1: Calvin and Hobbes cartoon. Bill Watterson. Copyright © 1991 by Bill Watterson. Reprinted with the permission of Universal Press Syndicate. All rights reserved.

Page 213: "The Uses of Meetings." Norman B. Sigband. From *Nation's Business* (February 1987). Copyright © 1987 by the U.S. Chamber of Commerce. Reprinted with the permission of *Nation's Business.*

Table 10.1: "Parliamentary Procedure: Table of Motions." From Michael E. Doyle and David Straus. *How to Make Meetings Work.* Copyright © 1976 by Michael Doyle and David Straus. Reprinted with the permission of Putnam Berkeley, a division of Penguin Putnam, Inc.

Figure 10.2: "The Problem-Solving/Decision Making Cycle." Edward Baum. Reprinted with the permission of Edward Baum. All rights reserved.

Form 10.1: "Meeting Leader's Checklist." Edward Baum. Reprinted with the permission of Edward Baum. All rights reserved.

Figure 10.3: "Forty-Nine Steps to a Successful Conference." From Don M. Schrello, *How to Market Training Programs, Seminars, and Instructional Materials.* Copyright © 1988. Reprinted with the permission of The Marketing Federation, 109 58th Avenue, St. Petersburg Beach, FL 33706. 813/367-4934.

Form 10.2: "Process Observer Form." Copyright © Learning Development Systems Publication. Reprinted with permission.

Form 10.3: "Process Observer Role Form." Copyright © Learning Development Systems Publication. Reprinted with permission.

Pages 237–240: "A Consulting Story from Anita C. James: Clarifying Who's in Charge." Anita C. James. Reprinted with the permission of the author.

Page 249: "Emergency Kit for Presentations." Adapted from T. C. Smith, *Making Successful Presentations: A Self-Teaching Guide.* Copyright © 1984 by John Wiley & Sons, Inc. Reprinted with the permission of the publisher.

Pages 262–263: "The Speaker's Checklist." Adapted from T. C. Smith, *Making Successful Presentations: A Self-Teaching Guide.* Copyright © 1984 by John Wiley & Sons, Inc. Reprinted with the permission of the publisher.

Pages 268–270: "A Consulting Story from Sue DeWine." Sue DeWine. Reprinted with the permission of the author.

Page 274: Excerpt adapted from Michael I. Harrison and Arie Shriom, *Organizational Diagnosis and Assessment: Bridging Theory and Practice.* Copyright © 1999 by Sage Publications, Inc. Reprinted with the permission of the publisher.

Form 12.2: "Team Development Scale by William G. Dyer." From William G. Dyer, *Team Building: Issues and Alternatives.* Copyright © 1987 by Addison-Wesley Publishing Company, Inc. Reprinted with the permission of Addison Wesley Longman.

Table 12.1: "Schein's Group Roles." From E. H. Schein, *Process Consultation, Volume I: Its Role in Organizational Development,* 2nd ed. Copyright © 1988 by Addison-Wesley Publishing Company, Inc. Reprinted with the permission of Addison Wesley Longman.

Form 12.3: "Broken Squares." Exercise portion from J. William Pfeiffer and John E. Jones, *The Encyclopedia of Team-Building Activities* (San Diego: Pfeiffer & Co., 1991). Copyright © 1991 by University Associates, Inc. Reprinted with the permission of John Wiley & Sons, Inc.

Pages 301–303: "A Consulting Story from Sandra Cheldelin and Sue DeWine: Can This Group Ever Work Together Again?" Sandra Cheldelin and Sue DeWine. Reprinted with the permission of the authors.

Page 315–316: "A Consulting Story from Judith Sturnick." Judith Sturnick. Reprinted with the permission of the author.

Form 14.1: "Communication Questionnaire." Adapted from C. Brammer, *Identification of Disruptive Communication Behaviors and Instrument Development* (doctoral dissertation, Ohio University, Athens, Ohio, 1993). Reprinted with permission.

Page 327: Excerpt from J. W. Pfeiffer from "Conditions Which Hinder Effective Communication" in *The 1973 Annual Handbook for Group Facilitators.* Copyright © 1973. Reprinted with the permission of John Wiley & Sons, Inc.

Form 14.3: "CMMS: Recall of Communication Behavior in Interpersonal Conflict." From R. Ross and Sue DeWine, "Interpersonal Conflict: Measurement and Validation" (presented at SCA, Louisville, Kentucky, 1982). Reprinted with permission.

Form 14.4: "Score Sheet for CMMS." From R. Ross and Sue DeWine, "Interpersonal Conflict: Measurement and Validation" (presented at SCA, Louisville, Kentucky, 1982). Reprinted with permission.

Pages 337–339: "A Consulting Story from David R. Seibold: The Admiral and the Loose Cannons." David R. Seibold. Reprinted with the permission of the author.

Page 341: Excerpt from Ian Cunningham from *The Wisdom of Strategic Learning: The Self-Managed Team Solution.* Copyright © 1999. Reprinted with the permission of The McGraw-Hill Companies, Inc.

Figure 15.1: "The Individual Risk Taker's Actions Are Influenced by Individual Tendencies and Externally by Organization Structure/Culture Factors." Based on Maggie Moore and P. Gergen, "Risk Taking and Organization Change" in Conrad N. Jackson (ed.), *Targeting Change: Organizational Development.* Copyright © 1986. Reprinted with the permission of the American Society for Training and Development.

Pages 347–348: Excerpts from L. E. Greiner and R. O. Metzger from *Consulting to Management.* Copyright © 1983. Reprinted with the permission of Prentice-Hall, Inc., Upper Saddle River, NJ.

Page 350: "The Sea Horse." Robert Mager. From Robert Mager, *Preparing Objectives for Programmed Instruction.* Copyright © 1984 by Pitman Learning, Inc. Reprinted with the permission of Lake Publishing Company.

Figure 15.2: "Goal Setting for Professional Associations." Communication Consultants. Developed by Communication Consultants, 190 Longview Heights, Athens, Ohio.

Figure 15.3: "The Applied Strategic Planning Model." From J. W. Pfeiffer, L. D. Goodstein, and T. M. Noland, *Applied Strategic Planning: A How to Do It Guide.* Copyright © 1986. Reprinted with the permission of John Wiley & Sons, Inc.

Pages 354–356: "A Consulting Story from Sue DeWine and Liane Gray Starner: Can a Strategic Plan Save Our Organization?" Sue DeWine and Liane Gray Starner. Reprinted with the permission of the authors.

Page 362: "Cures for Culture Shock." Adapted from J. Hanson and W. Fox, "Communication across Cultures" in *Training and Development* 49 (1995). Copyright © 1995. Reprinted with permission.

Form 16.1: "Intercultural Communication Behavior. " J. J. Zhao and C. Parks. Questionnaire and analysis from "Self-Assessment of Communication Behavior: An Experimental Learning Exercise for Intercultural Business Success" in *Business Communication Quarterly* 58 (1995). Copyright © 1995. Reprinted with the permission of the authors.

Case Studies (pages 378 and 379): "Thailand" and "United States and France." From N. R. Goodman, "Cross-Cultural Training for the Global Executive" in Richard W. Brislin and Tomoko Yoshida (eds.), *Improving Intercultural Interactions: Modules for Cross-Cultural Training Programs.* Copyright © 1994 by Sage Publications, Inc. Reprinted with the permission of the authors.

Figure 17.1: "Hierarchy of Evaluation Approaches." Based on Henry J. Sredi and William J. Rothwell, *The ASTD Reference Guide to Professional Training Roles and Competencies, 1 and 2.* Copyright © 1987. Reprinted with the permission of The McGraw-Hill Companies.

Page 403: Excerpt from Robert Mager from *Goal Analysis.* Robert Mager. Copyright © 1988 by Lake Publishing Company. Reprinted with the permission of the publishers.

Form 18.1: "The Learning Needs Assessment Scale." From Ray Bard and Leslie Stephen, "Developing Your Learning Plan" in Ray Bard, Chip R. Bell, Leslie Stephen, and Linda Webster, *The Trainer's Professional Development Handbook.* Copyright © 1987 by Jossey-Bass. Reprinted with the permission of Jossey-Bass, Inc., a subsidiary of John Wiley & Sons, Inc.

Page 444: Excerpt from Richard Ziehms from "How I Use Management Consultants" in *Journal of Management Consulting* 4 (1989). Copyright © 1989. Reprinted with the permission of the publishers.

AUTHOR INDEX

SUBJECT INDEX